Fascism, the War, and Structures of Feeling in Italy, 1943–1945

Fascism, the War, and Structures of Feeling in Italy, 1943–1945

Tales in Chiaroscuro

SIMONETTA FALASCA-ZAMPONI

Great Clarendon Street, Oxford, OX2 6DP,
United Kingdom

Oxford University Press is a department of the University of Oxford.
It furthers the University's objective of excellence in research, scholarship,
and education by publishing worldwide. Oxford is a registered trade mark of
Oxford University Press in the UK and in certain other countries

© Simonetta Falasca-Zamponi 2023

The moral rights of the author have been asserted

All rights reserved. No part of this publication may be reproduced, stored in
a retrieval system, or transmitted, in any form or by any means, without the
prior permission in writing of Oxford University Press, or as expressly permitted
by law, by licence or under terms agreed with the appropriate reprographics
rights organization. Enquiries concerning reproduction outside the scope of the
above should be sent to the Rights Department, Oxford University Press, at the
address above

You must not circulate this work in any other form
and you must impose this same condition on any acquirer

Published in the United States of America by Oxford University Press
198 Madison Avenue, New York, NY 10016, United States of America

British Library Cataloguing in Publication Data
Data available

Library of Congress Control Number: 2022948826

ISBN 978–0–19–288750–4

DOI: 10.1093/oso/9780192887504.001.0001

Printed and bound by
CPI Group (UK) Ltd, Croydon, CR0 4YY

Links to third party websites are provided by Oxford in good faith and
for information only. Oxford disclaims any responsibility for the materials
contained in any third party website referenced in this work.

In memory of my parents

Acknowledgments

In a book based on private journals, my sentiments of deep gratitude go first of all to the diarists (and their representatives) who allowed me to access and cite their personal writings. I wish to acknowledge their kindness and generosity. I am equally thankful to the archives that house these documents. In particular, at the Archivio della scrittura popolare (ASP) in Trento I owe an enormous debt of appreciation to Quinto Antonelli, who, now retired, was the director of ASP at the time of my research. Besides sharing his impressively extensive knowledge of diaries, Antonelli provided me with answers to questions I continued to pose him after I left the archive. His expertise and fine scholarship were of tremendous help to several matters of my study. Caterina Tomasi graciously assisted me during my stay at ASP, and Elisabetta Antonelli helped with last-minute requests, while Patrizia Marchesoni facilitated my preliminary contacts with ASP. The bulk of the diarists I surveyed came from the Archivio Diaristico Nazionale (ADN) in Pieve Santo Stefano. I am grateful to archivist Cristina Cangi for agreeing to all my requests of texts and for the additional work she had to bear in obtaining publication permissions from the diaries' right holders. I know it required a remarkable amount of labor. I also thank the director of ADN, Natalia Cangi, for the encouragement, the coffee breaks during long research hours, and the resolution of complicated copyright issues. The whole circle of volunteers and young researchers at ADN provided a friendly and cooperative environment. At the Archivio Ligure della scrittura popolare (ALSP) in Genoa, professor Fabio Caffarena offered me access to the archive's collection of ordinary writings, while in Florence I was able to examine the original manuscripts of Leonetta Cecchi Pieraccini at the Archivio Contemporaneo "Alessandro Bonsanti." In Genoa I also benefited from material housed at the Wolfsoniana. I wish to thank its curator, my friend Matteo Fochessati, as well as his wife Simona for their welcoming hospitality. Last but not least, Alvaro Tacchini, a master of local history, opened his archive to me in Città di Castello, the town where I resided during my research stays at ADN. From conversations with him, I became acquainted with two of the diarists that I eventually featured in the book. I also resorted to Alvaro for all sorts of questions during the writing phase of the book, including a request to reproduce one document from his archive. I stand in respectful awe of his scholarship.

During the research and writing of the book I received support from several institutions, including the incomparable service of Interlibrary Loan at the University of California, Santa Barbara. I would like to acknowledge funds from the Institute for Social, Behavioral and Economic Research at University of California, Santa Barbara as well as research grants from the Academic Senate at Santa Barbara. Most heartfelt gratitude goes to the National Humanities Center, where I spent the academic year 2018–19 as the Archie K. Davis fellow. It is hard to overestimate the value of a fellowship at the Center. Everything and everyone work indefatigably to guarantee the well-being of the fellows. I wish to thank President and Director Robert D. Newman and then Vice President Tania Munz, as well as Lynn Miller for all the logistics. A huge shout-out to the librarians who made our life as researchers so much easier and more fulfilling. Everybody on the staff, including in the kitchen, played exquisite hosts. Finally, I am indebted to the cohort of fellows for all the conversations, walks, events, and outings together. The affinity I developed with several of them is long-lasting. A special thanks to fellows Yan Xu for teaching me the art of Taiji and Matthew Rubery for those early breakfasts. I would also like to acknowledge librarian Joe Milillo for his meditation workshops.

For their continued encouragement throughout my career since the graduate school years and for their efforts on my behalf toward ensuring research funding for this project, Victoria Bonnell and Martin Jay stand out as irreplaceable. I am forever grateful to them. I would also like to acknowledge Walter Adamson's graciousness and wisdom as well as the camaraderie and support of Robin Wagner-Pacifici and Dylan Riley.

In Italy, my research visits were gifted with new relationships. In Città di Castello, Claudio Sgaravizzi connected me to his lovely friends Patrizia Calabresi, Beatrice Bocciolesi, and Paolo Montanucci. My sisters Ombretta and Stefania along with their families were supportive and extremely helpful, as usual. Hulla Bisonni ensured an image for the book. Bill Adams's suggestions about published diaries inspired me to develop a comparative case to complement the analysis of ordinary diarists. Students at my graduate seminar on everyday life pushed my understanding of the topic. In particular, Andrew Henderson's admirable will to continue reading Henri Lefebvre's multi-volume *Critique* in an independent study was inspiring during times of Covid-19 isolation. A huge thanks to Richard Kaplan for all the editing, patience, and positivity and to Edoardo Kaplan for being there. At Oxford

University Press I thank Matthew Cotton for his rare combination of professionalism and warmth, and Jo Spillane for answering all my questions. The anonymous reviewers solicited by the press provided helpful critical commentary on the manuscript. Although they might not be in full agreement with my revisions, I owe a huge intellectual debt to them.

This book is dedicated to the memory of my parents, who were barely teenagers in 1943.

Contents

List of Figures   xiii

   Introduction   1
     Betwixt Turns and Twists   2
     Of "Structures of Feeling" and the Past   4
     The Quandary of Experience   6
     Ordinary and Extraordinary   11
     Writing, Records, and Diaries: The Challenge of Authenticity   13
     Accounting, Value, and Aesthetic Laws: *Rédacteurs* and *Auteurs*   20
     Time and Narrative: Living in Time   24
     Everydayness and "Exception"   27
     The Case   35
     Chapters Outline   40

1. A Short, Long Summer   44
   Before the Fall   45
   War Is Over, or Is It? July 25   51
     Sidelining in freedom   61
   An Unending Summer: September 8   69
     Another surprise   71
     Tradimento!   74
   October 13: A Footnote?   86

2. Interpretive Ghosts   91
   Who Is the Enemy?   94
     Looking the enemy in the eye   98
     German, German not: The betrayed military   104
     Liberators? A linguistic game   112
     Brother, brother, brother   117
   Frolicking with the Fatherland   126
   Fascism, an Afterthought?   131

3. Every Day in the Everyday   138
   Along Came the Private   139
   Normalcy, Where Are Thou?   148
     Home and peace   150
     A house down on the plain   153
   Insanity by Reason of Indifference   157

Exceptional Normalcy — 161
  Shelling doom — 162
  Breathing without living — 164
  Gnawing hunger — 166
History, Power, Authority — 169
Styling Objectivity — 173
  An elliptical feast — 179
Closing In: A Roman Duet (In Place of an Epilogue) — 181

4. The Diary as Alibi — 190
  Why Write a Diary? — 192
  "It all ended too suddenly, too simply." — 203
  In Solidarity: Fatherland Reconsidered — 208
  Fascism, Fascism Not — 215
    Voiding fascism: The pure and the impure — 217
    We are all guilty — 223
    Fascism's imago — 226
    Redemption — 230

5. The Personal and the Political — 238
  Sentimental Fascism — 239
    The good fascists — 242
  Fascist Who? — 248
    Guilty, not guilty — 250
    Defascistization — 255
    "The Germans, the Germans, the Germans!" — 259
  Micropolitics: Glory and Misery of the Local — 262
  Banality and Drama: Enduring Instability — 268
    The morality of daily struggles — 269
    The order of things — 272
    "Bloody 'food'" — 275
    Sleepwalkers opening their eyes — 280

Conclusions — 287

Methodological Appendix — 305

Table of Diaries — 307
Bibliography — 311
Index — 331

List of Figures

1. Milan, July 26, 1943. Destruction of fascist symbols after Mussolini's fall. Footage supplied by Cinecittà Istituto Luce Historical Archive.   53
2. Rome 1944. War propaganda writing on a structure bombed by Allied forces. Bundesarchiv, Bild 101I-476-2094-17A/photographer: Gerhard Rauchwetter/1944.   118
3. Trento, May 14, 1944. Bombed city ruins. Fondazione Museo storico del Trentino, Album Pontalti.   152
4. Front page of *Il Popolo di Roma*, August 10, 1943 (with censored excisions).   209
5. Front page of the periodical *Rinascita*, July 27, 1943 (proofreading copy). Archivio dell'Istituto di Storia, Politica e Sociale "V. Gabriotti."   264

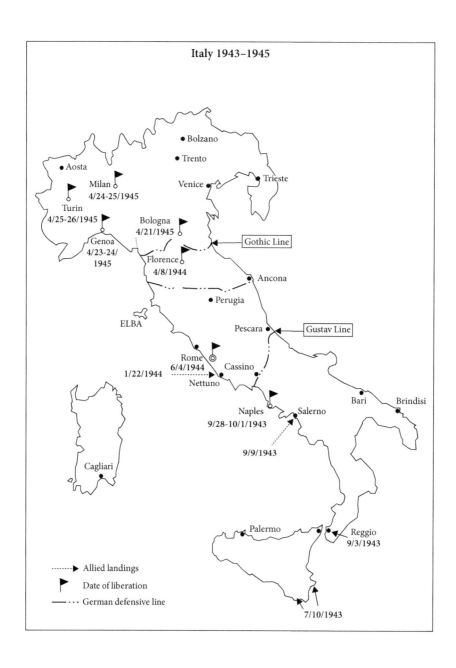

Introduction

> Above all, elucidation of the past must work to counter forgetting, a forgetting that all too easily goes hand in hand with the justification of the forgotten.
> Theodor W. Adorno*

This is a book about historical ruptures, extraordinary times, and political crises. It is an account of fascism's meteoric fall in Italy, of wartime life under Allied bombings and Nazi occupation, and of the lives of ordinary Italians in the midst of exceptional events. It is also a book about political subjectivity and the phenomenology of experience—a historical hermeneutics of the individual's relation to the social and political world gauged from the perspective of the everyday. Based on more than one hundred diaries written between 1943 and 1945, the book tracks the persistence of fascism by focusing on the imbrication of the lived with history. Against the tendency to transform "experience" and more generally human cultural activity into a finished whole—fixed interpretations and framings—the book illustrates the process through which Italians, entrenched as they were in the flux of the present, negotiated their historical situatedness following the collapse of Mussolini's dictatorship on July 25, 1943. I ask: What did Italians make of fascism and its role in the country's history as they witnessed the passing of the regime and its subsequent phantasmal reincarnation in the Italian Social Republic (RSI)? How did official narratives and the chaotic situation on the ground affect their understanding of their immediate fascist past? Ultimately, can we draw on people's experiences of this era to illuminate contemporary Italy's ambivalent relationship to its fascist legacy?

Inspired by Raymond Williams's concept of "structures of feeling," the book highlights changes in Italians' political subjectivity by synchronically relating those changes to the events that unfolded between July 1943 and May 1945. It argues that the dimension of lived experience involved in the everyday

---

* "Was bedeutet: Aufarbeitung der Vergangenheit," in *Gesammelte Schriften* (Frankfurt am Main: Suhrkamp Verlag, 1970), Volume 10. 2, p. 568. Thanks to Elisabeth Weber for help with the translation.

Fascism, the War, and Structures of Feeling in Italy, 1943–1945: Tales in Chiaroscuro. Simonetta Falasca-Zamponi, Oxford University Press. © Simonetta Falasca-Zamponi 2023. DOI: 10.1093/oso/9780192887504.003.0001

presents an ideal perspective from which to detect the deeply contradictory strands governing the Italians' responses to fascism and its fall. The indeterminacy of the quotidian caused by the fluid nature of its perpetual becoming offered diarists a grounded, albeit movable, platform on which to process their present. Centered in their everyday, journal writers built interpretive frameworks that fluctuated along with personal and collective vicissitudes. Constitutionally ambivalent, evanescent yet consistent, the everyday in wartime Italy functioned as a curse and a refuge. Plagued with tensions, it molded and affected people's perceptions of fascism and of the historical crisis in which they were immersed; it also helped underscore the close relationship that links individual fate to national destiny. An evaluation of Italians' understandings of this critical period through the analysis of private journals gives us a privileged, though by no means unproblematic, opportunity for approaching the past as lived present—a dynamic flow of time that defies presumptions of fixed identities, stable meanings, and narrative coherence. Considering the undeniable messiness of the historical context within which the long-standing fascist dictatorship suddenly came to a halt, an assessment of the Italians' mutable perspective at the time offers clues for addressing the unfathomability of fascism's current resurgence. More broadly, as we dig deep into the complex layers that make up one's political experience, historical analysis helps elucidate the critical question of ideological and cultural ambivalence.

Betwixt Turns and Twists

The end of Mussolini's regime in the summer of 1943 was cause for immediate celebration in a country that had withstood more than two decades of fascist rule. Images of smashed sculptures of Mussolini, along with the desecration of fascist symbols and monuments, were captured in film footage and became iconic signs of popular reactions to the dictatorship. Fascism's collapse seemed both inevitable and definitive. The regime's immediate reincarnation in the Italian Social Republic, however, soon proved that not everybody was ready to liquidate the fascist past.[1] Two critical years, spanning the Allied invasion and German occupation in summer 1943 until the war's conclusion in Europe in May 1945, tested the Italians' civic and political sentiments, along with their sense of unity, stamina, and resilience. This was a period of

---

[1] The RSI was formally instituted on September 23, 1943.

extreme confusion and traumatic changes as the liberating effects of the dictator's fall were counteracted by conflicts on multiple fronts. Having joined Germany's war effort on June 10, 1940, Italy eventually negotiated an armistice with the Anglo-American forces on September 8, 1943, following King Victor Emmanuel III's imprisonment of Mussolini and his replacement with Marshal Badoglio at the head of government. The forty-five-day hiatus between the end of the fascist regime and the armistice created uncertainty, especially among the military. Clashes between the Italian army and the civilian population (that demanded an end to the war) arose—harbinger of further divisions that would pit Italian against Italian in those two dramatic years. Meanwhile, Allied armies landed in Sicily and began advancing up the peninsula in a strenuous effort to push back the Germans. On September 12, 1943, Hitler's troops rescued Mussolini from prison and helped him set up the RSI puppet government in the northern town of Salò, eventually splitting Italy between the Nazi-occupied North and the liberated South. A patriotic war against the German invader unified antifascists especially in the North, but Italian resistance efforts were complicated by an internal conflict between partisan forces and the fascists of the Social Republic. Amidst momentous happenings, the overwhelmingly painful reality of the war affected everyone without distinction, as air raids and bombings added to the Italians' dismal conditions and misery. Coming to terms with a twenty-year dictatorship turned out to be an arduous enterprise made even more onerous by the emergent trope "war of liberation." Subject to the vagaries of semiotic instability and fluid interpretations, even categorizing who was the enemy became a challenge for the vexed population.

In an article drafted for *The New York Times* only a few months after the end of Mussolini's regime, noted philosopher Benedetto Croce hinted that those who had lived under the dictatorship inevitably desired "not to think of it and not to speak any more about it."[2] We do not know if Croce was right in his perception. Indeed, we have very little knowledge of what Italians felt and thought about fascism after its precipitous demise. This book intends to fill the gap in historical scholarship by assessing the Italians' lived present at a time of remarkable instability. Although invaluable studies have been produced on the memory of the war and the Resistance, none have focused on how ordinary people experienced the events of those years as opposed to how

[2] The article in question was "The Fascist Germ Still Lives," *The New York Times* (November 28, 1943). The cited sentence, although in the original draft, did not appear in the version published by the *Times*. For the original draft see "Il fascismo come pericolo mondiale," in Benedetto Croce, *Scritti e discorsi politici* (Bari: Laterza, 1963), vol. 1, p. 12.

they later remembered them. Moreover, while the fall of Mussolini in July 1943 finally offered Italians the opportunity to express their opinions openly, the nature and extent of their evaluations of fascism have been scarcely ascertained, if not misrepresented. Whereas Mussolini's dictatorial grip constrained people's behavior and has made it difficult for scholars to determine degrees of political opposition to fascism, interrogating the time immediately following the regime's collapse offers opportunities for attending to the historical conundrum of consent. Or, at the minimum, scrutiny of the biennium 1943–45 allows us to address the issue of Italians' evolving relation to fascism beyond the dominant liberation narrative of those years. The intention is not to provide a more "accurate" portrayal of history or an especially individualized version of it, but to tap submerged currents that, no matter how unarticulated they were at the time of their circulation, left an imprint on the political culture. The assumption is that those structures of feeling constituted the premises on which a post-fascist Italy was erected; they served as background for choices the reconstructed country faced in its pacified post-1945 phase.

Of "Structures of Feeling" and the Past

But why "structures of feeling"? A trademark concept in Raymond Williams's innovative understanding of culture, and originally envisioned as an analytical tool for literary analysis, "structures of feeling" was formulated by Williams to encapsulate the elusive idea of the "felt sense of the quality of life" at a particular historical time.[3] It was intended to emphasize "meanings and values as they are actively lived and felt," "social experiences *in solution*."[4] Countering the reductive tendency to transform "experience" and more generally human cultural activity into established relations and institutions, "structures of feeling" reflected Williams's overall theory of the social world as an ensemble of systems that are closely interwoven and not separable. It conveyed his intent to approach the totality of social relations as an active process and not an already predetermined, invariable reality to which we especially tend to

---

[3] Raymond Williams, *The Long Revolution* (London: Chatto and Windus, 1961), p. 63. Williams first introduced the concept of structure of feeling in *Preface to Film* (London: Film Drama Limited, 1954), a book he coauthored with Michael Orrom. See the chapter "Film and the Dramatic Tradition," where Williams used "structure" in the singular, although he later moved to the plural "structures."

[4] Williams, "Structures of Feeling," in *Marxism and Literature* (Oxford: Oxford University Press, 1977), pp. 132, 133. Williams first used the chemistry analogy "in solution" and its companion "precipitate" in *Preface to Film*: "We examine each element as a precipitate, but in the living experience of the time every element was in solution, an inseparable part of a complex whole," p. 21.

relegate the past. In Williams's words, "In most description and analysis, culture and society are expressed in an habitual past tense. The strongest barrier to the recognition of human cultural activity is this immediate and regular conversion of experience into finished products."[5]

Compartmentalizing different aspects of the social world and looking at them as prearranged and enclosed rather than fluid and mediated mutilates our understanding of people's experience of their present, whether we are dealing with a recent or distant past. Epistemological narrowness also leads to marginalizing the nonfixed ("all that is present and moving") into the category of the "personal" conceived as separate from the social.[6] The unknown or hard to grasp is then turned into the subjective and deprived of a wider meaning, while the social, now reduced to fixed form, ends up being denied its dynamic nature as a living process. Not that everything is always moving and there are no solidified social formations, Williams conceded. Nevertheless, experience always exceeds available articulations. The lived, as that which is not fully expressed, implies "disturbance, tension, blockage, emotional trouble."[7] These are all elements that contrast, or deviate from, existing ideologies. Oscillations counter the received thought of a time and expose the fluidity and indeterminacy of the lived present—its structures of feeling. As Williams insisted, what one "feels" interacts actively with the institutional and ideological levels and does not simply result from them. The analyst's critical task is to uncover the connections between all the different elements of the lived being mindful of the roots of "feelings" in the imaginary while still stressing their inherently social nature.[8] Values and beliefs should definitively not be privileged or considered in isolation. In contrast, one needs to illuminate the "interaction between the official consciousness of an epoch—codified in its doctrines and legislation—and the whole process of actually living its consequences."[9]

---

[5] Williams, "Structures of Feeling," p. 128. Williams also stated that one of the reasons why he ultimately opted for the phrase "structures of feeling" as opposed to "structures of experience" (experience being a more comprehensive word) was exactly to avoid the meaning of past tense generally associated with experience, p. 132.
[6] Williams, "Structures of Feeling," p. 128.
[7] Williams, *Politics and Letters: Interviews with New Left Review* (London: NLB, 1979), p. 168.
[8] By "structures" Williams meant to suggest that there was unity operating throughout literary works of a certain period, even if they were not connected in any other way, whereas the appositive "of feeling" evidenced a "pattern of impulses, restraints, tones," more than of thought (*Politics and Letters*, p. 159). Williams, however, insisted that the issue was not about "feeling against thought, but thought as felt and feeling as thought" ("Structures of Feeling," p. 132), although he confessed having never been happy with "the deliberately contradictory phrase" of "structures of feeling," *Politics and Letters*, p. 159.
[9] Williams, *Politics and Letters*, p. 159.

Williams's "structures of feeling" specifically targeted "emergent" relations whose articulations are filled with conflicting drives—social experiences "in solution" that only appear in full evidence at a later time, hence the suitability of "structures of feeling" for studying a past epoch.[10] In Williams's conception, this theoretical approach underscored the nature of cultural practices as forms of material production based on activities "of real people in real relationships" and engaged in actual processes of communication and reproduction.[11] As he stated, "there is some everyday commerce between the available articulations and the general process that has been termed 'experience.'"[12] The nature and direction of these transactions shape lived reality, even if they do not necessarily exhaust it. In a situation characterized by institutional uncertainties and historical unknowns, such as the one Italy faced between 1943 and 1945, feelings of incongruousness and confusion unsettled people's usual understandings and disrupted their conventional patterns of interpretation and action.[13] "Structures of feeling" helps direct attention to the several ways the evolving historical situation affected Italians' response to their uncertain present as they confronted a fascist past still wreaking havoc.

The Quandary of Experience

But what about "experience"? If, by Williams's own admission, "structures of feeling" is an elusive, hard to define concept, equally problematic and fraught with opacity and ambiguities is its accompanying referent: experience. As Martin Jay has reminded us in his historical analysis of the term, experience is ever slippery, complex, and multifaceted.[14] It can also be remarkably emotional, as when it is invoked to lament the loss of authenticity in the modern world. Ultimately, the aura surrounding the term does more to obscure than

---

[10] On Williams's understanding of "emergent" see chapter 8 of *Marxism and Literature*. On the productive challenges that "structure of feeling" poses to the conventional study of the past see Simonetta Falasca-Zamponi, "History, Ordinary Culture, and 'Structure of Feeling': Revisiting Raymond Williams," *Il Pensiero Storico* no. 7 (June 2020): pp. 99–118. Compared to affect theory or William Reddy's "emotives," the epistemological advantage of Williams's "structures of feeling" resides in its tight link to the past, i.e., its preeminent emphasis on historicity.
[11] Williams, *Politics and Letters*, p. 330.   [12] Williams, *Politics and Letters*, p. 172.
[13] Lynn Hunt suggests that in their analyses historians should also take into account the embodied self. See "The Self and Its History," *The American Historical Review* vol. 119, no. 5 (2014): pp. 1576–86.
[14] See Martin Jay, *Cultural Semantics: Keywords of Our Time* (Amherst: University of Massachusetts Press, 1998), especially "Songs of Experience: Reflections on the Debate over *Alltagsgeschichte*," "Experience without a Subject: Walter Benjamin and the Novel," and "The Limits of Limit-Experience: Bataille and Foucault." Also see his *Songs of Experience: Modern American and European Variations on a Universal Theme* (Berkeley: University of California Press, 2005).

to instruct and we are left with an assortment of meanings that resist all attempts at synthesis.

In the course of theorizing what he eventually named "structures of feeling," Williams was acutely aware of the dilemmas generated by any kind of referential nod to "experience."[15] Particularly objectionable he found the notion's purported assumption of the subject's privileged and genuine point of view—a supposition that, among others, failed to acknowledge the mediating role of cultural forms.[16] For Williams, there could never be an unmediated, direct relation to reality, nor should one ever postulate the existence of a pristine subject. Thus, his conscious choice not to use the semantically loaded "experience" when formulating "structures of feeling," even as he acknowledged the difficulty of finding replacement words for it: "one has to seek a term for that which is not fully articulated or not fully comfortable in various silences, although it is usually not very silent. I just don't know what the term should be."[17]

Without discounting the complexities inhering in the concept, in this book I resort to "experience," as well as its adjectival companion "lived," cognizant of the predicament the expressions implicate but also soberly aware of the lack of viable substitutes. The risks of semiotic confusion and oversignification entailed by using these terms are especially challenging when studying the past as lived present through the means of personal writings.[18] How can one avoid the epistemological pitfalls inevitably linked to this operation? Decades ago, Michael Oakeshott argued that historical experience is by definition a paradox, since interpreters inevitably appraise the past in light of the current moment and assume a presentist perspective—a chasm separates the particular past under consideration from the historian's account of it.[19] Although Oakeshott believed he could undo this Gordian knot by instituting the figure of the historian as neutral, masterful tamer of subjective

---

[15] Anticipated in *Politics and Letters* (p. 180), Williams added the entry "experience" in his revised edition of *Keywords: A Vocabulary of Culture and Society* (Oxford: Oxford University Press, 1983), originally published in 1976.

[16] On this point, see Joan W. Scott's stimulating discussion "Experience," in Judith Butler and Joan W. Scott eds., *Feminists Theorize the Political* (New York: Routledge, 1992), pp. 22–40. Scott particularly addresses the implications for historical studies of the predicaments linked to the concept of "experience."

[17] Williams, *Politics and Letters*, p. 168.

[18] A useful approach to historical actors as narrators and producers of history can be found in Michel-Rolph Trouillot, *Silencing the Past: Power and the Production of History* (Boston: Beacon Press, 1995). On personal accounts in social analysis see Mary Jo Maynes, Jennifer L. Pierce, and Barbara Laslett, *Telling Stories: The Use of Personal Narratives in the Social Sciences and History* (Ithaca: Cornell University Press, 2012).

[19] Michael Oakeshott, *Experience and Its Modes* (Cambridge: Cambridge University Press, 1933).

perspectives, in reality, and *pace* Oakeshott, the epistemological procedure involved in studying bygone eras is not unique to historians. On the contrary, its hazards are common to all efforts aimed at interpretation. From hermeneutics and phenomenology to pragmatism and, more broadly, interpretivism, philosophers along with humanists and social scientists have long grappled with how to turn the unfamiliar into something meaningful and understandable. Foreignness applies to the past as much as it does to ethnographic encounters. Indeed, the historian Robert Darnton approached his eighteenth-century subjects in the mode of an anthropologist looking to apply thick description to uncanny events such as a cat massacre.[20] Bizarre occurrences at a Parisian printing press, the meaning of which a twentieth-century sensibility could not fathom let alone explain, became fertile ground for a micro-level reading of cultural ideas and practices after the manner of texts. Coincidentally, in a 1995 essay on Raymond Williams, Stanley Aronowitz highlighted history's link to ethnography by characterizing Williams's work and methodological legacy as "historical ethnography."[21] In Aronowitz's evaluation, Williams powerfully transmuted literature into "a form of social and cultural knowledge" able to identify the signifying practices of a specific historical conjuncture.[22] Williams's ethnographic approach to literary texts sidestepped abstractions and illuminated that nebulous area of the lifeworld that, interspersed in a novel, emerges from the cracks left open by institutional structures and official perspectives.

Concerned with historical experience, and following his encompassing definition of culture as a way of life, Williams looked at cultural signs as constitutive of and constituted by social processes, whether these signs are located in literature and the arts or in everyday rituals and institutions.[23] By moving in between levels of material sociality and intellectual life, and at the same time engaging both quotidian practices and art forms while also emphasizing people's actively produced relations against views of reductive instrumentality, Williams tracked the *"changing practical consciousness of human beings."*[24]

---

[20] Robert Darnton, *The Great Cat Massacre: And Other Episodes in French Cultural History* (New York: Basic Books, 1984).

[21] Stanley Aronowitz, "Between Criticism and Ethnography: Raymond Williams and the Intervention of Cultural Studies," in Christopher Prendergast ed., *Cultural Materialism: On Raymond Williams* (Minneapolis: University of Minnesota Press, 1995), pp. 320–39.

[22] Aronowitz, "Between Criticism and Ethnography," p. 323. On Williams's epistemology as "historical hermeneutics" see R. Shashidhar, "Culture and Society: An Introduction to Raymond Williams," *Social Scientist* vol. 25, no. 5/6 (May–June 1997): pp. 33–53.

[23] See "Culture" in *Marxism and Literature*, pp. 11–20.

[24] "Language" in *Marxism and Literature*, p. 44. Williams relied on Russian linguists for theories on the creative capacity of language. On Russian linguists see Pam Morris ed., *The Bakhtin Reader: Selected Writings of Bakhtin, Medvedev and Voloshinov* (London: Arnold, 1994).

He stressed the lived character of experiences, be they unique or common, exceptional or ordinary. In the process, and critical for our discussion, he unhinged the past from its assigned fixity or prescribed standing. He put the spotlight on shifting beliefs and perceptions.

Williams's sensible attunement to the moods of history is particularly instructive for a study that deals with private writings, especially personal journals. Due to their defining features of subjectivity and regularity, diaries are often elevated to the status of privileged narratives; they are taken at face value both as illustrations of lives we don't often hear about (in the case of "ordinary people") and because expressive of routine activities that make up our existence more preponderantly than momentous events.[25] Diaries supposedly convey the experiences of common folks; we tend to see them as more accurate descriptions of reality based on a (questionable) trust in the transparency of personal accounts and a quasi-mystical belief in their redeeming, if not altogether progressive, power. One important lesson we draw from Williams, however, is the importance of de-essentializing subjective experience by setting it free from the fetters of uniqueness and authenticity normally attached to it. This is not to deny the singularity of people's histories. The goal is rather to underscore the dynamic interconnectedness between individuals and history. Williams expressly conceived "structures of feeling" with the purpose of highlighting modes of historical and social relations that are distinct from the official thought of a period.[26] At times, these modes could be articulating an area of experience; at others they might be exposing the silence that obscures existing but unexpressed experiences. In all cases, attention falls on the "complex whole," the inseparability of elements "in solution." As Williams wrote, "The most difficult thing to get hold of, in studying any past period, is this felt sense of the quality of life at a particular place and time: a sense of the ways in which the particular activities

---

[25] The use of the term "ordinary" is also problematic. Antonio Gibelli makes the case that, as compared to "popular," the term more aptly encapsulates an "epoch of marked decline of barriers and of static social hierarchies, as well as of the coming of standardizing social and cultural processes." See "Pratica della scrittura e mutamento sociale. Orientamento e ipotesi," in *Per un archivio della scrittura popolare. Atti del seminario nazionale di studi di Rovereto 2–3 ottobre 1987* (Mori (TN): Editrice La grafica, 1987), p. 8. However, in Italian, "ordinary" is expressed with "comune" as in "gente comune." In English, the equivalent would be "common man," whose meaning is not the same as "ordinary." All of these terms are loaded with significations that require further explanation. For lack of better alternatives, I will use "ordinary," keeping in mind its less-than-ideal straightforwardness, although I appreciate Nancy Bermeo's definition of "ordinary people" as those who "have no extraordinary powers vis-à-vis the states in which they live. [...] They spend most of their lives in personal endeavors—earning money, supporting families, and pursuing whatever leisure activities their social status allows." Bermeo, *Ordinary People in Extraordinary Times: The Citizenry and the Breakdown of Democracy* (Princeton: Princeton University Press, 2003), p. 3.

[26] Williams, *Politics and Letters*, p. 163.

combined into a way of thinking and living."[27] An underlying structure unifies those that might otherwise appear as distinctive experiences of individuals engaged with the complexities of the social world.

By addressing the issue of how communities lived their present in times past, "structures of feeling" invaluably challenges the understanding of past experiences as extraordinary or self-contained finished products. Moreover, and equally important, it suggests empirical tools for evaluating modes of historical relations. Williams proposed that evidence for structures of feelings could be found in the conventions and forms of literary or dramatic writing.[28] Being committed to freeing literature of its presumed insulation from social reality—a legacy of the nineteenth century's emphasis on creativity with its consequent belief in the separation of the realms of fiction and fact—Williams stressed the importance of formal elements while dispelling the belief that artistic claims would make creative writings immune to social analysis. Even more critically, he extended the applicability of his approach beyond literature and argued that all kinds of writing, as producers of meaning, could be analyzed via their modes of composition and pragmatic conventions.[29] The field of literature is not uniquely subject to formal analytical procedures, nor should reality be the exclusive focus of other, more scientific, types of texts. In truth, any writing practice is liable to be examined in terms of its underlying conditions of production and internal processes of composition, both of which are historically variable.

A type of prose, diaries would seem to fall within the range of works Williams designated for analysis of structures of feelings, even if as a "subjective" genre journal writing appears predisposed to that separation of the social from the personal that Williams saw as a dominant cultural mode.[30] Diaries adopt definite types of conventions and take on formal configurations that can be accounted for and examined within specific geographical and historical contexts. Diaries, in fact, offer a dual access to structures of feeling: first, through their formal composition, that is, the arranging and

---

[27] Williams, *The Long Revolution*, p. 63. For a theory of the subject that accommodates the collective and the temporal on the basis of the notion of structures of feeling see Sadeq Rahimi, "Haunted Metaphor, Transmitted Affect: The Pantemporality of Subjective Experience," *Subjectivity* vol. 9, no. 1 (2016): pp. 83–105. Also see Sadeq Rahimi, *Meaning, Madness and Political Subjectivity: A Study of Schizophrenia and Culture in Turkey* (London: Routledge, 2015).

[28] Williams retrospectively explained that, originally, structures of feeling "was developed as an analytic procedure for actual written works, with a very strong stress on their forms and conventions," *Politics and Letters*, p. 159.

[29] Williams, *Politics and Letters*, p. 326.

[30] See his discussion in Williams, "Structures of Feeling." On the uncertainty of diaries as a genre see Irina Paperno's acute observations, "What Can Be Done with Diaries?" *The Russian Review* 63 (October 2004): pp. 561–73.

combination of themes, arguments, and more generally sentences, as well as typography of punctuation; second, as records of events, personal reflections, and feelings, often annotated on a daily basis. When diaries are mostly composed by "common folks" and written not with publication in mind, their potential for testing the relationship between the articulated and the lived appears especially significant. Personal journals constitute a compelling site from which to observe the everyday "commerce" between articulations and experience evoked by Williams. They offer a glimpse of the ordinary.

Ordinary and Extraordinary

In 1958, Williams wrote a short article whose title became one of the best-known phrases associated with his theoretical orientation, "culture is ordinary."[31] Part of Williams's life-long intellectual project toward re-envisioning the meaning of culture through its historicization, the phrase unequivocally supported the anthropological understanding of culture as a whole way of life. Characterized by a commonality of meanings and directions, every society's mode of living expresses its shared purposes and vision, Williams proposed. Individuals organize available meanings and create new observations and discoveries from them: "These are the ordinary processes of human societies and human minds, and we see through them the nature of a culture: that it is always both traditional and creative; that it is both the most ordinary common meanings and the finest individual meanings." Culture is a ubiquitous and inclusive process where meanings are not prescribed but continuously "made and remade" as people engage in the business of living.[32] "Ordinary" is not a qualifier that delimits a certain area within a realm loosely defined as culture and that implies differentiation against a more valuable and privileged opposite. In contrast, "ordinary" connects to the general process of experience, even as it varies across generational, class, and gender lines, as well as space and time. Not special or unusual, "ordinary" highlights the everyday.

In historical studies, "ordinary" has come to designate a field of research that in the tradition of the Annales School steers away from big events and

---

[31] Williams, "Culture is Ordinary" (1958), in *Resources of Hope: Culture, Democracy, Socialism* (London: Verso, 1989), pp. 3–14.
[32] Williams, "Culture is Ordinary," pp. 4, 8.

characters and focuses instead on common people's quotidian experiences.[33] Through a considerable reduction of historical scale, related approaches such as history from below, microhistory, and *Alltagsgeschichte* highlight the agentic power of individuals often considered oppressed or marginalized.[34] To be sure, historians' forays into the normal frequently generate portrayals of exceptionality that are antinomic to the supposedly undistinguished, banal reality of daily existence. In most instances, however, the reiterative nature of the practices, habits, and beliefs of a specific community emerges from researchers' accounts. Emphasis falls on regularity and uniformity, even as efforts at documenting everyday reality tend to valorize neglected lives and actions.

Because the goal of histories of everyday life is to illuminate submerged perspectives, however, they often risk becoming self-referential. Their imperative to recover subjective experiences tends to rely on illustrative cases that, even when designed to track transformations, still describe groups and behaviors in their individuality. Single personalities are then taken as emblematic of a particular "state" of relationships in a specific era. In comparison, Williams's idea of ordinary is embedded within a cultural theory that focuses on "processes." It emphasizes the concept of social totality as composed of interwoven and historically variable systems to be studied in their active occurring. By embracing a dynamic rather than a static approach, Williams highlights the meanings produced by the encounter and clash of people's experiences with available articulations. Whereas passive reception hardly ensues, he suggests, new realities are continuously being created through interactions.

When it comes to journal writing, Williams's conception of the ordinary suggests that one can examine diaries not merely as records of the feelings and thoughts of ordinary folks, nor should diaries be read simply as subordinate groups' reactions (or even autonomous responses) to historical changes and society's norms, institutions, and conventions. In contrast, journals constitute means through which to gauge the pulsating tensions between official discourses and practical consciousness. They track the dynamic evolution of

---

[33] See Peter Burke ed., *New Perspectives on Historical Writing* (University Park: Pennsylvania State University Press, 2001 [1992]).

[34] Andrew Port, "History from Below, the History of Everyday Life, and Microhistory," in James D. Wright ed., *International Encyclopedia of the Social and Behavioral Sciences* (Amsterdam: Elsevier, 2015), vol. 11, 2nd edition. Also see Alf Lüdtke ed., *The History of Everyday Life: Reconstructing Historical Experiences and Ways of Life* (Princeton: Princeton University Press, 1995), and Geoff Eley, "Labor History, Social History, *Alltagsgeschichte*: Experience, Culture, and the Politics of the Everyday—A New Direction for German Social History?" *Journal of Modern History* vol. 61 (June 1989): pp. 297–343.

our acting in the world as we live through our present.[35] For, ultimately, when scholars intrude into the intimacy of private lives, they are looking for discrepancies in experience. They rise above the cacophony of individual voices in search of changes in the structures of feelings, patterns in ways of thinking and perceiving that communicate one's mediated relation to the social world. From Williams's perspective, available dominant interpretations are unable to meet or completely satisfy people's experiential understanding of reality; prevailing ideological standpoints cannot fully contain the sentiments that guide us in our day-to-day dealings—our life praxis. Without pushing the argument too far philosophically, one could state that official worldviews fail to catch the spillover of existence that occurs when we confront an inexhaustible horizon of decisions; they are unable to command the way we "cope" with situations. And this is the case not, or not only, because our intellectual acquisitions are embedded in pre-reflective, noncognitive habitus.[36] Rather, tensions and disconnections from sanctioned narratives define our sense of being in history, our distance from formally authorized versions of reality. Or at the minimum, Williams suggests, we should assume so. "Practical consciousness is always more than a handling of fixed forms and units" even when it is not expressed or articulated.[37] "Ordinary" captures a much richer terrain of meanings than normally understood. Despite engaging with repetitiveness and sameness, it is fluid and dynamic and is molded by and bends with time. The question is: How do these characteristics of flexibility fit with the imperative for objective accounts identified with diary keeping? What defines a diary?

Writing, Records, and Diaries: The Challenge of Authenticity

Writing is a form of "recording" both in the literal sense of registering something faithfully (the term is especially applicable to reproducible sounds and images) and in the wider meaning of testimonial: providing evidence,

---

[35] Drawing from Paul Ricoeur's distinction between identity as *idem* (similarity) and identity as *ipse* (individuality) (Paul Ricoeur, *Oneself as Another* [Chicago: University of Chicago Press, 1996]), Daniel Fabre emphasizes the nonmonolithic nature of the identity expressed in narration. Fabre focuses on the mobility of individuals as they express themselves in the text and argues that attention on movement highlights the "unstable fulcrum crystallized by narration" that is one's identity as *ipse*, the configuration of "a subject *in progress*." Fabre, "Vivere, scrivere, archiviare," in Quinto Antonelli and Anna Iuso eds., *Vite di carta* (Naples: L'ancora, 2000), p. 278.
[36] On this perspective see Maurice Merleau-Ponty's work and the whole phenomenological tradition.
[37] Williams, "Structures of Feeling," p. 130.

documenting.[38] Often drawn up in the form of reports, diaries too can be considered vehicles for the transmission of knowledge. Although personal journals are annotations of one's thoughts and experiences as they occur in the ongoing flow of the quotidian—they chronicle private, intimate events— they also recount facts that the journal writer either witnesses directly or hears second hand from official sources, newspapers, and other media of communication. Developed from the sixteenth-century practice of bookkeeping and the religious custom of self-monitoring, diaries were first fashioned after "memory books" (also called "family books"), a genre developed in the Middle Ages and whose popularity increased in the Renaissance, only to decline by the end of the 1600s.[39] Based on fixed formulas, similarly to books of mercantile accounts from which they derived, memory or family books registered data related to births, assets, debts, and deaths within a specific household. Mixing family matters with business notations, they were conceived as depositories of knowledge for the next generation—testimonial of a history that would survive one's own death through offspring's remembrance.[40]

Fundamentally focused on "registering" events and ensuring a faithful reproduction of reality, family books, whose text was organized around the external time of the calendar (not an interior time), also added a

---

[38] I do not intend to imply that writing is to be looked at as a technique that reproduces spoken language. As several scholars have argued, the relationship between orality and writing, or oral and literate modes of communication, is much more complex. For an early debate on the question that also addresses generative linguistics, see *Alfabetismo e cultura scritta nella storia della società italiana. Atti del seminario tenutosi a Perugia il 29–30 marzo 1977* (Bologna: il Mulino, 1978), especially the essay by Raffaele Simone, "Scrivere, leggere, capire," pp. 91–107; and Roland Barthes and Eric Marty, "Orale/scritto," in *Enciclopedia Einaudi* (Turin: Einaudi, 1980), vol. 10, pp. 60–86. On writing as a "scriptural economy" see Michel de Certeau, *The Practice of Everyday Life* (Berkeley: University of California Press, 1984). For anthropologically oriented perspectives, see the classic studies of Walter J. Ong, *Orality and Literacy: The Technologizing of the World* (London: Methuen, 1982) and Jack Goody, *The Logic of Writing and the Organization of Society* (Cambridge: Cambridge University Press, 1986), as well as Goody, *The Interface Between the Written and the Oral* (Cambridge: Cambridge University Press, 1987), in addition to Goody ed., *Literacy in Traditional Societies* (Cambridge: Cambridge University Press 1968). Also, in *The Domestication of the Savage Mind* (Cambridge: Cambridge University Press, 1977), Goody specifically examines means of communication in relation to modes of thinking, or the effects of writing on cognitive processes. For a phenomenological perspective on the issue in the tradition of Merleau-Ponty, see Georges Gusdorf, *Speaking (La Parole)* (Evanston: Northwestern University Press, 1965).

[39] See Angelo Cicchetti and Raul Mordenti, "La scrittura dei libri di famiglia," in Alberto Asor Rosa ed., *Letteratura italiana*, III, 2. Le forme del testo. La prosa (Turin: Einaudi, 1984), pp. 1117–59; Cicchetti and Mordenti, *I libri di famiglia in Italia*, I, Filologia e storiografia letteraria (Rome: Edizioni di storia e letteratura, 1985); Raul Mordenti, *I libri di famiglia in Italia*, II, Geografia e storia (Rome: Edizioni di storia e letteratura, 2001).

[40] According to Cicchetti and Mordenti, the merchants' habit of recordkeeping can be understood as a modality for guaranteeing the persistence of one's life in memory. Registering facts fostered the hope of overcoming humans' finality in the face of death. See Cicchetti and Mordenti, "La scrittura dei libri di famiglia," p. 1127.

compositional element to classic bookkeeping—brief comments sometimes accompanied straight numerical facts. Doubtlessly, the relatively short lapse between actual happenings and their reporting guaranteed that post-factum elaborations typical of retelling were kept to the minimum. Nevertheless, emotive factors began to color what was originally intended as the mere registering of news. Over time the narrative element expanded, eventually replacing tried-out formulas initially aimed at conferring veracity and authority to family chronicles. The writing style became more fluid too, while a shift towards intimacy and the private—combined with the emergence of modern Western conceptions of the self—gave rise to diaries as modern incarnations of family books.[41] Journaling expanded into a practice beyond the confines of the bourgeois class and its economic calculations.

A mixed genre that encroached upon the literary field, diaries took on a variety of goals spanning from self-perfection to self-creation. Sixteenth-century mystics' scrutiny of their own internal voyage of transformation, including accounts of the drives and desires that tormented them in their spiritual pursuits, became a preview of diaries later used by Pietists and Puritans as tool for self-improvement.[42] Then, beginning in the nineteenth century, the lay public increasingly resorted to narrative forms of individuation. Through the means of introspection, people annotated personal development and discovery.[43] In these instances, writing became an increasingly more private practice, as in the *journal intime*, although alternative models of diaries resonated with the original documentary purpose of family books.[44] A tentative nomenclature in French captures the hybridity of the genre:

---

[41] On conceptions of the self in the modern West, see the classic studies of Charles Taylor, *Sources of the Self: The Making of the Modern Identity* (Cambridge, Mass.: Harvard University Press, 1989); Jerrold Seigel, *The Idea of the Self: Thought and Experience in Western Europe since the Seventeenth Century* (Cambridge: Cambridge University Press, 2005). Also see Roy Porter, ed. *Rewriting the Self: Histories from the Renaissance to the Present* (London: Routledge, 1997); and Michel Foucault, *Ethics: Subjectivity and Truth*, edited by Paul Rabinow, translated by Robert Hurley et al., in *Essential Works of Foucault 1954–1984*, vol. 1 (New York: The New Press, 1997), and *The History of Sexuality*, vol. 3, *The Care of the Self* (New York: Vintage, 1988).

[42] On the case of mystics see Michel de Certeau, *La Fable mystique, XVIe–XVIIe siècle* (Paris: Gallimard, 1987).

[43] On this turn see Peter Boerner, *Tagebuch* (Stuttgart: Metzler, 1969). In France, the first work on diaries dealt with characterology in relation to the analysis of personality. See Michèle Leleu, *Les Journeaux intimes* (Paris: PUF, 1952). For a focus on French diaries from the 1800s on see Alain Girard, *Le Journal intime* (Paris: PUF, 1963).

[44] "Diary" and "journal" share the same etymological origin from the Latin term for "day" (*diarium*, from *dies* [day], was soldiers' daily allowance.) A technical distinction between diary and journal is sometimes drawn, where diary is a daily reportage and journal has less frequent entries. Also, in French *"intime"* accompanies *"journal"* as a way to differentiate diaries from newspapers. See Philippe Lejeune and Catherine Bogaert, *Le Journal intime. Histoire et anthologie* (Paris: Les éditions textuels, 2006), p. 23. Also see Françoise Simonet-Tenant, *Le Journal intime. Genre littéraire et écriture ordinaire* (Paris: Nathan, 2001).

journal intime, journal personnel, journal de reportage, journal externe, and even *journal extime.*[45] Each of these appellations reflects a particular emphasis, whether on private situations (*journal intime, journal personnel*), on the one hand, or history and facts (*journal de reportage, journal externe*), on the other, with the melting of the two captured in the neologism "*extime.*"

The impossibility of establishing a neat, catchall categorization illustrates the interpretive difficulties that inexorably confront the analyst of personal journals. While diaries are supposed to be receptacles of private reflections, they also purportedly offer accurate recounts of events and play a potential role as authoritative sources of information—a function made possible by diaries' key features. As Philippe Lejeune and Catherine Bogaert highlight, the first gesture of diarists engaged in journaling is to inscribe the day's date.[46] Without dates, there is no "diary" in its etymological sense of "daily," only an ensemble of unconnected contemplations. Often, the exact time, both in hours and minutes, will also be noted next to the current date. Dates and time anchor onto the actuality of daily contingencies what would otherwise be loose bits of information or even streams of consciousness. By adding context to the content of the entry, exactness helps specify the precise placement of people's writing activity within their daily schedule, it ensures the cogency of one's account.

The unadulterated status of single entries further contributes to conferring an aura of authenticity and reliability on the reported narrative—the originally written text remains untouched, with no edits, alterations, or revisions. (When modifications are applied, one might be crossing into the genre of memoir or autobiography.) Once jotted down in a diary, thoughts and facts, no matter how filtered, are forever fixed. As in a photographic still, the ephemeral turns into a memento, frozen in time—a testimonial that will be accessed by future potential readers in its entirety. Ultimately, diarists' personal investment in their journals stands as another guarantee of truth. One presumes genuineness and transparency from authors, especially when they initiate their diary with no expectations or desire to make it public—a "pure" status that is potentially tempered by other intervening factors, including the unconscious.

On the private realm and modernity see Alain Corbin, "Backstage," in Michelle Perrot ed., *A History of Private Life. Vol. IV. From the Fire of the Revolution to the Great War*, translated by Arthur Goldhammer (Cambridge, Mass.: Belknap Press, 1990), part of *A History of Private Life* series edited by Philippe Ariès and Georges Duby.

[45] Michel Tournier, *Journal extime* (Paris: La Musardine, 2002).
[46] Philippe Lejeune and Catherine Bogaert, *Le Journal intime.*

In truth, the sense of factual clarity emanating from diaries stands in paradoxical contradiction to the essentially subjective nature of journal writing, particularly if one considers the historical trajectory of this practice in the West up to its last incarnation as a vessel for adolescents' expression. Over the last century, young women have especially become associated with *le journal intime*—through daily entries in the pages of a reserved notebook, they engage in an intimate journey of self-exploration/confession.[47] Because personal, confidential, and often secretive, private diaries allow young writers to articulate inner feelings and thoughts they might not otherwise voice openly or share in public.[48] Diaries help authors carve a space away from the outside world and grant them the freedom to escape their social persona—a tendency already evident in the older memory or family books.[49] Although the chronicle style typical of the latter made it possible to separate private feelings from public events (at least in theory), we know that the division was spurious at best. An individual's driving factor for annotating particular facts was indeed the personal hope of surviving the transitory nature of life on earth—the scribe of the family book was leaving traces of his (and less often her) history with the expectation of being memorialized by future generations. Even the reporting of economic transactions was part of this overall effort to remember one's individual performance in the world. The line between the subject's inner realm and external "objective" reality was fundamentally blurry, and not only in terms of content but also of style.

Illustrative of formal fuzziness was the use of the narrative third person interspersed with first and second.[50] The switching of tenses from past to present and future demonstrated the same trend. Family books showed continuous movement between what Émile Benveniste sees as the two different planes of enunciation, history and discourse, as well as between their correlates, indirect speech and the dialogic (the latter involving an ideal

---

[47] See Philippe Lejeune, *Le Moi des demoiselles. Enquête sur le journal de jeune fille* (Paris: Éditions du Seuil, 1993). Young girls were not the only ones engaged in the practice, though. See Malik Allam, *Journaux intimes. Une sociologie de l'écriture personnelle* (Paris: L'Harmattan, 2000).

[48] In our electronic age, there are sites on how to keep the secrecy of a diary securely on the web. Some offer "locks" too.

[49] Ong claims that the diary "demands, in a way, the maximum fictionalizing of the utterer and the addressee." Writing "is always a kind of imitation talking," and diarists pretend to be talking to themselves, although we never actually talk to ourselves that way. *Orality and Literacy*, p. 102. Also see Paul John Eakin, *How Our Lives Become Stories: Making Selves* (Ithaca: Cornell University Press, 1999).

[50] On the use of pronouns see Émile Benveniste, "La nature des pronoms," in *Problèmes de linguistique générale* (Paris: Gallimard, 1966), pp. 251–66. Also see Michel Butor, "L'usage des pronoms personnels dans le roman," in *Répertoire II* (Paris: Minuit, 1964), pp. 61–72.

conversation with a fictional interlocutor).[51] Recourse to these mixed techniques points to writers' nervousness about the reliability of their statements—through stylistic choices they conveyed uncertainty about future readers and their perceptions. Later on, when family books metamorphosed into diaries and the modern individual emerged as a historical configuration with its own matured sense of self, the subjective point of view gained more currency and grew in legitimacy. The use of the first-person singular in modern diaries (along with the rise of autobiographies) signal this development.[52]

Methodologically speaking, the hybridity of personal journals means that assessing diaries' documentary potential is hardly obtainable through an exclusively literal reading. In contrast, one needs to contextualize single entries (and in some cases specific lines) within the overall tenor, goals, and direction of the individual diarist, while also keeping in mind the specificity of the historical time—a personal story's connection to the larger course of events. A fine-tuned explanatory operation becomes especially critical during periods of turbulence and change, when even those wishing to retreat from the outside world find it hard to do so. Considering that the separation of public affairs from one's private life is seldom achievable and appears ever more arduous in moments of social crisis, interpreting diaries based solely on the content of the written text would be insufficient.

A type of recorded communication that is socially embedded, diaries are akin to more traditionally defined literary works. Like them, they also follow

---

[51] Benveniste, "Les relations de temps dans le verbe français" in *Problèmes de linguistique générale*, pp. 237–50. Benveniste discusses use of the *passé simple* as "aorist," which, from the Greek, designates an event in the past. On "aorist" time also see Jean Starobinski's discussion in *La Relation critique* (Paris: Gallimard, 1970), pp. 87–8. Cicchetti and Mordenti talk about "mythical aorist" as the time of an event independent of the person of the narrator in "La scrittura dei libri di famiglia," p. 1130.

[52] On autobiographies see Karl J. Weintraub, *The Value of the Individual: Self and Circumstance in Autobiography* (Chicago: University of Chicago Press, 1978); Philippe Lejeune, *L'Autobiographie en France* (Paris: Colin, 1971) and *Le Pacte autobiographique* (Paris: Éditions du Seuil, 1975); James Olney, ed., *Autobiography: Essays Theoretical and Critical* (Princeton: Princeton University Press, 1980). For a history of Victorian autobiography, see Toni Cerutti, *Le vite dei Vittoriani. Breve storia dell'autobiografia vittoriana* (Bari: Adriatica editrice, 1981). On early autobiographies see Marziano Guglielminetti, *Memoria e scrittura. L'autobiografia da Dante a Cellini* (Turin: Einaudi, 1977). Also see Robert Folkenflik ed., *The Culture of Autobiography: Constructions of Self-Representation* (Stanford: Stanford University Press, 1993); and Michael Mascuch, *Origins of the Individualist Self: Autobiography and Self-Identity in England, 1591–1791* (Cambridge: Polity Press, 1997). For a critique of autobiographies' modern beginnings, see Georges Gusdorf, *Les Écritures du moi. Lignes de vie 1* (Paris: Odile Jacob, 1991), chapter 3, "L'acte de naissance des écritures du moi?" Gusdorf specifically cites the work of Georg Misch, *Geschichte der Autobiographie* (Leipzig/Berlin: Druck und Verlag von B. G. Teubner, 1907), a study that mapped the development of ancient and medieval autobiographies. Gusdorf also lists key works on the history of diaries. For an approach to autobiographical writing as egodocuments see Rudolf Dekker ed., *Egodocuments and History: Autobiographical Writing in its Social Context since the Middle Ages* (Hilversum: Verloren 2002). On ego-history see the special issue of *Historein* vol. 3 (2001) on "European Ego-histories: Historiography and the Self, 1970–2000," edited by Luisa Passerini and Alexander C. T. Geppert.

formal models whose particular features further contribute to define the meaning of the narrated text.[53]

Raymond Williams's discussion of "structures of feeling" underlined the importance of forms and conventions for the analysis of "actual written works."[54] The layer of meaning associated with the social context of the author (that is, with the mood of the author's particular social milieu) is embedded within formal narrative traits, he claimed. Conventional features embody and at the same time activate the values shared by a community. Indeed, etymologically, "convention" emphasizes the act of coming together through its connotative reference to agreement. Contrary to the negative association of "convention" with routine, unimaginative, and ultimately technique, the term's original sense highlights mutual understanding. More than modes of formal composition, "conventions" are products of the general social process and constitute usages of "a social language"—they are expressive means that, agreed upon via tacit consent, simultaneously convey and realize a particular structure of feeling.[55] In Williams's evaluation, every formal element is rooted in an active material basis and articulates specific relations.[56] As a form of practical consciousness, language reveals the "material process of sociality"; it sustains our active construction of the world by endowing us with the tools for describing that same world.[57] Language is both constitutive of and responsive to historical and social processes.[58] The relationship between form and content is therefore critical for assessing the production of meaning in any textual source. Williams's emphasis on the etymology of literature as the "ability to read," or "literacy," especially widens the range of potential texts to be considered under the rubric of "literary." It also reaffirms the constructive role of writing. Not merely recorded information, texts are the mediums through

---

[53] The debate on the literary status of diaries is especially engaging. See in particular Peter Boerner, "Place du journal dans la littérature moderne" and Jacques Chocheyras, "La place du journal intime dans une typologie linguistique des formes littéraires," in Victor Del Litto ed., *Le Journal intime et ses formes littéraires. Actes du Colloque de septembre 1975* (Genève: Librairie Droz, 1978), pp. 217-24 and 225-33. Also see Michel David, "Il problema del diario intimo in Italia," in Anna Dolfi ed., *"Journal intime" e letteratura moderna. Atti di seminario. Trento, marzo-maggio 1988* (Rome: Bulzoni: 1989), pp. 79-108.

[54] Williams argues that literature is a means of communication of experience or, more specifically, "Literature is communication in written *language.*" See Williams, *Reading and Criticism* (London: Frederick Muller, 1950), p. 107.

[55] "Genres" in Williams, *Marxism and Literature*, p. 185.

[56] "Forms" in Williams, *Marxism and Literature*, pp. 186-91.

[57] "Two Interviews with Raymond Williams," *Red Shift* 2 (1977), p. 16 (cited in John Higgins, *Raymond Williams: Literature, Marxism and Cultural Materialism* [London: Routledge, 1999], p. 119).

[58] "Language" in Williams, *Marxism and Literature*, pp. 21-44.

which authors become conscious of their experience while transmitting it.[59] Diaries, particularly those composed by ordinary people, exemplify the nexus of expression and competency achieved by the popular classes at a time of increasingly expanded access to education and knowledge.[60] The question is: are all diarists and all diaries the same?

Accounting, Value, and Aesthetic Laws: *Rédacteurs* and *Auteurs*

Historically, writing has been a valuable and restricted resource until mass literacy was achieved in the early twentieth century. Before then, access to writing was mostly limited to wealthy individuals, especially men, although in the case of private journals their rarity among females in premodern times is hard to ascertain. Samuel Pepys, whose diary is considered one of the first exemplars of personal journals in 1600s' Europe, reported that upon reading his wife's vivid notes in which she related her lonely life and sadness, he could not tolerate the idea of her papers being available to others.[61] Today, there is no trace of a Mrs. Pepys's diary. The bourgeois origins of journaling, rooted in the encounter of Christianity, capitalism, and individualism, could not but mark the genre as gendered. Women were not captains of industry, nor did they play leadership roles in religion.[62]

Male-dominated during their early stage of development, personal journals inherited the merchants' accounting habit, orientation to tracking, and constant attempt to balance the budget. As already discussed, financial items were at the forefront of diarists' narratives, while the practice of taking stock of bills helped individual scribes assess their position in life. Even more interestingly for our consideration, early diarists showed similarity with the merchants'

---

[59] Here, de Certeau's idea of writing as a form of travel and a connection, a *metaphorai*, is pertinent—stories link spaces together. Also see de Certeau's view of storytelling as performative activity in *The Practice of Everyday Life*.

[60] On the diffusion of reading and writing see the classic work by Carlo Cipolla, *Literacy and Development in the West* (Baltimore: Penguin Books, 1969) and Harvey J. Graff, *The Legacies of Literacy: Continuities and Contradictions in Western Culture and Society* (Bloomington: Indiana University Press, 1987). On mass literacy, also see David Vincent, *The Rise of Mass Literacy: Reading and Writing in Modern Europe* (Cambridge: Polity, 2000) and *Literacy and Popular Culture: England 1750–1914* (Cambridge: Cambridge University Press, 1989).

[61] Entry of January 9, 1663, cited in Béatrice Didier, *Le Journal intime* (Paris: Presses universitaires de France, 1976), p. 48.

[62] On diary-keeping by women over the last two centuries see Suzanne Bunkers and Cynthia Huff eds., *Inscribing the Daily: Critical Essays on Women's Diaries* (Amherst: University of Massachusetts Press, 1996). For an examination of women's diaries in nineteenth-century America see Jennifer Sinor, *The Extraordinary Work of Ordinary Writing: Annie Ray's Diary* (Iowa City: University of Iowa Press, 2002).

ethic of thorough and exhaustive recording—every single occurrence was deemed liable to be counted and registered, no matter its (numerical or qualitative) value. The compulsion to write everything down, which characterized diaries at their origins, was closely aligned with the core feature of journal keeping mentioned earlier: the short distance in time separating the happening of events from the diarists' actual reporting, usually on the same day. Due to time compression, very little room was left to scribes for processing life experiences and selecting the ones about which to write. Compensating for this inescapable limitation, it turns out, diaries became saving devices where everything was deemed worth keeping and in which nothing went to waste (as in the best Protestant ethical tradition of Weberian portraiture). Even time counted and was conserved in all its details, however menial. Lists of often uninteresting activities dotted diarists' tales.[63]

Within this logic of accumulation, journals served as repositories; written reports ensured availability of information for future use should one want to look back at what was recorded and "cash in" on its lessons.[64] Permanence on the written page created value, while failure to appear in ink equated with the nonexistent: it left no tracks. Paradoxically, private journals—that refuge from the bustling and hustling of the impersonal marketplace—did not escape the laws of capitalism. In the nineteenth century, when the individual subject more securely appropriated central stage in the diary's evolving history, the "I" along with time and memories became the most valuable capital to preserve and enhance.[65]

While the general shift towards intimacy preserved the privileged status of the private bourgeois individual, it also confronted the diarist with further predicaments. The journal's "objective" function of recording seemingly clashed with its supposed role as spiritual exercise—a way to oversee one's inner development. If, as a genre, diaries gradually began to veer toward the

---

[63] For a modern version of this compulsion to keep, see the magnificent work of Georges Perec. In "The Scene of a Stratagem," for example, he writes, "I began to be afraid of forgetting, as if, unless I noted everything down, I wasn't going to be able to retain anything of the life that was escaping from me. Scrupulously, every evening, with a maniacal conscientiousness, I began to keep a sort of journal. It was the exact opposite of a *journal intime*: all that I put into it were the 'objective' things that had happened to me: the time I woke up, how I spent the day, my movements, what I had bought [...]. With this panic about losing track of myself there went a fury for preserving and classifying. I kept everything: letters with their envelopes, cinema checkouts, airline tickets, bills, cheque stubs, handouts, receipts, catalogues [...]." In *Species of Spaces and Other Pieces*, translated by John Sturrock (London: Penguin, 2008), p. 171.
[64] Didier convincingly makes this economic argument through reference to surplus value. See *Le Journal intime*, especially pp. 50 and ff. Trouillot talks about the "storage-model" of history as memory in *Silencing the Past*.
[65] Didier, *Le Journal intime*, p. 54. Also see Daniele Marchesini, *Il bisogno di scrivere. Usi della scrittura nell'Italia moderna* (Rome-Bari: Laterza, 1992).

realm of the private and became essentially secretive because personal, in practice many journals still maintained their original connection to accounting through a parallel compulsion for reporting.[66] On this aspect, they shared newspapers' constant dilemma of keeping up their mission as recorders of daily events while facing the impossible reality of ever being able to cover all the news. A comparison of diaries with newspapers actually underscores key characters of daily written narratives. The challenge of having to handle facts in their unfiltered quasi-immediacy results in stylistic consequences for both. In the same way that time limitations affect the form and presentation of newspapers' articles, they mark diaries' entries: repetitions along with concise, telegraphic sentences are a generalized norm, while compositional structures show lack of unifying threads. In principle at least, diaries and newspapers can scarcely fulfill literary ambitions.

To be sure, diaries' writing style evolved over the course of a few centuries, and early journals' crude resemblance to books of bills eventually gave way to a model centered on self-absorption and introspective analysis. Past models of journaling were not eliminated. To the contrary, elements of previous incarnations came to coexist with more contemporary components. Although hybrid samples resulted from modifications and additions, in the end, two major and somewhat opposing tendencies remained characteristic of diaries into the twentieth century: attention to detailed chronicling and recourse to extended reflection. Each of these trends presented a specific style that in turn exhibited the artistic potential of journal writing, albeit its limits too. Jean Rousset, for one, argues that because of the genre's constraints diarists can never achieve the level of literary authorship asserted by a novelist (*auteur*). Diarists are forced to remain *rédacteurs*, even if Rousset acknowledges that wide expressive gulfs separate one model of journaling (chronicle) from the other (reflections).[67]

In truth, differences in style tend to run along class lines, suggesting that Rousset's dichotomous taxonomy of *auteur* and *rédacteur* should be applied

---

[66] Corbin suggestively hints that "techniques of self-comprehension developed for the confessional were being secularized. In the nineteenth century people became obsessed with accounting for their time. It was not only their obsession with sin that was responsible. Their need stemmed from the same fantasies of loss that impelled them to keep detailed household accounts and that engendered certain fears, such as the fear of squandering sperm or of watching life grow shorter with each passing day. A determination to stem these losses led to the keeping of private diaries." See Corbin, "Backstage," p. 498.

[67] Jean Rousset, "Le journal intime, texte sans déstinataire?" *Poétique* vol. 14, no. 56 (1983): pp. 435–43. *Rédacteur* might be translated here as "reporter." For an early analysis of diaries' literary qualities, see Robert Fothergill, *Private Chronicles: A Study of English Diaries* (London: Oxford University Press, 1974). On forms of diaries see Gianfranco Folena, "Premessa," *Quaderni di retorica e poetica*, issue on Le forme del diario, vol. 2 (1985): pp. 5–10.

to the practice of diary writing from within—some scribes are more *auteur* than others. Social status matters, and even taking into account the inevitable strictures to which the calendar schedule subjects journal entries, a range of modes of expression is available to diarists. Hence, the narrative approach that accompanies introspection, as opposed to the telegraphic, skeletal reporting of straight facts, offers a relatively higher degree of compositional freedom. It also grants diarists a broader command over the material about which they write. Conversely, the fragmentation that necessarily characterizes a diary due to the shifting nature of events from one day to the next (but also the use of repetition instead of continuity) becomes exponentially higher when one's account is limited to arranging facts on a list. In this latter case, the lack of an explicit conjoining logic to explicate the reported occurrences often signals one's inability to master writing, which as a practice, and more than speaking, requires engagement with the formal rules of language.[68] Skill differentials emerge that influence diary structure, raising the issue of ordinary people's relationship to the scriptural.[69] If, on the one hand, access to schooling and, more broadly, literacy heavily conditions the probability of one's taking up the habit, on the other hand, for those who can claim authorship, writing becomes a declaration of authority, a claim to one's right to speak.[70] Recourse to the "I," or the first-person singular, particularly indicates a willingness to claim jurisdiction over what one lays out on the blank page. Use of indirect speech, in contrast, is a form of delegation, a release of responsibilities, a defense against (perceived or real) inadequacies. Indeed, impediments to expression start from lack of basic language tools: What one says is

[68] On writing and its relationship to speaking also see Armando Petrucci, "Per la storia dell'alfabetismo e della cultura scritta: metodi—materiali—quesiti," *Quaderni storici* vol. 13, no. 38 (2) (May–August 1978): pp. 451–65.
[69] Roland Barthes distinguishes between *écrivains* and *écrivants*. The former writes in a disinterested way: literature is the goal, where literature works on and with language. The *écrivant* instead acts in the world: writing is a means to an end. See "Écrivains et écrivants," in *Essais critiques* (Paris: Seuil, 1964), pp. 147–54, translated into English by Richard Howard as "Authors and Writers," in *Critical Essays* (Evanston: Northwestern University Press, 1972), pp. 143–50. This distinction might be helpful to conceptualize stylistic differences in writing practices. However, it still fails to distinguish between occasional diarists, who might not be able to master written language, and those who, while not meeting the criteria of *écrivains* as theorized by Barthes, have a stronger command of linguistic rules and style. On the relationship between everyday language and literary language in diaries see Maurice Blanchot, "Le journal intime et le récit," in *Le Livre à venir* (Paris: Gallimard, 1959), pp. 252–9.
[70] See de Certeau's discussion of the problematics of enunciation in *The Practice of Everyday Life*. De Certeau addresses the question of what happens when ordinary people invade the privileged field of power operations. On the opposition between writing and style see Roland Barthes, *Writing Degree Zero* (London: Jonathan Cape, 1967 [1953]).

tightly dependent on how one says it. More than plagued by stylistic grossness, less literate diarists might suffer from a sense of tentativeness.[71]

We know that the ordinary folks who took up journaling most often opted for a stance close to the wholly impersonal observer—a posturing that, typical of scientific writing, relies on specific modes of composition to authenticate impersonal claims.[72] Taking class differentials into account, the question then becomes: How can we theorize the general relationship between journaling as a form of narration and the diarist's historical situatedness? More cogently, how does that relationship affect the status of diaries as historical sources?

Time and Narrative: Living in Time

In *The Past Is a Foreign Country*, David Lowenthal argues that we are accustomed to think of the historical past in terms of chronologies, sequences, and dates, which, organized together within a narrative structure—a tale—help give coherence to disparate occurrences.[73] A relatively recent turn in the way we approach history, the orientation to sequentially ordered events gives calendric specificity to the past; it salvages the past from the immense chaos of infinite deeds and characters that constitutes historical processes. In Lowenthal's words, "Historical facts are timeless and discontinuous until woven together in stories. We do not experience a flow of time, only a succession of situations and events."[74] Temporal precision helps shape history because ordering gives us a sense of our place in the succession of happenings. Together, dates and narrative provide unity; they help simplify the overwhelming synchronicity of events by turning them into manageable, comprehensible elements of unique stories. The linearity afforded by narrative accounts makes historical reality more accessible.[75]

Narrative sensibility is central to historical knowledge. In Paul Ricoeur's rendering, "Time becomes human time to the extent that it is organized after

---

[71] Mario Isnenghi argues that, in the case of ordinary people, writing, or the need to write, offers a venue for both creating and reinforcing an identity. The need to write reveals "a threatened identity that reintegrates itself and gets reconstituted (but also forms itself and diversifies) in the moment of writing. A threatened identity, but at the same time an identity in the making and made: I do not think it is verbal acrobatics, but a genuine dialectical situation." See "Intervento di discussione," in *Per un archivio della scrittura popolare*, p. 199. On the narrative self also see Judith Butler, "Giving an Account of Oneself," *Diacritics* vol. 31, no. 4 (Winter 2001): pp. 22–40.

[72] Williams provides an interesting point of view on scientific writing in *Politics and Letters*, p. 327.

[73] *The Past Is a Foreign Country* (Cambridge: Cambridge University Press, 1985), p. 219 and ff.

[74] Lowenthal, *The Past Is a Foreign Country*, p. 220.

[75] On a critique of linearity and the idea of history as progress see Siegfried Kracauer (with Paul Oskar Kristeller), *History: The Last Things before the Last* (New York: Oxford University Press, 1969).

the manner of a narrative; narrative, in turn, is meaningful to the extent that it portrays the features of temporal experience."[76] Connected to the human world via our own acting in it, narrative is able to represent human time or, more aptly, the human experience of time.[77] It addresses our need to make sense of life, that is, to make our lives intelligible to us—a desire that rests on and is inseparable from our natural relation to the past. As David Carr suggests, the past is there for us and "*figures* in our ordinary view of things, whether we are historians or not."[78] Narrative features are not external to the cognitive process. In contrast, they inhere in everyday experience—they stand as primary characteristics of our social life, an extension of the actions we take in the world. Storytelling can be considered one major way we organize our experience of time and understand it.

Writing a diary would seem to complement neatly our inclination towards conceptualizing the passing of time while accounting for our place in time—diaries relate one's living in time. As an activity, journaling puts into practice narrative sensibilities; it gives direction to and shapes our experience of the daily flow of events, and of life more generally.[79] Dates and the ordering of facts turn uncertain external situations into manageable occurrences that we can then categorize and make sense of as we communicate them onto a page. A reassuring operation, the reporting of selected observations out of myriad happenings simplifies reality and gives us the impression of mastering what occurs around us—it gives us the illusion of exercising a grip on existence. With its narrative's linear nature, chronicling dilutes complexity at the same

---

[76] Paul Ricoeur, *Time and Narrative* (Chicago: University of Chicago Press, 1984), vol. 1, p. 3. Over the last decades, the constructive role of language, and narrative more specifically, has been at the center of a vigorous debate among historians and literary critics, with Hayden White's work being especially influential. See his *Metahistory: The Historical Imagination in Nineteenth-Century Europe* (Baltimore: Johns Hopkins University Press, 1973) and *Tropics of Discourse: Essays in Cultural Criticism* (Baltimore: Johns Hopkins University Press, 1978). For the debate see W. J. T. Mitchell, *On Narrative* (Chicago: University of Chicago Press, 1981).
[77] According to Ricoeur, we experience time in two closely related and interactive ways: on the one hand linearly (cosmological time), and on the other in terms of past/present/future (phenomenological time). Ricoeur makes recourse to a threefold conception of mimesis to account for the process through which narrative represents human action. See *Time and Narrative*, vol. 3 (Chicago: University of Chicago Press, 1990).
[78] David Carr, *Time, Narrative, and History* (Bloomington: Indiana University Press, 1986), p. 3. Carr addresses what he calls "pre-thematic 'background' awareness."
[79] On the way that consciousness of time affected the prose of diary writing after the breakthrough of clock technology see Stuart Sherman, *Telling Time: Clocks, Diaries, and English Diurnal Forms, 1660–1785* (Chicago: University of Chicago Press, 1996). On the history of horology and measuring time see David Landes, *Revolution in Time: Clocks and the Making of the Modern World* (Cambridge, Mass.: Harvard University Press, 1983) (revised edition 2000).

time that it alleviates the burden of feeling overwhelmed by the multiplicity of situations.[80]

Unlike history accounts, in the case of diaries the time gap between the occurrence of an event and its recording is extremely limited, even if the same process of taking distance from the experience unfolds in both historical and journal reporting.[81] Jotting down notes at the end of the day insulates one from the chaos of stimuli and perceptions that make up the day; it turns external reality into a more familiar environment and might help domesticate the unspeakable too. Indeed, where chronicling prevails over reflections on one's inner life, diary writing signals emotional closure—a refusal to be subjectively involved, a type of defense mechanism against the brutality of the surrounding world. Keeping time helps living in time.[82] The everyday activity of reporting on the everyday contributes to scale down the often insurmountable magnitude of outside occurrences that make us feel powerless, a confirmation of our own insignificance.

Ironically, the ego-centered activity of diary writing reveals the fragility of the individual, the nonconsequentiality and helplessness of the self.[83] More critically, the tension between inner life and the experienced environment, a main feature of diaries, gets amplified in times of emergency, when not only laws might deprive citizens of their rights, but the overall weight of historical events becomes overwhelming.[84] In these instances, the ordinary and extraordinary interweave to create new expressive opportunities for those journal writers caught in the midst of eventful storms. As they navigate multiple contradictions, diarists epitomize the struggle to maintain inner balance in the face of dramatic circumstances—in the process of accounting for historical chaos, they strive to domesticate their own understanding of an unruly world. This was undoubtedly the situation many faced in Italy in 1943–45. How did

---

[80] Lowenthal, *The Past Is a Foreign Country*, chapter 5.

[81] On history as a new temporality and the acceleration of experience in modernity see Reinhart Koselleck, *Futures Past: On the Semantics of Historical Time* (New York: Columbia University Press, 2004). Also see Peter Osborne, *The Politics of Time: Modernity and Avant-Garde* (London: Verso, 1995).

[82] One could also refer here to the endurance of time in the sense of maintenance, as in Lisa Baraitser, *Enduring Time* (London: Bloomsbury, 2017), although she focuses on the experience of suspended time in grief, waiting, and other practices of care where time seems not to move.

[83] For an opposite argument see the case of intellectuals in Irina Paperno, *Stories of the Soviet Experience: Memoirs, Diaries, Dreams* (Ithaca: Cornell University Press, 2009). Paperno discusses how Soviet intelligentsia's autobiographical writings helped create a community.

[84] On the suspension of laws in a state of emergency see Giorgio Agamben, *State of Exception* (Chicago: University of Chicago Press, 2005). On the issue of how past, present, and future are understood in times of crisis see François Hartog, *Regimes of Historicity: Presentism and the Experiences of Time* (New York: Columbia University Press, 2015).

the confluence of ordinary and extraordinary under a state of emergency affect the writing of diaries then?

Everydayness and "Exception"

Although personal and increasingly more dedicated to the self, modern diaries are obviously not written in a historical vacuum.[85] A refuge from an outside world often perceived as uncaring and unsympathetic, diaries live symbiotically with the reality their authors are supposedly trying to bracket off and downplay. Surrounding contexts and events impinge upon the solitary act of journaling—self-examination and reflection hardly take place in the exclusivity of isolation. Because the majority of research on diaries tends to see the *journal intime* as the latest manifestation of the genre, however, models of diary-keeping that depart from personal introspection are scarcely considered, despite the fact that the inner dialogue presumed to characterize the *journal intime* is rarely achieved.[86] Studies of *journaux intimes* highlight the genre's historical evolution and emphasize the scribes' propensity to put the lived at a distance as they create an imaginary addressee in the guise of "dear diary." Little do these analyses recognize that the decades between the 1880s and the 1920s saw a surge in journaling among the popular classes enabled by an increase in literacy and an expanded access to writing. Motivated by the two critical phenomena of emigration and war, diaries became an expressive means to which soldiers, émigrés, and more generally common folks resorted in the face of extremely challenging circumstances.[87] Not overly intimate or reflective—in contrast, characterized by a pragmatic orientation—this model of journaling countered the inward-looking emphasis of the dialogic confessional typical of the *journal intime*.

As repository for tales of trying tribulations, diaries then offered historians a glimpse into the experiences of ordinary folks and became a critical source for illuminating the lives of those considered marginal. No longer amassed

---

[85] Nineteenth-century Russian intellectuals, for example, linked the development of their personality to the progress of history. See Jochen Hellbeck, "Russian Autobiographical Practice," in Jochen Hellbeck and Klaus Heller eds., *Autobiographical Practices in Russia–Autobiographische Praktiken in Russland* (Göttingen: V&R Press, 2004), pp. 278–98.

[86] On this point see Lejeune and Bogaert, *Le Journal intime*, p. 121.

[87] On diaries as well as private correspondence of Italian soldiers during the First World War see Antonio Gibelli, *La Grande Guerra degli italiani 1915–1918* (Milan: Sansoni, 1998) and Quinto Antonelli, *Storia intima della grande guerra. Lettere, diari e memorie dei soldati dal fronte* (Rome: Donzelli, 2015).

under the general umbrella of collective agent or meshed in the all-encompassing anonymity of large (nameless) numbers, the lower classes could be approached via personal accounts of their own.[88] Attention to their private writings highlighted the common people's active role in the making of their day-to-day life; it helped subjectivize the rhythm of their existence.[89] Recovering lost voices silenced by the traditional biases of dominant narratives was expected to illuminate the role of the downtrodden either as protagonists of individual acts of resistance or as participants in larger popular movements.

In this book, I wish to push the potentialities of marginalized narratives in a different direction. Beyond a trajectory of recuperation, I am interested in how people's interpretation of historical events from the standpoint of their everyday experience affected their responses to those same events and created new political sensibilities. Analytically, the juxtaposition of ordinary and extraordinary as applied to cases of historical upheavals directs our attention to the way individuals tentatively redesign new interpretive paths for themselves as they face the displacement of older frameworks. At times of momentous transformations, negotiating past understandings in the effort to confront present challenges is a necessary, albeit laborious, undertaking that knowingly or unknowingly all historical actors confront. While people strive to live their lives in as close a proximity to normalcy as possible, the encroaching of outside occurrences into the everyday flow of things, often in a violent manner, unsettles regular routines. Within a short timespan (sometimes merely minutes), individuals simultaneously need to filter new macro phenomena and coexist with their effects, even if only on a provisional basis. Adjusting becomes a survival skill that requires both flexibility and a willingness to reshuffle age-old habits and beliefs. The question is: How did the exceptional disruptiveness of the 1943–45 years affect Italians' evaluations of the past regime? How can diaries help us outline an answer?

The relationship between external events and the quotidian is central to the practice of diary writing. It is reflected in the genre's fragmentary nature as

---

[88] Martyn Lyons, *The Writing Culture of Ordinary People in Europe, c. 1860–1920* (Cambridge: Cambridge University Press, 2013). Also see Martyn Lyons ed., *Ordinary Writings, Personal Narratives: Writing Practices in 19th and Early 20th-Century Europe* (Bern: Peter Lang, 2007) and Quinto Antonelli and Anna Iuso eds., *Vite di carta*.

[89] On this point see Lyons, *The Writing Culture*. Also see Daniel Fabre ed., *Écritures ordinaires* (Paris: Editions P.O.L., 1993) and Daniel Fabre ed., *Par écrit. Éthnologie des écritures quotidiennes* (Paris: Editions de la Maison des sciences de l'homme, 1997). On the multiple aspects of writing, including cognitive, social, magical, and sacred, see Giorgio Raimondo Cardona, *Antropologia della scrittura* (Turin: Loescher, 1981).

well as open structure—features that transpire more plainly once diaries are compared to their kindred genre of autobiography. Here, narrative continuity is a trademark as the author can take advantage of the time lag between the happening of events and their reporting to reflect on issues in retrospect. This does not mean that individual autobiographies display no gaps in their stories or are free of sequential breaks. To the contrary, especially when they approximate the genre of the Bildungsroman, memoirs offer a coming-of-age lesson by outlining the moral-psychological formation of the protagonists/narrators as they handle the endless flow of life events. Because autobiographies count on the completed nature of the course of actions evoked, however, they can resolve the tensions in the narrative while also conveying the author's strong sense of command over the story. Courtesy of the past, autobiographers evaluate experience "with the detachment of an already concluded process."[90] Indeed, because autobiographical literature is presumed to be unambiguous, it has traditionally played a didactic role by providing *exemplum vitae* through realistic representations of one's existence at a particular stage of the life course.[91]

Diarists, in contrast, deal almost exclusively with the everyday, which one would assume contains by definition a degree of predictability, as it suggests routine and repetitiveness, and yet also conjures precariousness, as in the expression "live day by day"—a lack of an end goal or purpose. In the process of going through the day, any day, we are not being driven by a grand plan or master project; instead, we rely on expectations of familiar patterns. While chances are those anticipations will be met, single individuals can scarcely exercise control over daily happenings and events—occurrences slip past us. The everyday is in a sense the realm of what Hannah Arendt calls labor—a cyclical process that might be reassuring in its recurrent monotony but is also liable to different degrees of subjection.[92] In Arendt's view, we are condemned to labor willy-nilly, sucked in by its endless, necessary sameness that requires from us little more than compliance. We carry out our duties mindless of their logic and yet totally dependent on their successful completion for our own survival. In this situation, the act of following routines can become a

---

[90] Cerutti, *Le vite dei Vittoriani*, p. 13. Cerutti addresses the sense of static in autobiographies.
[91] Cerutti, *Le vite dei Vittoriani*.
[92] For Arendt, labor is the human activity aimed at satisfying the basic needs of reproduction and self-preservation. It is doomed to never have an end because basic needs can never be definitively satisfied, thus the repetitive nature of labor and its intrinsic futility. Arendt, *The Human Condition* (Chicago: University of Chicago Press, 1958).

superstitious ritual aimed at fending off uncertainty.[93] It shields us from the vagaries of history—if only we could maintain normalcy, the world (at least our small world) might not fall apart. The fact is, routines do not merely ensure stability—the regular unfolding of things the way we know them. They might also cover up a reality that is not especially friendly, favorable, or even equitable to us. Furthermore, routines, even when not disrupted, might coexist with traumatic and conflictual situations such as a war, a dictatorial political system, and generally a time of crisis or "state of emergency." What role do our daily practices play in these cases? How do they structure our relationship to the world?

In his study of Nazi Germany, Detlev J. K. Peukert attended to these questions by exposing the analytical liabilities as well as potentialities generated by juxtaposing the normalcy of everyday life to the exceptionality of totalitarian regimes.[94] On the one hand, Peukert feared that this comparative operation raised the ethical dilemma of diluting the contrast between supporters and opponents of the Third Reich by leading to relativism and the nullification of responsibility (in view of Hitler's extraordinary grip, was the population's compliance unavoidable?). On the other hand, he felt that examining daily life under the Nazi dictatorship offered critical opportunities for accessing the complexities of peoples' experiences, most especially their ambivalences. For the decisions we make on an everyday basis are not inevitable or neutral, nor should they be taken for granted. Although steeped in seeming normality, everyday life presents choices and requires decision-making at all levels and on a continuous basis. Indeed, the realm of the "social" (to use another of Arendt's terms) can also be looked at as a site of conflict and contestation and not merely of collusion (contrary to Arendt).

In the case of Nazi Germany, citizens reacted negatively to the Third Reich's imposition of new rules impinging on their lives. Resentful at the disruption of long-held traditions and daily habits, they opposed government's restrictions and ostensibly refused to follow orders. And yet their negative reactions only went so far. Peukert shows that Germans' criticism remained limited to few selected aspects of Nazi control and failed to address the overall nature of

---

[93] Rita Felski talks about "the pragmatic need for repetition, familiarity, and taken-for-grantedness in everyday life." See "The Invention of Everyday Life," in *Doing Time: Feminist Theory and Postmodern Culture* (New York: New York University Press, 2000), p. 95.

[94] Detlev J. K. Peukert, *Inside Nazi Germany: Conformity, Opposition, and Racism in Everyday Life* (New Haven: Yale University Press, 1982). Peukert expressly addressed everyday life under a state of emergency.

Hitler's regime.[95] The Nazi apparatus of terror, along with the atomization of social relations and the climate of resignation brought about by the war, fostered citizens' contradictory responses. Furthermore, a fragmented public opinion effectively worked to amplify personal inner conflicts, while individuals' retreat into the private realm helped advance compliance with the Nazi model of social conduct. Whether the result of deep conviction or of mere accommodation, support for the Third Reich remained solid.

The inconsistency of people's modes of actions and the difficulty of framing Germans' attitudes within a discussion of the classic duo "consent and opposition" highlights the relevance of political and cultural duplicity within the context of day-to-day routine practices.[96] Degrees of uncertainty injected into the regular rhythm of daily experiences affect the course of people's relationship to institutional power. The question arises: Does the "discreet charm" of normality—the appeal of regularity—exercise such sway that it leads people into accepting repressive systems and ideological manipulation? In the instance of the Nazi regime, Peukert suggests that much. A desire to believe in the re-establishment of order at a time of profound disarray clouded Germans' minds and drove them to have faith in those who promised a return to normalcy—the way things were.[97] As old forms of sociality faded, retrenching in the familiar allowed one to overcome the uncertainty of wartime. Wishful expectations, combined with the weakening of traditional structures of solidarity in a context of retreat from the public sphere, created the space for

---

[95] Peukert also raised the issue of oppositional opinion versus oppositional activity, the latter being much less frequent. On the case of the German working class see Tim Mason, "The Containment of the Working Class in Nazi Germany," in Jane Caplan, ed., *Nazism, Fascism, and the Working Class: Essays by Tim Mason* (Cambridge: Cambridge University Press, 1995), pp. 231–73. On consent in Germany see Geoff Eley, *Nazism as Fascism: Violence, Ideology, and the Ground of Consent in Germany, 1930-1945* (London: Routledge, 2013). For an important example of diary written under Nazism see Robert Scott Kellner ed., *My Opposition: The Diary of Friedrich Kellner. A German against the Third Reich* (Cambridge: Cambridge University Press, 2018). On the complexity of popular attitudes in the context of dictatorial governments see Alf Lüdtke ed., *Everyday Life in Mass Dictatorship: Collusion and Evasion* (Palgrave Macmillan, 2016), in particular Michael Wildt, "Self-Reassurance in Troubled Times: German Diaries During the Upheavals of 1933," pp. 55–74. For more recent contributions on everyday life and the relationship between private and public in the Third Reich see the forum "Everyday Life in Nazi Germany," *German History* vol. 27, no. 4 (2009): 560–79; and Elizabeth Harvey, Johannes Hürter, Maiken Umbach, and Andreas Wirsching eds., *Private Life and Privacy in Nazi Germany* (Cambridge: Cambridge University Press, 2019), which also has an updated bibliography on the topic. On the Italian case see Joshua Arthurs, Michael Ebner, and Kate Ferris, *The Politics of Everyday Life in Fascist Italy: Outside the State?* (New York: Palgrave Macmillan, 2017), in particular Geoff Eley, "Conclusion: Troubling Coercion and Consent—Everydayness, Ideology, and Effect in German and Italian Fascism," pp. 233–55.
[96] In her review of the book, Mary Nolan argued that Peukert's account blurred the line between good and bad Germans. "How Germans Saw Hitler," *The New York Times* (August 9, 1987), p. 27.
[97] Peukert claims that longing for normality became a critical factor in people's decision to support Hitler's regime. *Inside Nazi Germany*, p. 76.

trusting the authority of those already in charge, even though grand ideological frameworks often proved ineffective at mediating meaning at the micro level of the everyday.

The incongruous willingness of some Germans to go along with Hitler's regime while also resisting the strictures Nazism imposed on their private lives reveals the semantic gap separating official dispensers of political-cultural messages from the receivers of the intended communication.[98] Even more consequentially, the incongruity emphasizes the critical role played by day-to-day reality in the general structuring of people's relationship to their own historicity. Everyday life, Peukert's analysis insinuates, is the terrain where daily struggles take place, the space where existence is relentlessly put to a test, the context where one's relationship to the world is negotiated. And this is the case whether one lives in normal times or extraordinary ones, though in the latter instance the ordinariness of daily experience cannot but be ruptured by the violent intervention of the exceptional—people's sense of mastery undergoes enormous challenges. Facing the gray area of up-for-grabs signification constitutive of the everyday, citizens move tentatively, fumbling around in pursuit of a linearity they know is scarcely available. As the relentlessness of volatile events undermines the trademark predictability of the everyday, one has to readjust habits and correct the course. Processing a fast-paced reality requires new negotiating skills and novel approaches to time and space, while familiar rhythms and cyclical cadences have to be reimagined and recast within an ever-shifting historical panorama that presents unforeseen and unfathomable trials. Rooted in deeply entrenched and overly determined social disparities, daily life ultimately exposes subjective ambiguities, whether one deals with exceptional or regular times. As Peukert illustrates, uniformity and coherence are not to be expected in our quotidian living, to the contrary. Even political-ideological ambivalences mar daily life—a realm that is supposedly at a remove from politics and mostly concerned with mundane needs.[99]

---

[98] A different case is diaries written by Russians under Stalin. Here, individuals strove to adhere to a model of Soviet citizen, or Soviet self, that they perceived was demanded by the authorities in order to ensure the successful future of the revolution. See Jochen Hellbeck, *Revolution on My Mind: Writing a Diary under Stalin* (Cambridge, Mass.: Harvard University Press, 2006). Also see Igal Halfin, *Terror in My Mind: Communist Autobiographies on Trial* (Cambridge, Mass.: Harvard University Press, 2003). Although focused on autobiographies, Halfin's book details how Soviet Communists were supposed to examine and reassess their lives within the parameters of the party's ideal of the model revolutionary in unison with the progressive march of history.

[99] Alvin Gouldner claims that, as a concept, everyday life contrasts with heroic life. Because it is based on routine, everyday life constitutes a tacit critique of the political seen as focused on struggle, competition, and conflict. "Sociology and the Everyday Life," in Lewis A. Coser ed., *The Idea of Social*

In his pioneering three-volume treatise on the quotidian, Henri Lefebvre argued that daily life cannot be easily dismissed as the realm of the trivial, nor, for what matters, should it be liquidated as the site of the mystified. In contrast, everyday life needs to be reinstituted at the center of social analysis even as one recognizes its fundamental contradictions. Although Lefebvre evaded discussions of historical crises (his goal was to address alienation in consumption-oriented postwar France), he maintained that any transformative agenda in contemporary capitalist societies has to pass through that dimension of human experience we call daily life. After all, "Man must be everyday, or he will not be at all."[100] Contrary to the assessment of critics who deemed the quotidian a pragmatically based activity verging on the trite—a residue that eschewed the heights of philosophical and aesthetic engagement and thus forgettable—Lefebvre pointed to the indeterminacy of the everyday and its endless capacity for difference in spite of its constitutional sameness.[101] Structural constraints might limit our experience of daily life, he conceded; however, the way we live the present and understand it can also affect those same social forces that impinge upon us.[102] Ultimately, for Lefebvre the issue was not whether to glorify the everyday (the way the Surrealists did) or demonize it (like Heidegger and other philosophers), but to acknowledge its inevitable tensions and foundational ambivalence. "*Ambiguity* is a category of everyday life, and perhaps an essential category," he wrote in the Foreword to volume I of his *Critique*. "Everyday life is defined by contradictions: illusions and truth, power and helplessness, the intersection of the sector man controls and the sector he does not control."[103]

Structure: Papers in Honor of Robert K. Merton (New York: Harcourt Brace Jovanovich Inc., 1975), pp. 417–32.

[100] Henri Lefebvre, *Critique of Everyday Life* the One-Volume Edition (London: Verso, 2014), vol. I, p. 147 (first published in 1947). In the original, Lefebvre wrote, "L'homme sera quotidien ou ne sera pas" *Critique de la vie quotidienne. Tome I: Introduction* (Paris: Grasset, 1947), p. 140.

[101] Lefebvre did not deny the residual nature of the everyday but problematized it. See especially *Critique of Everyday Life, Volume II: Foundations for a Sociology of the Everyday* (The One-Volume Edition).

[102] Lefebvre suggested that, disconnected from its link to the sacred and community as well as the organic rhythms of cyclical time and impoverished by the process of privatization during the industrialized capitalism of the nineteenth century, everyday life contains the impetus for its own change. It is the source of unfulfilled possibilities. See *Critique*, vol. II, p. 312. As Michael Sheringham best summarized Lefebvre on this point: "everyday life harbours within itself the possibility of its own existential or ontological transformation," *Everyday Life: Theories and Practices from Surrealism to the Present* (Oxford: Oxford University Press, 2006), p. 12. On the potential for self-transcendence of everydayness see Agnes Heller, *Everyday Life* (London: Routledge and Kegan Paul, 1984).

[103] Lefebvre, *Critique*, Foreword to the Second Edition, pp. 40, 43. In "Sociology and the Everyday Life," Gouldner favorably compares Lefebvre to the ethnomethodologists, who, although focusing on the everyday, do not see it as containing contradictions. Gouldner emphasizes that philosophy's original interest in the everyday displayed a negative view—the everyday was a world of lesser value.

Lefebvre believed that exploding the confusing inscrutability of the everyday—what Georg Lukács deemed its "anarchic chiaroscuro"—would ultimately advance social critique and historical understanding, no matter how arduous the task admittedly was.[104] For, as noted by Maurice Blanchot, "the everyday escapes. This is its definition"—while it lives in us and with us, the moment we perceive it the everyday is already passed.[105] And yet even Blanchot pledged that, despite its "perpetual becoming," everyday life is where events come to a head in one person's experience. It is a level of existence in which humans are immersed and struggle both psychologically and physically.[106] Whether tedious or indeterminate, stagnant or unfinished, the everyday is what prompts us to raise the question of how to live.[107] In its immediacy and inescapability, it continuously confronts us with the concreteness of our existence.[108] And, one could add, this is even more the case during states of exception. Under dictatorial conditions and in times of war, the everyday stands to become a litmus test, a paragon of the past and a warning for the future—it helps us make sense of an unsettling world.

States of emergency understandably presented a double jeopardy to the diarists examined here: How does one write about the everyday in the face of the abnormal? Does the practice of writing (whether in its reporting or

[104] On Georg Lukács' phrase see "Metaphysik der Tragödie," in *Die Seele und die Formen. Essays* (Berlin: Egon Fleischel and Co., 1911), p. 328. In the English translation by Anna Bostock, "anarchic chiaroscuro" is rendered as "an anarchy of light and dark." See "The Metaphysics of Tragedy," in *Soul and Form* (London: Merlin Press, 1994), p. 152. In the German version, the term originally used is *Helldunkels*, which literally means chiaroscuro. Lukács opposed everyday life to real, "authentic" life and saw the former dominated by reification. (Heidegger echoed Lukács' negative assessment of everydayness, although he later modified his view. See Sheringham, *Everyday Life*, pp. 31–2.) Lefebvre was skeptical of Lukács' negative assessment of the everyday, even if he cited his phrase (Lefebvre addressed Lukács in volume III of *Critique, From Modernity to Modernism [Towards a Metaphilosophy of Daily Life]*). In his *Everyday Life* (p. 31), Michael Sheringham claims that the same skepticism also defines Michel de Certeau, who quoted Lukács' phrase at the end of *The Practice of Everyday Life*, but held a much more positive understanding of the unsettling potential of the everyday than Lukács.
[105] Blanchot, "Everyday Speech," *Yale French Studies* no. 73 (1987): p. 15 (issue on Everyday Life). Blanchot also quoted Lukács' reference to the chiaroscuro, apparently as cited by Lucien Goldmann in *Recherches dialectiques* (Paris: Gallimard, 1959), p. 273. See Blanchot, "Everyday Speech," note 4, p. 16. In the English translation of Blanchot by *Yale French Studies*, the term chiaroscuro is used for rendering the French "clair obscur."
[106] Blanchot talked about "the everyday in perpetual becoming." "Everyday Speech," p. 18. For Lefebvre, the everyday is the milieu in which all transformations take place. It is the site of mediation: "Everyday life is profoundly related to *all* activities, and encompasses them with all their differences and their conflicts; it is their meeting place, their bond, their common ground. And it is in everyday life that the sum total of relations which make the human—and every human being—a whole takes his shape and its form." See Lefebvre, *Critique of Everyday Life*, Foreword to the Second Edition, p. 119.
[107] Roland Barthes focuses on this issue in *How to Live Together: Novelistic Simulations of Some Everyday Spaces* (New York: Columbia University Press, 2013).
[108] For Blanchot, the everyday opens the way to its own transformation. Its indeterminate status escapes political structures and their authority, even though its amorphous status encumbers us. "Everyday Speech," p. 13.

reflective mode) affect one's experience of a present under duress? Whereas it would be unwise to separate the medium from the content, diaries complicate the work of historical interpretation. Nevertheless, as the following chapters will illustrate, an examination of journals written during the biennium 1943–45 gives us an entry into the Italians' multifaceted relationship to fascism. Amidst the ravaging reality of famine, bombs, and occupation, the meaning fascism held for millions of Italians took variable, assorted forms at a time when unpredictability came to define the quotidian rhythm of a country at war.[109] All the erraticism notwithstanding, and beyond the dichotomous categorization of pro- or antifascism, a close reading of personal journals allows us to capture the prevalent structures of feeling that emerged at the time. Diaries give us access to the Italians' forced reckoning with their fascist present/past, a hard-to-die reality that a century after its official beginning in October 1922 is still haunting us.

The Case

With the objective of tracking the Italians' relationship to fascism during the years 1943–45, the book's five chapters engage in close textual reading of personal diaries (and some occasional epistolary communications).[110] I initially focus on three key moments in 1943: the downfall of Mussolini on July 25, the

---

[109] Henri Lefebvre points at the importance of analyzing rhythm for understanding everyday life in volume I of *Critique*, p. 343. In volume II, he addressed the interaction between cyclic time ("natural, in a sense irrational, and still concrete") and linear time ("acquired, rational, and in a sense abstract and antinatural"). His thoughts on the issue were further developed in *Rhythmanalysis: Space, Time and Everyday Life* (London: Continuum, 2004), which is considered the fourth volume of *Critique*. In *Rhythmanalysis*, Lefebvre emphasizes the distinction between "cyclical" and "linear" rhythms. He differentiates between "presence" and "present" and highlights the interconnectedness of rhythm to space and time.

[110] In the Anglophone world, the use of private sources for the study of fascism has been pioneered by Christopher Duggan. Tapping the feelings of ordinary Italians through personal diaries, his *Fascist Voices: An Intimate History of Mussolini's Italy* (Oxford: Oxford University Press, 2013) explores "how men, women, and children experienced and understood the regime in terms of their emotions, ideas, values, practices and expectations," p. xii. An exemplary model of research featuring views from "below," Duggan's study focuses on the two decades of the regime's tenure and offers a crucial basis from which to evaluate the Italians' eventual change of perspective after fascism's collapse. My use of diaries is, however, different from Duggan's, as our projects have distinctive aims. While he examines the relationship between Mussolini and members of the public as a way to adjudicate fascism's appeal, I follow journal writers to track the process through which their understanding of fascism evolved (or not) over two critical years—a historical juncture that, though putatively free of the old dictatorial grip, presented people with considerable interpretive challenges. Also, I exclude memoirs and other kinds of a posteriori reconstructions from my sources (see Methodological Appendix), whereas Duggan, although noting potential epistemological issues arising from the use of memoirs (p. xiii), does not restrict his documentary material to private journals.

armistice of September 8, and Italy's proclamation of war against Germany on October 13. I then follow diarists' reactions to the liberation campaign as the Allied forces slowly marched north and drove out Hitler's armies. Throughout, and against the background of everyday life, my objective is to illuminate individual experiences that, in their uniqueness, also represent the spectrum of responses to the past regime as well as the cultural modes guiding people's interpretations of the traumatic era in which they were living. The arc of time I examine stops with the end of the Second World War, the defeat of the German occupiers, and the definitive collapse of Mussolini's short-lived government in Northern Italy.

Although the book concentrates on the biennium 1943–45, it does not cover all variety of experiences that punctuated those years. This is due in part to the types of diaries available at the archives I consulted, my own methodological imperative to avoid any a posteriori reconstruction based on memories (see Methodological Appendix), and the study's unique interest in assessing fascism's relevance among ordinary Italians.[111] Thus, the book only tangentially touches on the Resistance movement and the partisan struggle— critical issues that, simply stated, journal writers failed to address in their narratives. The rarity of references to these topics by the diarists examined here constitutes a historical puzzle of its own, maybe a further signal of the distance separating official views of the period from the experience of people on the ground. One should add, however, that the geography of war affected areas of the country differently. While the South suffered only a few weeks of German occupation and in the central regions comprising Rome and Florence the Allied forces were able to advance past the German defensive lines in summer 1944, only northern partisans had the onus of continuing the fight for Italy's liberation until late April–early May 1945. This means that one half of the peninsula, if not one third, bore the brunt of the armed struggle against both Nazis and fascists, severely limiting the number of diarists potentially addressing the matter. Still, paucity of reflections on this key aspect of the period is perplexing and deserving of further inquiry.[112] As for the private

---

[111] For a panoramic view of the period through the use of diaries and memoirs see Luigi Ganapini, *Voci dalla guerra civile. Italiani nel 1943–1945* (Bologna: il Mulino, 2012).

[112] In his preface to the diary of Carlo Chevallard—a young industrial manager in Turin— Alessandro Galante Garrone cites "prudent restraint" as a reason for the prevalence of silence on the Resistance. He remarks, "Chevallard says very little of the partisan actions propagating all over Piedmont, even when bands get close to the house where he evacuated." See "Diario di Carlo Chevallard 1942–1945," edited by Riccardo Marchis, in *Torino in guerra tra cronaca e memoria*, edited by Rosanna Roccia and Giorgio Vaccarino, with a Preface by Alessandro Galante Garrone (Turin: Archivio Storico della Città di Torino, 1975), p. xiii. Galante Garrone, however, believes that restraint

journals written by those active in the Resistance, they do not qualify as "diaries" by my definition, since most of them are re-elaborations. One of the first personal accounts on the armed struggle, *Banditi* by Pietro Chiodi published in 1946, for example, is reconstructed from memory. The same can be said of other partisan "diaries" printed over the years.[113]

Beyond issues of methodology, the question of the Resistance and the ensuing debate that has emerged in Italy over the last decades inevitably moves the focus of analysis onto a different level from the one I set up to explore in this study. Referencing the Resistance tends to separate Italians between those who participated in the armed struggle and the ones who remained passive observers, the latter often identified with the so-called "gray zone."[114] Such framing doubtlessly helps challenge the mythical image of Italians as united in the fight for freedom—a long-standing dominant interpretation of the period. It also refocuses attention on the different ways Italians confronted fascism after its crumbling. Ultimately, it reinjects politics (and its divisiveness) into the history of wartime Italy—all critical accomplishments.[115] At the same time, however, by adjudicating the entire field of players in terms of guilt and innocence, this interpretive frame fixes Italians into constructed categories that, in addition to being reductive and refractory to change, preclude a phenomenological analysis of how individuals create

---

alone might not explain the reticence about reporting on the growing phenomenon of the Resistance. On the issue of the availability of written sources on the partisan experience see Mario Avagliano ed., *Generazione ribelle. Diari e lettere dal 1943 al 1945* (Turin: Einaudi, 2006), especially pp. xix-xx. Avagliano presents an array of documentary material that he believes signals the existence of unmined sources.

[113] Pietro Chiodi, *Banditi* (Alba: Ed. A.N.P.I., 1946). Also see Ada Gobetti Marchesini Prospero, *Diario partigiano* (Turin: Einaudi, 1956). One notable exception is the diary of Emanuele Artom, which he kept until February 23, 1944, *Diario di un partigiano ebreo. Gennaio 1940-Febbraio 1944*, edited by Guri Schwarz (Turin: Bollati-Boringhieri, 2008). Captured by the Italian SS in March 1944, Artom was tortured and died in Turin on April 7 of that year. For an overview of partisan literature see Giovanni Falaschi ed., *La letteratura partigiana in Italia 1943-1945* (Rome: Editori Riuniti, 1984), preface by Natalia Ginzburg.

[114] The term "gray zone" was coined by Holocaust survivor Primo Levi with reference to those prisoners in the camps that collaborated with their oppressors. The appellation appeared in the second chapter of his collection of essays *The Drowned and the Saved* (New York: Vintage, 1989) originally published in Italian as *I sommersi e i salvati* (Turin: Einaudi, 1986). Later on, the category "gray zone" was adopted by historian Renzo De Felice to describe the majority of Italians who, after September 8, 1943, avoided taking sides with the Resistance but did not join the RSI either. See *Rosso e nero*, edited by Pasquale Chessa (Milan: Baldini & Castoldi, 1995), pp. 58-9. For a direct rebuttal of De Felice's thesis see Guido Bersellini, *Il riscatto: 8 settembre-25 aprile. Le tesi di Renzo de Felice, Salò, la Resistenza, l'identità della nazione* (Milan: Franco Angeli, 1998), especially pp. 62-6.

[115] Some of these issues are discussed in Nicola Gallerano ed., *L'altro dopoguerra. Roma e il Sud 1943-1945* (Milan: Franco Angeli, 1985). Also see Mariuccia Salvati, "'Tempo umano': a Roma dopo la dittatura," in *Passaggi. Italiani dal fascismo alla Repubblica* (Rome: Carocci editore, 2016), pp. 59-79.

cultural meanings in their day-to-day existence—an outcome that the concept of structures of feeling seeks to avoid.[116]

In his monumental work on the Resistance, the historian Claudio Pavone was among the first scholars to insist that one needed to interrogate "the behavior of the protagonists to understand the ideas that inspired them."[117] With the intent of assessing the "morality" of the period, that is, the area where "politics and morality meet and clash," Pavone moved away from traditional official sources, such as those of parties and organizations, and sought to identify how directives from above were received and "adapted to a rich gamut of individual and collective experiences."[118] Pavone's decision to approach the Resistance as a civil war—a gesture that helped re-evaluate the significance of the Italians' fratricidal conflict beyond the confines of the fascists' instrumentalized narrative—particularly illuminated the ethical dilemmas confronting those who chose to participate in the armed struggle.[119]

While Pavone lent an ear to the normally ignored voices of historical actors (in this case the Italians who joined the Resistance) and emphasized the often conflictual motives that guided people's moral and political decisions, he restricted his analysis to those who made the momentous resolution of becoming active members in the movement ("The choice" is the title of his book's first chapter).[120] The ordinary people, who purportedly did not make a commitment, end up lumped in the same broadly encompassing classification of spectators—those who, weary of politics, waited for things to resolve.[121] Within this interpretive context, the mass of the gray zone (or "the silent majority") becomes reified and frozen in time—its status permanently defined by its less than admirable "choice."[122]

---

[116] An attempt to defy the category of gray zone by telling the individual stories of "men in gray" is Carlo Greppi, *Uomini in grigio. Storie di gente comune nell'Italia della guerra civile* (Milan: Feltrinelli, 2016).

[117] Claudio Pavone, *Una guerra civile. Saggio storico sulla moralità nella Resistenza* (Turin: Bollati Boringhieri, 1991), p. ix; English version, *A Civil War. A History of the Italian Resistance*, translated by Peter Levy with the assistance of David Broder and edited with an Introduction by Stanislao G. Pugliese (London: Verso, 2013), p. 1.

[118] Pavone, *Una guerra civile*, p. x.

[119] Pavone described the Resistance as characterized by three wars: a civil war, a class war, and a war of patriotic liberation.

[120] A side effect of the focus on the Resistance, with its attention to Northern Italy where the partisans engaged in warfare with fascists and Nazis, was the marginalization of Southern Italy and other parts of the country. See Gallerano ed., *L'altro dopoguerra*.

[121] Pavone distinguished between passive resistance and gray zone as well as civil resistance (see his Preface to the 1994 edition of *Una guerra civile*, p. xv). "Attendista" was the term indicating all those waiting for the Anglo-American arrival. It comes from the French "attentiste," which in 1941 referred to the politics of waiting in regard to Germany.

[122] In a later article, however, Pavone discussed the limits of the gray zone as a notion that ends up generalizing the Italian experience and turns the population into an undifferentiated mass

This book, in contrast, places at its center the diverse and often contrasting ways Italians processed their relationship to the fascist past over the two years following the collapse of the regime. It shifts the analytical focus away from the gray zone as an inhabited *category* of predetermined, negative valence and emphasizes *modes* of being and thinking, along with their often conflicting and varied expressions. Without denying the reality of Italians' ambiguous stances, the book embeds people's creation of meaning in the interstitial area where sociocultural history and daily existence interact. And it argues that the clash of values, hopes, and expectations experienced by individuals occurred in the arena of everyday life. The everyday, characterized by the contrasting presence of light and dark, or heroic and prosaic moments, becomes the lens through which to assess structures of feeling in the new exceptional normalcy of wartime and occupation. Against the "blending" meaning inherent in "grayness" (its uniformity and dullness), the book highlights the dramatic features of daily life's "anarchic chiaroscuro."

The first three chapters are based on narratives composed by ordinary people. Approximately two thirds of them were written by men, with the authors' overall ages ranging from as old as sixty-eight to as young as eight. Young diarists of both genders constitute a substantial bulk, while in terms of educational level the authors almost split down the middle, with about half holding a high school or university degree. Geographically, the sample represents a variety of Italian regions, with a strong prevalence for Northern and Central Italy. A similar diversity applies to the writers' class as well as occupation. It includes students and professionals, housewives and service workers, artists and teachers, state employees and artisans, in addition to those serving in the military and prisoners of war. Whether or not these scribes can be considered representative of the whole population, the goal is to highlight elements of unity that characterize the seemingly subjective nature of their personal narratives.

Adding a comparative perspective to this set of private documents, the last two chapters consider a number of diaries (thirteen) authored by prominent national and local figures among Italian journalists, novelists, and politicians (they will be referred to as "intellectual diarists" for lack of a better term).[123]

---

characterized by moral and material passivity. Stating that "one does not belong to the gray zone once and for all," Pavone argued that "'ordinary' people need to become subjects of specific historiographic studies." See "Caratteri ed eredità della 'zona grigia,'" *Passato e presente* vol. XVI, no. 43 (1998): pp. 9, 7.

[123] Although I am hesitant to use the term, by "intellectual" I am emphasizing the diarists' level of expertise at composing a journal—they are practiced diarists as opposed to accidental ones—this is their distinguishing trait. In other words, I am not considering these diarists in their role as

Differently from the journals of ordinary people, these diaries were drafted with the specific goal of reaching a broad audience and all saw the light of print—a few of them were even published immediately after the war.[124] The issue of writers' intent is critical for evaluating the content of these journals (and the genuineness of their statements) when compared to the productions of "accidental" diarists. Did their aim to go public affect the type of information and reflections intellectual diarists conveyed in these journals? Conversely, and most critically, what does the examination of these writings help reveal about the perspectives of ordinary diarists? Mirroring the analysis of the initial chapters, in this final part of the book I scrutinize intellectual diarists' responses to the main events of summer/fall 1943. I review their assessment of the regime, the war, and the German occupation, and I report on their experiences of daily life under the duress of the ongoing military conflict.

Chapters Outline

Chapter 1. A Short, Long Summer

Chapter 1 examines reactions to three major events early in the period considered: the announcement of Mussolini's fall in July 1943, the declaration of armistice between Italy and the Allied forces in September 1943 (when Italy switched its allegiance away from Hitler's Germany), and Italy's official declaration of war against Germany in October 1943. As an initial test of the country's perspective on fascism, diaries' entries on and around July 25, 1943 immediately present interpretive challenges. Elations at the news of Mussolini's resignation appear mixed with, if not motivated by, hopes for an end to the war, thus mudding all attempts at differentiating evaluations of fascism from broader reactions to the war crisis. Diarists' interpretations of the armistice as "betrayal" present similar predicaments, as they appear to neglect that the option of preserving the country's "honor" by continuing to fight alongside Hitler meant upholding decisions made by Mussolini's dictatorial regime in a war that most agreed was "not wanted." Journals' muted reactions

---

representatives of the intellectual class, even if they can be deemed intellectuals in the sense generally assigned to the word.

[124] I have tracked all diaries published around, or right after, the end of the war as well as those written on the period 1943–45 but published later. The search resulted in the list of thirteen private journals examined in this study. I have, however, excluded diaries by political figures, such as Ivanoe Bonomi, and those that mainly dealt with political accounts, such as the journal written by Jo' Di Benigno. Also, I have not included memoirs and reconstructed stories.

to the October declaration of war against Germany confirm incongruities in people's shifting structures of feeling in the face of fascism's unraveling. Whether due to the fast pace of historical developments or lack of firm points of interpretive reference, contradictory attitudes characterize diaries' entries in the first three months following the regime's fall. Fascism had definitively faded from people's concerns.

Chapter 2. Interpretive Ghosts

Chapter 2 digs deep into scribes' ideological and philosophical ambivalences. It analyzes the semantic challenges presented by the "enemy"—a label that diarists seemingly found hard to assign and that further confounded the issue of fascism's historical responsibilities. It also shows that the difficulties at separating fascism from the "fatherland" steered attention away from two decades of Mussolini's dictatorship and demonstrates the effectiveness of the regime's ideological work in promoting patriotic motifs laced with dreams of glory and imperialistic drives. Ultimately, diarists' tendency to evaluate fascism by divorcing its objectives from actual results led to emphasizing fascism's supposed ethical posture and purity of intentions against its inability to achieve those ideals. In this scenario, corruption came to play the role of justificatory trope; malfeasance exculpated a whole political system. Admittedly, contemporary historical reality was an interpretive nightmare, and in poignant lines diarists voiced their incapacity to comprehend it. The ongoing civil war especially gave way to deep anguish, as people struggled to accept the unspeakable actuality of a brother-against-brother conflict. Particularly powerful are the stories of prisoners of war, whose inhumane treatment is still being documented. Although caught in feelings of shame at the collapse of the Italian military, IMIs (Internati Militari Italiani) refused to collaborate with the "eternal enemy." Captives of Hitler's army in German concentration camps, they had to disentangle their sense of the country's debacle from an assessment of the larger implications brought about by the fall of the regime. Italy and fascism had coincided for so long, the breakup of this unholy unity unleashed painful senses of culpability.

Chapter 3. Every Day in the Everyday

Chapter 3 excavates diarists' interpretive confusions by zeroing in on the personal, intimate level. I engage with the phenomenological categories that marked writers' responses, with particular attention to the duo private and public and the notion of normalcy. Emotional conditions, from fear and distress to cynicism and indifference and also desensitization, become keys to account for people's historical subjectivity—their evolving sense of self amid an external reality that ruthlessly confronted them with their own helplessness. I discuss diarists' rejection of public involvement and their strenuous defense of a private, orderly space away from the chaotic outside world, even as the "normalcy" of everyday life was irreparably altered by displacement, separation, food scarcity, and more generally an excruciating struggle for survival. A form of resistance to the overpowering of history, retrenchment into the personal (also through journal writing) allowed individuals to build distance from uncontrollable events while ensuring emotional numbness as a screen against suffering. With vivid portraits of people's experiential differences in terms of generation, gender, class, and geographical location, the chapter highlights diverse structures of feeling emerging out of situational distinctions. It emphasizes the impact on journaling of writing styles and the posture of objectivity.

Chapter 4. The Diary as Alibi

Switching to journals written by more practiced writers, the last two chapters focus on the sense of civic duty and the drive to bear witness that motivated a group of diarists to transform the private status of personal reflections into potentially public record. How did the authors' original determination to reach an audience affect their ultimate products? Stylistic and compositional choices suggest that the journals of intellectual diarists became alibis in the literal sense of the word. The writer is "elsewhere"—a distant observer whose objective sensibility tends to bleed into neutrality. Substantively, these diarists took positions that, although doubtlessly heterogeneous, exposed their political hybridity and connivance, such as when they attempted to artificially separate Italy from fascism and fascism from fascists. Similar incongruences also emerge from their reactions to the events of July, September, and October 1943. Like ordinary diarists, these practiced writers often sidelined fascism's guilt, although differently from the former they forcefully raised the issue of Italians' responsibility in the regime.

Chapter 5. The Personal and the Political

Focusing on social relations and everyday life, chapter 5 looks at the micro level of interaction as it surfaces from intellectual diarists' references to this dimension of the lived. It examines political hybridity in light of personal ties and highlights the struggle intellectual diarists experienced as they engaged in the operation of distinguishing friend from enemy. Within an environment saturated by the fascist past, old networks and sentimental connections complicated the work of assigning blame. The controversial process surrounding official attempts at "epuration" mirrored intellectual diarists' internal conflict as they contemplated how to minimize the deleterious effects of the twenty-year-long dictatorship. Eventually opting to look ahead rather than back, the diarists' choice of divorcing RSI fascists from the past regime carried long-term critical consequences for the country's process of "defascistization." The chapter examines normalcy as the notion through which diarists confronted the exceptional reality in which they were embedded. A countermeasure to a perceived sense of both material insecurity and psychological instability, the banality of daily rituals and practices helped intellectual diarists overcome despair at the same time that it led them to realize the inadequacy of their self-assigned role of reporters. Did writing have any meaning when all they jotted down was a repetition of the same? Although generally more reflective than ordinary scribes, intellectual diarists communicated similar negative feelings about their sense of impotence in the face of history.

Conclusions

The conclusions re-examine the constitutional ambivalence of the quotidian by linking ideological instability and exceptional circumstances to normal processes of daily experience as well as one's historicity. They reiterate the importance of analyses focused on the lived present and weigh the question of the Italians' failure to work through their fascist past. Ultimately, they address the normalization of fascism in contemporary Italy, thus raising the question: Should this re-emergence be considered an inevitable result of time passing or as rooted in misguided decisions back in the past?

1
A Short, Long Summer

> I was afraid it was a dream.
> (July 27, 1943)*

Memorable dates conventionally mark watershed events by singling out their supposed significance within a particular arc of time. Often the expected outcome of organic developments or alternatively arising as unpredictable manifestations of a period's idiosyncrasies, events and their dates would have no meaning if detached from the history that preceded them.[1] In most cases, their relevance would also remain opaque without considering the history that unfolded after them. In the instance of July 25, 1943, the state of the fascist regime and the country's mood up to that infamous night are critical for understanding the exceptional move by the Grand Council of Fascism to vote its lack of confidence in Mussolini.[2] Contextual conditions help explain the institutional repercussions of that seemingly audacious decision and the public's passionate reactions too.[3] As for the momentous character of the event, it is worth noticing that in its straightforward procedural nature the action of the Grand Council almost mirrored the equally nondramatic occurrence of Mussolini's initial appointment as prime minister of Italy in late October 1922. Ironically, the much-touted fascist violent revolution began and ended

---

* From the diary of Ettore Castiglioni.

[1] On theorizing events see Robin Wagner-Pacifici, *What Is an Event?* (Chicago: University of Chicago Press, 2017).

[2] The Grand Council was created as a consultative body of the fascist party in late 1922. It was "in theory the highest organ of the Italian state and of the fascist regime." See Philip Cannistraro ed., *Historical Dictionary of Fascist Italy* (Westport, Connecticut: Greenwood Press, 1982), p. 217. At the night meeting of July 24–5, nineteen of its members expressed doubts about Mussolini's leadership and elected to remove him. Eight members voted against the motion and one abstained. The next day the king had Mussolini arrested.

[3] The literature on July 25 and its aftermath is extensive. See among others, Ruggero Zangrandi, *1943: 25 luglio–8 settembre* (Milan: Feltrinelli, 1964); Gianfranco Bianchi, *25 luglio: crollo di un regime* (Milan: Mursia, 1963); Nicola Gallerano, Luigi Ganapini, and Massimo Legnani, *L'Italia dei quarantacinque giorni. Studi e documenti* (Milan: Istituto nazionale per la storia del movimento di liberazione, 1969). Also see Renzo De Felice, *Mussolini l'alleato 1940–1945*, 2 vols. Vol. I, *L'Italia in guerra (1940–1943)* (Turin: Einaudi, 1990); Gianni Oliva, *I vinti e i liberati. 8 settembre 1943–25 aprile 1945. Storia di due anni* (Milan: Mondadori, 1994); and Roberto Battaglia, *Storia della Resistenza italiana, 8 settembre 1943–25 aprile 1945* (Turin: Einaudi, 1964).

without the spilling of blood, while the dearth of theatrics in Mussolini's (semi)final act ran counter the regime's core tendency toward pageantry and spectacular politics.[4] As fascism's storyline derailed and its main narrative fell off script, the prosaic, normative feature of a democratically achieved committee vote led to the exceptional result of Mussolini's fall. In an unforeseen anticlimactic twist, the normal application of codified rules unleashed a happening of extraordinary proportions.

Before the Fall

Surprising as it was, the sack of Mussolini had come at the peak of a declining period for fascist Italy's economic-political fortunes and military fate as well. The regime's decision on June 10, 1940 to join Germany in the Second World War gradually but inevitably backfired, turning what was originally envisaged as a convenient solution to the challenges of domestic politics into a major catalyst for fascism's downfall. In truth, fearing potential involvement in the conflict, Italian public opinion had been caustically following the country's rapprochement with Germany for months. Well before Hitler's invasion of Poland on September 1, 1939, the event that officially started the Second World War, fascist party informers and secret police reports incessantly warned of Italians' negative dispositions towards a prospective alliance with Germany.[5] Besides harboring profound dislike for the enemy they had fought in the First World War, Italians unfavorably assessed Hitler's obvious penchant for violent conflicts. And although reasons for people's negative sentiments differed, we know that disapproval of the war ran high among all classes.[6] Even once Germany began scoring quick victories in early spring 1940 and it looked convenient for Italy to join the military effort, segments of

---

[4] Fascism's violence was however real. See, among others, Michael R. Ebner, *Ordinary Violence in Mussolini's Italy* (Cambridge: Cambridge University Press, 2011).

[5] See Alberto Aquarone, "Lo spirito pubblico in Italia alla vigilia della seconda guerra mondiale," *Nord-Sud* vol. 11 (January 1964): pp. 117–25; Pietro Cavallo, *Italiani in guerra. Sentimenti e immagini dal 1940 al 1943* (Bologna: il Mulino, 1997); Aurelio Lepre, *L'occhio del duce. Gli italiani e la censura di guerra 1940-1943* (Milan: Mondadori, 1992); Guido Leto, *OVRA. Fascismo Antifascismo* (Bologna: Cappelli, 1952), Part III, La guerra. (Leto comments on how the reports from provincial authorities did acrobatics to hide Italians' discontent. Confidential information, he states, was much more negative than reported.) Also see Loris Rizzi, *Lo sguardo del potere. La censura militare in Italia nella seconda guerra mondiale 1943-45* (Milan: Rizzoli, 1984); Piero Melograni, *Rapporti segreti della polizia fascista 1938/1940* (Rome-Bari: Laterza, 1979); Bino Bellomo, *Lettere censurate* (Milan: Longanesi, 1975); Simona Colarizi, *L'opinione degli italiani sotto il regime 1929-1943* (Rome-Bari: Laterza, 1991); Franco Martinelli, *L'Ovra. Fatti e retroscena della polizia politica fascista* (Milan: De Vecchi editore, 1967).

[6] Aquarone particularly points out the materialistic concerns shared by the economically dominant classes, "Lo spirito pubblico in Italia," p. 120.

the population still resisted the idea. In the supposedly "fascist" city of Florence, opposition to the looming possibility of Italy's intervention was pervasive, and the political police noted with alarm the Florentines' growing nervousness at the prospect.[7] Remarkably, antifascist organizations were able to advance their cause among young fascists at this time by making resistance to the war part of their agenda.[8] Popular apprehension about the practical consequences that the conflict might bring to the country prevailed over the potential benefits Hitler's military victories could accord even under the rosiest of forecasts.[9] Whether existentially driven or realistically motivated, Italians' assessments of the war were sobering.

Granted, fantasies of expansion did not magically die out in a country that had been fed imperialistic dreams for years. Moreover, the crowd cheered Mussolini when he announced Italy's declaration of war against Great Britain and France in his speech from Palazzo Venezia on June 10, 1940. According to witnesses, the enthusiasm running through those in attendance felt palpable.[10] With the conflict dragging on and the illusion of a war of short duration soon crashing, however, discontent rapidly mounted. Over time, relentlessly discouraging news on the paucity of military gains, combined with the grim reality of food insecurity and the rising cost of essential items, definitively moved Italians' opinions in the direction of antiwar. By the end of 1942 and early 1943, with cities in the industrial North suffering heavy bombings, the "home front" collapsed.[11] Concerns over the possibility (still felt as remote) that Italy might become a theater of war intensified.

Once Italy entered the conflict, police sources apprehensively tracked the rise of antiwar sentiments and nervously tried to decipher their political implications. With growing anxiety, official reports warned against underestimating expressions of nonalignment with the regime, even though the usual

---

[7] See Renzo Martinelli ed., *Il fronte interno a Firenze 1940–1943. Lo spirito pubblico nelle "informazioni fiduciarie" della polizia politica* (Florence: Stamperia Editoriale Parenti, 1989).

[8] Martinelli ed., *Il fronte interno a Firenze*, p. 26. Also see Franco Fucci, *Le polizie di Mussolini. La repressione dell'antifascismo nel "ventennio"* (Milan: Mursia, 1985).

[9] Letters caught by postal censors show this trend. See Lepre, *L'occhio del duce*, especially pp. 7–69. On Italians' wavering support for the war in 1941–43, also see Colarizi, *L'opinione degli italiani*, chapter 7.

[10] Martinelli ed., *Il fronte interno a Firenze*, p. 38. Also see the recording of the event, *10 giugno Anno XVIII. La dichiarazione di guerra* (Istituto Nazionale Luce, 1940), at the Archivio Storico Istituto Luce (http://www.archivioluce.com).

[11] See among others Philip Morgan, *The Fall of Mussolini: Italy, the Italians, and the Second World War* (Oxford: Oxford University Press, 2007), chapter 3; Angelo Michele Imbriani, *Gli italiani e il duce. Il mito e l'immagine di Mussolini negli ultimi anni del fascismo (1938–1943)* (Naples: Liguori, 1992), chapter 6; Gabriella Gribaudi, "The True Cause of the 'Moral Collapse': People, Fascists and Authorities under the Bombs. Naples and the Countryside, 1940–1944," in Claudia Baldoli, Andrew Knapp, and Richard Overy eds., *Bombing, States and Peoples in Western Europe 1940–1945* (London: Continuum, 2011), pp. 219–37.

parameter of "organized political opposition" poorly fit the situation at hand. Apathy, absenteeism, and more generally passivity and lack of participation were taken as worrisome symptoms of disengagement from fascism's core principles and objectives.[12] To those in charge of security, Italians' scarce enthusiasm for the war exposed a layer of ambiguity whose exact meaning they had difficulty interpreting but definitively took as communicating unhappiness. Even if barely muttered, discontent bore the mark of opposition.

And murmurs as well as louder forms of complaint surely abounded in wartime Italy. Despite higher levels of censorship and trumped-up propaganda, Italians burst out. Deteriorating living conditions within a militarized economy that visibly showed its failings weighed heavily on the majority of the population. Whereas in the late 1930s the uncertainty of the international situation partially mitigated the scope and spread of popular grievances, once war was declared and hopes for a quick resolution vanished, the floodgates opened. Citizens' dissatisfied mood even surfaced in epistolary correspondence—a significant phenomenon considering that letter writers knew of the monitoring activities censors conducted in their efforts to uncover antiwar sentiments.[13]

That the regime played a difficult balancing act vis-à-vis the conflict by manipulating, if not altogether eliminating, negative news did not help contain the protest.[14] Caught in street comments or at ubiquitous shopping lines, complaints about the war filled police reports on the Italians' mood. In Florence, the most common rumor circulating in the aftermath of Mussolini's official war declaration attacked the rationale for a war that "was not necessary and could and should be avoided."[15] As months passed, many displayed an avowed desire to curse those guilty of starting the conflict, with Mussolini bearing the brunt of accusations—as the charges went, he only acted

---

[12] Martinelli ed., *Il fronte interno a Firenze*, p. 37.
[13] The review of private correspondence for purposes of public order was summarized by censors under the neutral category "Statistics." See Rizzi, *Lo sguardo del potere*, p. 12.
Mail censorship had been instituted in Italy in 1915 as a device for controlling the opinion of military and civilians about the ongoing world war and for detecting potential diffusion of military secrets. Under Mussolini's regime, mail censorship extended to cover expressions of antifascism. Not by chance, censorship fell within the jurisdiction of the Ministry of Interiors and was considered an issue of domestic public order. Also see George Talbot, *Censorship in Fascist Italy, 1922–1943* (London: Palgrave, 2007); Elena Cortesi, *Reti dentro la guerra. Corrispondenza postale e strategie di sopravvivenza (1940–1945)* (Rome: Carocci, 2008); and Sergio Lepri, Francesco Arbitrio, and Giuseppe Cultrera, *Informazione e potere in un secolo di storia italiana. L'agenzia Stefani da Cavour a Mussolini* (Florence: Le Monnier, 1999).
[14] On the difficulties at the home front see Luigi Petrella, *Staging the Fascist War: The Ministry of Propaganda and the Italian Home Front, 1938–1943* (Bern: Peter Lang, 2016).
[15] Martinelli ed., *Il fronte interno a Firenze*, p. 74 (report of June 15, 1940).

motivated by personal ambition and lacked a sense of the nation's interests.[16] Hatred for Hitler and Germany soon added to the catalog of negative comments officials recorded among the population. The list included criticisms of Italy's military preparedness and skepticism about the country's chances of victory. At the end of 1940, one police report identified the Italians' lack of restraint in speaking their minds as the most worrisome development.[17] The mere fact that people felt free to express their opinions in the streets, the police rightly recognized, constituted a sign of the regime's failure. For beyond the specific content of what was being said, speaking up in public undermined fascism's role as the exclusive purveyor of beliefs and truth, the sole source of authority. Moreover, if initially the population avoided talking about the war and in this way indirectly communicated their lack of enthusiasm for the conflict, later on Italians did not keep quiet.[18] Complaints about the high cost of living, food scarcity, and economic aggravation abounded along with criticisms of the bureaucracy.[19] The sense of defeatism expressed by soldiers, when coupled with the inevitable, progressive crumbling of the home front, especially struck mail censors. The reality of worsening opinions looked undeniable.[20]

Not surprisingly, as the war situation deteriorated, 1941 and 1942 brought more bad news to those charged with monitoring public opinion. Police assessments persisted in emphasizing that the war was "not felt and not wanted by the people"—a phrase that would encapsulate the gist of popular discontent until the end of the conflict. In the meantime, Italians' sympathy for the British and Americans grew at the same rate as their criticisms of the German ally. Objections to Italy's dependence on Hitler became more common, while perspectives on Mussolini and his role in the situation exacerbated.[21] Although some still preferred to deflect guilt onto his collaborators or the fascist party, others accused Mussolini of launching a war without the necessary military preparation. Finally, if any illusion of triumph ever tempted Italians, including the disingenuous idea of a short war, all hopes began to fade once the Soviet Union entered the conflict in June 1941. At that point, a decidedly aggravated population came to the conclusion that, as long as the

---

[16] Martinelli ed., *Il fronte interno a Firenze*, p. 117 (report of December 12, 1940).
[17] Martinelli ed., *Il fronte interno a Firenze*, p. 121 (report of December 19, 1940).
[18] Postal censors signaled the trend. See Rizzi, *Lo sguardo del potere*.
[19] Martinelli ed., *Il fronte interno a Firenze*, p. 112 (report of November 10, 1940).
[20] This trend is also confirmed in sources cited in Nicola Gallerano, "Il fronte interno attraverso i rapporti delle autorità (1942–1943)," *Il movimento di liberazione in Italia* no. 109 (1972): pp. 4–32. See also Sandro Rogari, "L'opinione pubblica in Toscana di fronte alla guerra (1939–1943)," *Nuova Antologia* vol. 557, no. 2162 (April–June 1987): pp. 344–77.
[21] Martinelli ed., *Il fronte interno a Firenze*, p. 262 (report of June 7, 1942).

war ended, it did not matter if Italy lost. Indeed, as a report of July 27, 1941 dauntingly stated, many thought that the country would be ruined economically even if blessed by an unlikely victory. Among the popular classes, a defeat of the Axis (the military coalition that included Germany and Japan, besides Italy) was considered the only remedy to the multiple predicaments the country faced, which included recovering from the economic devastation, getting rid of the dictatorship, and avoiding subjection to German control.[22]

In a more ominous sign for the regime, even the middle classes appeared to be shifting away from fascism—a development the political police alarmingly flagged from early in the war years. Historically, antifascism had always been identified with communist organizations and the working class of the industrialized North. Also, because of a strict system of surveillance set up to contain potential expressions of dissent, manifestations of protests against the dictatorship had generally been rare and mostly oblique.[23] The war years, in contrast, exposed a diffuse lack of enthusiasm towards the regime's initiatives. Although harder to decode politically than direct acts of protest, this absence of participation when detected among the classes historically aligned with the regime especially put security functionaries on the alert. In an original (later modified) note of February 1941 that summarized the state of public opinion, the secretariat of the head of police drafted a dire diagnosis of the situation: "The depression of spirits is greater among the high classes and there are more and more cases of people who, although of undoubtedly fascist faith until now, strongly criticize the regime's actions in circumstances when they know they can speak freely."[24] The widening of disillusion among the middle strata, even if not as immediately oppositional as the Turin strikes that broke out in March 1943, was seen as spelling trouble.[25] Losing the support of traditional bourgeois constituencies deepened the crisis of a regime already besieged with problems of failing economic and military policies.

---

[22] Martinelli ed., *Il fronte interno a Firenze* p. 175.

[23] See Gianpasquale Santomassimo, "Antifascismo popolare," *Italia contemporanea* vol. 32, no. 40 (July–September 1980): pp. 39–69, and Luisa Passerini, *Fascism in Popular Memory: The Cultural Experience of the Turin Working Class* (Cambridge: Cambridge University Press, 1987).

[24] Cited in Rizzi, *Lo sguardo del potere*, p. 60. This sentence was erased from the final version. About the secret police's emphasis on the bourgeois classes' opposition, also see Melograni, *Rapporti segreti della polizia fascista*, p. 133.

[25] Tim Mason argues that the wave of strikes in Turin was "the most important act of mass resistance" under a fascist regime. See "The Turin Strikes of March 1943," in *Nazism, Fascism and the Working Class: Essays by Tim Mason*, edited by Jane Kaplan (Cambridge: Cambridge University Press, 1995), p. 275. Carlo Chevallard writes of the strikes in his diary, "Diario di Carlo Chevallard 1942–1945," edited by Riccardo Marchis, in *Torino in guerra tra cronaca e memoria*, edited by Rosanna Roccia and Giorgio Vaccarino, with a Preface by Alessandro Galante Garrone (Turin: Archivio Storico della Città di Torino, 1975). See in particular entries of March 9, 10, 11, 15, and 17, 1943, pp. 44–7.

While the conflict also threatened to jeopardize Italy's most recent conquests in North-Eastern Africa (her "empire"), the regime's relentless daily orders contributed to deepen people's sense of doom. Not a new development, the party's practice of imposing rules on Italians' daily life came to be particularly resented at this time. Official interference, when combined with bureaucratic incompetence, made it harder to maintain a semblance of normalcy in an everyday routine already disrupted by the actuality of war. As Allied bombings intensified at the end of 1942, the number of those still trusting the duce's foresight and strategic wisdom drastically declined.[26] A speech delivered by Mussolini on December 2 did not succeed in breaking the slew of criticisms—his power of persuasion had lost its aura. Ill at ease with these seemingly less legible instances of disagreement, police functionaries finally used the term "antifascism" to define the sentiment they detected, even if they added the qualifier "in the sense of manifestation of distrust."[27] The chickens had come home to roost.

Meanwhile, popular despair over the conflict was matched by the increasing realization that the war would be long lasting. The previously circulated suggestion of a separate peace abated, and even if the successes of the Soviet Union on the Eastern Front offered a glimpse of hope that a conclusion might be near, apathy and indifference marked the beginnings of 1943.[28] Three years of war had worn Italians down. They were now ready to accept any type of resolution, no matter its consequences, as long as it brought an end to the conflict. Faith in the regime appeared to have reached its nadir. By early summer 1943, the Allied forces invaded Sicily (July 9–10). Then on July 19, Rome suffered a devastating bomb raid that destroyed the working-class neighborhood of San Lorenzo, killing thousands. News of Mussolini's removal and arrest followed on July 25.

---

[26] After another incursion on Turin, Carlo Chevallard noted in his diary on November 27, 1942, "What is striking is the explosion of hatred against the regime, against the duce. Almost no one lashes out against the English who are doing their war, but everybody blames those who led us to this difficult situation." He added that all social classes were "united by a common denominator: panic." See "Diario di Carlo Chevallard 1942–1945," p. 27. For other ordinary Italians' views of the war see Christopher Duggan, *Fascist Voices: An Intimate History of Mussolini's Italy* (Oxford: Oxford University Press, 2013), chapter 11. "The English" was the standard noun Italians used to refer to the Anglo-American forces.

[27] See their 1942 report on the state of "public sentiment" in Martinelli ed., *Il fronte interno a Firenze*, p. 36.

[28] On Italians and the Eastern front see Guido Quazza ed., *Gli italiani sul fronte russo* (Bari: De Donato, 1982), especially Part IV. On personal testimonials from the Eastern front see Quinto Antonelli ed., *"La propaganda è l'unica nostra cultura." Scritture autobiografiche dal fronte sovietico (1941-1943)* (Trento: Fondazione Museo Storico del Trentino, 2015). Also see the several works of Nuto Revelli, including *Mai tardi. Diario di un alpino in Russia* (Cuneo: Panfilo editore, 1946) and *La strada del Davai* (Turin: Einaudi, 1966).

War Is Over, or Is It? July 25

"I wake up, what do I hear? Rumors running around, the Duce, has resigned, I didn't know what I was doing, I was overjoyed, overtaken by many hopes, during the day many things happened, protests, riots, things never seen."[29] With these opening lines, nineteen-year-old Zelinda Marcucci from San Casciano in Val di Pesa, near Florence, recounted the incredible news of Mussolini's fall in her diary entry of July 26. She had missed the official announcement of the event the previous night when, at 10:53 p.m., the national radio broadcast the message, "His Majesty King and Emperor has accepted the resignation from the position of head of government, prime minister, secretary of state of His Excellency the Cavalier Benito Mussolini and has nominated head of government, prime minister, secretary of state the Cavalier, Marshal of Italy, Pietro Badoglio."[30] Preceded by two warning cries of "Attention, attention" and delivered in stentorian tone by the official EIAR speaker, Giovanni Battista Arista, the announcement was followed by two separate proclamations on behalf of the king and Badoglio. It concluded with the music of the royal march symbolically marking the end of fascism. For, as perspicaciously noted by *The New York Times* reporter Daniel T. Brigham, this was the first time in twenty-one years that radio programs did not end with the fascist hymn *Giovinezza*.[31] Airwaves immediately registered and emblematically conveyed the sudden reality of an incommensurable political change.[32]

---

[29] I'm maintaining her incorrect punctuation and I will do the same for all diarists. Typographical stylistics will also be preserved throughout the citations, including, italics, bold, underlining, etc.

[30] The announcement was supposed to be delivered during the regular newscast of 22:45, but was apparently late. In order for official information to be disseminated by radio and newspapers, it had to be first transmitted by the Agenzia Stefani, which was under the control of the regime. See the director of the Agenzia Roberto Suster's diary for an account of the circumstances surrounding the July 25 news and its diffusion, "Cronache per una storia d'Italia del 1943," in *Per una storia d'Italia del 1943. Le cronache di Roberto Suster e altri scritti*, edited by Gianni Faustini (Trento: Museo storico in Trento, 2005). According to Faustini, Suster's diary might have been rewritten in parts.

[31] See *The New York Times* of July 26, 1943, front page: "For the first time in twenty-one years the Italian radio signed off a nation-wide program by playing only the royal march. '*Giovinezza*,' the fascist anthem, like fascism, is dead." (In the past, both musical pieces would be played together. However, "Giovinezza" only began to be played on the radio in 1924, not in 1922 as Brigham assumes.) Don Antonio Rossaro made the same comment in his diary: "The first time that the broadcast is announced and concluded without the fascist hymn but only with the Royal March" (July 25, 1943), in *Diario 1943–45. Il tempo delle bombe* (Rovereto: Museo storico italiano della guerra, 1993), p. 31. Similarly, Giuseppe Prezzolini annotated from his American residence, "I then heard the Italian bulletin: they indicated the year the old way, without the fascist era, they did not play the fascist hymn but only the Royal March. With this they believe they can skip twenty-one years." See Ardengo Soffici and Giuseppe Prezzolini, *Diari 1939–1945* (Milan: Il Borghese, 1962), p. 316.

[32] According to Brigham's report in *The New York Times*, a communiqué was supposedly aired by Eiar in between the king's and Badoglio's proclamations. It stated, "With the fall of Mussolini and his

Stunned, the few Italians who were listening to the news that late in the night woke friends and neighbors, initiating a bacchanalian surge of celebrations that culminated in the next day's destructive festival of everything fascist (Figure 1). Reactions were visceral and striking, as Zelinda Marcucci's reference to "things never seen" intimates. Forty-seven-year-old Concetta Bucciano reported from Rome, "In the evening, and already in bed, we hear a ruckus; cheers, music, cries of jubilation; what happened? Great news; Mussolini's government has fallen." In Bologna, twenty-one-year-old A.M. unsympathetically described "a whole population in ferment at the news of the Duce's resignation: everything that spoke about him has been torn, destroyed, trampled on; the hatred contained for so long erupts in the gestures of those maniacs that, screaming in the squares, tear pennants apart, take down his portraits and spit all over them" (July 28, 1943). Her peer Bruna Talluri, a student from Siena, offered a gentler account:

> Popular demonstration has been enthusiastic and spontaneous, and has surprised even the most optimistic observers. Fascist pins have ended up in the gutters. In the street I stopped an acquaintance, a gentleman who was still wearing the pin in his buttonhole. I told him, "Don't you know that fascism fell.?. That Mussolini was replaced.?." "Really?." he cried out. Then, receiving confirmation, he flew his pin in the air and, with tears in his eyes, hugged me.
> (July 26, 1943)

Although not all groups and areas responded to the event in the same manner, astonishment unified both supporters and opponents of the regime.[33] Even antifascist organizations were caught off guard by the news.[34] In East Africa, fifty-three-year-old Sicilian surgeon and prisoner of war Francesco Agnello described his fellow soldiers as "stunned" and "dumbfounded" (July 27, 1943). From the border with Switzerland, the middle-aged publicist Dino

---

band, Italy has taken the first step toward peace. Finished is the shame of fascism! Long live peace! Long live the King!" I have been unable to ascertain the veracity of this occurrence. If real, the pronouncement contradicted Badoglio's words soon to follow, which unequivocally stated, "The war will continue."

[33] There were differences in the way popular manifestations unfolded over the territory, with variations depending on local history and traditions. Overall, the destruction of fascist symbols was widespread, while more politicized acts, such as the liberation of political prisoners, remained limited to a few urban centers. Oliva, *I vinti e i liberati*, p. 18.

[34] In a number of industrial centers, especially in the North, spontaneous reactions eventually morphed into workers' rallies and combined labor disputes and wage claims with political demands. Unplanned, strikes confirmed the extemporaneous nature of the protests that united the country at this exceptional moment. According to Oliva, what makes this event a "historically extraordinary phenomenon" is the fact that it was "not mediated." *I vinti e i liberati*, p. 14.

Figure 1. Milan, July 26, 1943. Destruction of fascist symbols after Mussolini's fall. Footage supplied by Cinecittà Istituto Luce Historical Archive.

Villani, riding the train to Milan on the morning of July 26, observed the reverberations of the abrupt political turn on his fellow travelers. While "the truly fascists [*i fascisti fascisti*] remain silent, they are stunned, devastated and are waiting to hear more," a mixture of "excitement" and "disbelief" pervaded the rest of the passengers. When Villani first arrived at the departing station, he guessed from people's demeanor that something momentous, though decidedly not undesirable, had occurred. Still unaware of the news, he reported in a lengthy diary entry, "The expression on faces reveals wonder, maybe incredulity, but not sadness or apprehension. As a matter of fact, some are even pretty cheerful and gesticulate with vivacity." Unable to hide his own bewilderment when he finally learned of the unforeseen political change, Villani initially tried to establish the facts: "Mussolini resigning? The news is so unexpected and the event so far from being plausible that all doubts are legitimate, and one needs to know the precise text of the announcement before ascertaining the situation." Resorting to the principles of accuracy and objectivity as rational means to establish facts (rules followed by most fellow diarists), Villani tried to determine the correctness of his reporting in order to make sense of events he found hard to believe. Once the train approached Milan, the spectacle of unmistakable enthusiasm animating people in the streets confirmed his intuition of an extraordinary happening. And yet as he watched the Milanese joyously waving flags, he still could not shake off his disbelief:

> Who had told the crowd that with Mussolini's resignation fascism had fallen, that they could pronounce the word "freedom" after twenty years, that yesterday's institutions could be stormed and destroyed as unjust, that people could be insulted as traitors?
>
> Newspapers had not had the time to come out, people could not have had contacts with each other and therefore no agreement could have been reached.

Villani's entry brimmed with perplexed questions that highlighted the enormously consequential effects of the sudden regime's end. At the same time, his queries expressed the mystifying reality of the change while also acknowledging the impromptu nature of popular enthusiasm: "It was a spontaneous explosion that had been maturing over time, but that, in part, perhaps also caught the authorities by surprise. /Newspapers are disoriented too."[35]

---

[35] The bracket (/) stands for new paragraph in the original. Even Goebbels found the events unfathomable. See *The Goebbels Diaries 1942–1943* (Garden City, NY: Doubleday, 1948), edited, translated and with an introduction by Louis P. Lochner. Goebbels wrote on July 27, 1943, "It is simply

In truth, the sudden turn of happenings had been in preparation for months. After consulting with his entourage as well as revisionist fascists, moderate antifascists, and the military, King Victor Emmanuel III eventually decided on liquidating Mussolini, provided that the stability of the existing institutions and the role of the monarchy could be ensured. Notably absent from his final plot was any plan to end Italy's participation in the conflict—a war that had weakened the regime and undermined its support in the first place.

Although taken by surprise at the news, and generally unaware of the behind the scenes maneuvering that led to Mussolini's removal, Italians wholeheartedly embraced the unexpected change. In spontaneous manifestations throughout towns and villages, from north to south, across regions and localities, people hailed the king and the fatherland as strongholds in the country's struggle against the fascist regime's destructive spiral. Milanese Ester Marozzi found the general excitement genuine. A retired teacher in her early fifties, she had received notice of Mussolini's resignation in the early hours of July 26, first brought by her son shortly after 12 a.m., then a neighbor, and finally a friend. Evidently, the enormity of the event justified these late visits. In an entry quickly written in the middle of the night, Marozzi reported the information received. Once the momentous night passed, she woke up the next morning to witness the effects of the unfathomable happenings. Her diary entry for the day reported in large characters, "Monday July 26, 1943. /Italy is master of her freedom again. /Today she takes the first step towards her revival. /The execrated tyrant has fallen." Having emphasized typographically these critical facts, she then continued in regular typescript:

> The Italian people is delirious with joy, nobody went to work, the trams are not running, the death of fascism is a great national holiday, the streets and piazzas are filled with flags, on the walls and shop windows there are graffiti deprecating the hated tyrant. Joy is on everybody's face, while mouths can finally open to express thoughts repressed by twenty years of abuses and violence.

---

shocking to think that in this manner a revolutionary movement that has been in power for twenty-one years could be liquidated," p. 407. He also believed the Allies had sponsored the crisis in order to affect Germany. Still, he deemed the events very confounding: "Despite the fact that every hour brings us additional news, often of a conflicting character, the whole crisis is still hard to understand," p. 409. Goebbels had a respectful understanding of fascism's historical role and considered it "a twenty-one-year-old revolutionary work of reconstruction of historical significance," as he again wrote in his long entry of July 27 (p. 413). Then on July 28, "It is very regrettable indeed that Mussolini's resignation gave world Fascism such a heavy blow. After all it was his movement that gave a name to the doctrine of the authoritarian state. I can hardly imagine that Fascism has thereby ceased to be a fact," p. 417.

The Milan newspaper *Corriere della Sera*'s felicitous front-page confirmed, "Italy can finally smile." Many among its audience happily subscribed.[36]

But what exactly were Italians celebrating? How did they understand the facts of July 25? Interpretive battles over meaning readily emerge from the newly designated government's response to the popular outburst—a response that suggests degrees of incomprehension, if not altogether total distance, separating people from the authorities. To begin with, the government immediately instituted curfews and a state of siege and enforced them through violent repressive means. Over a mere four days, there were eighty-one people killed and more than three hundred wounded in addition to over one thousand arrests.[37] Anticipating fascism's resistance (which did not materialize) and ready to crush it at any sign of agitation, in actuality the new government exerted a military iron fist on groups suspected of sedition qua representatives of antifascist organizations.[38] Should one have any doubts, the coup d'état supported by the king was intended to maintain a monarchic state founded on established capitalist economic relations. Actions by law enforcement agencies conveyed this message and exposed the new administration's ideological makeup, while laying bare the government's fundamentally myopic view of Italians. For, as it turns out, concerned with suffocating any aspirations to social revolution, Badoglio blatantly ignored a central feature of Italians' joyous agitation: hope for peace. No matter how unrealistic, that desire dominated people's understanding of the institutional crisis and blinded them to the fact that, caught between the Allied forces' demands for unconditional surrender and the threat of German reprisal, the new Badoglio government simply pleaded for time and did not have a hint of a strategy in place. Indeed, that indecision gave Hitler's Wehrmacht the opportunity to organize a plan ahead of Italy's signing of the armistice with the Anglo-American forces in early September.[39] Lack of resolve also created the premises for the dire developments that rocked the country next.[40]

Meanwhile, with the belief that their long-held desire for peace would come to fruition, Italians identified Mussolini's fall with the end of the war.

---

[36] Among the diarists who cited this article in the *Corriere della Sera* were Dino Villani, Antonio Maestri, and Magda Ceccarelli De Grada.

[37] Oliva, *I vinti e i liberati*, p. 29. Also see Nicola Gallerano, Luigi Ganapini, and Massimo Legnani, *L'Italia dei quarantacinque giorni*, Appendix III.

[38] According to Guido Quazza, *Resistenza e storia d'Italia. Problemi e ipotesi di ricerca* (Milan: Feltrinelli, 1976), and Oliva, *I vinti e i liberati*, anti-left politics is fundamental to explain the events of July 25 and after.

[39] This was the plan Achse (Axis) previously called Alarich (Alaric).

[40] According to Oliva, although hard to accomplish, breaking up the alliance with Germany through an armed confrontation had more chances of success in July than later, *I vinti e i liberati*, p. 61.

From the village of Calliano near Trento, the elderly Luigia Visintainer had no qualms about the powerful effect of that equivalency, however misleading:

> On July 25 with very great wonder but with immense jubilation the duce handed in his resignation to the king—or better the duce was forced to hand in his resignation. With this act the people believed that the war would come to an end and instead it continues—but fascism with this act was abolished.

Visintainer plainly recognized that, although there was no denying the regime had exhausted its life, the same could not be said about the war, which "continues." As reality and popular aspirations faced a standoff, however, hope for peace did not abate.

Because Mussolini's "resignation" came after three years of war that had deepened the country's economic crisis and severely affected its quality of life, Italians could not but read the event within the context of the ongoing military conflict. Opposed to the idea of entering combat since the late 1930s, they found themselves ever more eager to end a war started against their will. Realistically or not, their expectations surged at the dictator's fall, even though Badoglio's proclamation following the official announcement of the change of guard on the night of July 25 unequivocally stated, "The war will continue." Young A.M. was caught in that misperception: "Thank God, everything would be over: the anguish and the fear, the uncertainty over our tomorrow! / But my hope, everybody's hope, faded all too soon because General Badoglio [...] immediately declared that the war continues. And now here we are again, nothing has changed, the war continues" (July 28, 1943). After suffering tremendous shock in the bombing of Bologna on July 24—an air raid that destroyed dozens of buildings and injured hundreds of victims, some fatally—A.M. took the news of Mussolini's resignation as harbinger for the war's end. Despite the fact that Badoglio's statement had been issued at the same time as the announcement of Mussolini's dismissal, and not days or even hours later, she initially simply refused to believe her ears. A desperate desire for peace led her to ignore reality until it hit her hard, crashing her hopes. War was not over.

Similarly oblivious to that idiosyncrasy was the usually pragmatic Bruna Talluri. Remarkably for somebody as civically engaged as she was (she began expressing antiwar sentiments from the start of her diary in 1939 and would join partisan forces in the Resistance movement in the next months), she did not seem to register the significance of Badoglio's proclamation. On July 28, she was still maintaining, "Everything leads to believe that the war will end."

To be fair, she did complete that sentence by asking "but what will happen afterwards.?." In many people's minds, whether they had reached this conclusion emotionally or through extended considerations, the turmoil ignited by Mussolini's resignation could not but lead to peace. References to potential resolutions were ubiquitous in personal journals. In light of Italy's suffering, the expectation of a separate agreement allowing Italy to exit the conflict appeared particularly enticing. Middle-aged Fortunato Favai, a teacher turned hotelier from the Veneto region, reported his clients' comments: "Most of them are of the opinion that we are now approaching the moment of a separate peace with the Axis powers. I share this view, because, in the present situation, to continue fighting against much more superior forces would be equivalent to committing suicide" (July 25, 1943). For many Italians, the path ahead was clear.

War (and peace) were dominant concerns even in the case of die-hard fascists such as eighteen-year-old V.R. Well aware of her fellow Italians' negative perspectives on the military conflict, which she blamed for the regime's troubles, she asked, "Is it plausible because the war is going badly for us to repudiate so viciously who, when announcing this same war, was then applauded and approved! Is it moral and ethical to repudiate who cannot manage to win?" (July 26, 1943). In her judgment, selfish opportunism as opposed to grateful loyalty reprehensibly emerged from the Italians' reactions to Mussolini's fall. Although V.R. did not seem to recognize that wars are not just won or lost but are also a source of pain, she still identified the war as pivotal for explaining Italy's unfathomable historical turn as well as the Italians' supposed change of heart toward their dictator. A twenty-year-old from Genoa, Giulio Repetto, agreed, "They forgot all Mussolini has done for his people. They forget that he loved his people" (July 25, 1943). Neither V.R. nor Repetto could disentangle the military conflict from Mussolini, even if they chose to focus on the Italians' lack of gratitude for the warmongering leader rather than consider people's experiential suffering, the woes, and miseries inflicted by the ongoing fight. They disturbingly failed to register war's unsettling, devastating effects.

In contrast, seventeen-year-old Angelo Peroni, a student from Milan whose critical analysis of July 25 did not spare the newly anointed government, resented the arrogance that transpired from Badoglio's announcement. How could they continue "the war that everyone opposes, that was not wanted by the people but by fascism's criminal politics, that the people in their cowardice have been unable to reject, this war is still continued! The alliance with Germany is kept; the German occupation is reaffirmed!" (July 26, 1943). In

Peroni's eyes, such blatant disregard of popular will exposed the king's opportunistic motives and power-grab orientation. He felt disillusioned. Similarly dumbfounded was Magda Ceccarelli De Grada's reaction to the *coup d'état* late in the night of July 25:

> I feel bewildered but not as happy as I expected. It's strange how I don't sense in me the kind of enthusiasm I expected at such astounding news, which is fulfilling my most ardent vows. Other people are excited, and act almost offensively towards me. I feel an unusual calm that allows me to assess the situation in a flash. "The war continues," the proclamation said, thus there is no change for now to this state of siege.

For the fifty-year-old Ceccarelli De Grada, one could not but parse the significance of Badoglio's portentous statement: "The war continues." She returned to the issue the next day, "Some things are not to my taste: in the proclamation they still talk about the Axis and the promise made. I recognize that the government has a difficult task and inherits a horrific legacy. It will be hard to liquidate the Germans." Even as she rejoiced at the novelty of a post-regime reality, Ceccarelli De Grada responded to the fall of Mussolini via reference to the ongoing conflict. Apprehensions over war and peace mitigated her enthusiasm for fascism's collapse and also dampened her hopes in a democratic future. Come July 27, she admitted, "In the first moment of euphoria everybody believed that the war would end. Today there is a sense of discomfort." Unable to disentangle the breakup of the regime from concerns about the war, she ultimately came to the realization that her hopes were moot. Anna Menestrina, a fifty-nine-year-old from Trento, agreed, "Badoglio issued a proclamation to the Italian people. The king also made an appeal: calmness, serenity, trust. Let's not believe that the war is over. No unfortunately! We have commitments, Badoglio says, that we cannot break" (July 28, 1943).

In a matter of a few days, as the actuality of the contorted geopolitical situation imposed itself, the original excitement for the end of the dictatorship turned into a darker mood. How could peace be achieved when the country was tied to its ally Germany? The specter of the war loomed large even in the mind of fifteen-year-old Olga Garbagnati, who mostly used her diary to confide thoughts about her sweetheart. An adolescent dealing with romantic matters, Olga was struck so deeply by the tumult of current historical events that she felt the need to notate them in her journal. As a child of fascism born and raised during the dictatorship, she could be considered a product of the system—her references, language, and sentiments reflected fascist teachings.

The entry she wrote after the Allied forces landed in Sicily in early July 1943 is telling—she resorted to nationalistic rhetoric to help her process the extraordinary occurrence: "Will my Italy then be oppressed by the foreigner again? The thousands of young lives that sacrificed themselves for your grandeur, were they in vain? The empire and colonies are lost, and now also the Motherland" (July 14, 1943). By evoking past glories, Garbagnati filtered the reality of war through the bombastic ideology she had been educated to embrace from birth. A couple of weeks passed, however, and, her ideological upbringing notwithstanding, she changed tone. Commenting on the consequences of Mussolini's sudden exit from government, she abandoned her high-flouted oratory seemingly mediating between personal understandings, drawn from her own life circumstances, and the effects of the regime's work of indoctrination. Besides switching to common parlance, Olga's entry stands out for the way it addresses the challenges presented by fascism's collapse—she ultimately identified war as the principal impediment to a successful resolution of Italy's problems:

> Down with the Duce. All around there are echoes of this scream! Fascism is finally gone with the Duce's fall. Freedom, that's the scream that we hear in the streets of my beautiful Milan [...] those hateful fascists are locked up in their houses and are machine-gunning the population from up on the roofs. The state of siege is still on. [...] Oh! If at least this war was over, everybody would return home and then everything would be different.......
>
> (July 30, 1943)

Disoriented by the dramatic happenings in her native Milan, Garbagnati trusted that the end of the conflict alone would ensure that Italy would see the better future that people were longing for. Like many other Italians, she did not realize the unlikelihood of such an aspiration.

In this charged atmosphere of confounding messages and uncertain outcomes, the rumor of a peace supposedly signed on July 28 sparked a surge of popular celebrations.[41] Zelinda Marcucci fell victim to it:

---

[41] As it is the case during all wars, rumors circulated during the Second World War. In Italy, they often took a turn toward the miraculous, with saints appearing and announcing imminent peace to children and other "chosen" people. See Quinto Antonelli, "'Bombe e Madonne': Vita quotidiana nel periodo dell'Alpenvorland (1943–45)" (conference paper, cited with permission of the author). On rumors and war see Marc Bloch, "Réflexions d'un historien sur les fausses nouvelles de la guerre," *Revue de synthèse historique* vol. 33 (1921): pp. 17–39.

Memorable day. Around 11:30 there was a voice, enough that I heard it, screams, clamors, people coming and going, there was a voice screaming "Peace." What did I do? I quickly rushed down the stairs, I made it to the piazza, people were running from all around, everybody was hugging, I didn't know if everything I was witnessing was real or just a dream [...]. At a certain point the radio announced that it was a false story, but the people did not want to believe it, it was "Peace" and they rejoiced with happiness. Soldiers lined up, with their muskets pointed at the very excited population. By 12:15 everything had crumbled, a false story, what a time, I felt insane. Bells were ringing, people were yelling, crying, screaming. Even men were moved. In my life I never found myself in similar situations and now I don't know what to think.[42]   (July 29, 1943)

Zelinda was crushed, befitting the elder Mario Tutino's disconsolate observation: "The people believed that with the fall of fascism the war would end. I strive to explain to as many as I can and to the extent I can the absurdity of such hope. And moods are already darkened. Some already begin to doubt the advantage of the newly acquired freedom" (July 27, 1943).

Sidelining in freedom

While the actuality of war and a desperate desire for peace overwhelmingly defined people's responses to the regime's crumbling, the sudden change of guard, no matter how militaristic and authoritarian, presented Italians with the opportunity to contemplate all the dictatorship had taken away. Freedom particularly stood out as a long-lost privilege, a wondrous miracle. Surprised by its unexpected reappearance, Dino Villani noted in his entry of July 26, "I hear from an approaching truck the first scream, 'down with Mussolini.' People still look around and are surprised to hear a phrase that a mere few hours earlier no one would have dared pronounce." For twenty years, any insult to the dictator had been forbidden. More significantly, restrictions had been placed on all forms of speech and communication. To Villani, who had lived his whole adult life under the regime, the abrupt dissolution of those controlling rules could not but feel strikingly uncanny.

---

[42] On the false rumor of peace see among others the diary of Giulia Minghetti, in *Firenze in guerra 1940–1944. Catalogo della mostra storico-documentaria (Palazzo Medici-Riccardi, ottobre 2014-gennaio 2015)*, edited by Francesca Cavarocchi and Valeria Galimi (Florence: Firenze University Press, 2014), p. 171.

In the case of eighteen-year-old Ada Vita, the excitement she expressed about freedom of the press is especially endearing, if not altogether moving. With disarming simplicity, her entry of July 28 captured the new situation emerging out of the unexpected political shake-up: "Newspapers have no censorship!! One needs to read them—they report many news." While her use of exclamation marks celebrated the end of a repressive practice, her statement that there was now "many news" meant that a different, more expanded version of the world was opening up in front of her eyes and everybody else's too.[43] All it took was accessing information the regime had long negated—an opportunity young Ada was experiencing for the first time. It was illuminating.[44] No better word than "freedom" quintessentially embodies the basic right most denied by dictatorships.[45] It was the chanting of "freedom" that struck young Olga Garbagnati in Milan at the fall of Mussolini. The same chants inspired eighteen-year-old Liana Ruberl, who started her diary entry of July 25 with "Hurray!!! Long live freedom." In the instance of Lieutenant Ettore Castiglioni, the evocative meaning of the word led him to muse about the term's symbolic and practical valence as he described the circumstances in which he apprehended the news of Mussolini's resignation:

One Monday morning [...] my attendant enters my room and announces with the most naïve expression that Mussolini had packed up his bags. I could not believe it [...] I was afraid it was a dream. [...] We still did not know anything, but we immediately felt that fascism had waned forever, that a new era was opening up for us, that beginning with that morning everything had radically changed. Freedom: that word each one of us had kept

---

[43] For a similarly surprised reaction to freedom of the press see Maria Carazzolo, *Più forte della paura. Diario di guerra e dopoguerra (1938-1947)* (Caselle di Sommacampagna: Cierre edizioni, 2007), entry of July 27, 1943, pp. 88–91. Also see her entry of July 26, where she states, "I was able to listen to Radio London with doors and windows open: this is freedom," p. 86.

[44] Umberto Eco's retrospective memory of the July 25 events as an eleven-year-old boy similarly highlights his surprise at the accessibility of news and the variety of its sources: "On the morning of July 27, 1943, I was told that, according to radio reports, fascism had collapsed and Mussolini was under arrest. When my mother sent me out to buy the newspaper, I saw that the papers at the nearest newsstand had different titles. Moreover, after seeing the headlines, I realized that each newspaper said different things. I bought one of them, blindly, and read a message on the first page signed by five or six political parties—among them the Democrazia Cristiana, the Communist Party, the Socialist Party, the Partito d'Azione, and the Liberal Party. Until then, I had believed that there was a single party in every country and that in Italy it was the Partito Nazionale Fascista. Now I was discovering that in my country several parties could exist at the same time." Eco, "Ur-Fascism," *The New York Review of Books* (June 22, 1995), p. 8.

[45] The continuation of Eco's passage cited above is befitting here: "The message on the front celebrated the end of the dictatorship and the return of freedom: freedom of speech, of press, of political association. These words, 'freedom,' 'dictatorship,' 'liberty,'—I now read them for the first time in my life. I was reborn as a free Western man by virtue of these new words."

inside as a secret treasure for twenty years or had whispered under the breath without daring to utter it loud. (July 27, 1943)

Awed at the new possibilities unlocked by the impromptu turn of political events, thirty-five-year-old Castiglioni endowed "freedom" with quasi-magical, community-building powers:

> Even in our small way, we felt the same sentiment that all Italians felt on that day. We found each other, we recognized each other, we all felt like brothers, we all felt Italian, and only Italian. Miracle of a word, explosion of an innate and inextinguishable feeling that for twenty years had been suffocated and repressed. (July 27, 1943)

Identified with sacredness, the appeal of freedom did not even spare Angelo Peroni, despite his disillusioned perspective about all forms of power: "Now at last everybody says and thinks as they want, and does what they wish" (July 28, 1943). Unbeknownst to him for all his life, freedom appeared as a new welcome reality, even if it kept him wondering whether people "will know how to be free?" (July 29, 1943). Whereas fascism had undeniably managed to "sedate" its citizens throughout two decades, Peroni believed that fear and cowardice had contributed to the Italians' subjection. Caught between the contrasting sentiments of confidence in people's strength and skepticism about their ability to resist authority, Peroni vacillated. Still, freedom remained at the center of his reflections—an exhilarating experience he shared with fellow citizens. On July 28 Magda Ceccarelli De Grada noted about the Milanese, "The crowd is happy, not at all scared, and still believes in the freedom promised." In spite of the violence, the wounded, and the dead that marked the days following Mussolini's fall, Italians were moved by the newfound condition.

Regretfully, once the elation dissolved, the hardship of adjusting to the recent changes struck some as daunting. Young Bruna Talluri bitterly admitted, "We can barely manage getting used to this new freedom" (July 28, 1943). The past seemed hard to wipe out, and the achieved severance from the authoritarianism of the regime did not necessarily ensure a fresh beginning, be it of political institutions or of one's ideas and emotions. Notably, the freedom from fascism that Italians had finally gained was met with repression by the militarized state—a somber counterpoint to the popular euphoria that greeted the king's and Badoglio's announcements on the night of July 25. While the government's brutal actions worked to suppress the general excitement, another element negatively affected people's buoyant spirits: uncertainty. In brief but poignant statements, diarists expressed their uncomfortable sense of disorientation at the prospect of things to come. Thirty-five-year-old Aldo Lanzoni, a self-taught artisan from Ferrara on military duty in Corsica, put it simply, "Today July 26 I learn that the fascist government, after dragging Italy to ruin, decided to capitulate. /I don't know, being away from the fatherland, how this is going to end." In Trento, Anna Menestrina marveled at the "sensational" event of Mussolini's resignation, "And now what will happen?…" (July 26, 1943), while Concetta Bucciano intuitively felt flabbergasted by the complex scenario facing the country. She simply asked, "Will it be a good thing, will it be a bad thing? Who knows?" (July 25, 1943).

Whether instinctively feared or following extensive reflection, Italians were struck by the unpredictable future ahead. In this situation of emotional whirlwind, as individuals were torn between existential worries and joyful hope for an elusive peace, the reality of the regime further faded from their consciousness. The past became mixed in with the present and the future, while the drive to neglect immediate history stopped people from analyzing and understanding it, or simply from bursting. How, indeed, did July 25 help Italians define their experience under the fascist dictatorship? Or did it? Judging from diaries, words miserably failed writers, and only a few attempted to convey the significance of a historical phenomenon that in some cases had lasted their entire life. Even among those few who approached the subject, their assessments often boiled down to single lines or exclamations. In a quick summary written in indirect speech, the elderly Luigia Visintainer described the immediate aftermath of July 25: "Reprisals ensued—dead that were thrown out the window—hangings—severed heads—and everything that an enraged people can do to take revenge of a life of terror endured for over twenty-one years." In Visintainer's succinct evaluation, the "life of terror" the regime had dispensed during two long decades more than sufficiently explained people's fury at the news of Mussolini's resignation. Terror had to be met with terror, ugliness could only be responded to with more ugliness. Unforgiving, her appraisal of the era was condensed in a few sharp sentences that only implicitly revealed her feelings.

In the case of the much younger Bruna Talluri, a focus on the regime's dysfunctions and shortcomings became the springboard for mounting a critique of the future. More than the target of scrutiny or self-reflection, the past served to identify current impediments to progress. As she perspicaciously wrote on July 28, "But where will we find functionaries capable of NOT stealing, willing NOT to scam, resolved NOT to speculate over the surrounding misery .?." Targeting the regime's institutional culture, she worried about the consequences of twenty years of dormancy. "Hibernation is over," she proclaimed. What would the Italians do now? The easiness with which people were turning antifascist in a matter of hours was not necessarily reassuring. How could one evaluate their good faith and move forward? She found no easy answers.

One among a handful of diarists who in the days immediately following July 25 engaged with the fascist past, Angelo Peroni wrote a series of entries that particularly centered on the Italians' responsibility during the regime. If, he reasoned, people were currently waking up from their lethargy and "all are wondering how they were able to stand this enslavement for twenty-one years" (July 28, 1943), one could not neglect that those same people had been "ready until yesterday to go to the piazza and clap in front of their executioner" (July 26, 1943). It was then "useless to assign blame to one man: it's convenient, but absurd. /All of us are responsible for what has happened: some more, some less. /[...] We are all guilty" (July 29, 1943). Granted, Peroni reasoned, Mussolini was responsible for "duping, betraying, and ruining Italy" (July 26, 1943). Also, there was no denying that Italians exploded with joy at the fall of fascism. However, he bitterly noted, the majority of popular reactions generally end up being mere vents, outlets for rage. In post-regime Italy, the challenge was to overcome the illusory sense of achievement felt at the fall of Mussolini. It was imperative to continue the fight cognizant that a different oppressive system was entrapping the country.

Ironically, because Peroni looked at the relationship between people and fascism from within a broader critique of power, his analysis ended up diluting fascism's singular perniciousness: "I'm certainly not rejoicing because fascism fell. The orchestra's director has changed, but the music is still the same. /It's all governments, of all kinds, that must fall: it's all the current rotten and absurd social system that opposes the new level of consciousness" (July 26, 1943). Two days later he called the king's government "a new fascism with a changed label" (July 28, 1943).

Although Peroni ended up sidelining fascism's speciousness, his honesty on the critical issues of fascism's ability to survive and the public's role in this outcome is disarming, especially considering that diaries of the time rarely exhibit the kind of deep soul-searching exemplified by this young man. A question arises about the scantiness of personal reflections among other diarists, even taking into account the sudden nature of the July 1943 events. The fast tempo of history certainly limited one's ability to collect thoughts and evaluate the past, and the continuous surge of novel challenges required equally constant shifts in attention. In the end, as events outpaced people's ability to process them, fascism either took a backseat or came to be revisited against the background of newly developing crises. Mussolini's hurried liquidation paradoxically led to dismissing twenty years of national history.

In his densely packed diary, Ettore Castiglioni attempted to sort through the challenges of the fascism-less reality he unexpectedly found himself confronting. The notes he wrote on July 27 about the reactions of his military unit to Mussolini's exit especially reveal the emergent paradoxical impasse: if, on the one hand, fascism's malign deeds were indelible, on the other hand, most Italians desired to eliminate all evident signs of fascism. In not so many words, Castiglioni identified the reason why the festival of destruction that followed the news of the dictator's fall seemingly exhausted people's reactions to the regime: the absence of a violent revolution. That fascism's end had taken place with almost no show of force helped contain antagonizing actions. The peaceful nature of the finale elicited people's contained responses via celebratory rituals of collective cleansing:

> As dark as the future looks, we have to appreciate that the event which could have been the bleakest and most tragic, the fall of fascism, occurred with no shocks and almost no bloodshed. Because fascism was so rotten, it did not have any strength left to even put up a desperate resistance. With frenetic joy we demolished all the fasces and all the vestiges of an epoch that by now belonged to the past: at hotels and lodges we destroyed Mussolini's portraits. I ordered that his name be erased from the external walls, registries, postcards. In our small way, we did whatever we could, what every Italian did all over Italy. In a few hours and a few days everything fascism had done for twenty years was completely erased.

In Castiglioni's analysis, fascism had collapsed from the inside because corrupt to the core. Fatuous and vacuous, it had exhausted itself and could not but dissolve along with all traces it had harrowingly imprinted on the country. Its only survival would be as "a deep and very bitter mark in our memories and a very sad page, unfortunately indelible, in the history of Italy." Almost anticipating Benedetto Croce's thesis of fascism as parenthesis, Castiglioni deemed the regime painful but ultimately negligible or, better, ineffective—a paper dummy that showed its true emptiness right as it fell apart.[46] But if in

---

[46] On the concept of parenthesis in Croce see Pier Giorgio Zunino, *Interpretazione e memoria del fascismo. Gli anni del regime* (Rome-Bari: Laterza, 1991), pp. 132–42. Later, Zunino tracked the origin

view of its insubstantiality fascism needed to be dismissed, at the same time, and somewhat contradictorily, Castiglioni recognized that fascism had inflicted such profound damage on Italians that he expected it to live forever in their memory. Two conflicting theories drove his reasoning, although both seemed to lead to the same conclusion: fascism amounted to merely external appearance—once its symbols were knocked down, it was forever dead.

One wonders if the regime's aestheticizing impulses, though failing to achieve prospected goals, succeeded in circulating a hollow image of itself. The confusion of form and substance that many even among the regime's hierarchy lamented as one of the leadership's liabilities seemed to preside over people's reception of the fascist dictatorship.[47] Wasn't the young Peroni displaying this orientation when he weaved together reality and representation, overlapping them in the same paragraph?

> One thing is however certain: the fascist regime has fallen, fascism with all its filth is gone forever. /The stupor has ended: one spark was sufficient to awaken sleepy souls [...]. All symbols of fascism have disappeared under the mortar or scalpel [...] and now everybody marvels at having managed to bear this enslavement for twenty-one years. (July 28, 1943)

But was fascism gone forever only because its symbols had been destroyed? In truth, and contrary to Mussolini's grandiose artistic design, form and substance rarely overlapped under the regime, nor did fascism simply evaporate once its emblematic signs came down. While the dictator's inability to achieve his artistic project and build "new men" could not cancel out the deeply violent and repressive nature of his totalitarian aims, the annihilation of symbols did not modify the reality of twenty years of abuses and manipulation either. As satisfying as the cleansing of fascist markers felt in the hours following the news of July 25, rituals alone could not eliminate a system that had indefatigably, if ineffectively, worked to colonize Italians' private and public lives. Still, the serendipitous course of historical developments contributed to semantic confusion and complicated popular reactions. Interpretive clues seemed out of order, and more familiar logics failed to apply. How should one understand Mussolini's resignation, for instance? It was not only hard to fathom but also

---

of the metaphor to fascist commentators in 1925. See Zunino, *La Repubblica e il suo passato. Il fascismo dopo il fascismo, il comunismo, la democrazia: le origini dell'Italia contemporanea* (Bologna: il Mulino, 2003), p. 286, footnote 4.

[47] On fascism's aesthetic orientation see Simonetta Falasca-Zamponi, *Fascist Spectacle: The Aesthetics of Power in Mussolini's Italy* (Berkeley: University of California Press, 1997).

incredibly elusive, as forty-year-old Milanese trader Roberto Cohen expressed with a plethora of punctuation flair, "Mussolini resigned! The curtain falls on fascism after 22 years of power! If I step back kill me are his words......!! Mussolini resigning to the king!! Certainly not the end of a dictator!" (July 25, 1943).

Cohen found something amiss with that picture of collapse. Other elements in the story also appeared to be lacking the usually expected common referents and felt incongruous: an internal revolt of the Grand Council was complemented by a military coup; a forever-compromised monarch supported a regime change; a dictator peacefully met arrest; loyal fascists did not put up a revolt. In this sequence of events, the rules of the political game (as normally understood) were turned upside down, with the narrative's main logic seemingly deprived of the usual coherence. Over the next weeks (the so-called forty-five days), the ensuing general sense of wonder did not abate and many continued to feel clueless about the future. On August 31, Bruna Talluri reported her dismay:

> Poor Italy: it went from bad to worse! What terrible days we are living and what blizzard is hitting over our heads...The government is acting in the most contradictory way imaginable. They force us to be ashamed of being Italian...We are paying every day for the consequences of our inertia. What is this ghost government doing.?. What is it preparing for us.?.

Unpredictability spelled troubles, especially in view of Badoglio's inconsistent moves over that summer.[48] As uncertainty fueled fear, the apparently seamless way in which the dictatorship crumbled came at the cost of inadequate political vision and poor strategic planning.

Because the unexpected, unfathomable fall of a twenty-year dictatorship occurred in bewildering historical and political circumstances, it is difficult to extricate popular reactions to the regime's collapse from more pressing

---

[48] Loss of popularity for the king and Badoglio was registered soon after July 25. Ester Marozzi reported on July 28, "The first day, there was a wave of sympathy and affection for the king and Badoglio. Now I have to observe that the wind is changing. There are accusations of weakness and ineptitude against the king and of a too accommodating stance against Badoglio." Other Italians raised stronger criticisms. In a letter of July 27 caught by the postal censor, the sender wrote, "The king declares that he does not want recriminations and invites us to genuflect in front of the wounds he has procured. Those who had, they had. And those who stole or profited, they keep. Well, gosh! The king should have said, 'Don't make recriminations now, but be united to defend the country.' You understand that this is not an issue of form but of substance. Those who drafted the proclamation should have thought about the suspicion held by every Italian that the king too is seriously guilty and is only trying to comfortably minimize his responsibilities." Cited in Lepre, L'occhio del duce, p. 193 (from a letter from Stresa Borromeo [Novara] examined by the censor and written on July 27).

concerns about the war. The (delusional) belief that the crumbling of fascism would lead to a "separate peace" for Italy made the regime's fate inseparable from the popular dream of a pacified nation. In addition, the handful of diarists who spent a few lines evaluating the past regime failed to register the gravity of the previous twenty years, even if they feared its impact on the future. As the conflict progressed and Italy precipitated into darker and more agonizing times, fascism ceased to have a part in peoples' lives. Although the regime was the root cause of the devastations the country suffered at the hands of both Germans and Anglo-American forces, it came to occupy a less prominent role in the Italians' immediate concerns. The state of emergency created by the war absorbed all energies and deflected attention away from the regime. Amidst scenarios of disaster and ruins, as well as a dire struggle for survival, the specter of fascism inevitably receded into the background, leaving open epistemologically challenging questions on the Italians' relationship to two decades of fascist ruling.

An Unending Summer: September 8

The month of August was particularly hard on Italians. As Anglo-American forces began their occupation of the country after their initial landing in Sicily, bombings became regular occurrences—a form of geopolitical blackmail meant to force the Italian government into accepting unconditional surrender. Northern industrial cities, including Turin and Genoa, were particularly targeted, while a series of heavy air raids on Milan caused the highest number of deaths and destructions.[49] In the South, Rome suffered its second bombing on August 13. Naples, which had been pounded since the beginning

---

[49] On bombings and the urban experience in Italy see among others Ugo Cappelletti, *Firenze in guerra. Cronache degli anni 1940–1945* (Prato: Edizioni del Palazzo, 1984); Gaetano Casoni, *Diario fiorentino. Giugno–Agosto 1944* (Florence: Stabilimento tipografico Civelli, 1946); Gabriella Gribaudi, *Guerra totale. Tra bombe alleate e violenze naziste. Napoli e il fronte meridionale 1940–44* (Turin: Bollati Boringhieri, 2005); Marco Gioannini and Giulio Massobrio, *Bombardate l'Italia. Storia della guerra di distruzione aerea, 1940–1945* (Milan: Rizzoli, 2007); Umberto Gentiloni Silveri and Maddalena Carli, *Bombardare Roma. Gli Alleati e la "città aperta" (1940–1944)* (Bologna: il Mulino, 2007); Cesare De Simone, *Venti angeli sopra Roma. I bombardamenti aerei sulla Città Eterna (19 luglio e 13 agosto 1943)* (Milan: Mursia, 1993); Marco Patricelli, *L'Italia sotto le bombe. Guerra aerea e vita civile 1940–1945* (Rome-Bari: Laterza, 2007); Luigi Ganapini, *Una città, la guerra. Lotte di classe, ideologie e forze politiche a Milano, 1939–1951* (Rome: Franco Angeli, 1988); Achille Rastelli, *Bombe sulla città. Gli attacchi aerei alleati. Le vittime civili a Milano* (Milan: Mursia, 2004); Giorgio Bonacina, *Obiettivo: Italia. I bombardamenti aerei delle città italiane dal 1940 al 1945* (Milan: Mursia, 1970). On memories of civilians' experiences see Giulio Bedeschi ed., *Fronte italiano: c'ero anch'io. La popolazione in guerra* (Milan: Mursia, 1987).

of the war, underwent a massive attack on August 4. It was a difficult summer no matter one's location.

In the northern city of Bolzano, where she had relocated from her habitual residence in Milan, eighteen-year-old Ada Vita filled the August pages of her diary with all kinds of military information. She recorded the Germans' movements in the North, reported rumors of the Britons' bad behavior in Sicily, and kept an accurate chronology of bombardments hitting Italian cities. Strictly sticking to facts, her writing style gained emphasis from typographical amplification when, on September 2, she experienced the drama firsthand. "**Bolzano has been bombed for the first time**," she announced. After recounting all the details with great precision, she concluded, "**Memorable day!!**"

When war struck, it struck violently. How could anybody not be impressed by its violence? War was the event. With the ugliness of the conflict spreading throughout the Italian territory, an undying desire for peace continued to animate people's expectations. Hope is indeed last to die, as the popular saying goes. Twenty-one-year-old Sicilian Pietro Massolo wrote to his mother from the military base in Padova where he was stationed, "My very dear Mother, […]. How much desire for peace! It's an enormous desire! Will that happy day come?" (August 17, 1943). Massolo's yearning for an end to the war was so great that on that same day of August 17 he reiterated verbatim a line from the letter in his diary, "How much desire for peace!" On September 10, Pietro fled his barrack as German troops approached.

That the war had become the defining phenomenon of summer 1943 finds confirmation in workers' strikes, which, launched on August 17 in reaction to heavy bombings, spread throughout the Northern and Central industrialized regions. The cities of Milan and Turin, followed by Reggio Emilia and La Spezia and, further south, Foligno, joined in the protest. Despite being met with repressive military intervention, the mobilization extended to a four-day event, featuring at its forefront direct demands for peace. The swelling movement of workers' protest only abated after the government gave reassurance of imminent peace talks.[50] For, as it turns out, behind the scenes Badoglio was negotiating with the Anglo-Americans. On September 3, he signed a "short" armistice at Cassibile. It was made public on September 8.[51]

---

[50] Oliva, *I vinti e i liberati*, p. 78. For reports of the August strike in Turin see Chevallard, "Diario di Carlo Chevallard 1942–1945."

[51] The "short" armistice of Cassibile was followed by a "long" one signed in Malta on September 29, which detailed all the conditions pertaining to Italy's surrender to the Allied forces. On the armistice

Another surprise

When she started her diary on the first day of September 1943, twenty-year-old Irene Paolisso found herself wondering at the beauty of nature as the "hurricane of the war" swirled around her with threats of unpredictable changes. Halfway between Rome and Naples, the town of Formia, where she lived, was witnessing a flurry of military maneuvers that filled the atmosphere with worrisome portents. With the Anglo-American enemy expected to strike, the imminence of war loomed somberly over this southern little town by the Tyrrhenian Sea. Gloomily, Irene noted, "Peace is far away." The dream of a return to normalcy that stirred so many Italians in the aftermath of July 25 appeared to her forever extinguished. Instead of joy, the grim actuality of an intensified war occupied people's thoughts and directed their actions. Decisions whether to evacuate or find air raid shelters or how to address food shortages weighed on everyone's daily existence. If fascism was ever a matter of apprehension to Italians, by now that concern had faded, replaced by the urgent need to respond to the war's more mundane challenges.

While hope for an end to the conflict had risen in the days following Mussolini's resignation, during the month of August that optimism all but dissolved as a barrage of heavy bombings battered Italian cities. The new government's erratic behavior eroded the little confidence people still had in the possibility of a change of course. With the war fully engulfing the country, there seemed to be no way out of the horror. Unsurprisingly, when news of the armistice began to spread on September 8, a mixture of incredulity and bafflement characterized immediate reactions. How Italians interpreted this unexpected twist in the tormented saga of that summer 1943 became another piece in the puzzle of their complicated relationship to the fallen regime.[52]

As Elena Aga Rossi has masterfully demonstrated in her historical reconstruction of the armistice, the politics behind the pact was complicated.[53] Not only did its origins go back to the time Italy joined the conflict in 1940. Over the years, it also underwent several transformations up to the conclusive

---

see Elena Aga Rossi, *Una nazione allo sbando. L'armistizio italiano del settembre 1943* (Bologna: il Mulino, 1993).

[52] Some of the reactions are reported in Duggan, *Fascist Voices*, last chapter.

[53] Elena Aga Rossi, *Una nazione allo sbando*. Also see the book's augmented edition, *Una nazione allo sbando. L'armistizio italiano del settembre 1943 e le sue conseguenze* (Bologna: il Mulino, 2003). For the English translation see Elena Aga Rossi, *A Nation Collapses: The Italian Surrender of 1943* (Cambridge: Cambridge University Press, 2000).

outcome of September 3.[54] At first, the Allied forces considered Italy the "weakest link" in the Axis, and the British contemplated the possibility of a separate peace with her on the assumption it might encourage Italians to abandon the regime. The Americans, however, disagreed with the British over military strategies and tactics, while different currents within each respective government also held dissenting positions. Eventually, the Allied forces came to the conclusion that the war would be resolved in Normandy and on the Eastern front, hence the need to eliminate Italy as a main site of the conflict and concentrate efforts where they would be most beneficial. The Anglo-American offer of armistice to the Badoglio's government, predicated on unconditional surrender, was part of a calculation according to which Italy only played a secondary role in the war.[55]

For her part, Italy had been pursuing a contradictory and often ambiguous course in the negotiations—the government fundamentally withheld a firm commitment to both the Allied forces and Germany. Not being able to pick sides, Badoglio and the monarchy tried to do a little of both, with results nothing short of disastrous. Their indecision left the country vulnerable and unprepared.[56] Meanwhile, amidst all the misperceptions and failing games at second-guessing, as well as the ineptitude in assembling the pact, on September 8 at 19:42 Badoglio announced the armistice in a message broadcast from the EIAR station. It aired about one hour after General Eisenhower made his own announcement on Radio Algiers.[57] Badoglio's statement was carefully calibrated. Besides declaring that an agreement had been reached, it presented the reasons for such decision. It also called for the end of violence

---

[54] Aga Rossi, *Una nazione allo sbando* (1993 edition), pp. 21–2. Also see among others Ruggero Zangrandi, *L'Italia tradita. 8 settembre 1943* (Milan: Mursia, 1971); Giorgio Rochat, "L'armistizio dell'8 settembre 1943," in Enzo Collotti, Renato Sandri, and Frediano Sessi eds., *Dizionario della Resistenza*, Vol. I, *Storia e geografia della Liberazione* (Turin: Einaudi, 2000), pp. 32–42; Gianni Oliva, *I vinti e i liberati*, chapters 5 and 6. For a general overview in English see Morgan, *The Fall of Mussolini*, chapter 5.

[55] The formula of unconditional surrender was also connected to the geopolitics of alliance with the Soviet Union. In reality, the policy of unconditional surrender was interpreted differently by the powers involved. See Aga Rossi, *Una nazione allo sbando* (1993).

[56] According to Aga Rossi, the government was fearful of the Germans' reaction and acted accordingly, thus creating a paradoxical situation. "Badoglio waited to contact the Anglo-American governments for fear of the Germans getting suspicious, while the Germans were convinced that the negotiations for the armistice were already taking place, and they were trying to find proofs of the 'Italian betrayal' so to have the pretext to break cover." *Una nazione allo sbando* (1993), p. 80. Italy had no opportunity for serious talks with either side. In addition, Italy overestimated her leverage over the Anglo-Americans based on her ability to offer neutrality as opposed to a scenario with German occupation and a new fascist government. In reality, Aga Rossi argues, strategically speaking the Allied forces would have preferred the latter situation, pp. 74–83.

[57] As Aga Rossi argues, a still uncertain Badoglio was finally forced by the circumstances, *Una nazione allo sbando* (1993). Badoglio's wavering shows in the delay of the announcement, which had been expected to happen at the same time as Eisenhower's. See Zangrandi, *L'Italia tradita*, chapter 4.

against the Anglo-Americans and ultimately concluded with an ambiguous sentence. To the statement "Consequently, any act of hostility against the Anglo-American forces by Italian forces must cease everywhere," the marshal added, "They will however react to eventual attacks from any other source."

Popular responses varied—confusion overtaking joy and vice versa.[58] Something did not quite feel right. That last sentence, in particular, hung like the sword of Damocles over people's renewed hopes, considering how desperate for peace Italians had been and how disillusioned they had become. In an entry marked Summer 1943, a teenager from the Treviso area, Albertina Roveda, unequivocally interpreted the armistice as "an ephemeral, treacherous pause," while Zelinda Marcucci's only line on September 8 read, "an armistice, even worse." Conveying their dismay in short phrases, the two young girls failed to explain the motivation for their negative assessments. They were not, however, the only ones at a loss for words. Vitruvio Giorni, a young carpenter from Anghiari, Tuscany, stationed at a military base in Albania, simply wrote, "War is over!?!?!?" He confessed praying to the Madonna that all the blood would not be in vain. Less dramatically, the elderly Anna Menestrina laconically reported, "Suddenly tonight the news began to circulate that Italy asked for an armistice. It's a vague rumor that elicits hopes and concerns. It seems that Badoglio has accepted unconditional surrender. And now?..." Whether expressed hermetically or in more elaborate sentences, with detailed precision or approximately, doubts over the meaning and consequences of the surrender filled people's immediate responses. Fifty-two-year-old Roman Barbara Garrone expressed her puzzlement: "What confusion in my poor head! Will it be good? Our dear Italy! [...] I don't know if I should cry or rejoice."

Uncertainty over the meaning of the pact haunted many, even though not all reacted with caution at the news. Traveling from Bologna to the small town of Lendinara, Veneto, for the annual festival of the Madonna, twenty-one-year-old A.M. thought the armistice could not have come at a better time: it fell on the birthdate of Mary. She welcomed the announcement with excitement, and the same did the people of Lendinara, of which she reported upon her return home:

> I will never be able to describe what happened in that small village when the news of the armistice arrived.

---

[58] Oliva argues that information on the war had been scarce until September 8 and newspaper reports were mostly redacted. This situation contributed to the general unpreparedness at the news of the pact. See *I vinti e i liberati*, p. 102.

Everybody only saw it as the end of the war and the return of soldiers to their families. On a first impulse of enthusiasm, people came out of their homes, to the piazza, and made noise while the men, after taking out their flags, marched toward the church to thank the Madonna, having recognized in this event the sign of divine intervention.   (September 9, 1943)

A.M. felt overwhelmed: "I was moved and had a lump in my throat. If anybody would have said only one word, I would have started to cry. [...] I was taking deep breaths as if an enormous weight had dropped from my heart freeing it." Disillusion would soon catch up with her: "I was deceived like everybody else. I was inebriated by the ruckus, the lights, the music, the merry-go-rounds, the bells that continued to ring in celebration. They rang until midnight. They were the same special bells that mother heard at the end of the First World War" (September 9, 1943).

Tradimento!

Historians have characterized September 8 as a watershed moment in the history of contemporary Italy, a dramatic crisis point that reverberated onto the country's future and its post-fascist reconstruction. To some commentators, the armistice exposed Italy's moral debacle and ushered in the death of the fatherland both at the level of national sentiment and in terms of actual unity of purpose.[59] Others have positively interpreted the event as the catalyst for the country's resurgence after the shame of fascism—an occasion for active redemption.[60] Interpretive divergences aside, the enormity of the consequences unchained by the armistice, most prominently the institutional void created by the catastrophic failing of political and military elites, has been documented and discussed in several studies. Thus, we know that, although a German reaction to the agreement was to be expected, those at the head of

---

[59] A little volume by Salvatore Satta, *De profundis* (Padova: Cedam, 1948) is generally credited with introducing the trope of the "death of the fatherland." In 1996, Ernesto Galli della Loggia took up Satta's trope in *La morte della patria. La crisi dell'idea di nazione tra Resistenza, antifascismo e Repubblica* (Bologna: il Mulino, 1996). Renzo De Felice argues that on September 8 there was a "moral strike" in Italy. See *Rosso e nero*, edited by Pasquale Chessa (Milan: Baldini & Castoldi, 1995), p. 43. Guido Bersellini contests De Felice's argument in *Il riscatto: 8 settembre–25 aprile. Le tesi di Renzo de Felice, Salò, la Resistenza, l'identità della nazione* (Milan: Franco Angeli, 1998), especially pp. 85–8.

[60] September 8 marked the beginning of the Resistance as a homegrown movement for the defense of the nation. Not by chance, the Committee on National Liberation (Comitato di liberazione nazionale or CLN) that presided over the Resistance was founded in Rome on September 9, the day after the armistice, by the leaders of the antifascist opposition with the goal of coordinating the Italians' resistance to Nazi-fascism.

government proved unable or unwilling to take on the responsibility of ordering resistance against the predictable occupation. As German divisions approached Rome, Italy's military leadership renounced defending the capital—Hitler's troops prevailed in a mere three days despite being at a numerical disadvantage. The king also declined to take any strong initiative. In contrast, preparations were made for transferring him away from the capital and preserve intact the institution of the crown. Early in the morning of September 9, the king and his family, joined by Badoglio and all the highest officers of the Italian army, fled to the Adriatic town of Pescara, having abdicated all responsibilities.

Amidst this power vacuum, and with the structure of military command paralyzed, the complete disarray of the royal army ensued. Defection became the order of the day as soldiers abandoned their barracks in a desperate attempt to reach home and avoid capture by the Germans. Italian troops deployed in the occupied territories suffered an even worse fate (especially in the Balkans). Left with no directives by their commanders, they remained at the mercy of the ex-ally with hundreds of thousands ending up in German internment camps.[61] Meanwhile, as the country failed to put up the necessary defense at such a crucial juncture, a lengthy military occupation by Hitler's armies began. The next nineteen months would prostrate Italians to a degree few would have imagined possible only a few weeks earlier. Considering the magnitude of the events and their tragic turns, what reactions transpired on the ground? Once the initial confusion passed, how did the sobering reality of September 8 translate at the level of ordinary Italians?

Magda Ceccarelli De Grada at first responded with excitement at the announcement of the pact:

At the café with Pea, I hear some news. Impossible? The Armistice! But soon after I see people flooding the streets as if gone mad. War is over for Italy! Italians and Germans rejoice together and drink. I rush home. Nobody knows anything.

At eight Badoglio's proclamation. It's certain. But the Germans? Hitler, the Brennero? Against all logic, this time I truly, blithely feel happy!

(September 8, 1943)

The armistice gave concrete embodiment to people's desire for peace, and Ceccarelli De Grada could not but be thrilled at hearing the news. As a matter

---

[61] This topic is discussed in chapter 2.

of fact, she felt happier than at the fall of the regime on July 25, although, in the back of her mind, she knew there was little reason to be overjoyed. "But the Germans?" She wondered—the Germans, indeed. Called by a neighbor who told her "in a voice choked with emotions that 'everything is over,'" Ester Marozzi asked, "What is over?" The neighbor replied, "The war. Radio London broadcast that Italy asked for the armistice."[62] Initially perplexed, once she heard the announcement on the national radio Ester admitted, "Every doubt dissolved upon this communication. A sense of relief opened our hearts: the threat of the incursion dissipated. However, a concern immediately clouded that sense of liberation. And now the Germans will come and take revenge." Concetta Bucciano succinctly summarized that fear in her short entry, "For a moment we rejoice, but then thinking about it: and Germany? Will it submit?" The gravity of the question was undeniable, and the answer to it remained the great unknown, or, more accurately, people sensed that the question could only lead to an undesirable answer—and they were haunted by that eventuality.

Young Ada Vita was not as tentative when she reported the news in usual typographical flair: "A few minutes ago the radio broadcast **Badoglio's speech announcing the end of the war**. /Everybody is in the street screaming out of joy, but who knows what will happen here?!! The Germans will revolt!!" Since she lived in Bolzano, a town where the majority of the population was German-speaking, Ada expected them to oppose the new political development. More ominously, she felt that the announcement (which like many other Italians she interpreted as stating the end of the war rather than a mere cease-fire between Italian and Anglo-American forces) would unleash violent reactions. Her Milanese peer, Liana Ruberl, seemingly agreed. Combining excitement with a strong dose of realism, Ruberl welcomed the cease-fire but gloomily anticipated the Germans' threat: "The Armistice! /Hurray! It's over! Hostilities against the English stopped but now the war against the Germans begins anew! Now the terrible moments come! Let's try to resist! God forbids that if we do not kick out the Germans quickly, they will have the time to kill us all."[63] The Germans threatened to be the next worst nightmare, and Leo Baldi, an employee at the Ministry of Foreign Affairs in his mid-thirties, had no illusions about them. Upon hearing the news on the radio, he noted:

---

[62] Marozzi wrote "everything is over" in larger characters.
[63] After this entry, Liana interrupted her diary. She resumed it on April 26, 1946, with a chilling note: "I will not write ever again […] I cannot even speak about these three years."

On Corso Vittorio Emanuele the populace rejoices with cries of long live peace, long live Badoglio, long live the pope. I don't find much reason to be happy: we are a conquered people, and besides Badoglio's last sentence that Italian forces will put up resistance against offenses that might come from other sources hints that we will have to fight against the Germans.

(September 8, 1943)

Even without knowing any of the future developments that followed the announcement, including the humiliating behavior of the government leadership, Italians appeared to have few illusions about the country's ability to avoid the Germans' wrath, although not everybody expressed mixed feelings about the pact. E.R. freely dispensed exclamation points, including one at the end of the day's date, to convey her joy about the resolution: "Wednesday 8 September 943! [...] The radio gave communication of the armistice! All night long it broadcast the news along with Badoglio's proclamation!!" Her enthusiasm continued the next day: "Thursday 9 Sept. 943! Memorable day!"[64] In truth, E.R.'s elation was not widely shared. Most Italians readily recognized that the long-awaited peace was but ephemeral—Badoglio's declaration suggested that much. Among a roller-coaster of emotions (alternating between exhilaration for the moment and fear over the future), another sentiment began to surface that exposed the twisted ways in which fascism had tied Italians to its fate. A Florentine middle-aged milliner with a boyfriend at the front, Maria Alemanno, illustrates this trend. Here is how she described her experience on September 9:

> It was about 8 pm, women walking fast, children running, men standing and talking, then there was some shouting "War is over." /I don't know why, as I was running home, I felt pressed with so much anguish. "War is over." How, why??! Later I learned of Badoglio signing the armistice...good or bad?!! Everybody is worried.

Then, upon reflecting, she commented:

> At first, I also believed in a great joy and great relief and my thought immediately flew to him, "He is going to return soon..." Now I know it is not the

---

[64] In both entries, she also underlined the date twice and the text once.

case. /[...] I don't dare saying anything but from what we hear it is evident that all hell is breaking loose in Italy. Germans run rampant and take possession of our cities.

Finally, Maria dropped the critical word: "They have been betrayed; everything is a betrayal."

Although not all diarists were able to articulate as directly as Maria the bout of anxiety they experienced at the announcement of the armistice, the trope of betrayal, however unqualified, immediately surfaced in their narratives. Irene Paolisso, sparingly but to the point, remarked, "Italy has signed the unconditional armistice with England and America. /We are all suspicious and nervous: we look around with caution. We keep telling ourselves that such a decision cannot but be understood by the Germans as a betrayal." Throughout Italy and beyond, reactions appeared eerily similar. In a note of September 8, Francesco Agnello painfully parsed the meaning of the armistice from his prison camp in Africa:

> Thus, the curtain has suddenly fallen on the big drama. But is this the end we were waiting for after three years of war and sacrifices?
>
> To the damage of the defeat follows the shame of a dishonoring surrender. What will happen to the future of poor Italy? But is the war really over for us? Badoglio's admonition at the end of his proclamation is quite telling and a new war with yesterday's ex-ally seems inevitable.

A member of the army, Agnello particularly focused on the issue of dishonor—he struggled to find reasons to justify Badoglio's historical misstep. Ruminating on the terms of the armistice three days after the surrender, he found them objectionable based precisely on the argument of betrayal. The pact, he wrote, "made us deserve the German violent reaction, by marking us with Machiavellism and treachery" (September 10, 1943). To Agnello's eyes, Italy was unquestionably guilty of disgraceful behavior and could not lay claim to any ethical stand from which to raise legitimate objections against the ex-ally. The country warranted the Germans' ferocious response, he ostensibly concluded, even though he realized that such position played into the hands of the die-hard fascists among his comrade-in-arms. For them, "The Germans are not our traditional enemies any longer, or those who dragged us along, but the betrayed friends; therefore, any reprisal by them is viewed as legitimate" (September 26, 1943). In a war of shifting symbolic values, "betrayal" and "reprisal" had turned into battle cries. To invoke those terms, especially in the case of both Germans and Italian fascists, stretched to the limit the meaning of honor and revenge.

The fact that denunciations of betrayal had such immediate currency among Italians of different ages and locations is puzzling and certainly goes counter to interpretations that impute invocations of betrayal mainly to the fascists.[65] As for the Germans, we know that well ahead of the armistice (indeed in the aftermath of the regime's fall and throughout the summer) they had raised the question of betrayal in anticipation of the eventual split from Italy. Joseph Goebbels expressed doubts about the Italians soon after receiving news of Mussolini's resignation back in July. Upon hearing the king's statement on the momentous change of guard, he wrote in his diary, "The King, too, addressed an appeal to the public. The noteworthy thing in this appeal is a sentence stating that Italy remains true to her tradition and her word. You can't do much with that!" (July 26, 1943). The next day he added, "The Fuehrer is firmly determined to see to it that Italy does not betray the German Reich a second time." Come the armistice of September 8, an unrestrained Goebbels unleashed his rage:

> In the morning the British and American papers were already able to report the news—which proves that the Italians have cheated us to beat the band. [...] The Italians are deserting us in our most critical hour. But I suppose they realize fully that they have thereby chosen the most disgraceful political fate that history can record. They have lost face. Certainly, one cannot break one's word twice in the course of a quarter century without smirching one's political honor for all time to come.   (September 9, 1943)

Not satisfied with this verbal assault, a few days later Goebbels promised no mercy: "The Italians by their infidelity and treachery have lost every claim to a national state of the modern type. They must be punished most severely, as the laws of history demand" (September 11, 1943).[66]

---

[65] Renzo De Felice argues that the political literature of the RSI focused on the betrayal of the king and Badoglio. See *Mussolini l'alleato 1940-1945*, 2 vols. Vol. II, *La guerra civile (1943-1945)* (Turin: Einaudi, 1997), footnote 1, p. 137. For a broad view of how the betrayal trope was applied after the armistice see Claudio Pavone, *Una guerra civile. Saggio storico sulla moralità nella Resistenza* (Turin: Bollati Boringhieri, 1991), chapter 1.3. Il tradimento.

[66] *The Goebbels Diaries 1942-1943*, pp. 406, 410, 427, 445. Apparently, Hitler too immediately cried betrayal on July 25 (cited in Hans Woller, *I conti con il fascismo. L'epurazione in Italia, 1943-1948* [Bologna: il Mulino, 1997], p. 33). On "betrayal" and its aftermath in the form of the Germans' occupation see Lutz Klinkhammer, *L'occupazione tedesca in Italia 1943-1945* (Turin: Bollati Boringhieri, 1993); Paolo Emilio Petrillo, *Lacerazione/Der Riss. 1915-1943: I nodi irrisolti tra Italia e Germania* (Rome: La Lepre Edizioni, 2014). On betrayal as the excuse for punishing Italians see Gerhard Schreiber, "Gli internati militari italiani ed i tedeschi (1943-1945)," in Nicola Labanca ed., *Fra*

Historical and strategic reasons doubtlessly underlay the Germans' adverse attitude towards Italy, and the choice of framing Italy's behavior in terms of betrayal fit those calculations.[67] When it comes to the Italians' approach to "betrayal," however, a more complicated interpretive knot emerges, and two parallel impulses appear to have inspired people's sense of guilt: dishonor and shame. The two sentiments organically grew out of a basic understanding of human relations. Even to those striving to remain ideologically neutral, they felt natural. Fortunato Favai, for example, was well aware of Germany's role in creating the "betrayal" narrative. As he wrote a few days after the armistice, "The Italian troops and people at first cheered, but the German ex-ally cried betrayal and immediately adopted repressive measures" (September 14, 1943). Favai recognized that "betrayal" had become a catchword, an excuse for Germany to engage in extreme war measures. Nevertheless, he felt one could not discount the negative ethical implications of the armistice. Most crucially, he thought Italy's behavior should not be condoned: "After all, Italy was solemnly tied to a pact with the ally Germany to resist together until the end. Germany had sacrificed in the fight for Italy thousands of combatants and precious war material" (September 14, 1943). In Favai's moral universe, "betrayal" logically applied to Italy's duplicity. Intuitively and factually, and in light of the available information, that negative judgment was something that made sense to him, and he declined to consider any other element that would complicate his interpretation.

Carried by their everyday principles and values, Italians' reactions to the pact were baffled. Dino Villani confessed experiencing a feeling of extreme sorrow: "People happily walk in the street but I'm sad, very sad because this is probably one of the worst days of our lives as humans and citizens" (September 8, 1943). Even those very critical of fascism, such as young Angelo Peroni, could not escape the heaviness of the mystifying decision: "We have come to the ending of twenty years of criminal politics: the armistice, unconditional surrender, betrayal, the stabbing in the back secretly plotted against yesterday's allies." He confessed having smiled upon hearing the announcement at first, "But I was soon to cry thinking of what the name 'Italian' means: traitor, coward, buffoon. [...] The most lurid, complete, refined, egregious, disgusting betrayal of all" (September 9, 1943). Peroni's loathing of the government's

---

sterminio e sfruttamento. Militari internati e prigionieri di guerra nella Germania nazista (1939–1945) (Florence: Le Lettere, 1992), pp. 31–62. On the view of betrayal as perpetrated by Germany instead see Erich Kuby, *Il tradimento tedesco* (Milan: Rizzoli, 1987).

[67] According to Renzo De Felice, the Germans feared Italy's exit from the war even before July 25 (and they had different plans for before and after July 25). See *Mussolini l'alleato*, vol. II, p. 45.

pact with the Allied forces (which he considered a shady backroom dealing) even eclipsed his pacifist orientation. Indeed, his contempt for Italy's "betrayal" appeared to have no bottom. After hearing about the conditions of the armistice, he blurted, "These terms are something humiliating, repugnant, disgusting: one feels revulsion for the traitors who today, with a proclamation, incite Italians against Germans" (September 12, 1943).

In Peroni's view, Italy had committed a serious crime, a morally dubious act that completely discredited her reputation. Antonio Maestri, a thirty-one-year-old knife sharpener from the Trentino region in active military duty abroad, shared Peroni's opinion. With basic prose, he described his battalion's reactions to the armistice on the evening of September 8:

> At around 7 pm the news circulates among us that Italy signed the armistice with America and England. Later on, around 8 pm the radio confirms it. We took note of the news not at all satisfied; in contrast, we realized that it was too early and that this had to be a big betrayal.

While Maestri did not elaborate on the reasons for judging the pact a betrayal, he dramatically depicted Italy's and the Italian army's capitulation as signifying nothing less than "everybody's ruin."[68]

Unsurprisingly, those Italians more sympathetic to the regime expressed outraged reactions at the unfathomable pact. From his prison camp in Africa, forty-six-year-old Florentine Carlo Ciseri sadly saw it as a sign of Italy's moral debacle. A fervent believer in fascism, to the point of volunteering to join its colonial troops, Ciseri mourned the termination of what he believed was Italy's ethical stand. Contrary to other fellow citizens, Ciseri believed that the war was necessary and "wanted." Still his moral outrage at the armistice fit the generally negative reaction, and it would be mistaken to dismiss his indignation as preposterous.[69] Especially for soldiers (whether or not they aligned with fascism), the collapse of the Italian military in the aftermath of the armistice was a sad proof of the carelessness with which the government acted.

As a member of the Alpine corps, Ettore Castiglioni felt the same humiliation as Ciseri, despite the fact that his ideas stood at the opposite end of the political spectrum. Granted, Castiglioni did not endorse the "betrayal" narrative upheld by Ciseri and was clearly torn between the desire for the end of the war and his pride as a military man loyally serving the nation.

---

[68] He wrote the phrase "everybody's ruin" in other scattered pages also dated September 8, 1943.
[69] Ciseri features prominently in Duggan's history of the period as narrated in *Fascist Voices*.

Fundamentally, however, he felt deeply wounded by the armistice and resented the dishonor he associated with the army's capitulation and the dereliction of duty demonstrated by the military hierarchy. Lack of reaction to German occupation, as well as people's general apathy in the face of depredations and stealing at the abandoned barracks, also contributed to his dejection. "I had to witness scenes that I would have never wanted to see, I had to live days that I would have never wanted to live," he lamented. With the fall of fascism, he had hoped Italians would unite in a fight against the "eternal" German enemy and regain the honor lost in the "ignominious" war: "But maybe it was the crumbling of this hope and of any illusion that has made the days of the armistice so desperately sad and humiliating." Castiglioni was disconsolate, unable to "fathom how long it will take before we will be able to redeem our honor as humans, before we will be able to raise our heads and look at the world without blushing from shame and humiliation" (September 26, 1943).

Strikingly powerful, the gravity of Castiglioni's sentiments brings to light the interpretive challenges Italians confronted as they tried to process an event pregnant with symbolic meanings and loaded with factual reverberations. In the case of Castiglioni, shame resulted from a deeply painful contemplative assessment and was grounded in a complex set of values, as well as expectations and conditions, that were hardly reconcilable. His first reaction at the news of the armistice is telling: "When someone pronounced the word 'Armistice,' we did not want to believe it. It was like the liberation from a nightmare, the end of a long tragedy" (September 26, 1943). From welcoming the armistice as an emancipating moment to damning it as a total debacle, Castiglioni's change of heart testifies to the cognitive confusion the pact generated for him. In a matter of weeks, he had recast the event of September 8 within a morally infused frame in which concern with honor and humiliation became the main interpretive thread. Although no other diarist matched his eloquence, the issue of the country's ethical stance stood at the center of countless other Italians' responses to the armistice. Prisoner of war Francesco Agnello summarized his sentiment in a few words: "To each Italian, to each soldier the accusation and the mark of traitor burns" (September 14, 1943). Or as carpenter Vitruvio Giorni reflected from Albania, "I have to note however that for a soldier the surrendering of weapons is one of the biggest humiliations" (September 10, 1943). No matter that Giorni was deeply religious and opposed war in principle on the ground of his Christian ethic, as a member of the army he found himself unable to ignore the disturbing impact that unconditional surrender exerted on his sense of honor.

As for the people who rejoiced at the announcement, the consequences of the armistice still lurched in the back of their minds. At the parish of Robecco Pavese in Northern Italy, Don Luigi Serravalle felt his emotions pulled in different directions as he simultaneously tried to draft an objective report of the facts:

Armistice!.....

This evening the long-awaited news arrived. It was 7:45 pm when, by chance, I turned on the radio. Just then, the sound tone indicated the start of the broadcast, and they promptly announced that Marshal Badoglio would speak.

From the first words, one could immediately guess that the armistice was the matter, as it was indeed announced. But one could hear an anguished voice and from the overall proclamation something sad transpired.

(September 8, 1943)

Though initially elated at the proclamation ("Armistice!....."), shortly thereafter Don Luigi felt the need to exercise caution and restrain his excitement. He sensed the equivocality of the situation and even detected a sorrowful tone in Badoglio's announcement.[70] As he continued, "At first I thought of ringing the bells, but then, upon reflection, I did not think it was right to celebrate while we were facing but defeat." Well aware that Italy had not engaged in the treaty as a winner, Don Luigi wondered about the legitimacy of joy in the absence of victory. Troubled by this Gordian knot, he struggled to decide whether to behave as if it was an ordinary day or acknowledge the exceptional nature of that September night. In his homily, he gave the news of the armistice but warned that the pact "could not bring as much joy as the one of 1918, because we were winners then, we are losers now." Pragmatic in his approach, Don Luigi represented a middle of the road perspective—he welcomed the armistice for bringing peace after so many years of war, but was wary of its potential complications: "And the conventions to be agreed with by the winners, how will they be? /And the consequences of the defeat?" Reality appeared complicated and so did the armistice. Sitting at the table as a winner or loser obviously made a difference to Don Luigi. Unlike other Italians, however, the issue of honor and betrayal did not cross his mind, at least not on that momentous night.

---

[70] Newspapers also reported that same interpretation of Badoglio's tone. See Oliva, *I vinti e i liberati*, p. 101.

If Don Luigi ignored or seemed unaffected by the dilemma of Italy's supposed duplicity, a handful of diarists adamantly rejected the notion of betrayal and denounced it as deeply problematic. "Many are talking of betrayal. We didn't betray anybody, in contrast, we were betrayed by the fascists first and then the Nazis," Bruna Talluri wrote on September 8. In a few terse words, she brought back the regime to the center of discussion. By refusing evaluations rooted in ahistorical moral categories, Talluri reclaimed her right, as a victim, to single out responsibilities. Hence, she forcefully separated oppressed ordinary citizens from their fascist oppressors—fascism and Italy were not the same thing, and she deemed aspersions of guilt and self-flagellations simply out of place.[71] Ester Marozzi agreed, "Mussolini handed us over to the Germans bound hand and foot." Criticizing those "idiot Italians" who were lamenting, "Ah, we are disgusting, we'll go down in history as traitors," Marozzi retorted:

> We should shoot these people because they constitute a permanent enemy among our ranks. Who is a traitor? Us? But we are the ones being betrayed by Mussolini and his accomplice Hitler for they knew that the whole Italy did not want to fight alongside Germany in a war against her allies of 1915 [...]. The ones being betrayed is us.   (September 8, 1943)

Assuredly combative, Marozzi did not feel any less devasted: "Italy facing defeat. /Immense humiliation, a cry from the heart that freezes inside. [...] We will have to empty the bitter cup until the last drop" (September 9, 1943). Convinced that fascism's responsibilities could not be superseded by newly constructed moral arguments, she stoically confronted the unwelcome situation.

Fifty-eight-year-old Milanese Mario Tutino had been questioning essentialist judgments about the Italians' behavior ever since the regime's crumbling, for he believed that people's conduct needed to be contextualized within the current historical conditions. Considering Italy's very peculiar situation, how could she preserve national interests while maintaining her honor? "To stop fighting would be cowardly, but one doesn't know why and for whom one is fighting. [...] Agonizing days" (July 31, 1943). Although he continued to hope that Italy would emerge from the conflict "without dishonor" (August 3, 1943), the news of the armistice opened up a whole new phase of painful

---

[71] After this entry, Talluri wrote another one on December 12, then stopped the diary altogether only to resume it on August 24 of the following year. Meanwhile, she joined the partisan struggle.

considerations for him. He deemed unconditional surrender "the most humiliating and complete defeat" (September 10–11, 1943)—a sobering conclusion. Despite this unforgiving diagnosis, however, Tutino refused to take the armistice as an excuse for shaming the country or, even worse, for withdrawing from a fight for the future. After meeting an acquaintance (an ex-fascist in "good faith"), he recounted:

> He too at some point repeated the sentence that today is on the lips of too many and most disparate individuals, "I'm ashamed, he said, of being Italian!" And here I gave out all the outrage the sentence provokes in me. He was the fifth, sixth person that within two or three days told me the same thing. A sentence of foolish arrogance, of voluntary and stupid detachment from a well-identified position of humanity to which one belongs, of cynical handwashing, of sly and doubly guilty intention to find a personal alibi. When, where, how does shame start? And what's in this guilt we certainly have on our conscience that is specifically Italian? But above all what is there that cannot be redeemed? And even redeemed immediately because the chance is here, is present, indeed is urgent?[72] (September 13, 1943)

For Tutino, acknowledging one's involvement in fascism was a necessary first step in the pursuit of a pragmatic course of actions based on a "sentiment of solidarity in guilt, of solidarity in repentance, of solidarity in will of redemption" (September 13, 1943).[73] One could not approve of those who, because of Badoglio's controversial decisions, seemed to be having second thoughts on the regime—it was a false dichotomy. No matter the current government's mistakes, "If one is not for tyranny, everything that happened from July 26 till today can be understood and justified. It's absurd to talk about the king's or Badoglio's betrayal today. If the king betrayed, it was long ago when he opened the doors to fascist violence." Tutino defied people's uncertainty and posed the stark choice to be "either for tyranny or freedom" (September 17, 1943). Or, as he later summarized, "Today hatred against the Germans is the only true measure of hatred against fascism" (September 20, 1943).[74]

---

[72] The prevalence of the statement "I'm ashamed of being Italian" is also lamented by Chevallard, "Diario di Carlo Chevallard 1942–1945," p. 139 (entry of October 20, 1943).

[73] Tutino's thoughts resonate with Claudio Pavone's moral argument about the Resistance in *Una guerra civile*. The timing of Tutino's reflections is also important as Mussolini had been liberated by the Germans from his mountain prison the previous day (September 12) in the so-called operation Achse.

[74] Carazzolo seems to anticipate Tutino in an entry written in the wake of the Anglo-Americans' landing in Sicily on July 17, 1943: "This is not a war of nationalisms, but a war of principles. On the

86 FASCISM, THE WAR, AND STRUCTURES OF FEELING IN ITALY

With a philosophical sleight of hand, Tutino reversed people's moral argument according to which Italians were guilty of betrayal for turning their backs on Germany. To the contrary, there was but one option: to fight against the Germans. This sole course of action would help overcome fascism, even if it implied engaging in a civil war. By rejecting false idealisms, Tutino recognized that sometimes circumstances force us to make less than perfect choices, and he understood that many Italians would prefer to finish the war first before taking care of fascism. To him, however, this argument amounted to a mistaken dichotomy. It was "a hypothesis of idyllic resolution of a tragic situation, and for that reason false and anti-historicist" (October 3, 1943). In order to move forward and take initiative, Italians' responsibilities for fascism needed to be recognized as a starting point, the crucial issue being not atonement but practical engagement against a fascist war. If dishonor happened to have stemmed from the armistice, it was the undesirable result of the necessary and crucial goal of defeating fascism. Like the younger Talluri, Tutino brought fascism back into the equation. Honor and dishonor were not pertinent paragons of evaluation for assessing the country's course, even in the face of the armistice's discomfiting reality.

October 13: A Footnote?

With all the commotion raised by the issue of betrayal, in actuality Badoglio's announcement of the armistice had only made an oblique reference to fighting the Germans. That vague allusion became a certainty on October 13, when, as representative for the government, Badoglio committed Italian troops to cooperating with Allied forces.[75] Steeped in diplomatic rationales and legalities (including assigning legal status to Italian soldiers that had been without one after September 8), the declaration clarified a situation that the official statement of the armistice had left murky and confusing, albeit unequivocal in practice: the war continued and Germany was now the official enemy. Due to the critical developments that followed the armistice, notably the Germans' liberation of Mussolini on September 12 and the establishment

---

one side there are autocracy and enslavement, on the other democracy and liberalism. One is either on this side or the other. It is not an issue of Italy or England; it is an issue of Nazi-fascism or democracy." *Più forte della paura*, pp. 80–1.

[75] Italy's Kingdom of the South, the current territory under the king's jurisdiction, was however considered a co-belligerent, not an ally.

shortly thereafter of a reconstituted fascist government in Northern Italy, the declaration also gave veracity to a fear people had been anticipating for some time: Italians would now be at war with each other.

Oddly for such a momentous event, reactions at the war announcement were almost muted, and only a few diarists commented specifically on it, with Don Luigi Serravalle simply reporting, "In the evening, the radio broadcast that today Italy declared war to Germany." In a similarly laconic entry, Anna Menestrina added an expression of concern: "Declaration of war on Germany from Badoglio's government. And now?..."

In truth, the reality on the ground had foreshadowed Italy's official decision—German troops had occupied the country immediately after the armistice, sparing no brutality. Badoglio's declaration of October 13 matched factual conditions and eerily reminded people of the reality in which they were immersed. Only, the war was evidently going to turn uglier, as Anna Menestrina realized after her initial subdued reaction to the announcement: "Now the situation will get even worse. The Germans rule at home and fight on our land. [...] Our poor, poor Fatherland!" (October 14, 1943). Similarly focused on the graver repercussions of the declaration, Leo Baldi reported from the capital, "The more pessimist among us believe that the Germans will not leave one single man in Rome that will not end up in the military, or in work services, or in concentration camps. Any reprisal and abuse against us by the Germans will become legitimate" (October 13, 1943). Expect no mercy, Barbara Garrone expressed in Latin, "Poor us. Vae victis!..." (October 13, 1943).[76]

A small number of diarists lent the announcement little more than a few words. In Rome, Fedora Brenta Brcic, a native of Croatia in her mid-forties, buried her one line within a longer account of her daily mundane activities.[77] In Schio, Leone Fioravanti's telegraphic chronicle showed his practical preoccupation with survival.[78] Fatigued by the emotional roller-coaster experienced since July 25, the Italians had no response to the war declaration. The fear people held throughout the late summer and early fall that the worst had

---

[76] From the Latin, the phrase means "Woe to the conquered."
[77] While writing about a few foods she had indulged, she guiltily reminded herself of the privations suffered by her admiral husband, prisoner of the Germans, and drew a connection: "The complication of the formal war declaration dampens my hope of seeing you soon" (October 14, 1943). Then she quickly moved on to more sentimental affairs.
[78] "Declaration of war against Germany by the Badoglio's government. Ironic comments by the Germans. We'll see about the consequences. Meanwhile, food is in short supply and firewood is no longer distributed. The allowance of milk, butter, and oil is decreasing. They are not distributing the ration cards yet" (October 13, 1943).

yet to come prepared them for the undesirable but inevitable sequel of October 13. Meanwhile, fascism kept disappearing from their radar.

Amidst the prevailing negativity, twenty-year-old Second Lieutenant Giorgio Crainz found an uncommon silver lining. Taken prisoner by the Germans after the armistice, he reacted to the news of October 13 with a hint of optimism: "Good! Perhaps, if the mass of Italians joins Badoglio's government and behaves accordingly, it will be possible to save something" (October 14, 1943). Little elaborated, but sustained by the hope of regaining a degree of dignity, the reasoning behind Crainz's optimism was the idea that the country's terrible mishaps might be rectified by fighting on the right side.[79] Mario Tutino agreed. For him, the ex-ally "was the true enemy. The true enemy is Nazi-fascism, and those Italians that help Nazism are enemies as much as the Germans" (October 13, 1943).

By reframing the significance of Italy's "betrayal," Tutino fully embraced the harsh reality of having to fight against fellow Italians if that was the only way to achieve freedom from oppression and defeat tyranny. Due to shifting alliances and the resurgence of fascism in German-occupied Italy, he recognized that the ongoing war required a new map of friends and foes. And he guessed that the realignment would force Italians to confront the issue of fascism so hurriedly liquidated in the frenzied rush after July 25. More fundamentally, Tutino understood that one critical, unanswered question remained: what were Italians fighting against? Or, most consequentially, did they realize the weightiness of fascism, and how were they to handle that predicament while trying to survive the terrible circumstances of a world war tragically turned internecine?

In this chapter we have taken the events of July 25, September 8, and October 13, 1943 as historical moments through which to begin examining the Italians' reckoning with fascism after its sudden demise. What were people thinking about the regime once they were relieved of its yoke, and how did they relate to that immediate past considering that the dictatorship fell in the absence of a revolution from below? Looking for clues in the writings of diarists, we have found that little retrospective analysis took place in the days after Mussolini's resignation. Most importantly, in the majority of cases, the significance of July 25 was adjudicated in relation to the course of the war. A paramount hope for peace meshed with and affected popular reactions to the end of fascism, making it difficult to extricate the two. The incongruences

---

[79] This is the "morality of the Resistance" in Pavone's interpretation, *Una guerra civile*.

that arose out of this ambiguity gave rise to interpretive fallacies that exploded at the time of the armistice, when feelings of shame at the country's supposed betrayal blinded Italians from understanding the implications of a continued alliance with Germany. Standing alongside Hitler meant upholding Mussolini's misconceived politics and the Nazis' destructive agenda—September 8 as well as the declaration of war of October 13 could not be disentangled from fascism and its resurgence. Yet fascism seemed to be fading from people's immediate concerns, as if it had been a passing malady now resolved. A cognitive dissonance of great historical, political import ensued.

The chapter has brought to light the shifting evaluative terrain on which ordinary Italians built their interpretations of current history—their clashing views and contradictions. It has also exposed the distance that separated people's assessment of their present from officially dispensed messages and interpretations. Especially in the case of September 8, understanding the armistice as betrayal was a diffused, spontaneous conclusion that even preceded its eventual ideological exploitation by the fascists. The format of daily entries characteristic of personal journals has proved ideal for tracking the cultural process through which Italians voided established frameworks. Diaries show that, by mediating between historical phenomena and practical experience, people created their own meanings and values—a cluster of structures of feeling that, though often unarticulated and underdetermined, as Raymond Williams suggests, were nevertheless commonly held. At the same time, diaries say very little about the substance of the historical events that marked the summer/fall of 1943, events whose magnitude cannot be minimized. And diaries are especially short on evaluations of the fascist regime. Although at times expressive and revealing emotions (such as the widespread surprise on July 25), journal writers mostly stuck to facts and were keen on establishing the accuracy of their reports. In several cases, their orientation to chronicling constrained them to detailed descriptions that tended to isolate feelings. Only typographical devices intervene to help give flair to their dry informative notes. Ultimately, how substance and content interact in the composition of entries, or more precisely, how the genre of journaling restricted the scribes' creative output remains in question and certainly does not explain diarists' laconic reactions on October 13.

The next chapter will dig further into the structures of feeling of Italians, being mindful of the ambivalence diarists expressed toward the events of and after summer/fall 1943, while also remaining alert to the disconnection with the fascist past that transpires from people's interpretive tentativeness. Although most often sidelined, abducted, and deflected, fascism's ghostly presence officiated over the ways the country navigated the crises that followed July 25. As Italians confronted the most consequential phase of a devastating war that shattered familiar patterns, they had to rebuild their evaluative categories and adapt to a continuously changing reality. In the process, it turns out, the past re-emerged from the fissures of a summarily buried regime now rising from its ashes.

2
Interpretive Ghosts

> This is what happened: Italy is divided in two.
> (September 8, 1943)*

"Who occupies the place of honor in offices today? The king?...Mussolini?... Barely two months ago they removed Mussolini's portrait and left the one with the king. Then they removed the king and hung Mussolini again. And now? It seems they are thinking of a coat of arms with the Republican fascio..." (November 7, 1943). With a keen eye to the elusive reality of political symbolism, Anna Menestrina's entry of early November 1943 encapsulated the schizophrenic unfolding of history following the fall of fascism in Italy. A resident of Trento, Menestrina was particularly aware of the epochal maelstrom that over mere months had engulfed the country and upended its political structure. One of the capitals of irredentism during the late nineteenth century, annexed by Italy after the First World War, Trento was now under the control of the German territorial subdivision of Alpenvorland.[1] Artificially split between two administrations—the German military on the one hand and the reconstituted fascist authority on the other—Trento was doubly subjected to the confusion of symbolisms highlighted by Menestrina. In truth, the rapidity with which political scenarios shifted in Italy over the summer and fall of 1943 fueled feelings of disorientation beyond that region. Despite the ritualistic destructions that marked July 25, fascism had returned to haunt Italians. Newly reconfigured in the Italian Social Republic (RSI), and thanks to the military support of the Third Reich, Mussolini's government reclaimed sovereignty over more than half the peninsula.

---

* From the diary of Michelina Michelini.

[1] The Alpenvorland was an operational zone in the Italian sub-alpine area established by the Wehrmacht in response to the armistice of September 8. For literature on the Alpenvorland see Lutz Klinkhammer, *L'occupazione tedesca in Italia 1943–1945* (Turin: Bollati Boringhieri, 1993). Also see, among others, Istituto Veneto per la storia della Resistenza, *Tedeschi, partigiani e popolazioni nell'Alpenvorland (1943–1945)*, Atti del convegno di Belluno 1983 (Venice: Marsilio, 1984); Enzo Collotti, *L'amministrazione tedesca dell'Italia occupata 1943–1945. Studio e documenti* (Milan: Lerici, 1963); and Enzo Collotti, "L'occupazione tedesca in Italia," in Enzo Collotti, Renato Sandri, and Frediano Sessi eds., *Dizionario della Resistenza*, Vol. I, *Storia e geografia della Liberazione* (Turin: Einaudi, 2000), pp. 43–65.

Although fascism was an actual force to be reckoned with, the new government appointed by Victor Emmanuel III in the Kingdom of the South curiously relegated it to a secondary, if not altogether negligible, role.[2] Marshal Badoglio instead focused his ire on "German arrogance and ferocity," which he saw especially unleashed in the aftermath of September 8. In his proclamation to Italians issued on October 13, Badoglio cited German terror as the main justification for engaging in war:

> We had already seen some examples of their behavior in the abuses of power, robbery, and violence of all kinds perpetrated in Catania while they were still our allies. Even more savage incidents against our unarmed population took place in Calabria, then in the Puglie and in the area of Salerno. But where the ferocity of the enemy surpassed every limit of the human imagination happened at Naples. The heroic population of that city, which for weeks suffered every form of torment, cooperated with the Anglo-American troops in putting the hated Germans to flight.
>
> Italians! There will not be peace in Italy as long as a single German remains upon our soil. Shoulder to shoulder we must march forward with our friends of the United States, of Great Britain, of Russia, and of all the other United Nations.
>
> Wherever Italian troops may be, in the Balkans, Yugoslavia, Albania, and in Greece, they have witnessed similar acts of aggression and cruelty and they must fight against the Germans to the last man.[3]

Rid of any ambivalence left lingering at the announcement of the armistice a month earlier, Badoglio's words could not have been clearer. This was a war against the one and only enemy, whose alleged violence—beyond the pale of imagination—demanded an equally radical response: not "a single German" should be left roaming on Italian territory. With this hefty mission bestowed upon the country, and seemingly ignoring internal conflicts, Badoglio elicited

---

[2] After fleeing Rome on September 9 and eventually reaching Brindisi, the king maintained the administrative structure of the Italian Kingdom in areas of the South occupied by the Anglo-American forces. Badoglio remained at the head of the government in what came to be referred to as the Kingdom of the South (which initially only comprised four provinces). For a chronicle of this period see Agostino Degli Espinosa, *Il Regno del Sud. 8 Settembre 1943-4 Giugno 1944* (Rome: Migliaresi Editore, 1946). Also see Ennio Di Nolfo, *Le paure e le speranze degli italiani (1943-1953)* (Milan: Mondadori, 1986), chapter IV "Dal regno del Sud a Roma."

[3] The citation comes from the English text of the proclamation as delivered by Badoglio to the Commander-in-Chief of the Allied Forces, General D.D. Eisenhower. It is conserved at the Franklin Delano Roosevelt Presidential Library (FDR speech file). Retrieved online.

Italians to realign their fighting efforts and salvage the fatherland—the final goal being political self-determination in free elections. As the country was joining new "friends," Badoglio encouraged his compatriots, "The present arrangement will in no way impair the untrammeled right of the people of Italy to choose their own form of Democratic Government when peace is restored."

While Badoglio's call for unity was meant to reassure the population about the role of the Anglo-American allies as well as to gain the latter's trust, it officially sanctioned the Germans' inimical status and left Italians to confront yet another interpretive dilemma.[4] Allies of Hitler for more than three years and having fought alongside Germany on numerous battlefronts, they were now asked to switch sides and support the Anglo-American "friends," even if the latter's continuous bombings were wreaking havoc among the population. Who was the enemy and how was one to judge them? Centered on the existential threat raised by the conflict, Italians' concerns about "the enemy" fluctuated, often shaped by individual experiences more than official labels. As a war of meanings accompanied the harsh reality of the struggle on the ground, many redeployed the accusation of betrayal, turning it around and challenging its original intent. Meanwhile, fascism and Mussolini continued to lose relevance in the arena of public debate (Badoglio failed to mention them at all in his declaration of war), and the Germans offered a convenient scapegoat behind which to hide internal divisions and responsibilities. Feeling like pawns in a grander game of which they had few clues, Italians resiliently kept hoping that the current destructive course would rapidly come to an end. Whereas some hesitated to take the Anglo-Americans' side, others particularly agonized over the ensuing tragedy of the civil war. Identifying the guilty within this multiplicity of actors proved to be a mystifying task of phenomenal consequences. Interpretive clues were not lacking, whether provided by historical precedents or suggested by the authoritative voice of those in power. People, however, did not impassively acquiesce to and adopt those pointers.

---

[4] Aware of the need for Italy to abide by the Allied forces' view of the war as a fight against Nazism in defense of democracy, Badoglio's proclamation demonstrated his government's acceptance of the Anglo-Americans' position. It also encouraged Italians to join the fight in an eventual Italian corps of the Allied army. In his study of the Italian memory of the Second World War, Filippo Focardi summarizes the main themes of Allied propaganda efforts in Italy from the beginning of the conflict. Those themes were reiterated in the message Roosevelt and Churchill sent to Italians a few days before the invasion of Sicily. The message "differentiated between the Italian people and the fascist regime, unloaded on the latter the responsibility for the war, and pointed to Germany as a false ally exclusively concerned with its own interests and ready to betray its unwary Italian follower." See Focardi, *Il cattivo tedesco e il bravo italiano. La rimozione delle colpe della seconda guerra mondiale* (Rome-Bari: Laterza, 2013), p. 4 (also see chapter 1 for studies on the Anglo-American propaganda).

Instead, they used them as scaffoldings on which to build their own response to the historical puzzles—structures by which they expressed their feelings on the issues at stake.

Who Is the Enemy?

When Anglo-American forces occupied Sicily in early July 1943, fifteen-year-old Olga Garbagnati was at first anguished by the idea that Italy might be under foreign control again.[5] Writing about the situation in her diary, she highlighted the cruelty of the occupiers in the unfolding drama: "Alarms upon alarms, victims upon victims, but are they heartless? When will this scourge end?" (July 14, 1943). Beset by Italy's atavistic obsession with the foreigner, Olga loathed the Anglo-American invaders from the safety of her Milan, some 1,500 kilometers away. Probably influenced by the regime's propaganda at the time, she changed her perspective two and a half months later, whereupon she showed no reservations to switching her anger towards the Germans: "The armistice was signed!!! The joy of this event has been spoiled by the Germans' invasion of Italy. Italy, my dear fatherland, is now subjugated by the enemies" (October 2, 1943). With the Germans taking the grave step of occupying the country in the wake of September 8, they turned into the foe for Olga or, even worse, into Italy's quintessential foe: "The Germans, our eternal enemies, that for years have been considered friends but now we realize the mistake and are paying the price for it" (October 19, 1943). Apparently subscribing to Badoglio's recent negative characterization of the Germans, Olga relied on the trope of "eternal enemy" (a legacy of the Risorgimento struggles and the Great War) to make sense of otherwise complicated geopolitical realignments and strategies. Although she saw the question of friend and foe in simple terms, she exactly captured the gist of Italy's tortuous historical conundrum.[6]

A wife and young mother of three in her thirties, Wanda Africano-Marabini did not have the assuredness that comes with adopting a simple Manichean view of the world as displayed by young Garbagnati. To the

---

[5] The association of the foreigner with the enemy—an invader and despot—was central to the Risorgimento's view of history. On the role of Risorgimento ideals in the "patriotic war" of 1943–45 see Claudio Pavone, *Una guerra civile. Saggio storico sulla moralità nella Resistenza* (Turin: Bollati Boringhieri, 1991), chapter 4 "La guerra patriottica", section 1 "Alla conquista dell' identità nazionale," pp. 169–89.

[6] For the existential distinction between friend and enemy see Carl Schmitt, *The Concept of the Political*, translated by George Schwab (Chicago: University of Chicago Press, 1996).

contrary, her engagement with the "enemy" was in part tied to the vicissitudes of her husband—a soldier whose currently unknown fate left Wanda in great distress. Cognizant of the possibility that the Germans might have imprisoned her spouse—and in the attempt to re-establish some form of communication with him, be it merely at the emotional level—she began a diary on October 2, 1943. A sense of loneliness and vulnerability, in addition to grueling uncertainty, transpires from her entries composed in epistolary form— letters directed to her loved one in an ideal dialogue that forever missed its interlocutor.[7]

In these entries/missives, Wanda expressed both fear and outrage at the Germans, whom she ironically addressed as "dear allies," questioning their behavior as befitting a partnership and calling them "cowards" for making unreasonable demands on Italy. Without mincing words, she labeled their conduct a form of betrayal, unmistakably rejecting any suggestion that the Italians were the ones to blame. In her very first diary entry, she asked her spouse, "And you, what are you thinking at this moment??! Do you know what is happening here and what our dear allies are up to? Anything but betrayal by us! They are the cowards who demand the impossible from an agonizing nation, which is what our Italy is reduced to!"[8] In Wanda's view, the question about the Germans boiled down to issues of character and behavior, although she did not consider their wickedness unique. Indeed, while scornful of the Germans' arrogance, she was not quite sure about the British either: "Naples too has been occupied by the English, who are now marching towards Rome. Oh my God, what will happen! Here we are caught between two fires and I don't know under whom we'll be better off" (October 3, 1943). Guided by a heightened practical sense and inspired by her own personal experience, all the while heralding an instinctive distrust of those in power, Affricano-Marabini assessed the present with little idealism: "I say, the Germans by now know us and we realize what they are capable of, but the English too, I don't believe they are all saints!" She expressed skepticism about lending support to another foreigner when there was no evidence of their virtues. Most of all, she

---

[7] Several diarists adopted this epistolary style at a time when postal communication came to a halt and civilians were no longer able to exchange letters with military personnel. On the use of private letters from the eighteenth century to the twentieth century see Maria Luisa Betri and Daniela Maldini Chiarito eds., *Dolce dono graditissimo. La lettera privata dal Settecento al Novecento* (Milan: Franco Angeli, 2000).

[8] On the importance of the "you" in one's life story see Adriana Cavarero, *Relating Narratives: Storytelling and Selfhood* (London: Routledge, 2000). Cavarero views politics and ethics in terms of a relational ontology in which the subject (I) implicates the other (you) as necessary; they are interdependent. Also see Judith Butler's comments on Cavarero, "Giving an Account of Oneself," *Diacritics* vol. 31, no. 4 (Winter 2001): pp. 22–40.

was concerned about the country's future. Her awareness of Italy's dominated status was unmistakable, albeit still disarming, and she confronted it pragmatically, while punctiliously trying to take stock of the advantages and disadvantages the two occupying forces might bring. On the one hand, the Germans were the main cause of the war and its continuation. Moreover, they had annexed territories in Northern Italy (the Alpenvorland as well as the Adriatic Littoral in Italy's northeastern shore), and Wanda wondered about the perverse logic that allowed them to be reaping rewards at Italy's expenses.[9] On the other hand, how could one trust the English? All things being considered, Italians were still facing the choice between two ruling powers, neither of which she felt could be trusted.

An obviously harrowing issue, the dilemma vexed Wanda greatly, so much so that she returned to it in the next days, never quite resolving it: "Don't we have two enemies at home?! Which one might be better in the end?" (October 21). Despite Badoglio's official rebuke and her own risk of being persecuted by Nazi-fascism for her Jewish origins, she did not lean against the Germans (but she did call them "assassins" after their raid of the Jewish ghetto on October 16). In truth, her perspective was tempered by a realistic view of the situation that appeared ominously bad for Italians no matter the perspective. Focused on practical matters, Wanda acknowledged that all foreign dominations were to be loathed. Idealism did not agree with her daily suffering.

The decision over friend and foe, which seemed to trap Wanda in a non-committed position on the enemy, also presented an unresolvable quandary for Don Luigi Serravalle. Inclined to tolerance in his role as priest, he looked at people from the standpoint of the equalizing category of humanity. Germans were no exception, although he admittedly resented their insolence. On a Sunday evening in early September 1943, having convened a meeting of the Catholic Action, the father noted that, sadly, only four men were in attendance. He explained the reason for such a poor outcome with the fact that Germans were roaming the village causing fear over their potentially malign behavior[10]—a situation that in an apparent non sequitur led him to a further consideration:

Tonight at the tavern the Germans sang until midnight. They said we are good people. Certainly, if taken individually, they too are like our soldiers,

---

[9] The Operational Zone of the Adriatic Littoral comprised territories in present-day Slovenia, Croatia, and Italy. The capital of the zone was Trieste.

[10] Tales of ransacking by Germans were prevalent in the letters written by Florentine priests to their bishop. See Preti fiorentini, *Giorni di guerra 1943–1945. Lettere al Vescovo* (Florence: Libreria editrice Fiorentina, 1992), edited by Giulio Villani, Preface by Pier Luigi Ballini.

away from their families because forced to. And yet if one thinks that we fought for so long against them in the 1915–18 war and that so many died in order to chase them out of Italian soil, looking at them almost acting as masters of the place now!..... (September 5, 1943)

Even before the Italian government negotiated the armistice with the Anglo-Americans and Germany was still considered an ally, memories of the First World War affected Don Luigi's sentiments. Germans obviously made him uncomfortable. Although he did not explicitly state it, the ellipsis at the end of his entry spoke volumes, and matters only worsened after the armistice. Instead of happiness, doom seemed to befall the small community: "Not a day of joy, but of trepidation today. Early in the morning we immediately learned that the bridge on the Po was occupied by the Germans. They disarmed our soldiers and took them prisoners" (September 9, 1943). Still restrained in his judgment, or better avoiding one altogether, Don Luigi was noticeably struck by the incident. Two months later, when that same area suffered heavy bombings by the Allied forces, he burst out, "What times are we living in!...One could almost say that we do not know which are our allies and which our enemies" (November 8, 1943). Incessant bombings by the Anglo-Americans did not help Don Luigi resolve his confusion, even if he seemed to be taking the side of the Allied powers. He could not rely for help on official definitions either, unless, that is, he made a choice between whose words to follow: those of Badoglio in the Kingdom of the South or the ones of the Fascist Republic of Salò under whose jurisdiction he resided.

Layers of complexities made the question of the enemy hard to resolve for many. To the puzzlement caused by the changed coalitions in the conflict and the consequent switching of roles between friend and foe, one had to include the paradox of having to suffer destruction at the hands of the new ally. Meanwhile, the Germans remained a central figure in the Italians' ongoing semantic struggle. Both symbolically and in practice they embodied enmity, however ill-defined. The propaganda unleashed by the Allied forces, and supported by Badoglio and the king as well as varied representatives of Italian antifascism, played a large role in circulating the inimical picture of the German. Through the historical connection with the Risorgimento wars for independence, the German was framed as the barbarian invader, quintessentially violent and outside of civilization—an irredeemable villain that one could not but fight to the death.[11]

---

[11] On the representation of the German as villain see Pavone, *Una guerra civile*, chapter 4 "La guerra patriottica," especially section 3 "Il nemico ritrovato," pp. 206–20. Pavone points out that many

These highly charged images were disseminated abundantly in Italy via radio and other means, and there is also no doubt that dislike for the Germans was widespread among the population. Diarists' accounts, however, present a more nuanced picture of people's experiences of the German, one that contrasts the monochrome postwar narrative of the conflict.[12] Granted, Italians were not insensitive to rumors, stereotypes, and old beliefs that demonized the Germans. Also, they might (or might not) have internalized the government's official position on the "enemy" in the aftermath of the armistice. In the end, however, their relationship to the ex-ally-turned-occupier and enemy-invader was especially filtered through the sieve of individual perceptions, personal knowledge, and specific circumstances. Moreover, their "hatred" for the Germans grew over time as Nazi crimes mounted. Far from being a straightforward affair, hatred, it turns out, could not be simply commanded.

Looking the enemy in the eye

Tuscan teenager Perla Cacciaguerra found the designation of friends and foes baffling. The daughter of a fascist *podestà* with a complicated family tree that included an American mother and a grandfather of German origins, Cacciaguerra was a free spirit who lived the wartime events from a privileged class position. Her household in the Arezzo countryside often hosted German officers for dinner gatherings and film viewings (at least until the war declaration of October 13), even if her family was divided between supporters and opponents of fascism. Perla counted herself among the latter. Critical of the consequences of the military conflict especially on civilians, she claimed to be professing socialist ideas. When it came to the Germans, however, she appeared less self-assured—personal experience made judgment complicated. At times, she could be mildly critical (such as on November 14, 1943: "We hosted three of those villains for dinner," without explaining why she considered them villains); at others she was praiseworthy, as when she played poker

---

antifascists rejected this depiction of the German because based on national attributes rather than on the critical issue of Nazism. Also see Focardi, *Il cattivo tedesco e il bravo italiano*, chapter 3.

[12] See Focardi, *Il cattivo tedesco e il bravo italiano*, for an account of how Italy's memory of the Second World War has been constructed. In particular, Focardi argues that the myth of the "evil" German as opposed to the "good" Italian began to be delineated after the armistice and gained full speed in the two years following the end of the conflict. Although Focardi's focus is on the false narrative of the good Italian that emerged out of the contrast with the German, he provides useful background for understanding the image of the Germans in Italy during the war.

with a "very good German who also gave us an accordion concert" (November 28, 1943). The familiarity she entertained with foreign military hampered her from confronting the question of their role in Italy's ordeal—the association between fascism and Germans, or even Germans and Nazism, was lost to her. Indeed, as war events evolved and the Resistance against the Nazi occupiers solidified, Perla continued to admire the Germans: "I'm now listening to the Italian radio that is doing nothing more than spitting out futile, useless chatter. It would be good to have more facts and less talk. That's what Germans, who are a fine people, do" (February 11, 1944). She commended the Germans even more for repelling the Allied forces' advance towards Rome ("These Germans demonstrate an unheard-of courage" [March 19, 1944]). Somewhat idiosyncratically, she did not call them the enemy, no matter her professed antifascism. To be fair, she did not call them friends either, though she certainly appreciated the good rapport established with some of them. After another German "invasion" of her country house, Perla recounted meeting three paratroopers twenty-four, twenty, and twenty-three years of age, "full of life, nice, cheerful." Basking in youthful fun, "we played cards, […], sang and conversed." They were drifters, as it turns out, and caused some trouble, and ultimately had to depart two days later: "They left happily and promised to come back after the war if they didn't die" (June 27, 1944). Eternal enemy they were certainly not.

Cacciaguerra's perspective on the Germans was guided by a focus on personal relations, rather than political-ethical motivations, and she obviously sidelined the official views both of the Badoglio government and the Anglo-American forces. Other diarists also ignored master narratives and elaborated original approaches to the war events, often in a fluid way. In the instance of Maria Alemanno, although human empathy and a strong pragmatic inclination helped her make sense of the perplexing armistice of September 8, she did not hold onto a fixed position. Hence, she seemingly subscribed to the trope of Italy's betrayal and took it as the reason for the Germans' ruthless occupation. At the same time, she undermined the legitimacy of the charge by declaring that "everything is a betrayal" (September 9, 1943), a statement that, by spreading the guilt of treachery widely, challenged the purported explanation of Italy's egregious duplicity. More than logic, however, let alone ideology, an independent-minded Alemanno preferred to rely on her contextual reality to evaluate, almost on a daily basis, the exceptional facts of which she was the unwilling witness. Not surprisingly, throughout the months of September and October her impressions of the Germans consistently fluctuated, though she always maintained a wary outlook about them. When

Hitler's army occupied Florence, she expressed trepidation: "In these first moments we fear them and maybe this fear is not unfounded" (September 11, 1943). One day passed, and her note assumed a definitively animated tone: "I've seen Germans for the first time, not the way I had seen many so far, but in their abominable role of invaders and bosses, I understand how one can hate them, whether betrayed or not [...], they are enemies that have taken possession of our beautiful city" (September 12, 1943). Still questioning the narrative of betrayal, Alemanno had no qualms designating the Germans the "enemy." A few days later, though, she felt slightly more relaxed. Having become habituated to the military occupation, she examined soldiers in their condition of fellow human beings: "The Germans are not the devil after all [...] I feel sorry for some of them: inexperienced young boys suddenly out of their homes and fatherland, subjugated by an iron fist" (September 16, 1943).[13] The sight of barely grown-up men softened Alemanno's perspective on the occupiers. Looking at them up close, in psychological terms if not literally, mitigated her antagonism and assuaged her judgment.[14]

War's crude reality forced people to make choices even when, as in the case of Alemanno, she preferred not to take sides and mostly cared about peace, regardless of who originated the conflict. Still, Alemanno declined to take a principled stance. By early October, the Germans had turned into such a familiar reality that she was led to observe, "If I don't talk any longer about the Germans, who are continuously roaming up and down, it's only because we got so used to seeing them that they don't affect us anymore" (October 2, 1943). Unluckily for her and many in the area of Florence and Tuscany, that state of lull would change dramatically in only a few months.

Marisa Corsellini's and Michelina Michelini's dislike for the Germans escalated upon witnessing the sad fate of their besieged Florence in summer 1944. Initially, Marisa's and Michelina's assessments on the ex-ally were less severe.

---

[13] In quite a striking coincidence, in Turin Claudio Chevallard reported on September 17 (almost the same day as Alemanno's entry), "Life is beginning not so much to get back to normal, I'd say, but to feel less anxious. One can get used to everything, unfortunately, even to the Germans." See "Diario di Carlo Chevallard 1942–1945," edited by Riccardo Marchis, in *Torino in guerra tra cronaca e memoria*, edited by Rosanna Roccia and Giorgio Vaccarino, with a Preface by Alessandro Galante Garrone (Turin: Archivio Storico della Città di Torino, 1975), p. 113.

[14] For a similar reaction see Maria Carazzolo, *Più forte della paura. Diario di guerra e dopoguerra (1938–1947)* (Caselle di Sommacampagna: Cierre edizioni, 2007), p. 115. Carazzolo considered the young age of the soldiers and concluded, "I am not able to hate them. Hatred for the mass dissolves once one descends to the individual, maybe I would not have the courage to kill them" (entry of October 1, 1943). A few lines earlier she had denounced the Germans' vile methods, stating, "By now we all realize it and we hate them for this." She came back to the issue of soldiers' youth and compassion on September 5, 1944 and then again on September 25, 1944. By the end of the war, she wrote that maybe exterminating all Germans might not be sufficient punishment for their evil actions, p. 265 (entry of May 4, 1945).

After hearing of the unspeakable massacre of 210 farmers in a nearby village, for example, seventeen-year-old Corsellini simply invoked the superior authority of religion to express her deep abhorrence: "To God the judgment!!" (July 15, 1944). When Florence was liberated from German control and the bells rang all around, she only made a scant reference to the Germans, focusing instead on the festive mood in the city (August 11, 1944). Once she witnessed firsthand the destruction surrounding Ponte Vecchio, however, her reaction became harsher and uncensored: "I will never cease in all my life to curse the Germans, I will never be able to hate them as much as they deserve; that they be annihilated till the last generation!" (August 13, 1944). Her abhorrence had grown unsparing.

In a similarly spiraling tone, Michelina Michelini's repugnance toward the Germans reached a boiling point by the time of Florence's liberation. Previously, in an entry addressed to her absent husband, she recounted an episode involving one of their children:

> Last week about one hundred Germans slept in the barn. I cannot tell you how scared we were. The officer told us they were Austrians coming from Cassino where, they say, there had been an infernal battle. Maria naturally ended up in his arms. He asked for her name and told her that his wife's name was also Maria. He held her in his arms and sang her a song in German. All the other soldiers sang in a chorus. [...] Finally, I said it was time for the children to go to bed and I took them away. Whether or not they were Austrians, I think that they too must have enough of this war.[15]
>
> (June 4, 1944)

Driven by an empathetic impulse, Michelina took stock of war's quirky twists and felt a connection with the invaders—fellow human beings subjected to the same horrors she was suffering. After watching their devastating acts and "terror," however, she wrote to her husband, "I've always hated the Germans, but now my hatred is tremendous, you can't imagine what they have done to our beautiful Florence" (letter of September 7, 1944). The human closeness Michelina felt for the Germans earlier in the occupation was forever gone, superseded by the reality of utter evil she encountered. There could be no good sentiments left in her for the ex-ally.

---

[15] Pavone claims that the Austrians were considered among the most humane of the Nazi military. See *Una guerra civile*, p. 219.

Mario Tutino confronted a similar mental struggle with regard to the Germans. Watching a military unit listen to their superior in a street of Milan, he reflected:

> When you look at their faces, one by one, these Germans are good and handsome boys. This is, after all, the way I knew them when I was in their country as a youth. [...] Nevertheless, inside all of us, day by day, hatred against the German grows, and we almost wish not to look at them in the face, we do not want to perceive them as single individuals so that we can detest them even more passionately.   (September 18, 1943)

Determined not to be trapped in sentimental thoughts, Tutino decided one could not wait to see what kind of wicked acts the Germans were capable of. Differently from Michelina Michelini, he made the principled choice of siding against them no matter the moral and emotional challenges he doubtlessly faced. The Germans could not but be the legitimate target of Italians' aversion; hesitations or doubts were not admissible.

As a mature person with a reflective inclination (but also because driven by antifascist ideas), Tutino had the strength to hold on to an ethical viewpoint about the Germans. Other Italians found it hard to achieve a similarly firm stance. Hence, young Irene Paolisso initially displayed a raw hatred for Hitler's troops, whom she viewed as a terrifying force, almost nonhuman: "Our blood freezes as soon as we see one. What kind of living being is a German for us by now? Not a man, not anymore. We are unable to imagine anything more dangerous than a German" (September 14, 1943). Months later, when she and her family happened to encounter a Nazi drifter in their desperate flight from the war zone of Formia, she still relied on her previous construction of the "enemy," only this time to undo it: "We got the chance to meet for the first time, after many months, a truly German man: a twenty-five-year-old blond brother, professor in Berlin, as worn-out as us if not more. [...] He was handsome as only the Albion can be: finally, not an enemy any longer" (April 3, 1944). Free of the filters she would normally apply to the Germans, Paolisso related to the young soldier as a human being, even though one might surmise that his status as a rebel influenced her benevolent perspective. Whatever the reason for Irene's kind attitude, that spirit of generosity was a luxury she could not continue to afford. After her family ended up in a camp for displaced civilians run by Nazi troops and she was able to obtain food distribution favors from another "blond German," she had to remind herself of what that meant: "It is at this point, dear brother, that I have to make an effort to remember that the blond is and remains a German, an enemy by now" (April 6, 1944).[16] Private feelings had to be suppressed and personal interactions canceled in the face of an anonymous yet real collective foe that was sowing chaos in the life of countless Italians. The German was an enemy, no questions about it, even if Irene seemed to have forgotten exactly why that was the case.

Diarists' opinions of the German occupiers demonstrate the unsettled and often rupturing way in which Italians reshuffled commonly accepted categories, such as the one designating the Germans' enemy status, and reconceived them anew. This ongoing process of valuation took place in parallel with the changing historical circumstances and was most often at odds with officially sanctioned views. People showed a degree of reticence at embracing the qualification of "enemy" unconditionally—that label did not acquire a real meaning to them until they experienced its actuality on their own skin. Judgments could not be entrusted to depend on abstract classifications, no matter how well grounded. Conversely, principles could be followed, but sometimes halfheartedly. Thus, the Germans elicited a degree of hatred that could be either appeased or heightened contingent on personal stories and according to the vagaries of war developments.[17]

Members of the Italian military who were imprisoned by Hitler's troops on September 8 and declined to collaborate (Internati Militari Italiani or IMIs) were among the few who held on to a definite attitude towards the ex-ally.[18]

---

[16] Paolisso wrote many of her entries by addressing her brother away in the military. He had been deployed on the island of Crete a year earlier, and the family had no recent news of him.

[17] It should be noted that a few diarists raised the issue of Italians' hatred toward the Germans. Chevallard wrote entries on the topic. At some point, he explained the hatred as a "difference of mentality." He believed that Italians could not share the Germans' cruelty and brutality and were temperamentally much closer to the Allied forces. See "Diario di Carlo Chevallard 1942–1945," p. 177 (long preface to the beginning of year 1944). Magda Ceccarelli De Grada was actually surprised at the Italians' milder aversion for the Anglo-Americans, who were bombing their cities with no apparent restraint, than for the Germans. She explained the Italians' anti-German feelings as rooted "in the blood." See her entry of October 7, 1943.

[18] On the IMIs see among others Gerhard Schreiber, *I militari italiani internati nei campi di concentramento del Terzo Reich 1943–1945: traditi, disprezzati, dimenticati* (Rome: Stato Maggiore dell'Esercito-Ufficio Storico, 1992); Gabriele Hammermann, *Gli internati militari italiani in Germania. 1943–1945* (Bologna: il Mulino, 2004); Nicola della Santa ed., *I militari italiani internati dai tedeschi dopo l'8 settembre 1943. Atti del Convegno di Studi* (Florence: ANEI, 1986); Nicola Labanca ed., *Fra sterminio e sfruttamento. Militari internati e prigionieri di guerra nella Germania nazista, 1939–1945* (Florence: Le lettere, 1992); Mario Avagliano and Marco Palmieri, *I militari italiani nei lager nazisti. Una resistenza senz'armi (1943–1945)* (Bologna: il Mulino, 2020); and of the same authors, *Gli internati militari italiani. Diari e lettere dai lager nazisti (1943–1945)* (Turin: Einaudi, 2009). On prisoners' personal memories also see Erika Lorenzon, *Lo sguardo lontano. L'Italia della seconda guerra mondiale nella memoria dei prigionieri di guerra* (Venice: Edizioni Ca' Foscari, 2018).

German, German not: The betrayed military

It might not be a surprise that highly negative reactions to the Germans came from Italian officers and soldiers left stranded on the battlefields of foreign lands after September 8.[19] With no directives from their superiors, and immediately apprehended and transported to prison camps by Hitler's armies, they became prey to the Nazis' relentless efforts at coopting them. Those who rebuffed solicitations were subject to an unremitting campaign of persuasion that included physical and emotional privations. Humiliated and victimized, and denied their rights as prisoners of war, IMIs struggled to maintain a sense of sanity—the agony of psychological torture often superseding the aches caused by starvation.[20] Predictably, resentment for the abusers ensued, and several among the IMIs vehemently expressed bitterness toward the Germans. Somewhat less predictably, they did not look at their captors as enemies, although they did not deem them friends either. Their perspective on the ex-ally was tightly linked to the trope of betrayal, which they reconsidered in new meaningful and often unforgiving combinations. Calling into question the trope's original target, members of the Italian military who had decided not to "opt" refused to be labeled traitors and built their decision of noncollaboration on a reinterpretation of the armistice. From this particular evaluative angle, they found themselves revisiting more than Italy's recent history. They also reassessed the significance of their own role as soldiers, patriots, and citizens.

Captain of Artillery Pompilio Aste was stationed in Ljubljana (Slovenia) when he heard about the armistice. In the chaos that unfolded, he was offered the chance to collaborate with Hitler's Germany, an option that would have spared him the undesirable prospect of internment. Finding the proposal repulsive, Aste refused to sign the "Declaration of Commitment" required by the Germans as condition for releasing the Italian soldiers taken into custody. He transcribed the "Declaration" verbatim in his diary as an aberrant memento "of what was the most devious, ferocious, inconceivable offer one

---

[19] Figures on the IMIs continue to be evaluated, but it is estimated that between 650,000 and 750,000 Italian prisoners refused to collaborate with the Germans. According to Elena Aga Rossi, although initially estimated at 600,000, the number of IMIs should be updated to approximately 750,000, *Una nazione allo sbando. L'armistizio italiano del settembre 1943 e le sue conseguenze* (Bologna: il Mulino, 2003), p. 25. On IMIs figures and personal biographies also see the online data bank: lessicobiograficoimi.it. For an account of Italian soldiers in the Balkans up to and in the aftermath of the armistice see Elena Aga Rossi and Maria Teresa Giusti, *Una guerra a parte. I militari italiani nei Balcani (1940-1943)* (Bologna: il Mulino, 2011).

[20] Because they were not captured in combat, Italian military were deprived by Germany of all rights granted prisoners by the 1929 Geneva Convention.

"To opt" was the technical term used for the choice of joining the Germans.

could make to an ally." Adamantly and unequivocally adverse to the possibility of collaborating, Aste's denunciation of the Germans anticipated Badoglio's negative language of October 13:

> Very bitter tears on the faces of all of us, who were part of a very beautiful regiment and in no time are being reduced to anonymous mass, prisoner of German brutality. [...] I am reminded of the sentiments that animate my wife, grown in the climate of pure Trentino patriotism, and I promise myself never to consider the option of collaborating voluntarily with this people of oppressors and bullies, who will only bring grief and affliction to Italy.
> (September 8, 1943)

In part a legacy of the First World War and the struggle for irredentism but also following an atavistic sense of allegiance to the idea of fatherland, Aste declined to submit to the Germans. As he confided in a letter to his wife and son drafted on November 11 and never sent, he especially resented the accusation of betrayal leveled against him—being called a traitor and treated as one:

> Today's day has been particularly hard because of the physical and spiritual sufferings they imposed on us: exposed to the cold for a long time, malnourished and with little covers, we had to listen once again to the vulgar speech of a sold-out general, as they again proposed the problem of the option to us, in very harsh terms, and with covert threats to those that did not think their duty to join. It goes without saying, my dear ones, that again I have not considered, not even for a second, the possibility of opting, and not because I feel especially tied to an oath, but only because I do not want, I who did not betray anyone, to have to deal with the Germans.
>
> But it is not simply today's torments that have caused me this crisis of discouragement, it is the whole infinite sum of privations, hardships, adversities that have piled up during my two months of life inside these fences. First of all, they are spiritual sufferings, such as being considered traitors, us, who were the first to be betrayed [...].

Within an environment that denied soldiers the dignity of military treatment and forced them into impossible choices, Aste's adverse assessment of the Germans deepened at the same rhythm as the miserable conditions in the camps worsened. Considering his personal history (he had been an active participant in Mussolini's regime by holding the position of secretary of the Bolzano fascio and then as volunteer in the army at the outbreak of the

Second World War), Aste's rejection of the betrayal narrative and concomitant harsh valuation of the Germans appear all the more significant. Germany's ruse of calling Italian military "traitors" and (mal)treating them as such especially hardened captive soldiers. Through a spurious and abusive reinterpretation of the military code of honor, the ex-ally's intent to take revenge appeared unashamedly obvious. Demanding that the Italians fight under the German flag was a despicable act of vileness meant to debase Italy's standing and her right as an independent nation.

Massimo Campregher was among the more than 650,000 Italian officers and soldiers refusing to join the German army.[21] A thirty-two-year-old farmer from the Trentino region captured in Bulgaria after the armistice, he began keeping a personal diary on September 24 (stopping it shortly thereafter on January 16, 1944). Never complaining about his miserable condition as prisoner, the detailed descriptions he drafted of the relentless struggle to procure food while in captivity are touching. And this is so not because Campregher presented his accounts with any palpable emotion. To the contrary, his diary lacks both self-pity and rhetorical excess. Rather, what strikes the reader is the way he dwelled on the few occasions in which he managed to feel satisfied with a meal. His entries expose the bare reality of detention exactly because unadorned, expressed in direct, rudimentary phrases that better than any elaborate discourse manage to amplify the mortifications endured by prisoners:

> Day 27 of October, I as well as about forty comrades, the Germans stripped us down in order to dress the fascist volunteers who were the shabbiest vagabonds of all and in the morning because of propaganda these scumbags volunteered, and so we, stripped since noon, remain in our underwear until five in the evening.

Considering the humiliating vexations to which he was subject, Campregher's refusal to collaborate appears all the more remarkable. Oddly, he never mentioned any reason for his decision not to join. The same can be said of

---

[21] On the military that decided to opt, which is estimated between 10 and 20 percent (officers opted more than soldiers), see Alessandro Ferioli, "Dai lager nazisti all'esercito di Mussolini. Gli internati militari italiani che aderirono alla Repubblica Sociale Italiana," *Nuova Storia Contemporanea* no. 5 (September–October 2005): pp. 63–88. According to Aga Rossi and Giusti, the figure is closer to 22 percent. *Una guerra a parte*, p. 402. Also see Claudio Sommaruga, "Dati quantitativi sull'internamento in Germania," in Angelo Bendotti and Eugenia Valtulina eds., *Internati, prigionieri, reduci. La deportazione militare italiana durante la seconda guerra mondiale* (Bergamo: Istituto Bergamasco per la storia della Resistenza e dell'età contemporanea, 1999).

thirty-year-old Agostino De Pedri, another native Trentino who only a few weeks before the armistice of September 8 had returned home from the military campaign in Greece. Taken prisoner by Hitler's army from his station in Bressanone (South Tyrol), then transported to Eastern Europe, he battled with severe hunger throughout the years of internment. Although the lack of food was an excruciating condition of which he wrote incessantly and almost exclusively in his scant diary entries, the possibility of being forced to collaborate with the Germans haunted De Pedri more.[22] As he wrote on November 21, 1943, "This would be the worst infamy that they could commit—sending prisoners to fight for those who hold them captive." Like Campregher, his stubbornness against joining Hitler's army remained undying.

An ardent admirer of Mussolini from Emilia Romagna, twenty-three-year-old Mario Corbolini was more forthcoming than Campregher and De Pedri about his choice not to support the Germans. Stationed in Athens when news of the armistice arrived, he questioned the rising call to take up arms against Hitler—to him, it felt like stabbing yesterday's ally in the back, a form of betrayal. Once imprisoned by the Germans and presented with the option of pledging obedience to them, however, he refused: "How could I still fight without wearing the Italian uniform? It's true that the armistice had broken my heart; I was aware we had betrayed our ally, but why didn't they organize some units like we were hoping? The German uniform never" (no date). Corbolini did not contest the narrative of Italy's treachery; nevertheless, he refused to come under German authority. The only way he would fight alongside Hitler's army was in a separate Italian corp. Absent that condition, symbolism took over pragmatics, and he preferred to become a prisoner than renounce his identity as an Italian combatant. The humiliation (what De Pedri called "infamy") was overbearing—it amounted to a cancelation of Italy's nationhood. By the time Corbolini arrived at the Cholm lager in January 1944, he conceded, "Now we hated the Germans too much" (January 1944).

Whether they acted out of ideological convictions, or because guided by patriotism, or due to moral principles, IMIs resisted Germany's attempt to enlist them. Seeing that the option of enrolling was incessantly pushed and that the consequences for refusing amounted to endless abuses, the prisoners' resolve signals an indubitably courageous stance. Yet uncertainty accompanied their seemingly firm decisions. Reports of debates involving officers and subordinates alike fill pages and pages of prisoners' diaries, giving us a glimpse

---

[22] His diary stopped on January 13, 1945.

of the dilemmas Italian military faced as they evaluated their options. "Thus, every day, at all times, everywhere, we argue, we torture ourselves, we suffer a pain that would not exist otherwise," Pompilio Aste wrote at the end of November 1943. Giorgio Crainz, a second lieutenant in his late twenties stationed in Milan when the Germans captured him soon after the armistice, recounted similar Hamletic doubts. Immediately confronted with the choice of joining Hitler's troops, he at first resolutely rejected the idea. Subsequent diary entries show that, in time, he and his comrades were overtaken by hesitations. On September 21, after yet another German offer to enroll in the SS, Crainz reported, "Big discussions. Many appear undecided. They fear the consequences of their refusal. Rumors say we will be taken to Poland." Then again on October 3, "It looks like tomorrow morning the German Command will ask each one of us if we are willing to go and fight in Italy under the orders of Mussolini. Discussions do not even stop at night. In the dark about the events as we are, it is impossible to make a decision."

Lack of information about the exact state of affairs back in Italy supposedly made Crainz and fellow prisoners vacillate. In actuality, with the Germans continuing to lure them with the promise to fight for Mussolini, captured soldiers were looking for some type of leverage to justify whichever determination they might be reaching. Absent any exemplary leadership, they scrambled for solutions to their predicament. In the case of Crainz, he relied on a personal set of ethical principles to help guide his actions—moral tenets that, combined with a pragmatic orientation, led him to focus on the sacredness of the nation. In the name of "Italy's interest," all Italians should gather around "that sucker of Badoglio" and unite in the fight against the Germans, he proposed (October 3, 1943). Two days later, with defections rising, he jotted down, "Here it seems that the mass has opted for the Republic, but all with the intention to cut and run. I continue to be very undecided."

An exhausting dilemma consumed Crainz, even though fighting alongside Hitler was not a viable option to him no matter how deceptively the opportunity was being presented. As assuredness alternated with doubt and the Germans continued their relentless efforts to persuade and threaten prisoners, Crainz's entry of November 1 is telling: "I'm very steadfast about the decision I took yesterday. I think that if they promised to send us home, provided that we give our word not to take up arms voluntarily against Germany, I would refuse." Crainz sounded simultaneously unwavering ("I'm very steadfast") and hesitating ("I think…I would refuse"). That the Germans offered appealing forms of collaboration, outside of enrolling in the SS, certainly made decisions harder on the Italian soldiers.[23] And yet Crainz even declined proposals to do civilian work for the German army—he feared it might help Hitler's war efforts. Rationally, he seemed to know where to stand. In practice, however, his emotional turmoil did not find any relief in that certainty. Or maybe he was not fully aware of his determination. If dreams are in any way enlightening, the one Crainz retold on October 30, 1943 offers a glimpse of his endless agonizing:

> Last night I dreamed of returning home where mammà immediately informed me that father was decidedly Republican and pro-German. It scared the life out of me and I screamed, "What? I remained one year in that hell for fear of taking a different position from my family?!"
> But this dream is absurd! I'm sure that dad's thinking has evolved in the same way as mine...
> If I wasn't in the dark about what is happening![24]

A child of the regime, Crainz was not naturally inclined to doubt a system under which he had lived most of his life and that his family had also presumably supported. Presently facing a different reality, he incessantly obsessed over the best course of action, weighed all the pros and cons, and continuously reassessed the wisdom of his resolution. In truth, he and fellow prisoners lived their situation as a complicated historical experience, not a straightforward black and white one. The burden on their shoulders felt unbearably heavy, due in large part to the reversal of roles in Italy's designation of the "enemy." Disappointment at the behavior of their military leadership additionally contributed to IMIs' distress.

Indeed, IMIs' contempt for the Germans could not be disentangled from both the Italian government and the army's top-ranking officials—they were responsible for the debacle. A Ligurian in his early thirties originally dispatched in Montenegro, Sergeant Giacinto Mario Guala denounced from Stammlager XI:

> I start this diary the day that we received the news that the fatherland, having capitulated, abandoned us in foreign land.

---

[23] Mussolini was supposedly working behind the scenes to make collaboration with Hitler more palatable to the IMIs.
[24] Crainz continued to have dreams featuring the same nightmare scenario of his parents not understanding his position. In reality, families that had adhered to fascism might have found themselves at odds with their sons' refusal to join the Republic.

I will try to illustrate the best I can what our dear officers did and tried in order to sell us to the highest bidder. I hope these truths will reach my children even if I don't make it back, so they will know and all Italians as well what kind of disgraces and terrible miseries the soldiers of the Balkans had to endure, victims of having done their duty over four long years.

(September 12, 1943)

Guala spent the next twenty-one months in German detention camps having resolved not to collaborate.[25]

By virtue of their resolution not to assist the ex-ally, IMIs assumed their distance from the Germans. They did not call them enemy, nor did they toy with labels and designations. In contrast, their actions spoke louder than words, even if the motivations for their stances varied. While a sense of patriotism prevailed and humiliation and shame played a substantial role in their decision not to opt, the Italian military also reacted to the charge of betrayal by reinterpreting the term and contesting its premises. Isolated in prison camps with little access to the outside world, they constructed and applied their own categories of judgment, resisted shaming classifications, and denounced the leadership that abandoned them—if anything, soldiers were the ones being betrayed, they charged. It remains unclear how fascism's past and current manifestations fared in their decisions and whether IMIs assigned any antifascist meaning to their refusal to cooperate.[26] Fascism seemed like an absent interlocutor in their reflections, much in the same way that the past regime was being shrouded in silence by fellow Italians in the homeland.

An aside: Drifters

Back in Italy, Alpine officer Ettore Castiglioni witnessed firsthand the military leadership's failure to stop the nation's debacle. When the news of the armistice arrived, Castiglioni's unit was ecstatic and immediately clamored for action. Inspired by patriotic enthusiasm, recruits were eager to stop Hitler's

---

[25] Antonio Rossi epitomizes the ethical commitment that sustained many prisoners. An IMI suffering inhumane conditions in several camps throughout Poland and Germany, by early January 1945 he unequivocally proclaimed the primacy of his inner needs: "I feel weak, tired, thin, but absolutely serene. My resistance is not any more a question of monarchy or republic, king or duce, fascism or antifascism, all things by now distant and outdated. My resistance now means only survival of my freedom. It might cost me my life, but the trial is necessary" (January 11, 1945). Personal integrity was the only principle he felt worth following. Beyond ideologies, it was what helped him maintain a conscience able to oppose any form of bondage or abduction. In his interpretation, an individual sense of duty was the only guarantee for the righteousness of one's decision.

[26] For an interpretation of IMIs in terms of resistance see Mario Avagliano and Marco Palmieri, *I militari italiani nei lager nazisti*.

armies at the mountain pass, but "we wait for orders that do not come. At the headquarters there is nobody left or they lost their mind. Nobody takes up the responsibility to give any order whatsoever." Many, especially among the young, decided to desert even at the risk of being caught by the Germans. Castiglioni was crushed. As he watched soldiers giving up their guns and uniforms, he moaned, "I am anguished and shaken; I almost feel like crying." Dejected over the behavior of his superiors, he admitted, "I too wished to toss away that uniform that now weighed on me like a sentence, like a dishonor" (September 9, 1943).

Soldiers on the run (*sbandati*), including Castiglioni's comrades-in-arms, became a common sight throughout the country, a shocking phenomenon whose effects reverberated among the civilian population, further complicating their understanding of the war, the armistice, and betrayal.[27] Who was a victim in this ever-evolving drama? South of Rome, young Irene Paolisso caught a glimpse of the *sbandati* in the afternoon of September 9, as her whole family went into lockdown following the news of the armistice: "They knocked and asked for civilian clothes: they couldn't wait to throw away their uniforms. They wanted to flee; they were in a hurry to disappear." In Bologna, A.M. reported:

> I'm witness to miserable and humiliating spectacles. Now it's the interminable view of soldiers, our soldiers, ragged and tattered, who after gaining freedom on September 8 are trying to return to their families on foot. They have their uniforms torn or better literally in tatters, they are dirty and their faces reflect nothing more than sadness and confusion. They are barefoot and they were Italy's soldiers! Some of them are wearing civilian clothes and are trying to be in disguise so not to get into trouble, but one can recognize them anyway. I truly feel sorry for them. (September 12, 1943)

Diarists were struck by the phenomenon of *sbandati*.[28] The miserable sight of a long column taken captive by the Germans shocked Ester Marozzi in Milan.

---

[27] On the *sbandati* see Gabriella Gribaudi, *Combattenti, sbandati, prigionieri. Esperienze e memorie di reduci della seconda guerra mondiale* (Rome: Donzelli editore, 2016).

[28] In addition to reporting the sad scenes of soldiers on the run, some journal writers noted the incredible efforts of the local population to help drifters find civilians clothes and escape. In Chevallard's words, "It seems impossible that, with so much shortage of clothes and two years of ration cards, thousands of people were able to be dressed and get shoes." "Diario di Carlo Chevallard 1942–1945," p. 102 (entry of September 12, 1943). Maria Carazzolo reported the rumor that some of the soldiers were even wearing women's clothes. See *Più forte della paura*, p. 107 (entry of September 12, 1943). For some commentators, the civilians' assistance to the drifters should be regarded as a form of "non-armed struggle in the Resistance." See Antonio Parisella, *Sopravvivere liberi. Riflessioni*

Her reactions reflected almost verbatim A.M.'s depiction: "Depressed, tired, pained faces. Our soldiers! Shabby, ragged, filthy clothes!" (September 12, 1943). From the observation point of his hometown of Livinallongo in Northern Italy, Fortunato Favai chronicled the endless stream of runaways. As he registered the "continuous coming and going" in the village, he perceptively brought out the predicaments entangling the thousands of Italian soldiers let loose on September 8:

> There are about fifty local militaries who returned home after the signed armistice. Of the not-returned, nobody heard any news and their relatives are very concerned. Those who returned recount the adventurous escape and feel generally very humiliated. Indeed, how could they not be? After serving the Fatherland faithfully for years and years, they are now back, treated as if they accomplished nothing, branded as traitors by some, and with the additional risk of being taken to other unknown destinations.
> (September 19, 1943)

Were Italian soldiers at fault of betrayal or were they the ones being betrayed? How did the drifters' story fit within leading interpretations of the armistice? Ordinary Italians pondered the questions. Meanwhile, summer 1943 was winding to an end, and confusions appeared to be piling on top of more confusions. After weeks in occupied Sicily, the Allied forces had advanced onto the mainland following the armistice. They were Italy's new "friend," a status that, as it turns out, did not imply a scot-free acceptance. After all, the Anglo-Americans had been Italy's enemy in the war until then. Furthermore, they represented a threatening foreign invader and were indiscriminately bombing Italian cities. How did Italians respond to their arrival on the national scene?

Liberators? A linguistic game

On September 1, 1943, in the very first entry of her newly minted diary, Irene Paolisso addressed the imminence of the invasion by the Allied forces. In the atmosphere of uncertainty that surrounded her small town of Formia, she mentioned people's fear "that the *liberators* might land on our coasts." Using the term "liberators" in the original English, she underlined the idiosyncratic

---

sulla storia della Resistenza a cinquant'anni dalla Liberazione (Roma: Gangemi Editore, 1997), chapter 3, which also raises the issue of women's role in the history of the Resistance.

reality facing Italians. In a situation worth the theater of the absurd, Italy was being invaded, but the invaders claimed to be liberating her. In truth, British propaganda had been hammering the message of liberation for some time while the Anglo-Americans forces prepared to initiate the Italian phase of their operation in the Mediterranean. By adopting the word "liberators," Paolisso proved the success of that campaign of persuasion, which reached many Italians via broadcasts of Radio London—a critical source of news during the war years.[29] Paolisso's somewhat ironic use of "liberators," however, also suggests that reactions to the organized psychological warfare were not necessarily all approving. A sense of skepticism accompanied Italians' recognition of the confusing reality they were living, with the line between enemies and friends growing increasingly blurry. Here is Paolisso again:

> The *liberators* have landed in Calabria. [...] Strange how, sold either to the one or the other, we haven't been able to resist this game in which we only represent puppets or pins that are maneuvered according to rules of a machination of which we don't understand the goal and even the meaning. Arriving from whichever part, man in the guise of enemy is the personification of the brute force that annihilates and tramples on what other men have built with labor and sacrifices over years and centuries.
>
> (September 4, 1943)

Irene did not think of the Anglo-Americans as enemies, but she sensed that their presumed "liberation" implied the fettered and powerless status of her country. She wondered about the seemingly irreconcilable nature of this paradox and wished to clarify the Allied forces' relationship to Italians. Could one simply assume a pragmatic attitude towards them, as one of her friends suggested? "Rita is very clear. For her, Americans or English or French, all will be welcome, because only then will the fascists and Nazis cease to exist and to sow hatred and ruin. They are just a means, then, not 'friends' or 'allies': in any case, this role playing is unpredictable" (September 4, 1943).

---

[29] On Radio London see Ester Lo Biundo, *London Calling Italy. La propaganda di Radio Londra nel 1943* (Milan: Unicopli, 2014); "'The War of Nerves.' Le trasmissioni di Radio Londra da El Alamein all'operazione Husky," *Meridiana. Rivista di storia e scienze sociali* no. 82 (2015): pp. 13-35; and "Voices of Occupiers/Liberators: The BBC's Radio Propaganda in Italy between 1942 and 1945," *Journal of War and Cultural Studies* vol. 9, no. 1 (2016): pp. 60-73. For an inventory of the British broadcasts in Italy see Maura Piccialuti Caprioli ed., *Radio Londra 1940-1945. Inventario delle trasmissioni per l'Italia* (Rome: Ministero per i Beni Culturali e Ambientali, 1975). Also see Maura Piccialuti Caprioli, *Radio Londra 1939-1945* (Rome-Bari: Laterza, 1979). Chevallard composed his diary notes by reporting on the news he heard daily on Radio London. See "Diario di Carlo Chevallard 1942–1945."

The feeling of being hostages to a strategic game was upsetting to Irene, and she could not but be torn about the Anglo-Americans: "I wouldn't in any case know how to judge our 'liberators,' who are so meek and contemptuous of the sufferings of a helpless people" (October 29, 1943). With a huge gap separating the Allied forces' objectives from the population's needs, several factors complicated the locals' perceptions of the Anglo-Americans, most especially the actuality of continuous devastating bombings and the slow pace of liberation (see chapter 3). As time and place affected the dynamics of war, Italians' responses to their new "friends" evolved, exposing a series of historical fallacies and interpretive contradictions.

From near Caserta, Lucio Macchiarella experienced the Allied forces' occupation far in advance of the rest of Italy. Early in October 1943, as British troops joined Neapolitans in successfully pushing out the Germans, American soldiers reached Macchiarella's small village of San Leucio, some twenty miles further north.[30] A musician, Macchiarella benefited from a close relationship with the Americans and drew substantial personal advantages from working for them. All the gains notwithstanding, he never managed to overcome the sense of humiliation felt at being occupied. To his eyes, Italy as a subjugated country represented a case in moral degradation. Besides, Macchiarella was caught in the tangle over enemy and friend created by Badoglio's perplexing decisions. His diary entries in the aftermath of the armistice are filled with bitter comments about Italy's switching of sides and her presumed two-faced behavior. He especially lamented the situation in his village, where Germans had been displaced by the Americans: "How the political world changes! /In Italy it comes down to this: we have no character any longer. We do about-turns following current needs" (October 19–20, 1943).

Macchiarella's unhappiness was irredeemable and his cynicism seemingly unstoppable. Whether responsibility for foreign occupation fell on Italy's ineptitude or on the invaders' cunning appeared to make little difference to him. Even if he hoped for the defeat of Germany, he still took the presence of the Anglo-Americans on Italian soil as a negative sign. His comment on the attendance of Americans at a New Year's Eve party showed no qualms: "Last year, in our homes, there were Germans to celebrate this traditional holiday!!!" (December 26–31, 1943). What more evidence did one need for the country's lack of spine and weak ethical stance?

---

[30] Known as "the four days of Naples," the local insurrection against the German occupiers took place between September 27 and 30—a first among European cities. For direct observations on the events see Filippo Caracciolo di Castagneto, '43–'44. Diario di Napoli (Florence: Vallecchi, 1964). For a summary account see Aldo De Jaco, La città insorge (le quattro giornate di Napoli) (Rome: Editori Riuniti, 1956).

The sense of resentment Macchiarella felt against the Allied forces was not caused by a preference for the Germans. Indeed, on the last week of November 1943, for example, he bemoaned Rome's fate (where his cherished fiancée Anna resided) under "the iron heel of the enemy" (November 25–December 1, 1943). He knew how to assign roles—Germans were the "foe" according to the official assessment of Badoglio's government, and Macchiarella did not question that classification. Indeed, he criticized fellow Southerners' attacks on the king for risking losing sight of the real and most urgent struggle.[31] Germans remained the indisputable enemy in Macchiarella's book. Still, his ambivalence towards the Anglo-Americans remained. Although more sympathetic to the British, he definitively denounced the immorality and alcoholism present among the American military (January 2, 1944). Adding an extra layer of racism to his sense of national defeat, Macchiarella's negative sentiments for U.S. soldiers were blatant: "Just the humiliation before the negroes is enormous! (Uncle Tom's Cabin... in reverse.) They rule over us... and how much! The bread we earn is very bitter" (January 17–23, 1944). Foreign occupation, no matter if by enemy or friend, was an embarrassing indication of Italy's failing status. Macchiarella could barely tolerate it.[32]

Further north in Rome, fascist supporter V.R. had no reservations when it came to challenging the value of the Anglo-Americans. She especially questioned their role as "liberators" and pointed out blaring contradictions in their behavior, including their destruction of the abbey at Montecassino. Playing on the emotive, V.R. denounced the Allied forces' false claims of friendship and wondered how people could not see through those aberrations. She felt dejected: "I want to leave. I can't stand these Romans any longer who wait for the enemy and call it the liberator" (May 26, 1944). Being unable to stop her fellow citizens from welcoming the Americans' arrival, she eventually switched to denigrating the results of the Allied forces' intervention: "It has been ten days since the 'liberators' are in Rome and already people are figuring out that after all they brought neither the freedom nor the so much touted well-being" (June 14, 1944). Clear evidence of "enemy" propaganda's

---

[31] Vittorio Emanuele III became the target of criticism by many in Italy and among the Allied forces, especially after he abandoned Rome and fled to Pescara. In June 1944, after the liberation of Rome, he transferred most of his powers to his son, Prince Umberto, who became Lieutenant of the Kingdom.

[32] Macchiarella's is one of the few diaries from the South that addressed the moral degradation due to the American occupiers. The Americans' presence contributed to the difference in experience in the South compared to the rest of Italy. See Nicola Gallerano ed., *L'altro dopoguerra. Roma e il Sud 1943-1945* (Milan: Franco Angeli, 1985). For a discussion of the impact of American culture in the South see Rosario Forlenza, *On the Edge of Democracy: Italy, 1943–1948* (Oxford: Oxford University Press, 2019), chapter 3, "America is Coming, America is Coming!"

effectiveness, though in reverse, V.R.'s critique exactly mentioned the two points that the British Political Warfare Executive had planned to instill in the population: 1) this was a war for freedom from fascism and not against Italians; 2) the Allies would be able to guarantee Italians better living conditions.

Another Roman resident, the less politically motivated Fedora Brenta Brcic, continued to call "enemy" the Anglo-American forces well into June 1944, when, having finally reached the capital, they liberated it from the German occupiers. To be sure, in Brenta Brcic's case the idiosyncratic use of linguistic terms was not accidental—she plainly avowed her lack of sympathy for the Anglo-Americans. Just one week before Rome's liberation, in distress at their imminent arrival, she penned in her diary, "The day is approaching that so many are awaiting and that I am fearing. The Anglo-Americans are now in *Velletri*! [...] Rumors going around say that the enemy is already near *Albano*" (May 27, 1944). Eventually, she switched from "enemy" to "Allies," but still wished the Anglo-Americans would vacate the capital promptly. Cynical about their actions, Fedora finally addressed them as "liberators" only in order to cast more blame on them—she could not quite consider them saviors. With a daily life vexed by restrictions that forced her to engage in a relentless struggle for subsistence, she was unforgiving and only expected positive material results out of the Allied forces' victories. Meanwhile, she began writing about the Germans in negative terms and was happy to report their losses in the war. Ultimately, her assessment of the military situation depended on the effects of the conflict on her personal world. In one instance, she regretted the Anglo-Americans' advances in the north only because it might compromise assistance to her husband, a navy officer imprisoned by the Germans.[33] Fedora never developed a strong sense of allegiance for the coalition fighting against Hitler. In contrast, she remained focused on her own afflictions, even when she stopped speaking of the Allied forces as "enemies."

Italians' confused sense of the Anglo-Americans was doubtlessly aggravated by the change in war coalitions as well as the ongoing historical developments, all factors that helped produce an overabundance of political interpretations (the Anglo-Americans as enemies, allies, and liberators). Young Ada Vita noted the mystifying muddle early in September 1943, when Bolzano was taken over by the Germans: "**Strange thing**!!: English and Italian

---

[33] "Newspapers say that the Allies broke through the front arriving from Nice. This news saddens me as I fear that Gino will be unable to send you packages any longer" (September 3, 1944).

soldiers, first enemies now prisoners, hug each other and the English offer chocolate to Italians" (September 16, 1943). Rationally calculated or as a slip of tongue, in some instances the Allied forces were even called simultaneously enemies and liberators, as by Caterina Gaggero Viale, a tavern owner in her fifties from the northern region of Liguria. Throughout 1944 in her chronicle of the war, Gaggero Viale inevitably shifted back and forth between "enemy" and "liberator" (and also "allies") when addressing the Anglo-Americans, although by the end of the year "liberators" prevailed.[34] Intriguingly, she maintained the proper name for "the Germans" and did not qualify their role. Although she never called them "friends," she did not refer to them as "enemies" either. Unlike other diarists, Gaggero Viale did not exercise any irony when talking about the Anglo-Americans, although her use of quotation marks around "liberators" shows she shared the Italians' sense of the twisted nature of their liberation (Figure 2).[35] She seemed to adjust her vocabulary to the war developments and let the events determine her relationship to history.[36]

Brother, brother, brother

The Italians' perplexities about Germans and Anglo-Americans were not merely a matter of semantics aimed at adjudicating the status of "ally," be it

---

[34] On January 24, 1944 she wrote, "Since last night German trucks keep passing by full of troops. People say they are going south, where the enemies landed." Or May 23, "Our enemies are advancing very slowly, but they are holding on to the conquered positions: Cassino, Pignataro, Formia." Then on May 30 made the switch: "Vercelli was bombed and the population machine-gunned, Tuscan centers still under attack by the 'liberators.'" On July 20, "The Allies keep advancing on the Tyrrhenian coast." On July 21, "The liberators bombed Riva Ligure, Borgio Verezzi, and other localities in the surroundings." While she referred to "the Allies" in many of her notes, her use of the term probably followed official appellations, and was not necessarily meant in the sense of "our" allies. But her use of "liberators" appeared to increase along with the desire of being liberated. See for example November 5, "Let's hope the good weather continues so that maybe our 'liberators' will finally advance."

[35] In his "Diario di Carlo Chevallard 1942–1945," Chevallard reports that on a visit to Milan he noticed on "very many" houses the inscription "House destroyed by the liberators," which he deemed "evidently obligatory" (May 16, 1944).

[36] She also switched terms when it came to another key figure/protagonist of the time, those she called the "rebels." Sometime in the summer of 1944, she began to talk about them as "patriots." Gaggero Viale was aware of the implications, both political and ideological, that certain words carried, and she made a point of noting in her diary that by patriots she meant rebels. Thus, when recounting one of the rebels' actions, she wrote, "The rebels, that from this moment on we will call 'patriots'" (July 22, 1944). At some point she even added a qualification, "true patriots," just in case there was any risk of confusion. Even with this self-warning, however, she continued to use terms interchangeably. Don Luigi Serravalle did something similar: "From the hills, there came down the rebels, or partisans or patriots as they like to call themselves" (October 11, 1944). Most diarists referred to the Resistance fighters as "rebels." In post-liberation official parlance, "partisans" displaced "rebels." Forlenza claims that partisans called themselves "patriots." See *On the Edge of Democracy*, p. 159.

Figure 2. Rome 1944. War propaganda writing on a structure bombed by Allied forces. Bundesarchiv, Bild 101I-476-2094-17A/photographer: Gerhard Rauchwetter/1944.

old or new. Depending on one's particular interpretive choice, personal beliefs also affected one's relationship with fellow countrymen and women, besides being a matter of individual conviction. Those who subscribed to the Germans' claims of betrayal, or any notion of treachery, unchained a series of political and social dynamics with highly divisive potential. The prospect of conflict between brothers (and sisters) appeared not only inevitable but threateningly violent too. Another figure then came to complicate the Italians' views of the enemy: the enemy brother.

Camicia Nera (Black Shirt) Aldo Bacci, as he proudly liked to sign his diary, began to evaluate fellow Italians through the frame of "betrayal" even before the infamous armistice of September 8. A Tuscan in his early forties taken prisoner by the Allied forces in early July 1943 in Sicily, he accused his Sicilian compatriots of being "traitors" for not defending the Italian military during the American invasion of the island. In a few high-sounding sentences, he anticipated the tragedy of what was yet to come:

> Even brighter than the day that dawns, we see the betrayal, we know we were sold, we know that our Fatherland is about to face a period of suffering, terror, sacrifices. The coward will rejoice, but I am crying. [...]

It is the crumbling, the collapse of the grandiose work built over twenty-two years of struggle and sacrifices. It is the crazy attempt to kill fascism and Germany.

Bacci wrote these lines on July 22, 1943. Mussolini was forced to resign three days later. Reality would prove more unforgiving than Bacci's bleakest forecast.[37]

After the events of September 8, the possibility of die-hard fascists fighting alongside Hitler and, consequently, against other Italians became increasingly tangible. Whether or not the fascists grasped the full meaning of this uncanny twist, which turned the friend–foe formula upside down, their support for the Germans could not but be the prelude to the civil war—an eventuality many fellow nationals found abhorrent. If, when the armistice was first announced, Italians expressed concerns about loss of honor and felt ashamed at the country's perceived duplicity, gradually but inevitably the prospect of a looming domestic conflict entered their consciousness. The actuality of having to take sides and fight on opposite fronts weighed ominously on everyone's mind.

In 1991, Claudio Pavone's historical analysis of the Resistance caused shockwaves with his interpretation of the period as a "civil war" (in addition to a patriotic and class war).[38] Among the polemical debates that ensued, some claimed that no civil war had occurred in Italy at the time. Historian Renzo De Felice, in turn, argued that during 1943–45 references to "civil war" were only present among the fascists and that very few of the antifascists, especially on the communist side, recognized this aspect of the liberation struggle.[39] Opinions on the appropriateness of civil war as a category of analysis were mostly expressed by those who had been active participants in the Resistance movement, and the debate took on ethical and political tones often based on matters of principle. Little concern was raised about how the

---

[37] Sustained by an undying faith in fascism, Bacci continued to plot vengeance against fellow Italians throughout his captivity. On June 18, 1944 he threatened, "My poor fatherland, how much suffering and what martyrdom your evil children imposed on you, but you will be avenged. The Fascists suffer silently and silently they await the day of punishment. And this day will come, it's not too far." Two months later he reiterated, "The only goal in my life is vengeance, my orders are death to traitors" (August 27, 1944). Once Italy was liberated, he did not give up his faith. Not surprisingly, on April 30, 1945, his diary recorded the duce's words in capital letters: "IF THEY KILL ME, AVENGE ME."

[38] Pavone *Una guerra civile*. Pavone first advanced the idea of civil war in 1986 in "La guerra civile," *Annali della Fondazione Luigi Micheletti* no. 2 (1986): pp. 395–415. For a view of the 1914–45 period as a European civil war see Enzo Traverso, *A ferro e fuoco. La guerra civile europea 1914-1945* (Bologna: il Mulino, 2008).

[39] On the first view see Parisella, *Sopravvivere liberi*, p. 90. On Renzo De Felice see *Mussolini l'alleato. II. La guerra civile (1943-1945)* (Turin: Einaudi, 1997), footnote 1, p. 69.

concept related to the concrete experience of people who lived through that era. In contrast, and *pace* De Felice and others, the diaries examined here demonstrate that the civil war was a reality of which ordinary Italians were painfully aware since the announcement of the armistice. Once the government aligned with the Anglo-Americans and dropped the German ally, the prospect of a war of brothers arose immediately in people's awareness. To Italians, that possibility was blatantly menacing, and one did not need to wait for interpretive instructions to understand the significance of its consequences. In Florence, young mother of three Michelina Michelini recounted popular disappointment at the realization that the pact of September 8 was not bringing the war to an end. As she described the sad spectacle of German troops making their way into the city, Michelina instantly evoked the image of a split country:

> German soldiers look at us in the face as if they owned our land.
>
> The question everybody is asking is, "What is the government doing?" Impatiently, I turn the knob on the radio [...]. I find a fascist radio, what was the purpose of July 25? [...] This is what happened: Italy is divided in two.
>
> (September 8, 1943)

Some hundred kilometers to the north in Bologna, A.M. witnessed with dismay the degradation of civil society in the aftermath of the armistice. With social relations newly reconfigured, the distance separating fellow citizens struck her hard: "Some fascists dared to come out of their hiding places and are now showing off by lending a hand to the Germans. This provokes deep pain, because they are working against their own brothers" (September 12, 1943). A.M. mostly focused on the symbolic significance that a split country entailed, but she feared that such a discord would soon be physically rooted in the territory too and, one could not but presage, would be splashed in blood. On the same date she penned this note, the Germans liberated Mussolini from his undisclosed prison in the mountains of Abruzzi. Four days later, young Ada Vita in her usual detailed account of the period reported, "In Rome Germans and Black Shirts fight against the Romans. In Germany, the freed Duce has already begun to call the shots and pushes the Black Shirts against Italians" (September 16, 1943). The internal rift had become real, as Ada's apparent denial of any form of national belonging to the fascists demonstrates (Black Shirts fighting against Romans/Italians).[40] Meanwhile,

---

[40] The issue of the fascists as "foreigners" was advanced by Nuto Revelli in an interview that counteracted Pavone's thesis of the civil war. See Pavone's comments in "Sulla moralità nella Resistenza.

Mussolini's reconstitution of the government in the Italian Social Republic provoked an upsurge of violence by his supporters. If July 25 had failed to incite notable reactions among fascist followers, the country was now geographically cut in half. To those who fell under the RSI in the territory controlled by the Germans, the situation felt especially taxing.

From the small Tuscan town of Calcinaia, thirty-year-old municipal clerk Manilio Tartarini brooded at the start of his diary, "The civil war is flaring in all its cruelty. On the riverbank of the Volturno and around Campolano Italian soldiers fight alongside Anglo-American troops against German troops supported by their Italian allies. This is insane!...Where will we end up?" (October 15, 1943). Tartarini continued by marveling at the sad turn of events in a country only recently unified and whose independence struggles were still vivid in people's hearts. Italians were fighting one another instead of a common enemy—it was truly a war of brother against brother. Or, as teenager Gian Carlo Stracciari put it: "From one, two governments arose, each one of which more or less allied to a foreigner. Two Italies again, like a hundred years ago and this time set armed against each other" (December 23, 1943).[41] Often overlapping, the themes of brotherly conflict and a divided country filled people's diaries in the days following September 8. The declaration of war of October 13 brought the foretold drama to its breaking point. In the words of forty-three-year-old Leone Fioravanti, "Italy becomes the protagonist of one of the most horrendous tragedies that history can remember. The fratricidal war begins" (October 13, 1943). Or, as Irene Paolisso summarized it: "Now officially two Italies exist" (October 16, 1943).

The tragedy of a brotherly conflict was vividly real, and some found it too excruciating to accept. With the added emphasis of underlining, the elder E.R. wrote on the day Badoglio declared war against Germany (one among the few diarists who commented on the event):

> I've cried a lot begging clemency from God for me and our Italy: how painful it is for me to see our Fatherland being mutilated, offended, ransacked, torn by many men that proclaim love of the Fatherland and denigrate each other, and accuse each other, slander each other, go one against another, pit brothers against brothers.

Conversazione con Claudio Pavone condotta da Daniele Borioli e Roberto Botta," *Quaderno di storia contemporanea* no. 10 (1991): pp. 19–42. For Revelli's interview see Antonio Gnoli, "Fucilavamo i fascisti e non me ne pento," *La Repubblica* (October 16, 1991).

[41] The last phrase (*l'un contro l'altro armato*) was a direct citation from the poem "The Fifth of May" by Alessandro Manzoni.

Sensing that a whole world of ideals and beliefs risked collapsing under the sweeping stroke of the conflict, E.R.'s venting drew from deeply felt core values and old patriotic principles, including the trope of "mutilation" originally launched by the poet Gabriele D'Annunzio at the end of the First World War.[42] E.R.'s despair radiated broadly to encompass unspecified "men" responsible for what she saw as the travesty of their pretended love for the country. Beyond accusations of guilt, E.R.'s entry expressed the pain she suffered at the undeniable spectacle of brotherly divisions and antagonisms.

Similarly struck by the degenerating conflict that threatened to tear Italy apart, Anna Menestrina bemoaned, "What a terrible thing would be a civil war! God forbids!" She hoped that the discord would not transform into a full-blown fratricide, even though by the time she wrote her note on November 18, 1943 the nation's divisions were unequivocally set. Against all evidence, and despite the fact that the specter of civil war followed her as she moved from bombed-out Trento to the nearby countryside, she continued to be confident. Only months later she reported, "Carnages, dead, assassinations, destructions... this is what the fatherland has come down to" (July 6, 1944).

For teenager Perla Cacciaguerra, the moment of truth about the fratricidal nature of the domestic conflict came at the RSI's trial and execution of fascist functionaries, those that had dared cast a vote against Mussolini on that infamous night of July 25. When Perla heard the verdict in early January 1944, she launched into a discussion of the meaning of voting that, albeit naïve and seemingly ignorant of fascism's undemocratic character, exposed the brotherly drama:

> I didn't really know that those who vote are under death penalty if they don't do it according to the goals of those at the helm of the state. Then what is voting worth, if one has to do it not according to one's opinion but to that of one's boss? [...] This principle is very bad and I feel it is the harbinger of even more horrendous things: carnage on a massive scale, convictions, executions and what is even worse civil war where brothers against brothers will fight to the death.   (January 9, 1944)[43]

The specific episode of the trial and the drama of its death sentences, including capital punishment for Mussolini's son-in-law, Galeazzo Ciano, had all

---

[42] D'Annunzio lamented Italy's treatment at the negotiating table and decried her "mutilated victory" (*la vittoria mutilata*).

[43] In the published diary, the date of this entry is January 11, 1944.

the elements of a bloody family conflict, a "brother-against-brother" fight. As Perla rightly understood, they were killing their own.[44] But, in truth, few diarists made the connection between the internecine fight and the fascist regime. "Brothers" were never addressed as fascists or antifascists—they belonged to an undefined other. To be sure, differently from the confusions that arose about the inimical German and the Anglo-American liberators, people were aware that one of the two camps in the brotherly division belonged to supporters of the regime. Nevertheless, they seemed to be treating the civil war as happening in an ideological and historical vacuum—they seldom drew connections between past and present. Mario Tutino lamented his fellow Italians' blindness at fascism's role in the country's current drama:

> So it happens that no one is yet able to realize that this war, in whichever way it was born or provoked, was from its onset the very beginning of the civil war, and it is now its outlet; war that was intrinsic to fascism since its beginnings, and was the leaven of all its development, and would fatally lead to its dissolution. [...] This one is above all and exclusively a civil war.
> (November 2–3, 1943)

With his usual acumen, Tutino turned attention to the original cause of the drama currently ripping the country apart: the twenty-year-long dictatorship. Few of his fellow nationals followed suit. Only sympathizers of the regime seemed to recognize the country's internal division from early on. Among them, young Roman V.R. lived the brotherly conflict literally. A zealous believer in fascism—so much so that she even wanted to enlist and fight in the war—she had a brother and father who did not share her ideas, although her mother did. The break with her brother was particularly hard on V.R., and the more so once he became close to the partisan movement. With tensions rising at home, she disconsolately lamented:

> Italy is divided in two and so is our family.
>
> How sad, how sad. And poor little mom, how much she is suffering as she watches her beloved son getting farther and farther away from the path of honor, of what is right, of true patriotism.

---

[44] The news of the trial struck several diarists. It felt grim. See among others Magda Ceccarelli De Grada, Anna Menestrina, and Leone Fioravanti. The latter commented, "Even the Germans must turn up their nose at the stench emanated by fascist filth" (January 10, 1944).

If we lose the war, it will only be because of the communists' skilled, deceitful, sneaky propaganda that manages to brainwash the weak.

(May 4, 1944)

For V.R., attachment to fascism counted more than anything else, including fraternity with fellow Italians—those she believed were indoctrinating her own brother. Firmly convinced that Italy had betrayed her Nazi ally, she found Germans' violent reactions against the Italian population "normal." At the news of the massacre of 335 at the Ardeatine caves on March 24, 1944—one of the worst atrocities committed by the Nazis during their occupation of Rome (supposedly executed as reprisal to the partisans' attack on a special SS police regiment that killed thirty-three soldiers)—she had no doubts about where to cast guilt.[45] "The German command unfortunately exaggerated. It could have sentenced the same number of poor innocents," she conceded. In essence, she did not hold the occupiers responsible. Much guiltier she found fellow Italians, the Resistance fighters: "I'm only praying for those poor dead and their heartbroken families, victims, in my opinion, of that vile little group of partisans more than of the Germans" (March 25, 1944). Ideological conviction influenced V.R.'s perspectives and affected her values, no matter how untenable or contradictory her views turned out to be once checked against reality. Wasn't her own brother by blood a partisan sympathizer? How should one define a brother, and would it ever be legitimate to kill one? To overcome her own emotional conflict, V.R. resorted to blaming others, whether "the communists" or government leaders. Turning political opponents into "vile" mobs helped her deny fellow Italians their right to be part of the "family."

The same negative strategy of demeaning "the other side" was pursued by Aida Rinaldi Gatti. Mother of Rinaldo Rinaldi, a prisoner of war in India since the heyday of the conflict, this upper-class woman from Genoa was understandingly concerned about the fate of her son in captivity. Even more troublesome, however, she found the choice Rinaldo would have to make upon his return to a divided country. In a letter to her son's fiancée, she wished he "would be left down there until the end of the war [...]. Just thinking that he could be taken away and sent back to fight against us, as it seems they

---

[45] On the massacre see Robert Katz, *Death in Rome* (New York: Macmillan, 1967); *Morte a Roma. La storia ancora sconosciuta del massacro delle Fosse Ardeatine* (Rome: Editori Riuniti, 1967). On the memory of the event see Alessandro Portelli, *The Order Has Been Carried Out: History, Memory, and Meaning of a Nazi Massacre in Rome* (New York: Palgrave, 2007). For the first mention of the massacre see Carlo Trabucco, *La prigionia di Roma. Diario dei 268 giorni dell'occupazione tedesca* (Turin: Borla, 1954).

would ask him to do at first, makes me ferociously exasperated." Aida preferred "a thousand times over to know him prisoner than fighting among Badoglio's troops, against one's own brothers" (October 5, 1943). The chasm between Italians was more than apparent to her, and she did not want her scion, as member of the Italian royal army, to be battling fascism's supporters. After all, he had been taken prisoner defending Mussolini's Italy—fascist Italy, her Italy. She was not ready to see her family give that up. Although she still called nonfascist Italians "brothers," she resorted to a string of highly negative appellations to lessen their human value. By addressing them as "traitorous bandits," "godless," and "foul hyenas," she erected a barrier separating her and her kind from those who had renounced Mussolini's regime.[46] And she did not seem to find that symbolic division objectionable or hard to carry out. Aida was operating from an abstract ideological standpoint devoid of direct interlocutors—actual people with whom she was in relation and at whom she could point her finger as deviant. When one descends to the micro level of social interaction, however, the question of "strangers" takes on a different valence. It implicates "us" in deciding how we deal with "them," those we consider different. As the case of V.R. testifies, the "other" could involve a family member. How was one's political faith going to fare when confronted with the inviolability of blood ties?

This and other idiosyncrasies exposed the hiatus between theory and practice as well as abstract ideals and concrete daily life that characterized the Italians' response to the events triggered by the fall of the regime on July 25. Deeply embedded in their lived environment—their day-to-day experience—people appeared at the same time plainly disenchanted and surprisingly out of touch. While they recognized the reality of civil war as a matter of fact—a state of things that could not be debated—they did not accompany that recognition with an analysis of responsibilities or even a precise characterization of the two sides of the divide. Who was against whom? Vague invocations of "brothers" often failed to mention that one of the two camps was comprised of fascists. It almost seemed as if the reasons and context for the dramatic split Italians were experiencing had no relevance. Meanwhile, fascism continued to influence the fate of the country and people's existence as well. Supposedly buried, it remained, in contrast, very much alive—a spectral presence that lurched in the shadows. Even more uncannily, fascism's unchecked impact continued to bind Italians with invisible ties that proved to be especially resilient around the issue of fatherland and national pride.

---

[46] "Bandits" was how the RSI's propaganda referred to members of the partisan movement.

Frolicking with the Fatherland

Research suggests that when comparing Italians' views in the First and Second World Wars, opposition to the conflict was widespread in 1915–18 and led to acts of insubordination, including desertion, among soldiers. In 1940 and thereafter, in contrast, dissent remained limited and was mainly manifested in words rather than actions. Despite the fact that the general population disapproved of military intervention and hoped it would be avoided, conscripts did not protest or refuse to join the army—they appeared unwilling to disavow their call to serve. According to Loris Rizzi, because fascist Italy was on the side of the invaders, it could not but justify the current war within a highly nationalistic discourse that, as the regime had been preaching for years, emphasized restoring power to an old civilization steeped in glory.[47] Most Italians did not seem to understand the country's role in the present conflict, nor did they realize the difference between a war of defense and a war of attack. Seemingly natural and innocuous, the cross-referential overlap of fascism and patriotism, and the regime's ability to associate its ideological mission with a glorified concept of fatherland, had profound political effects.[48] As Rizzi argues, "Confused by twenty years of nationalist rhetoric, many Italians end up believing that the war of the regime is a war to defend the fatherland, the last Italian war for independence, as a matter of fact, and that the soldiers of Mussolini's army continue the work and are the inheritors of the Risorgimento's heroes."[49]

Trapped in these semantic confusions, once the regime came apart many Italians found themselves wondering about the meaning of their patriotic beliefs. Mario Tutino confessed to having fallen for the nationalistic myth along with his friends:

> I was in favor and optimistic about the war, Agostino was in favor of the war and fascism [...]. In any case, how wrong we were, and how we let ourselves be led (or at least I did) more by desire, by the deformed and deforming passion for the fatherland's power, than by a realistic assessment of facts, a

---

[47] Loris Rizzi, *Lo sguardo del potere. La censura militare in Italia nella seconda guerra mondiale 1943–45* (Milan: Rizzoli, 1984), p. 96. On the perspectives of the military about the war also see Giorgio Rochat, *Le guerre italiane 1935–1943. Dall'impero di Etiopia alla disfatta* (Turin: Einaudi, 2005).

[48] Christopher Duggan details the regime's ideological work in this area in *Fascist Voices: An Intimate History of Mussolini's Italy* (Oxford: Oxford University Press, 2013), chapter 9, "A Place in the Sun."

[49] Rizzi, *Lo sguardo del potere*, p. 97.

true and solid comprehension of Italy's true needs, of her possibilities and her true destiny of grandeur. (November 9, 1943)

Despite his aversion for fascism, Tutino had shared the regime's imperialist aspirations. As it turns out, his support for a vision of patriotism that overlapped with expansionism was not unique. When Perla Cacciaguerra objected to a "Sicilian fascist" who badmouthed Italians and wished them a defeat, she relied on those principles:

> We cannot forget the dead in East Africa, the Duke of Aosta, the dead in Greece, in Albania, in Russia (see Armir) that gave their lives to the Fatherland. [...] We will have our Fatherland back, it will return to being great, maybe more than before and we will surely not be ashamed of proclaiming our nationality.[50] (May 21, 1944)

Cacciaguerra salvaged the country's reputation by emphasizing the dead, those soldiers that fought and fell on the battlefields. In truth, not only did she refer exclusively to the military campaigns launched by the fascist regime (due to her young age, they were obviously more familiar to her), she also did not seem to mind that territorial expansion was the ultimate goal of those operations. Fascism had accustomed Italians to think of themselves as conquerors. By expanding their reach to foreign lands, Italians supposedly enhanced the fatherland; by winning wars, they would guarantee the country's well-being. Little did people acknowledge the terrible record in human rights violations scored by fascist soldiers in the occupied territories.[51] In contrast, a romanticized vision of conquest prevailed. Hence, Dino Villani believed that Italians had been "sensible" colonizers (October 4, 1943), while Mario Corbolini expressed the indulging delusion that the Greeks adored the Italian occupiers ("We fell in love with Greece and Greece with us. We had surely conquered the Greek land but most of all we conquered the Greek soul").[52] More credibly, IMI M.D. exposed the hypocritical naïvety behind those myths. With a sense of atonement at the funeral of a fellow prisoner at the camp, he brooded, "I'm reminded of the grief, the ruins, the dead and

---

[50] Armir indicated the Italian Army in Russia.
[51] Among the substantial literature on the topic see Angelo Del Boca *Italiani, brava gente? Un mito duro a morire* (Vicenza: Neri Pozza Editore, 2005); Davide Rodogno, *Il nuovo ordine mediterraneo. Le politiche di occupazione dell'Italia fascista in Europa (1940–1943)* (Turin: Bollati-Boringhieri, 2003); Eric Gobetti, *Alleati del nemico. L'occupazione italiana in Jugoslavia (1941–1943)* (Rome-Bari: Laterza, 2013); Elena Aga Rossi and Maria Teresa Giusti, *Una guerra a parte*.
[52] This is how Corbolini remembered the situation, writing from his prison camp in 1944.

suffering we left behind in our tragic and absurd imperial march in the world." The responses he recorded from his comrades were flat out denials: "But we never completely abandoned our humanity"—"Do you remember in Cattaro (Kotor) how many people came to greet the Italian occupiers, prisoners of the Germans."—"Don't forget that we also left good memories of us."—"We never committed the atrocities of the SS"—"Come on, M., they called us the 'Sagapò Army' in Greece!"—"The army of love" (June 28, 1944).[53]

Part of the regime's enduring legacy and the underlying motif guiding fascism's dream of "legitimate" expansion, the link between fatherland and conquest was also invoked by IMI artillery Captain Pompilio Aste to justify his participation in the war. In a letter drafted for his wife, Itala, and son, Sandro, he wrote:

> I also need to tell you a few words about love for the fatherland: Itala, you know, and Sandro will soon get to know, with what enthusiasm I answered—after much asking and insistence—the call of the nation at war, and how faithfully I served her in the more than two and a half years as soldier. I had one sole ambition: one day to be able to tell my son of my modest contribution to the victorious war from which he and his generation would be able to draw some benefit.   (November 11, 1943)

Devoted to an idealized concept of patriotism—an encompassing notion independent of specific political references or affiliations—Aste suffered at the idea of the fatherland fallen in ruin. Held captive by the Germans on the 1943 anniversary of the fascist Day of Faith (originally held in December 1935), he reminisced with fondness about that landmark celebration and underlined its symbolic meaning as a unifier of national conscience:

> Day of faith. I think back at the cold and snowy day in which, eight years ago, Itala and I rushed to offer our sacred gold to the Fatherland, so to make it greater. How much patriotic ardor, how much moving devotion we had then. Even now, though, after so many events, even painful ones, we always hold very high in our trusting heart the undying flame of love for the true

---

[53] On the myth of the good Italian see Del Boca *Italiani, brava gente?* Also see David Bidussa, *Il mito del bravo italiano* (Milan: Il Saggiatore, 1994); Filippo Focardi, *Il cattivo tedesco e il bravo italiano*; and Filippo Focardi and Lutz Klinkhammer, "The Question of Fascist Italy's War Crimes: The Construction of a Self-Acquitting Myth (1943–1948)," *Journal of Modern Italian Studies* vol. 9, no. 3 (2004): pp. 330–48.

Italy. When everything is over, we'll start living again at the undying cry: Long live Italy!   (December 18, 1943)

In his apotheosis of the fatherland, Aste did not mention the regime, despite the fact that the gold he so willingly gave on the Day of Faith was directed to fund fascism's aggressive, imperialist conquest of Ethiopia. Maybe he was not aware of any brutality the Italians inflicted on the local population, or maybe that reality simply did not register in his mind. Still, he believed it was worth making sacrifices, including giving up one's own gold possessions, if those actions enhanced the "greatness" of the fatherland. As he licked his spiritual and physical wounds in the prison camp of Cholm, the effects of fascism's patriotic rhetoric on him were proving resilient years after that evocative ritual.

At the start of the civil war, patriotic and sentimental entrapments remained plentiful in the ideological web spun by the regime. "Fatherland," even when disconnected from fantasies of imperialism, offered Italians a common ground from which to evaluate the country's current predicament. References to the fatherland helped the "apolitical" Don Luigi Serravalle make sense of events that suddenly and brutally turned his familiar worldviews upside down. Pessimistic about September 8, the father compared it to another armistice, the one signed with the Austrian-Hungarians at the end of the First World War: "What a difference between that day and today!... At that time, Italy was victorious and celebrating.... Today Southern Italy is invaded by Anglo-American troops, and in Central and Northern Italy German troops are roaming free" (November 4, 1943). Winning was a value that even Don Luigi could not renounce, although in the specific circumstances of 1943 the alternative to peace and the armistice meant fighting alongside the Germans. Should it have been the path to follow? The father did not seem able or willing to make that call. A year later, his evocation of the same anniversary was short and nostalgic: "November 4!....How many memories!....." (November 4, 1944).

Between ambitions of victory on one side and the reality of disarray on the other, Italians were pulled in different directions. And yet the notion of fatherland remained at the center of their concerns even when they expressed criticisms of its current valence. Summoned to serve in the RSI military, seventeen-year-old Gian Carlo Stracciari decided he should follow his cohort's decision and enroll. Holding no qualms about the wisdom of his resolution, he appeared cynical about the value of the service he was about to offer. Hence, he immediately rationalized his decision by denying any viable significance to the notion of fatherland, which he saw as inexorably defiled: "Today it would seem that love of the fatherland does not exist any longer. With all the events that have recently taken place, one does not know if the true Fatherland is the one of Badoglio, in the South, or this one, just born, thanks to the work of Mussolini, or so they say" (November 1943). If in the past the criteria for joining the army would have included patriotism, that principle did not apply to present-day Italy. What was the fatherland? Stracciari could not quite make it out.

Twenty-year-old Milanese Danilo Durando similarly made the decision to enlist in the RSI army out of fear for his family.[54] Dismissive of the whole initiative and completely disaffected with the ruses of power, he was aware of the patriotic ideals being flaunted at young people like him—a sad, if not sinister, manipulation. Barely one month into his conscription, he penned in his diary, "It seems impossible, but the fatherland must always be saved. Always. The beauty of this is that, according to some, we are the ones saving the fatherland, while, according to others, let's call them our brothers-enemies, they are the ones who are saving it" (March 19, 1944). Durando exposed the contradictions, if not the hypocrisy, inherent in the various appeals to the fatherland. While that rhetoric did not match his experience, it impacted the course of his existence and that of million others. After reporting the first death in his unit, Durando wryly commented of the deceased, "Fallen for an unfortunate accident, but fallen for that famous fatherland that they say, we too should be saving. Dang it" (April 6, 1944).[55]

---

[54] The fact that Durando's mother was married to a British man made his family's situation worse, although, in general, all young males were under pressure to enroll at this time. Magda Ceccarelli De Grada wrote a series of entries on the crude methods adopted by the RSI to force conscription. On February 25, 1944, for example, she commented, "Mussolini calls young people to arms, first with flattery, then with threats, finally with the coercion of brutal decrees. /The poor ones that after much hesitation, discomfort, and crisis decide to enroll are immediately sent to Germany. Some flee, others, weaker and less decisive, follow their fate as slaves." Chevallard and Carazzolo, however, report RSI's failure to attract conscripts despite the many threatening calls. For Chevallard, see for example entries of September 20 and December 14, 1943, and of April 24 and May 15, 1944 in "Diario di Carlo Chevallard 1942–1945." For Carazzolo, see entries of February 16, April 20 and 26, and December 21, 1944 in *Più forte della paura*.

[55] The story of twenty-six-year-old Michele Barile is telling. As he was journeying his way back to Italy from a German prison camp in Yugoslavia at the end of the war, his enthusiasm was mitigated by fears that the country he left as a young soldier might be completely transformed. He became concerned that his patriotic sentiments might not find a place in the new environment. To him, fascism epitomized love for the fatherland, and he could not extricate the one from the other: "Grown up under a different regime, **we don't know how to make sense of the big political changes in Italy** of the last few years and we are therefore disappointed. We can't erase suddenly all that sense of the fatherland and feeling of loyalty that fueled us during our youth" (July 20, 1945) (bold in the original). For an exception to this prevailing view see Carazzolo, *Più forte della paura*. To Carazzolo, fatherland was a "sentimental notion" secondary to the "rational principles of freedom or enslavement," p. 81 (entry of July 17, 1943). She insisted on the importance of freedom in other entries too.

Fascism, an Afterthought?

Fascism cast a long shadow over Italy's identity, and it would be disingenuous to think that after twenty years of dictatorial rule its effects had dissipated along with the regime's fall. Even the skeptical-sounding Gian Carlo Stracciari, who resented having to join the RSI army while all he wanted to do was to be left alone, seemed nostalgic about the past, if in a self-mocking way, and appeared to appreciate the importance of believing in an idea whether or not inculcated: "And I who not too long ago was dreaming of going to war at the sound of trumpets, and accompanied by the smiles of the Young Italian Girls!" (November 30, 1943). Stracciari was not necessarily a warmonger, nor did he actively advocate fascism's bellicose plans. Still, he lamented the loss of past bliss as well as of higher moral grounds or, more simply, of trust, regardless of its object. Feeling dejected, he reminisced of the regime's years as a golden age in the utopian/mythological sense, including the time Mussolini announced Italy's entry into the Second World War (admittedly, he was only fifteen then): "I think of June 10, 1940. Mussolini from Palazzo Venezia declared war on France and Great Britain. I was on the big balcony of our house in via Pier Crescenzi with Loredana and Wanda. We were playing cards, carefree and happy" (March 10, 1944). Stracciari thought that the conflict would only last a short time. Although he now recognized the delusionary character of that credence, he still retained a sentimental image of life under fascism.

Nationalist feelings were hard to disentangle from the regime, as IMI Giorgio Crainz's personal recollections of military life attest. Although definitively opposed to the emergent Italian Social Republic, Crainz wrote nostalgically about his past military service in Italy's Libyan colony (October 30, 1943) and became very emotional at the sight of Italian officers entering the prison camp in step: "I've got my heart in my throat and I feel a bit moved. It's like watching the spectacle of the review of the Empire again…" (November 1, 1943). Against the paradoxical scenario of forced cooptation in a German lager, past images of army solidarity filled Crainz's memory. In retrospect, and compared to his current status as an imprisoned Italian combatant, the time he shared with fellow soldiers might have seemed golden. More crucially, separating Italy from the regime, or the fatherland from fascism, was an arduous task—a tie that had been knotted for over twenty years could not be undone overnight through a mere cleansing frenzy. The unwilled union—a forced marriage—was one of the reasons that made it difficult for Italians to single out Mussolini and his movement as the abusers. Fascism was a homegrown phenomenon that had affected every fiber of the country, including its identity. In disguise under all these tangles, fascism was now having an afterlife beyond the RSI, and, even worse, its nefariousness remained unexamined. Contributing to this outcome were popular considerations of the regime in terms of corruption, which, while sparing Mussolini from any criticism, discounted the dictatorial dimensions of fascism.

Although a tyrannical system, fascism was reduced by many to a problem of misgovernment and maladministration—a perspective that was not new. In his work on the *ventennio*, Christopher Duggan has shown that accusations of malfeasance were characteristic of views exculpating Mussolini throughout his tenure as head of government.[56] Additionally, Paul Corner's research has documented how criticisms of the fascist party along the line of corruption ran parallel to the idolization of Mussolini.[57] What remains puzzling, however, is the persistence of these opinions past July 25. At the fall of the regime, Dino Villani noted people's satisfaction at the fact that "this government of thieves" had finally come to an end. He subscribed to this interpretation and later on returned to it, wondering whether stealing and nepotism had caused Italians' exasperation. Eventually, he agreed with a friend that, even though Mussolini had made many terrible mistakes, a good internal cleansing would have changed things for the better (August 3, 1943). Based more on practical matters than principles, Villani's evaluation ultimately absolved fascism as circumstances allowed. When the Germans liberated Mussolini, he welcomed the news convinced that the dictator possessed the necessary resources to solve Italy's complicated political quandary—he was willing to give Mussolini the benefit of the doubt. Then, as fascism regrouped in the RSI, Villani followed the development of the government in formation, criticized its details but not its substance, and appeared to place great hopes on its future actions. News of a nearby massacre of Jews disturbed him (September 27, 1943). Yet he continued to ruminate over the reasons for fascism's weaknesses and pointed his finger at external causes, such as, again, the fact that corruption had exerted corrosive effects on the movement (January 10, 1944). By the end of 1944, he still had not given up expectation that Mussolini could make a comeback.

Whether in good or bad faith, the issue of malfeasance offered a convenient framework from which to evaluate the regime and archive it. As tales of

---

[56] See Duggan, *Fascist Voices*.
[57] Paul Corner, *The Fascist Party and Popular Opinion in Mussolini's Italy* (Oxford: Oxford University Press, 2012). On fascism's pattern of corruption also see Paolo Giovannini and Marco Palla eds., *Il fascismo dalle mani sporche. Dittatura, corruzione, affarismo* (Bari-Rome: Laterza, 2019).

morality unfolded, political and ideological principles took a backseat—a trend that Fortunato Favai observed in the national and local press, "Newspapers are reporting extensive accounts of confiscation of property from gerarchi and other members of the Fascist Government, properties that they had improperly obtained. [...] According to the same newspapers it seems that these gerarchi enriched themselves enormously, dishonestly, and on the back of the hapless Italian people" (September 8, 1943).[58] Car mechanic Leone Fioravanti subscribed to that compelling narrative. Drawing on personal observations collected in his own town of Schio, Fioravanti put forward a harsh critique of fascism's malfeasance. Although he did not ignore the regime's tyrannical nature, the theme of corruption took center stage in his negative assessment—it was the divisive factor pitting the dominated against those in power. The less well-off particularly had to endure enormous hardships "in order to fatten the fascists and sustain their shameful war" (October 16, 1943), he charged. Even for the die-hard fascist Carlo Ciseri the regime's corruption was not in question. To the contrary, it explained the unfortunate downfall of Mussolini. Having misplaced his trust, Mussolini naïvely confided in unscrupulous collaborators and remained unaware of their malign behavior—he was now paying a price for his magnanimity.[59] As Ciseri concluded, "Were there some mistakes? We will consider them and judge them. So far, we can only attribute him one: too much generosity, which in a man of government can be considered a weakness" (August 4, 1943).

Through denials, displacements, and deflections, the assessment of fascism followed serendipitous routes. Whereas scapegoating (including of the king and Badoglio) became an additional means for minimizing the degree of the regime's vacuousness, many people were simply caught in the web of fascism's ideology. Unable to extricate themselves from its coils, they were stuck in intractable contradictions. Self-flagellation often characterized their response, especially among the military. Having come to recognize their past mistaken views, soldiers and officers mostly blamed themselves and were at loss to provide a more concrete diagnosis of the regime's remarkable ability to endure for over twenty years. Calls for personal responsibility fit Pompilio Aste's vision of spiritual rectitude as he invited his fellow prisoners "to repudiate our national past, in order to reconstruct from the foundations a new life for

---

[58] Badoglio instituted a committee of experts to inquire about prominent fascists' illegal wealth. Although of limited effectiveness, that measure was propagandized and successfully drew public attention to the question of corruption. See Hans Woller, *I conti con il fascismo. L'epurazione in Italia, 1943–1948* (Bologna: il Mulino, 1997), p. 40.

[59] However, other fascist supporters, such as Paolino Ferrari, included Mussolini among the corrupt.

ourselves, on principles of greater Dignity" (end of November 1943). With a transcendent ethical anguish, Aste evaluated fascism as a sign of Italians' moral weakness, a self-inflicted wound.

From his prison camp in India, the Ligurian Giacomo Agnese regretted the choices he originally made against the wishes of his own father, a socialist. A volunteer with Mussolini's Black Shirts, which he joined for the 1935 African campaign at the age of twenty-nine, Agnese was taken prisoner by the British in 1936 and held in captivity until the war's end. In his missives to his spouse, he expressed atonement along with a readiness to repudiate his fascist faith: "Having managed to free myself, through pain, of the dross that was not mine and that only the environment and bad education imposed on me, I have matured and reached those moral conclusions that were inevitable for a person endowed with disinterest and idealism, generosity and spirit of sacrifice" (September 20, 1944). Agnese rationalized his political enthusiasm for the regime as a youthful sin, albeit one based on authentic commitment and genuine faith. He conceded to having been blinded, but now being able to see through all the smoke. In truth, he remained unable or unwilling to verbalize what needed to be eliminated from that wasted past. As he eschewed concrete assessments of a system that had deceived him and many others, his personal apology was based on idealist values and abstract principles. The wounds of which he lamented were mostly spiritual, caused by the collapse of his romanticized view of fascism.

In many cases, the disappointment ran so deep and regrets over the crimes committed in the war felt so haunting that many soldiers simply wished to forget. The Piedmontese surgeon Gualtiero Marello, another military who decided not to opt, confessed to his wife that he had witnessed horrors he thought could never be recounted: "I don't even know if I will want to tell everything [...] to forget, to forget everything because everything is ugly, painful, dark, shameful" (July 25, 1944). Marello usually wrote very intimate, personal letters to his spouse Angela. On this first anniversary of fascism's fall, in contrast, his missive revisited the odyssey of the collapsing Italian army and gave him the occasion to state his refusal ever again to serve ideas that had "betrayed and abandoned" him and his fellow soldiers.

The harshness of war magnified the confusion Italians faced at the unexpected fall of the regime. At the same time, the desire to end the conflict superseded most other issues. Within this context, it might not be surprising that, although the accidental collapse of fascism left many gasping for answers, very little efforts at examination ensued. In truth, as the reality on the ground grew more dramatic, extreme conditions often numbed people, and in spite of a diffused anger suffering only occasionally spurred reflections—almost an ascetic's delirium. Irene Paolisso, who experienced acute spasms of hunger, realized that moral standing could barely be maintained when physical dereliction was in play. Like others, she wondered whether fascism had contributed to deprive people of personhood, leaving them in a state of semi-conscience that only responded to the solicitation of primary needs—a condition in which, she confessed to her next of kin, she found herself:

> The other night I felt very sick, and the same last night. Dear brother, a nice steamy plate of pasta would be the only remedy able to give everybody strength and courage. It is mundane, I know. But only now we manage to understand the spring that pushes a crowd of starving beggars to violence as they find obstacles to their pressing needs.
>
> I wonder, brother, where all our starving people are, if in the republic of Salò, enlisted in the Republican army, or alongside the oppressor Germans, and why not on the mountains and, all united, here next to me.
>
> (March 25, 1944)

Lamenting the lack of popular resistance around her, Paolisso believed the regime had sapped thoughts and energy out of individuals; it had left them unable to take action even when their despair hit the lowest point. Fascism appeared too resilient to be overcome. In actuality, the ravages of the world conflict forced people to engage in unending efforts to survive both the physical damages they suffered and the mounting emotional scars.[60] Within such a dire state of ruin, to many the fascist regime felt like a distant memory, if not an unfathomed better time filled with dreams of greatness and imperialistic claims. With the impelling demands of the moment affording few opportunities to reflect on the past, the urge to look forward rather than back did not facilitate any kind of reckoning either. As the next chapter indicates, the misery of everyday experiences helped shape Italians' responses to the vagaries of history.

In this chapter we illustrated the interpretive idiosyncrasies that continued to confront Italians in the aftermath of the institutional crisis provoked by the fall of Mussolini and the signing of the armistice. Whereas the previous chapter examined the Italians' structures of feeling around the three main events

---

[60] On pain see Elaine Scarry, *The Body in Pain: The Making and Unmaking of the World* (Oxford: Oxford University Press, 1985).

of summer 1943, here we focused on the dominant reality of the period—the war, with its twists and turns. We tracked the phenomenology of people's moods and opinions especially in relation to the figure of the enemy, around which definitional confusions arose. Caught between ex-allies and new ones, Italians struggled to untangle the multiple manifestations of enmity that emerged from the historical context. While Badoglio's declaration of war on October 13 painted a picture of the Germans as the quintessential foe, diaries reveal that Italians' evaluation of the enemy followed a more nuanced process that shifted over time and also deviated from official labels. At first perplexed by the Germans' switching roles from friend to foe, Italians eventually expressed deep hatred for them. As for the Anglo-American enemy now turned "liberators," many accepted them with a good dose of irony and a great amount of skepticism. Most significantly, the Italians recognized the internecine character of the struggle unleashed by the armistice and grieved the reality of a brother-against-brother civil war. Enemies were not only foreigners but nationals too, they were quick to realize.

While bringing to the fore the fluidity of Italians' structures of feeling, the chapter has also highlighted the persistence and effectiveness of fascism's cultural-political ideals despite people's symbolic rejection of the regime in the wake of July 25. On issues of how to define the enemy or why one should subscribe to the narrative of betrayal, the Italians' responses reveal the vitality of interpretations that, though autonomously elaborated, owed more than one debt of gratitude to fascist principles. Via references to the fatherland, honor, and national grandeur, the stories Italians constructed to make sense of a world gone astray showed the mark of a long-standing cultural subjection to fascism's worldview. While not exclusive to the regime, those core values filled people's imaginary and guided their interpretations. Reductive familiar metaphors, including love for the fatherland and fears of brotherly strife, turned the actual conflict into an abstract parable that was disconnected from history and divorced from concrete analysis of social forces. Those perspectives in many ways elevated Mussolini and the fatherland to unreflective objects of trust and love and commingled them with the glorification of the Italian people. Struggling to overcome the dire consequences of Mussolini's irresponsible war politics, people remained caught in fascism's ideological fetters, be they in the guise of habits, traditions, or ways of thinking and feeling. Popular opinions of the regime as corrupt contributed to divert attention from the political significance of the dictatorship, while individualized assumptions of guilt in the face of fascism's rottenness further exposed the

Italians' inability to confront the most consequential phenomenon of their recent history.

The next chapter will continue the discussion of fascism's relevance in Italians' existence by moving the analytical lens onto the quotidian. It will focus on how retrenchment in the private sphere contributed to distance Italians from political issues, even if that retreat also offered people a venue for expressing their discontent. In particular, a closer analysis of daily life in occupied Italy illuminates the instances of chiaroscuro that, as Henri Lefebvre theorized, define the everyday. Through attention to the micro-level of experience, the chapter probes the ambivalences that marred the Italians' relationship to their history, especially as they navigated the exceptional normalcy of wartime. While giving ampler space to diarists' narratives and life stories, the chapter also assesses the impact that formal aspects of journaling exerted on diaries' written content. Following Raymond Williams's suggestion on how to identify structures of feeling, we test the relationship between the articulated and the lived as shaped by the practice of diary writing.

3
Every Day in the Everyday

> In this interminable wait anything can happen.
> (November 18, 1943)*

A pervasive, all-around colonization of the private sphere had been among the key objectives of the fascist regime's domestic policy. In accordance with the totalitarian logic guiding its political project, Mussolini's dictatorship required of Italians continuous participation in mandated parades and ceremonies, besides active membership in all sorts of fascist organizations, party-sponsored sports, youth clubs, and summer leisure programs. Additionally, the dictatorship produced a system of rules and laws that applied to individuals' personal, even intimate, life and controlled it. From language usage and body shape to clothing wardrobe and reproductive prescriptions, the regime's mission of capillary politicization was intrusive and encumbering. Paradoxically, this vast apparatus of coerced involvement and extreme scrutiny promoted the citizenry's eventual retreat to the private realm. The desire to withdraw into one's own inner circle—hopeful refuge from an overly saturated public domain—was a side effect of forced spectacularized rituals. Obligingly compulsive, the duty of citizenry under fascism wore people out.

Once the regime's scaffolding tumbled and loosened its grip on Italians, flight into privacy became the partial legacy of an authoritarian system that had fostered political engagement through blind faith and obedience more than a civic sense of duty. By mid-1943, far from being reassuring, the domain of politics appeared unable to solve the predicaments of a volatile wartime situation soon to be aggravated by the upstaging event of fascism's sudden collapse. With the once-familiar world turned upside down, to many the sphere of privacy became an anchor to hold on to, if not in actuality at least in aspiration.

---

* From the diary of Irene Paolisso.

Fascism, the War, and Structures of Feeling in Italy, 1943–1945: Tales in Chiaroscuro. Simonetta Falasca-Zamponi, Oxford University Press. © Simonetta Falasca-Zamponi 2023. DOI: 10.1093/oso/9780192887504.003.0004

Along Came the Private

Focus on personal life defined the story of Maria Alemanno. This middle-aged Florentine (she was born in 1900) approached the extraordinary events of summer 1943 through the lenses of her own pained condition. With her partner Nando away at war, she lived in fear for his safety. Instinctively skeptical about institutional changes, Maria applied a disillusioned perspective to the historical upheavals she was witnessing while mostly taking stock of their effects on her private drama. Animated by a cautionary spirit, she fundamentally refrained from evaluating the current political situation beyond its immediate refractions on her romantic liaison. On September 8 at 4 p.m., when she started her diary just a few hours before the announcement of the armistice, she revealed her priorities unequivocally:

> Today it came to me to start writing a diary: a few words on events and facts that will be able to tell me, when I read them again one day, what this horrible war was truly like. Certainly, my first thought as I jot down these lines is for him, far away, doubly separated from me by the continuing overpowering reality of tragic facts.

Lured by the aura of memory (to be kept alive for future purposes) and trusting the power of reporting, Alemanno was motivated to write by the power of her love for the sorely missed companion. Having spent a long agonizing week with no mail, she had just received a much-desired letter from her beau. A miraculous surprise (she had even prayed the Madonna for it) and a source of infinite pleasure, the missive made her feel closer to Nando.

For Alemanno, life revolved around her beloved, no matter that he was physically distant. In her daily notes, she regularly paired short factual descriptions of local and national events with direct, emotional appeals to him. His presence hovered over her lived reality regardless of the occurrences she described. When recounting the extraordinary news of the armistice, for example, she wondered about Nando's reactions: "Everybody is concerned. And him?! What might he be thinking?" (September 9, 1943). As she reported on clashes in town between civilians and soldiers, she sighed, "What might he be doing, what might be happening down there?? Nobody says" (September 10, 1943). In Maria's mind, the great pain that tortured her as a consequence of the world conflict was not factored into the calculations of those with the power to make decisions. "These are things of no importance in a war like this one. What matters if some creatures suffer for their separation?? It's the war!!!" (September 10, 1943). Almost obsessive in her evocations of Nando, she continued to raise the same anguished interrogatives when Hitler's armies began their occupation of Florence: "And him?? This is the nagging thought that never leaves me. What might be happening down there??" (September 11, 1943). Ever sadder, her sorrow reached a boiling point once the Germans imposed a moratorium on private correspondence, her only remaining link to Nando: "They forcibly ripped something out of my heart. The mail was everything for me, I always waited for it anxiously. Now nothing more" (September 13, 1943). With her postal privileges taken away and her only communication channel with Nando brutally cut off, Maria resolved to use her own diary as replacement:

> When I begin to write my one little daily page, I feel as if I was starting a letter to him, and I barely avoid addressing it the way I used to, "Nando dear." In truth, now that they blocked me from writing and I don't receive anything anymore, these are almost like letters I send to him and I write for him here.   (September 19, 1943)

Composing a diary filled the void; it drew a bridge between her and the person she cared about. Desperate over the absence of news about her beloved, Alemanno began imagining his return. When at home, she would continuously look out the window not to miss his arrival. Watching a film at the theater, she kept turning around "to see if he comes!" (September 19, 1943). Not oblivious to the changes that in unending succession were striking the country during that late summer and early fall 1943, she hung on to the steadiness of her love relationship—it was the one secure thing in her life. Even the reconstitution of the fascists under the banner of the Social Republic did not motivate her to take a political stance: "Today I have no preference for this or that party, I will give my love later to those who will save us from ruin and return Nando to me! /For now, I feel dislike and repulsion for everybody" (October 4, 1943). Whether or not she was tantalized by the resurgent fascist movement, she remained impervious to any commitment: "I am not saying anything, I have no preferences, nor sympathies. I only think of him" (October 26, 1943).

In her evasive reaction to old and new fascism, Alemanno focused on Nando's return (he was now prisoner in a German camp), although even this private concern required guessing which strategic/political conditions might best advance the cause for which she cared most exclusively. Guided by self-interest, when faced with the prospective arrival of the Anglo-Americans in January 1944, Maria candidly acknowledged her dismay: "My thinking is simply selfish: I think that if they arrive in Florence, I will be separated from him and from his mother once again without even the hope of these postcards that give me strength and hope" (January 26, 1944). Entirely absorbed by her love relation, Alemanno could not make up her mind on the Allied forces, nor was she willing to evaluate their role in the liberation campaign. She consciously refused to assess war developments beyond their immediate impact on her aggrieved sentimental relationship—the postcards Nando's mother shared with her were more precious than any political stance or moral obligation. Or maybe Alemanno just felt emotionally unable to make principled decisions. Like a bystander, she was waiting for things to happen, conscious of her own impotence in the face of historical happenings that were seemingly insensible to her personal agony.

A young spouse and mother of three, Wanda Affricano-Marabini also suffered the torment of separation from her adored military husband. For months after the cataclysmic armistice, she remained in the dark about the fate of Captain Luigi Marabini—she could only conjecture he might have fallen captive to the Germans. Lacking any information about his status, Wanda started a diary on October 2, 1943:

> Already for some days I've had in mind to begin a sort of diary of this life of mine without you, my loving husband, and to dedicate to you day after day, every one of my actions and every one of my thoughts, since I am unable to express them in person or by letter the way I did over these last two and a half years.

Deprived of the precious outlet of mail correspondence, which had sustained her during her husband's years in deployment (the same predicament suffered by Alemanno and countless others), Wanda lamented her utter state of despair at the absence of news from the spouse. The diary replaced the lost medium of contact she had with the captain. Aware of the Italian military's disbanding after September 8, including in Greece where Luigi Marabini was stationed, she fantasized about his whereabouts with an anxious sense of urgency and a persistent dose of wishful thinking:

> And if I think that [...] you could have been imprisoned by the Germans and might run the risk of who knows which retaliations, I feel my head spinning! I also think that maybe like many others you changed into plainclothes

and found shelter with some acquaintance there. That would be the best thing! But I don't see it as something possible and compatible with your temperament and character, so honest and straight in everything! Unless you all did it and, thinking of us, you did it too to avoid the worst!

Addressing her husband directly, Wanda expressed hope that he would be "thinking of" them when making decisions. Surely, she hinted, he was not sacrificing his family's well-being for his ideals. Surely, he would not do anything that would cause her unhappiness. Surely, he wanted to fulfill her wish.

In truth, hers was a dialogue with a missing respondent, literally and metaphorically a dialogue of the deaf. For besides being unable to hear her, Luigi Marabini had taken exactly the position she suspected and had been dreading all along. Contrary to her desire that he bypass the predicament of political or ethical stances, he followed his principles and ultimately refused to collaborate with the Germans—an outcome Wanda could only be guessing. In the evening of November 28, still ignorant of his fortunes but more knowledgeable about the options available to captured soldiers, she commented, "I've heard that they will pose you the dilemma: either remain in concentration camp or enroll in the Fascist Republican Party and maybe be sent back home." She did not add any other comment on the topic, although the reported news was replete with drama considering the weighty choices Italian military personnel were forced to confront. Eventually she found out that the reason for her husband's continued captivity was his resolution not to opt. At that point, her anger exploded:

> How could you make such a decision?! And didn't you think that it might be the last straw that could irreparably worsen our situation? Why did you let yourself be influenced by Angeli and by an ideal that by now does not exist anymore?! Your first concern should have been for your family, and you missed a chance, that might not repeat itself, to come back to us and defend the interests of your wife and children!!!... (April 19, 1944)

Railing against the supposedly persuasive impact of a comrade-in-arms, and citing the risks the family was running because of her Jewish origins, Wanda became furious:

> For now there have been no consequences, but they could go dig up information on the families of those who did not join and...what would happen to us?!

> Is it possible that you did not think of this probability! [...]
>
> Even regardless of the fact that you could be here with us by now, how could you not think that with this refusal you might worsen your situation and ours too?!

In Wanda's mind, her husband should have put family first. In contrast, and to her chagrin, he acted according to his "wounded pride." Repeating the same point over and over throughout her lengthy entry, she insisted that he should not have neglected the children's welfare "in order to follow your ideal that might be in the right, I won't deny it, but is gone by now!" She questioned whom her loyal husband was defending considering that the monarchy had showed its grave limitations and the army leadership had miserably failed. The more she wrote, the more her resentment escalated:

> One needs to be decisive, strong men, and you demonstrated not to be one on this occasion! [...] You needed to think of our interest and not of grudges and pride. What did you obtain? That you are still there suffering and have no possibility of getting out until the war is over. And.... don't deceive yourself, it will not be over so soon!

The culmination of months of suffering and uncertainty over her husband's fate, Wanda's rage was so unbridled that she felt the need to revisit the issue that same evening, picking up her writing from where she had left it earlier that day. With a pragmatic sense, she chastised her spouse for failing to obtain any concrete results from his decision. Her irritation barely concealed, she lamented his scarce rationality and lack of practical logic in the face of her endless daily struggle for survival—this was not the time to play hero. Berating his "idealism," she refused to accept the legitimacy of his point of view. Indeed, she turned the tables around: "No, sorry if I say it, but you did not show character in this circumstance!" All in all, the whole matter had become a deep personal grievance for her. Weeks later, when Rome was celebrating its liberation, she wrote with disarming sadness, "I always regret that you did not want to come back" (June 8, 1944). Wanda interpreted her spouse's decision not to opt as a conscious choice not to rejoin his family. She took it personally, in sum, although she also continued to worry to death about his fate in the renowned "barbaric" German concentration camp.[1] In

---

[1] She had just read an article on the treatment of Italian soldiers in Hungary.

her experience, official institutions had mistreated her, hence she would not put any trust in them, nor did she think they deserved any devotion or sacrifice. The family unit was the only value she would uphold against a hostile and often indifferent outside world. Under duress, she was not open to any other argument or perspective.

Having an imagined dialogue with her husband through the pages of a personal journal made Wanda "feel better" and closer to him (October 2, 1943). It also recentered priorities in her life. In a similar way, thirty-three-year-old Corrado Di Pompeo focused on the private as the only secure point of reference in an unsettling historical era. On October 30, 1943, he began writing his diary as a series of letters to his wife, Antonietta, who had evacuated to native Molise along with their two children. Echoing Alemanno and Affricano-Marabini, Di Pompeo stated the reason for starting a journal: "It has been a few days I've had this idea in my mind: to write for you, my adored Antonietta, a short little page daily to freeze in time at least some of the many thoughts that overload my brain." Pushing the private nature of the genre to its limits, Di Pompeo turned the diary into a receptacle of personal messages— the means to share intimate reflections with his cherished spouse. Afflicted by a strong sense of guilt, for he had been the one insisting that the family would be safer away from Rome, he regretted his decision. It turned out that the eastern side of Italy, where wife and children had moved, was no less at risk than the capital. The thought of what could happen to them consumed Corrado incessantly, gnawing at him from inside, especially since he was deprived of any news about their well-being. Sad reminders of the unbridgeable separation setting them apart haunted him with "return to sender" messages stamped on the several letters he desperately but obstinately continued to mail. Completely absorbed by his own drama, he avowed exclusive interest in the welfare of his loved ones and explicitly rejected any commitment to political ideas, programs, or groups.

Di Pompeo's personal situation was peculiar to say the least. Originally employed at the Ministry of Corporations, he held on to his post after Mussolini's fall and also following the fascists' regrouping in the wake of the Germans' occupation. Hoping for a quick end to the war that would allow him to rejoin his family back in Molise, Di Pompeo rooted for the Anglo-Americans while being officially loyal to the Republic of Salò. In many ways, he did not really care for either side, possessed as he was by one only wish: to reunite with his wife. Everything occurring around him he filtered through the narrow scope of the advantages it might bring to his cause. Exhausted by the painfully slow pace of the Anglo-Americans, and in an emotional seesaw of joy and dejection, he welcomed the vaguest sign of the Allied forces' advance but felt completely crushed when learning of their failures to deliver:

> If I hear a bombardment, I think that German men and vehicles have been destroyed and I rejoice. If I see Red Cross convoys carrying the wounded, I'm not taken by pity. If I see vehicles heading to the front, I wish they would not make it, I wish I could signal their passing to the English. When American airplanes fly over, my heart celebrates. And this happens to me not because I hate the Germans, for after all these others are almost more obnoxious than them, but because I would like for everything to be over, because I would like to have the way cleared to rejoin all of you.   (February 25, 1944)

Di Pompeo's adoption of a quasi-cynical attitude allowed him to reaffirm his strong link to wife and children even as he struggled to survive in perilous conditions. With an almost obsessive insistence on the private, he tried to assuage his tremendous fears in the face of an overpowering historical reality. Rather than getting caught up in frustrations, he believed it was better to tune out. Not that this goal was easily achievable—he needed to stay abreast of war news in the eventuality it might turn in his favor. Under the grip of misery, and as uncertainty corroded his confidence, Di Pompeo relied on pragmatism, combined with a good dose of misanthropy, to help sustain him in his disconsolate solitude. Definitively refusing to get involved or take an ideological position and make choices, he adopted a strategic attitude. Hence, he evaluated every outside occurrence, act, and decision against the larger context of the war situation, but still according to their potential impact on his personal goal of reuniting with wife and children. Weather conditions were included in his appraisal: "After a few sunny days, over the last two or three days a shower occasionally comes. I would in contrast demand a fine and mild weather that would not hinder the march of our 'friends' from whom all my calculations depend. Indeed, with every advance they make, the time to come back to you shortens" (December 4, 1943). Or as he wrote a month later, "The cold is not about to lessen. Even the weather is contributing to slow down the Americans' march that, maybe if they found a milder season, would be here by now and I with you…" (January 7, 1944).

Di Pompeo's own individual predicament depended on the larger collective drama whose irresolute status appeared to redouble his frustration at the difficulties of rejoining the family. A solid diarist with an inclination toward self-reflection, he was aware of the peculiarity of his views. As he confessed to his wife:

Perhaps if I was close to you, I would be more engaged with the ongoing fight, but because we are separated my selfish spirit prevails; I ardently wish for the Americans to advance so I could see you again or at least be able to have your news. Afterwards I may regain the conscience of being human and Italian, afterwards I will be able to conceive the pro and con, but for now my only desire is to come to you and my children and I admire and value the work of those who will be able to clear the way for me…

(December 5, 1943)

Feeling dehumanized, Di Pompeo exhibited an almost schizophrenic relationship to the war, one that was replete with emotional detachment, on the one side, and a compulsive interest in its progression, on the other. In truth, as some of his entries attest, he could not suppress his concern for human misery, even if he certainly tried hard, nor could he avoid acknowledging the reigning desolation. Nevertheless, by focusing on his personal ordeal, Di Pompeo tried to smooth out the adversities he experienced under the dramatic conditions of German occupation and the relentless torment of military conflict. He built an alternative world that, though still miserable since it was made up of worries and unfulfilled wishes, allowed him to carve out a space away from the devastating reality that surrounded him. In his daily narratives, skepticism, the personal, and normalcy interweaved together to erect a barrier around feelings of love and intimacy that worked as a countermeasure to despondency and agony.

In truth, his stance of active defiance against the overbearing weight of History was a measure of his inevitable resignation in the face of those same consuming forces. He recognized that his neurotic reactions were a function of the rising war drama: "The hardships and concerns brought by the war get ever bigger; the spirit has become tough, insensitive to everything. No matter what might happen to you, your face does not express anything any longer and you don't rebel against anybody either, one is in a state of complete stupor" (November 11, 1943). This was the new normalcy, Di Pompeo realized—a mixture of apathy, indifference, and numbness that found its rhythm and space in an inescapable everyday reality altered at its core. The anticlimactic sentence that followed his reflections above is telling: "Not even the English advance is going the way we were expecting."

With the situation deteriorating in the city, family remained the sole anchor of salvation for Di Pompeo, a reason to endure even at the worst of moments—and there were many. As he agonized over the Anglo-Americans' slow progress, the first half of 1944 was tough on Romans. German raids on civilians, combined with Allied forces' bombings, afflicted a starved population ever more desperate for a resolution that appeared closer and closer by the day and yet still agonizingly too far. Interestingly, in the case of Di Pompeo, he never called the Anglo-Americans "enemies" or "liberators," and kept referring to the Germans as "the allies." Unencumbered by issues of semantics, he had a clear vision of the future at stake and continued to hope for the defeat of the Germans and their ouster from Rome. Short on ideological pronouncements and political evaluations, Di Pompeo exuded emotional distance—he rarely judged either warring party beyond their relative military abilities. On the last day of his diary, however, right after Rome was liberated, he had a few piercing words for Germany: "The grief and destructions she caused with her brutality are about to be paid back. I've been watching the viciousness of her soldiers for nine months. By now everybody hates them. They stripped and starved us" (June 8, 1944).

The personal diaries of Alemanno, Affricano-Marabini, and Di Pompeo reflect the authors' desire to engage with the realm of the private in order to isolate themselves from the ravages of an unforgiving and brutal war, if only temporarily. As a practice, writing a journal already requires carving out of one's daily routine the time and space to take distance from the outside world. In addition, by focusing on personal matters, journaling constitutes a validation of one's autonomy—it offers authors the ability to engage with a different set of priorities than the ones imposed by geopolitical necessities or institutional demands. In the instances of Alemanno, Affricano-Marabini, and Di Pompeo, keeping a diary, regardless of its content, helped them proclaim their right to be selfish in the face of enormous suffering. It allowed them to indulge in the small things ignored by the domain of History, such as love relationships and family affects. It also facilitated their responses against the continued state of emergency through affirming the primacy of personal interests. At the same time, no matter how much they strove to escape the demands of historical time or how far they were pushing their assertions of normalcy against all odds, Alemanno, Affricano-Marabini, and Di Pompeo depended on external forces for the resolution of intimate matters. Despite their attempts at contesting the political and separating themselves from it, their personal fate was inextricably interweaved with the larger situational context. Ignoring that link came to their peril. It threatened to nullify all their efforts toward exercising control over the precarity of existence—a control that could scarcely be achieved in the midst of a war where unruly routines were the norm.

Normalcy, Where Are Thou?

The devastating experiences of war and destruction often demanded the kind of emotional shield erected by Di Pompeo and others, a degree of insensitivity to the outer world as guarantee against succumbing to trauma. Building a psychological armor became eighteen-year-old A.G.'s necessary response to the facts she witnessed on August 12, 1944 on the hills near Lucca:

> Today was a terrible day worth of being called "bad" ("nera").
>
> I feel as if I had a fever so many facts have happened whose only thought horrifies me. This morning at dawn SS Germans climbed up to Capezzano, captured some civilians that were unwisely trying to return to their houses, both men and women.
>
> From the group of men, they selected ten who, once they arrived at a wood, were shot. As I'm writing, I hear the desperate, harrowing screams—they pierce one's heart—of a poor mother whose very young son was slaughtered and she saw with his head smashed. Then they say that some in Valdicastello were also murdered but we do not know if it is really true. A rumor also goes around that the small village of S. Anna was completely burned down like Farnocchia.

In a series of raids that culminated with the now infamous massacre of Sant'Anna di Stazzema, SS units had effectively committed the crimes mentioned by A.G.[2] Once she found confirmation of the facts the next day, she wished not to be alive:

> Today I am so demoralized that I almost envy the dead.
>
> We learned of certain things that make one cringe with horror. S. Anna was completely burned and the horrible thing is that the whole population died in it.
>
> A poor woman who lost a sister and niece there but managed by chance to save herself recounted things that possess the unbelievable.

---

[2] On the Sant'Anna massacre see Paolo Pezzino, *Memory and Massacre: Revisiting Sant'Anna di Stazzema* (New York: Palgrave Macmillan, 2012). According to Pezzino, only a small percentage of massacres (19.5 percent) were committed as reprisals for partisan actions. On the German politics of massacre see Michele Battini and Paolo Pezzino, *Guerra ai civili. Occupazione tedesca e politica del massacro. Toscana 1944* (Venice: Marsilio, 1997). The authors argue that massacres were part of the political and military strategies of the Wehrmacht. In Italy, the Germans followed the blueprint earlier applied to the occupied territories of Eastern Europe. Also see Carlo Gentile, *I crimini di guerra tedeschi in Italia 1943–1945* (Turin: Einaudi, 2015). On the particular structure of the German occupation in Italy see Lutz Klinkhammer, *L'occupazione tedesca in Italia 1943–1945* (Turin: Bollati Boringhieri, 1993), and chapter 8 for an overview of the fight against partisans.

Overtaken by the events, A.G. desperately tried to make sense of something that she found fundamentally unexplainable. Looking for reasons, she resolved to follow a legalistic logic—villagers failed to comply with the German order that had dictated evacuating the areas:

> At dusk, SS soldiers arrived there, started searching through houses, and found arms and clothes belonging to partisans, thus confirming their suspicions. They became enraged (indeed one can say that the partisans' headquarters were in S. Anna). [...]
>
> I really cannot understand why people didn't leave given that they received the same order of evacuation as us.
>
> If everybody complied like we did, today S. Anna would not be reduced into a cemetery.

A.G. attempted to rationalize the massacre by blaming it on the combination of two causes: people's failure to follow the rules and partisans' irresponsible meshing into village life.[3] Despite desperate efforts at explanation, however, she could not contain her horror. When she resumed writing on August 29, after days with no entries, she could not be more candid about her state of mind: "Over these days, no events occurred worse than in Sant'Anna. /That famous day I suffered such a big shock that now I feel I have become so hard I almost frighten myself; I remain indifferent to everything, I don't feel either pain or joy any longer, I feel I'm living like an automaton."

Unspeakable occurrences numbed A.G. to the point of nonrecognition; she needed to be desensitized totally in order to overcome suffering.[4] As time went by, her diary notes expressed a desire for normalcy. She focused on mundane interactions as occasions through which to re-engage with the surrounding reality and gain back her older sense of self. Hence, we read about peaceful scenes of German soldiers playing the accordion, joining in a chorus, and inviting girls to dance (September 13, 1944). On another instance we hear the story of one German soldier who helped A.G.'s family in their chores, even serving food. His parents and sister were dead, and A.G. empathized,

---

[3] To this day, resentment against partisans is still felt in another place of German massacre, Civitella della Chiana. See Giovanni Contini, *La memoria divisa* (Milan: Rizzoli, 1997). On that massacre see Leonardo Paggi ed., *Storia e memoria di un massacro ordinario* (Rome: Manifestolibri, 1996).

[4] On victims' reaction to traumatic events see Ronnie Janoff-Bulman, *Shattered Assumptions (Towards a New Psychology of Trauma)* (New York: Free Press, 1992). On trauma and narrative accounts see Jane Robinett, "The Narrative Shape of Traumatic Experience," *Literature and Medicine* vol. 26, no. 2 (Fall 2007): pp. 290–311; Jean-François Chiantaretto, *Écritures de soi et trauma* (Paris: Anthropos, 1998); Arnaud Tellier, *Expériences traumatiques et écriture* (Paris: Antrhopos, 1998).

"I was sorry because he seemed truly nice" (September 17, 1944). She built her emotional strength on scenes of domesticity—ideals of simple pastimes and sociality—no matter that those young soldiers were part of an army that was brutalizing the country. Her mental sanity required humanness, an openness to others that was based on overcoming divisions, especially those of the kind that leads to a fight to death. She prayed, "Oh my God, I wish nobody would die on one side or the other, unfortunately it is impossible" (September 19, 1944). A.G. was no fool and knew the gravity of war—the massacre of Sant'Anna had taught her that much. Nevertheless, because everyday reality was so ugly, she also seemed willing to hang on to those few idyllic moments that miraculously appeared to suspend wartime. She wished life to return to an appearance of normalcy, in whichever way one could define it. For many Italians, that normalcy was rooted in the concrete foundations of "home."

Home and peace

Although not every Italian confronted the traumatic experience lived by A.G., the all-around horror of war and German occupation were difficult to endure even for those, such as Anna Menestrina, who decided to keep a diary simply in order to bear witness. Like Di Pompeo, Menestrina followed the news assiduously to keep up with her task of chronicling (she also correlated her diary with newspaper clippings for supplementary evidence). Like Di Pompeo, however, she was a reluctant witness to the unfolding events of the time and wished to get away from it all: "Occasionally we get *L'Avvenire*. But it would be truly better not to read newspapers any longer. To be able to close one's eyes and reopen them the day of peace!" (November 25, 1943). Menestrina dreamed of a world where one did not have to worry about the next tragic news, a world where life could return to some kind of regularity. Deeply religious, she confided in God (and the Madonna) as the ultimate hope for breaking the impasse caused by human unwillingness to stop the conflict. This was a meager consolation considering that the war had lasted for years and had transformed people's lives in more than one way, bringing with it a string of miseries. Menestrina's detailed account of daily activities (especially of women) in and around Trento soberly conveys the harsh situations people faced. Her interjections condense, often in just one sentence, the collective sorrow: "For everybody life is hard with this war that doesn't want to end" (November 26, 1943). "Tears and pain everywhere. All darkness!" (November 29, 1943). "It's almost hard to think in the face of so many ruins"

(February 5, 1944). Or as she simply summarized it on January 1, 1944, "The year that is about to begin is year of war."

War prevailed over any other ill. It magnified pain to the highest degree and made it impossible for one to find a sense of stability; it also defied the laws of progress and the promises of a better future. Aerial bombings, in particular, distorted people's perceptions of safety and elevated impermanence to a universal condition, besides sowing terror and fear. "Today we heard airplanes…" Menestrina's entry of January 8, 1944 read. That was all she wrote for that day—no need for more words. Being displaced from one's home added an especially grave element to the number of disruptions. The abandoned home was where everybody left their hearts. In Menestrina's case, her family had vacated Trento for the nearby countryside in early September 1943. They remained away from the city for almost two years in the hope of avoiding the worst (Figure 3). But not even the idyllic landscape of mountainous Trentino offered guarantees of safety—aerial raids spared no one, and food scarcity was simply inescapable. By fall 1944, the bombings in the area increased in frequency and intensity. While Rome and Florence were liberated, the people of Trentino's agonizing wait for the war's end took nearly another year. Over that time, the thought of returning home in Trento sustained Menestrina in the same way that the hope of rejoining their loved ones helped Alemanno and Di Pompeo relieve their obsessive worries over the unpredictable fate of war. Differently from them, however, Menestrina did not eagerly await liberation. Indeed, there are no direct references to "liberation" in her diary and no mention of the Anglo-Americans as saviors either. On the contrary, Menestrina deemed their offensive destructive. As she commented on July 18, 1944, "The invasion of Europe continues."

Unfavorably disposed towards the Allied forces, Menestrina avoided taking sides (including on fascism). She however followed the Church's official view on the world conflict, which focused on promoting the neutral values of fraternity and reconciliation.[5] By continuously appealing to the more generic term "peace," she bypassed judgments on the political and moral questions raised by the war, including the critical issue of ending Nazi-fascism. Peace became her refrain—almost a religious belief, but also her lifeline—the only objective that could alleviate her mental and physical fatigue and guarantee a long-sought return home. "St. Luigi today but this morning I can't even go to

---

[5] In accordance with the Church's orientation, fear of the Russians featured prominently in Menestrina's accounts. Rumors of Sicilian children sent to the Soviet Union circulated widely at the time.

Figure 3. Trento, May 14, 1944. Bombed city ruins. Fondazione Museo storico del Trentino, Album Pontalti.

church. I feel truly sick. /However, if tomorrow peace came, I believe I would immediately heal," she wrote on June 21, 1944. A few weeks later she insisted, "And soon peace will come, yes it will come. It's not an illusion. It's faith in that suppliant omnipotence whose gentleness the Madonna let us experience many times" (July 6, 1944). Peace promised to rejuvenate the world and breathe new life into the faithful.

Alas, Menestrina's wishes did not materialize. Nevertheless, and regardless of the setbacks, she continued to expect a positive outcome. Months later, on her mother's eighty-sixth birthday, she fantasized that a true celebration "would be to tell her: There is peace! We go back home!" (November 14, 1944). Home was where the general and the particular well-being met, it was where Menestrina's inner peace could thrive, it was the reason she fought to remain alive. With her mother suddenly passing away in December 1944, she did not feel like keeping a diary any longer: "What for? She, for whom I was writing it in the hope she could read it in the comfort of her home, is gone forever! And she will never return home. [...] My God! What a pain losing her in this way, far from our home, amidst the horrors of the war that never ends!..." (December 30, 1944). In Menestrina's thinking, peace—a universal ideal—allowed normalcy to prevail. It recentered the good around everyday existence and family life, one's individual hearth.

While unceasing bombings and continuously deteriorating conditions tested Menestrina's resilience during the last months of 1944 and early 1945, the fate of the family home in Trento remained at the core of her concerns, even if she realized that the survival of the structure did not ensure that life would revert to normal. Once the war ended, and as she arranged to leave her countryside dwelling, Menestrina was especially aware that things had profoundly changed: "We are working to pack and prepare everything for our departure. We are so, so tired. And we feel great sadness at the thought of returning home without mother…" (July 20, 1945). Home, so much longed for, would not be the same—Italy's wounds reflected in one's own personal losses. With a last goodbye to her mother's resting place at the local cemetery, Menestrina mourned, "How painful to leave her here! She so much desired to return to her house" (July 21, 1945). The last bastion of emotional stability against the uncontainable madness of the outside world, "home" as it turns out did not remain unscathed in the mayhem unleashed by an unforgiving war.

A house down on the plain

For twenty-year-old Irene Paolisso, the experience of losing home was especially agonizing. With the war at their door, the family evacuated to the nearby mountains in early September, leaving their small town of Formia behind. Watching over the town from the height of their new shelter, they feared for their house's fate but felt a sense of reassurance by the mere fact of being able to keep an eye on it. Such was the comfort they drew from this visual connection that they remained in the area, moving from one bad accommodation to another, even when wisdom would suggest otherwise. Three months into their peregrinations, Irene observed:

> Many people are already heading to Rome. We still believe that leaving would be like betraying ourselves, declaring ourselves defeated, weak, inept […].
>
> And nevertheless, there is still a persisting hope that motivates us to go on another day, and another day, and another: that house down in the plain, whether standing or ruined it doesn't matter. But we see it, we caress it with our eyes and with our persistent thinking.
>
> War did not manage to eradicate this profound love for home, so old and still the same. In contrast, if we went elsewhere, what would we have that is ours, real, concrete?   (December 12, 1943)

The ideal of home, with its imagined features of domestic bliss, safety, and tranquility, became for many a way to counteract the overall despair and gloom of the biennium 1943–45, even though quiet life was an oxymoronic ideal—"normal" and yet so hard to attain. With a poetic inclination, Paolisso reflected on these matters when bombs began falling in her area at the end of summer 1943: "Here is the war, we begin to know it firsthand. And still, we keep going with almost normal gestures, acts, and thoughts. And I'm surprised. The same trains go by, at the same time, very crowded: and I keep watching them from the window, while they continue to take away a part of me, every single time" (September 6, 1943). Paolisso highlighted the uncanny feeling she drew from observing the ostensible continuity of normalcy during times that were nothing but extraordinary. Despite marveling at the idiosyncrasy, she hung on to what was the mere appearance of regularity. Months later, when she witnessed the German army destroy the railway tracks that held such symbolic value for her, she was crushed: "On those tracks, for a good eighteen years, I projected every second of my life and the very meaning of it. On them sped the trains of my desires. There will always be a train in the real world for me; and the train tracks will be the natural way towards the future and beyond. I can't imagine anything else." (December 16, 1943).

For Paolisso, normalcy made it possible to envision the present as well as what was yet to come; it allowed her to define her approach to existence. Refusing to forgo life as she knew it, she wanted to hold on to past habits and traditions—markers of a reality one could give up only at one's peril. "To take shelter in the normalcy of the past is becoming my habit, a natural need, a safety valve," she confessed (November 13, 1943). Aware that the time she longed for was not devoid of problems, she felt relief in thinking of it as familiar and regular; she expected everything to return the way it was. Most importantly, memory of past habits sustained her willingness to not give up in moments of grave suffering, such as at the end of 1943 when she reminisced about the previous new year's eves:

> Is it going to rain until this evening, tomorrow, and forever in order to cleanse the world of any traces of normalcy, in order to wipe from the face of the earth every person that still has memory of past well-being and of trust in others?
>
> But I do need to find shelter in the past, such as when I was setting the table with the embroidered linen tablecloth that smelled like out of the trunk [...].
>
> I need to feel again the same unique emotion when turning on the lamp of special occasions, all blue with the white shade [...].
>
> No, I can't become too estranged from this reality that is so true, the only reality one can live. To escape it to the point of losing touch with it might be too big a risk.

With the war persisting and people's misery growing ever more unbearable, Paolisso's crisis deepened. In a surprising turnaround, she almost wished not to remember the way things were before. As she told her brother at the end of winter 1944, after her family moved to a sheep stable higher up the mountains:

> Nino dear, if you knew how much anguish and how much dismay we accrued in the course of these months of life away from normalcy: it's as if we were dead and then reborn without forgetting the existence we previously spent. It would be easier to adapt if nobody reminded us that there existed and still exist values through which one can still acquire well-being and tranquility, possibly until death comes equally for all.   (March 1, 1944)

Because people were living in inhumane, primitive conditions, Paolisso felt it might be better to forget one's humanness—exceptional times required novel skills:

> Meanwhile, imagine us locked up for days on end in this more than cramped hut for sheep, twelve of us, so hungry that we are speechless and bitter to the point of hating whoever we can think of that might have better chances to satisfy their hunger.

Imagine, dear, a herd with no shepherd, no pasture, at the mercy of wolves, on the gray rocks of these naked mountains: this is us. (March 1, 1944)

With life reduced to its barest, no semblance of normalcy appeared recognizable. Once her family finally decided to depart the area at the end of March (with the hope of making it to Rome) and ended up in a refugee camp run by the Germans, Irene found herself responding to a young male friend flirting with her: "Scraps of normality, dear brother, under a sky that is uncertain and always full of risks" (April 6, 1944). Digging their way out of the grim reality imposed by war, sentiments and affects still emerged—free, spontaneous expressions of people's humanity or of what humans were supposed to be. As things stood, Irene could not avoid her attraction for "normal" feelings and emotions. Yet in an ironic reversal of situations, other people's normalcy offended her as a blatant denial of her unspeakable suffering. After her family eventually vacated the camp and reached their relatives in Rome, Irene confessed to her sibling, "I cannot hide, my brother, that I felt a certain sense of resentment mixed in with deep astonishment at the apparent normalcy with which they live here, everybody staying in their own home, among their usual furnishings and objects, with no sign of deprivation whatsoever" (April 9, 1944).

In truth, and contrary to Irene's claims, Romans did not fare well under the occupation—like most in Italy, especially in the South, they suffered from food shortages and daily roundups by the Germans, in addition to aerial bombings.[6] Irene, however, was thinking of another kind of normalcy. What especially upset her was seeing people in their home—something that as a "sfollata" (an evacuee) she had been forced to abandon months before.[7] To her, the gulf between her extreme experience and the apparent normal life of her relatives felt like a cognitive dissonance, two different realities facing each other in spite of sharing the common situation of wartime. Home and domesticity were lost to the "sfollati." And the sense of displacement Irene suffered from having to leave her house was deepened by the condition of being an "evacuee" and, especially, being labeled one. "In this little village hidden behind the hill we too are not but strangers, the 'evacuees' (sfollati), the have nots," she wrote in the early stage of her displacement (September 11, 1943).

---

[6] On the situation in Rome and the South see the volume by Nicola Gallerano ed., L'altro dopoguerra. Roma e il Sud 1943–1945 (Milan: Franco Angeli, 1985), especially Sezione Prima.

[7] On the "sfollati" see Elena Cortesi, Sfollati, profughi, evacuati. L'italia nella Seconda Guerra Mondiale (Pisa: Pacini Editore, 2022). For memories of the experience see Alessandro Portelli, "Assolutamente niente. L'esperienza degli sfollati a Terni," in Nicola Gallerano ed., L'altro dopoguerra, pp. 135–44.

A closed community deeply suspicious of outsiders, locals resented the newly arrived for breaking the "normalcy" of the place, the unspoken rules of habitual coexistence. Fearful of the evacuees, they guarded their belongings and buried all their goods. In this climate of unspoken tension, it was inevitable that violence would explode. Irene witnessed it in all its dramatic intensity:

> Do not curse us, you who will come after us, if you will get to know that a brother has killed a brother: he was not aware, he did not intend to. None of us is a saint, and it wouldn't make any sense to be one in these moments. It's fear that makes us remain unresponsive: those who have courage react, but often it's madness that gives courage.
>
> Yes, it happened that a villager shot an evacuee at the end of a quarrel: too tight a spring eventually will snap. One cannot be obsessing for three months, all the time with our arms folded, that is, one cannot let oneself die without reacting. And for the villager, who was the evacuee that dared to defy him, and for the evacuee, who was the villager that denied him his own, and does it make any sense today to say it's mine, it's not yours?
>
> (November 18, 1943)

Paolisso did not explain the minutest details of the episode, although one can guess them, but we know that by the time she wrote that entry, the anxiety caused by the unmet hope for the arrival of the Allied forces had been mounting in the area. As she put it, "In this interminable wait anything can happen. Our brains could explode too, breaking the limits of our endurance."

Insanity by Reason of Indifference

Having been deprived of the stability of a regular permanent dwelling, evacuees suffered more than physical mutilation or property damage. They also lost their equilibrium—a center of gravity. It was hard to maintain mental balance in a situation defined by temporariness and danger.[8] An overwhelmed Angelo Peroni described the fragility of his condition after attempting to rescue remnants from the ruins of his family apartment destroyed during the bombings

---

[8] Di Pompeo is very effective in portraying the difficulties of impermanence even for those still living in their homes. He recounts how traffic from the periphery to the center of Rome was a daily occurrence, with people carrying their belongings on trolleys, kids in tow, and headed towards parks and open spaces even in the middle of winter. Romans believed that the city center would be spared from attacks.

of Milan on August 12 and 13, 1943.[9] While moving around collapsed buildings, he felt no fear for his physical safety, but was instead assailed by a sense of despair at what he saw:

> No danger scares me, because I'm not afraid to die.
>
> Perhaps, it would be better to die than to live in this horrible world!
>
> Milan is not anymore, there is not one street that has not been gravely hit. Everywhere houses turned into dust or emptied by flames, everywhere dead that cannot even be buried [...]. When one witnesses the spectacles of people fleeing on their bikes with children, mattresses, and pillows, looking to sleep in a meadow under a mulberry tree; of hungry people weeping as they stretch out their arms for a piece of bread; of children screaming and pleading—such spectacles of destruction and death—one remains so despondent and cannot but cry and wish for death.   (August 22, 1943)

Lasting images of absolute misery after the terrible bombardment in Milan prostrated the young Peroni. That same destruction also left an indelible mark on Magda Ceccarelli De Grada, who added tales of utter madness and despair to Peroni's desolate depiction of urban and human devastation:

> I've heard a wild-eyed man screaming, "Let's burn them, let's burn them all, Mussolini and his family, like our houses are burning! At the stake, at the stake!"
>
> On the trolley a woman appeared to have gone mad: she tore away the rags covering her skinny chest, insulted the king, and insulted the government as bystanders assented. Only one person said, getting off, "Stop it!" but he was deluged with screams.   (August 20, 1943)

The massive movement of people and things caused by the war had disrupted rhythms and regularities and affected the nature of human interactions, besides transforming one's personal outlook. Normalcy almost felt like a contradiction, an unreal jolting experience. Ceccarelli De Grada described her own incongruous feelings in summer 1943, as she juggled life under Anglo-American bombings:

---

[9] On the bombing in Milan see Achille Rastelli, *Bombe sulla città. Gli attacchi alleati. Le vittime civili a Milano* (Milan: Mursia, 2000) and Marco Gioannini and Giulio Massobrio, *Bombardate l'Italia. Storia della guerra di distruzione aerea, 1940–1945* (Milan: Rizzoli, 2007).

We sleep in Monza. I feel much less safe than in Milan in Piazza Fiume. To see this clean little town, with orderly stores where one can shop, feels miraculous. I am rested for the first time after many days. There are quiet lights at dawn and dusk. Is there still a life that is not danger, misery, rags, ruins and where everything is not provisional and terribly tiring? (August 26, 1943)

Struck by the "miraculous" normalcy of a little haven not far from the city, Ceccarelli De Grada experienced welcome relief. At the same time, however, she found life in Monza almost artificial, its regularity out of place, even dangerous—it made her feel more at risk than in bombed-out Milan. For Ceccarelli De Grada, a sense of uncanniness emerged out of small moments in the rhythm of everyday life, as when in anticipation of Germans' raids in early September 1943 she cleared her little beach house of all things she held dear: "Still another tiring move, baggage, disorder. Life has lost every sense of kindness and harmony" (September 16, 1943). Impermanence, her note suggested, threatened one's small universe. Back in Milan, her sorrow stemmed from losing the network of personal relationships, the familiar circle of friends with which she used to socialize and that was dissipating as many joined the Resistance and went underground. With her children active in the opposition movement and herself an eager participant, Ceccarelli De Grada still felt that life was being mined at its core. When yet another friend left the city, she confessed, "There is not one day that doesn't bring some sadness" (September 29, 1943). Longing for small things—those that in the past might have appeared unimportant, taken for granted, and unappreciated—was the direct result of one's current sense of turmoil. A desire for stability, no matter how unrealistic, prevailed amidst the chaos.

In times of extraordinary uncertainty, ordinariness was a rare, sought-after commodity. Simple life inspired good feelings and reinstated personal relationships at the center of one's world. Presently, however, the exceptional was turning into the norm, or the new normal, in a cliché expression. It was replacing older and more familiar interpretive frameworks while inexorably tinting people's worldviews. Fortunato Favai recognized this state of facts in early fall 1943. Against all conflicting signs, and seemingly in denial, yet also aware of the paradox, he affirmed the idiosyncratic power of regularity:

Life would follow its normal rhythm if there wasn't the war with its painful consequences, which are getting ever more complicated and taking root, gradually, slowly, as if wanting to form in the spirit of the oppressed a habit, a premise of resignation to new, ever new and harder trials. As a matter of fact, the first inconveniences have become habitual, one accepts them by now as something that has always been there and will continue to be. The ration cards, pasta, and the bread, that is dark and small, mandatory blackouts and curfews, the fatal news of gruesome fights, of annihilating bombardments, everything comes to be absorbed by now with some kind of apathy, a certain indifference, precisely as if all these things had existed in continuity for years and practically depended on a superior and insolvent force. In the same way that the soldier fighting on the battlefields after a while remains indifferent to the fall, the death, of his comrade, so today's humanity begins to remain indifferent to the fresh drama in which it is locked. (October 15, 1943)

For Favai, the realization that something critical was being lost in the process appeared even more consequential: "In spite of all this, an incessant, exhausting grueling work takes place within the human soul; the microbe unobtrusively gnaws at its vital parts and destroys them. What's there more to say? How to find a treatment that would put an end to the terrible disease that has affected living beings and things everywhere?" He had no answer, or better he took a quasi-fatalistic attitude about humanity, convinced as he was that one could not but wait for "the last phase of the contagion" to be running its course and hope to learn a lesson for the future.

That disease of indifference to which Favai alluded affected Manilio Tartarini. Terrified at the prospect of the brutality Hitler's armies could unleash if matters did not evolve in their favor, Tartarini seemingly adjusted to fear and was surprised at his own blasé reactions: "I ask myself how it is possible to continue living in this state of mind!...The mere fact of writing with indifference about these things, in the same way that I could describe a walk in the moonlight, leads me to think that I too like others have become insane" (November 9, 1943). Strolling in the streets of Milan just days after the armistice, Ester Marozzi similarly expressed, "Indifference, as if the city was not living the war, is the absurd phenomenon that I am witnessing these memorable days" (September 13, 1943). Whether struck by people's unresponsiveness or merely feeling the meaninglessness of life, Marozzi noted that one continued as if everything was normal, as if there was not a war and an occupation. With the Germans roaming throughout the city, "the crowd goes about its business in a big hurry, doesn't even turn around to look, as if running towards a destination with no spare time to look around."

Uncertainty was turning people into automatons, or at the minimum it made them feel that way—something was deeply out of sync. In one of her daily "missives" to husband Luigi, Wanda Affricano-Marabini appeared to lament the waning of human values and dignity as she informed him of a neighbor's death: "Yesterday lawyer Strani, down below, died: can you believe it that one almost feels envious of these that are getting out of worries and know they will have their proper burial, while we could be bombed here any moment or massacred who knows how and after how much pain!" (November 14, 1943). Death as the conclusion of a natural biological cycle ensured decency, while the randomness of life in times of war threatened the integrity of personhood and undermined the fundamental rules of humanness. Burial rituals are, after all, one of the things that distinguishes us from the animal realm.[10] Exposed, unmarked corpses signal the collapse of "civilization," the dissolution of the line separating the sacred from the profane—an ultimate sign of the triumph of bare life. And yet even death was losing its aura of respect in the disrupted normalcy. Although Anna Menestrina kept quoting from the scriptures, "Blessed are the dead!" the bliss she evoked was vacuous.[11] And Caterina Gaggero Viale pragmatically (or profanely) wondered about the fate of the deceased: "Today is the day of the Dead and the thought we send them, even from home, is one that makes us sincerely desire to be dead ourselves. At least we would not be suffering any longer! I wonder whether their bones are still in the tombs or they blew up." (November 2, 1944). The same unemotional nonchalance was remarked by Irene Paolisso in the little village outside Formia:

> Meanwhile deaths are occurring ever more frequently here, and not only because of war accidents. The coffins, made of a few disjointed boards, are carried on the shoulder but with no followers. One hardly cries over a natural death any longer, one does not have the time nor the will to respect mourning, a luxury of normal times.   (October 22, 1943)

In the aberrant reality of war, the rules of normalcy had changed. So had the experiences that comprised people's daily life. Incessant bombings, endless wait for the Allies, inevitably unsatisfied hunger, in addition to continuous impermanence as people searched for safer locations, were the new norm.

Exceptional Normalcy

Once infrequent, cohabitation with risk, but also adjustment to desolating situations, became regular features of Italians' life, embedded within one's daily rhythms, almost unremarked and yet devastatingly distressing. The

---

[10] "Human" is etymologically linked to the Latin "humare" (inter) from "humus" (ground).
[11] See, for example, entries of October 15 and December 30, 1944 and January 5, 1945.

desire for normalcy paradoxically led to accepting as ordinary the exceptional reality of war and terror. As Carlo Chevallard noted, in retrospect "it will seem impossible that one could have kept going in such conditions."[12] But people did. Human adaptability, he concluded, was infinite. Meanwhile, shelled and starved, Italians tried to avoid going insane as they continued to hope for the return of peace and longed for a conclusion to their insufferable pain.

Shelling doom

Maria Alemanno was jaded after observing yet another bombing in Florence:

> The number of dead from the most recent raid is close to three hundred [...]. I didn't see anything because it's not a spectacle to watch, like many people do who take their walk to poke around. But I too have become a bit cold and careless, only thinking about saving my skin, the firm, and seeing him again. This is not very nice, but certainly what is happening every day doesn't help soften one's heart. (September 30, 1943)

In Bologna, A.M. confessed, "I'm devastated, I wish I would die immediately not to see anything any longer, not to witness, desperate and impotent, everything that passes before my eyes every day" (August 16, 1943). (And we know the worst in Bologna had yet to happen.) As anxiety filled people's days, Mario Tutino was especially wary of emotional deadness. In early September 1943, he recounted his sense of frustration upon returning to an emptied-out Milan following a heavy bombing:

> I'm here, more alone than ever. And not in the material sense, knowing that there is no life for a wide range around me, but because spiritually everything is beyond my reach. I feel as if every sentiment or family and friendship ties are dead. Any thoughts and feelings of affection are incommunicable.
>
> It is the tiredness of these days. And perhaps it is having suffered, in worthless thoughts, at the daily spectacle of this infinite misery, which one would

---

[12] "Diario di Carlo Chevallard 1942–1945," edited by Riccardo Marchis, in *Torino in guerra tra cronaca e memoria*, edited by Rosanna Roccia and Giorgio Vaccarino, with a Preface by Alessandro Galante Garrone (Turin: Archivio Storico della Città di Torino, 1975), p. 279 (entry of July 27, 1944).

wish to alleviate but in actuality is personally unable to and does not even know who could.   (September 4, 1943)

Whether or not one was under the threat of bombings, the mere fact of not knowing what the immediate future held caused enormous stress. Ester Marozzi recounted the harrowing experience of waiting for the raids:

> 1:40 am and I am very anxious. From midnight to 2:00 am is the critical time of waiting, generally 1 or 2 is when the RAF arrives. If it's past 2:30, it's less probable that they come, or at least until today they never conducted raids at sunrise.
>
> As long as I live, I will hear in my ears and in my soul the howls of enemy airplanes passing over our heads with the speed of a meteor and the eerie hissing of the bombs followed by the enormous crash after the explosion.
> (August 11, 1943)

People's relationship to the day was governed by the prospect of aerial raids, the coming and going of threats, the calculation of risks in going about one's daily chores. From his residence in Modena, fifty-six-year-old Sicilian E.R. took solace in the absence of bombings for one day, despite worrying about her native land, as well as the ferociousness of the war and the fate of her military sons: "My God! My God! No sirens—quiet night" (August 18, 1943). Living in anticipation of aerial raids felt overwhelming to Anna Menestrina: "The thought of bombardments is like a scary nightmare that grips us all with anguish" (November 24, 1943). Could one avoid that tension? The paucity of effective answers pained Wanda Affricano-Marabini: "For now everything is quiet, again, but...for how long? And then who knows how much longer we'll go on with this slow dying!!!...When will all this end?!..." (November 14, 1943). Uncertainty killed. Concetta Bucciano recognized the predicament early on. After the bombing of San Lorenzo in Rome, she thought back nostalgically to times of peace as the current precarity deprived her of the semblance of security that comes with predictability:

> Now everything is anguish and pain, and because of the uncertain tomorrow one lives hour by hour, never sure of getting up in the morning, never sure of going to bed in the evening. Oh, where is that blissful time of peace and quiet, when even despite the thousands of life's small adversities one could sit quietly in one's favorite corner at home, with a work or a book in one's hands, or peacefully converse with a friend?   (July 19, 1943)

As bombings intensified and insecurity reigned supreme, even alterations of sounds caused anxiety. "The cannon is quiet," Di Pompeo remarked as he despaired over the war quagmire (February 5, 1944). Silence being a casualty of the raucous conflict, its sudden reappearance triggered an unnerving experience. Ester Marozzi described the discomfiting feeling that invaded her when all around was quiet: "The silence is striking these nights in the streets of Milan. Not one light, not one noise, a terrible menace hovers on the city. […]. The silence of nighttime is tragic" (August 24, 1943). Rather than offering reassurance, the rare occasions of tranquility raised concerns—they disrupted the new normalcy of the state of emergency. What might peacefulness hold? Anxiety prevailed, as Gaggero Viale, who was long habituated to the clamor of war, reveals: "Last night and today too, absolute quiet. It doesn't even feel to be in a war. But we are not calm at all because we fear some unpleasant surprise" (October 7, 1944). Considering the highly volatile reality, expectations of the worst had become a fateful habit, a guarantee against false chimeras. One could not but be engulfed by a sense of continuous, impending doom.

Breathing without living

In this situation of permanent fear, the extenuating wait for the Allied forces' arrival felt like an eternity. Manilio Tartarini, who followed closely the war bulletins, was initially confident that the Anglo-Americans would promptly kick out the Germans, but was soon led to admit, "Heavens, this darn landing of the English somewhere in Italy makes us wait!" (November 8, 1943) For his own well-being (he was trying to avoid enrolling in the new fascist party while holding on to his job as town clerk), a quick resolution was critical. Things, however, did not quite go the way he wished. On November 19, he sadly reported, "They say that the English are retreating." Having tied his own fate to the Allied forces' advance, Tartarini's stress mounted; he kept hoping that it would only be a question of days. Months later, he was still waiting. Meanwhile, his not-too-distant neighbor Perla Cacciaguerra found the pressure of waiting unbearable. She especially agonized over the consequences of the Anglo-Americans' arrival for her family due to her father's fascist allegiance. By early June 1944, she burst out, "I am not reading, I'm not working, I wander around the house like a restless soul only wishing for one thing: the end of this torment that is oppressing me. Whatever is meant to happen it'd better happen immediately, because this way one does not live any longer, one merely vegetates" (June 3, 1944).

A significant source of anxiety, waiting was a torment, "Tantalus' torture," as Irene Paolisso described it (September 19, 1943). Day in and day out, rumors about the Allied forces' position fueled expectations. Any sound heard from afar became a sign of the long-anticipated advance. Irene was alert to these little holders of hope, and when nothing could be heard, she worried at the lack of progress: "The calm oppresses us" (October 2, 1943). People's relation to silence was fine-tuned, as in divination practices whose interpretation foretells the good or bad nature of the omen. Over time, with angst and tension rising, disappointment became much harder to take:

> In this unnerving wait everything can deceive us. No noise has a reason for being unless it is for what we want it to be. For example, for a long time we mistook a grinder for the echo of a faraway battle, and this fed in us an empty hope. When we finally realized the mistake, we were about to cry like disappointed children. (November 24, 1943)

The fantasy of an imminent arrival—a dream unfailingly killed—particularly vexed the expectant population, who found the slow pace of the Allied forces heartless. "The imperturbability of the 'liberators' crushes us," Irene Paolisso noted (December 18, 1943). Eventually, she came to realize that "in war a few kilometers might amount to an enormous distance" (January 12, 1944). It was a grinding process.

Corrado Di Pompeo had to learn that lesson. When he started his diary on October 30, 1943, he expected the Allied forces to arrive in Rome at least by Christmas of that year. In actuality, they only reached the capital in June 1944, those months of wait weighing heavily on Corrado's sanity. The slowness of the Anglo-American forces compounded the degree of his despair and incessantly tested his ability to be resilient. With relentless reports about the troops' "baby steps," his diary entries continued to post updates on arrival prospects to no avail. Not only did the anticipated Christmas deadline turn out to be ephemeral, but all calculations inevitably crashed: "Saturday, January 15, 1944. No news today. Everything is normal, and waiting is ever more intense. When will the English arrive?" With liberation appearing ever more elusive, Corrado's wait assumed the dimensions of a Beckett play, with a Godot that never seemed to materialize: war was not abating. In early March 1944, as Rome continued to be vexed by alarms and bombings, he complained, "I'm tired and disheartened by this life of waiting" (March 2, 1944). To counteract the discouragement of unfulfilled desires, Di Pompeo erected an emotional armor around himself. He wished to be preserved from the frustration of unsatisfied projections, even if he kept holding on to hope—the thought of his family remaining his single steady source of emotional support: "My sweet Antonietta, I want to be strong, I want and must resist, but sometimes I feel broken, crashed" (February 3, 1944). The incessant seesaw between anticipations and disappointments produced misery and sorrow and made it impossible to escape the ever-growing sense of defeat.

In this dismal scenario, it was hard not to succumb to a fatalistic perspective. Irene Paolisso struggled to preserve her mental stability under the condition of displacement, all the while lamenting the absence of community among the nonreactive evacuees. When they all gathered in the village church on a Sunday morning, she noted little social solidarity: "Only a few know each other, many ignore each other, almost all are gloomy, surly, guarded" (December 5, 1943). She wondered how the future would look back on them, on the "tedium, this civil death, this breathing without living that makes us crazy, vicious, ruthless toward one another" (December 18, 1943). She found no redeeming features emerging out of the evacuees' common status of misery and powerlessness. Forced cohabitation produced no good fruits. In search of balance, and as the only resource for upholding normalcy, Irene relied on her diary—a luxury in the eyes of others. How could one write in the middle of mayhem? And yet the alternative to writing was not necessarily active engagement but, instead, retrenchment, if not apathy. Journaling allowed one to connect with history and show vigilance; it constituted an act of testimonial. It also proved that one was still spiritually alive.

In contrast, even air-raid alarms failed to shake people's dejectedness. Like bombings, alarms had become casual everyday occurrences. From Rome to Turin, diarists reported having become so used to sirens that they no longer cared about them, nor did the rest of the population. Indeed, some of the bombardments' highest casualties resulted from failure to reach shelters. As suggested by Caterina Gaggero Viale, indifference characterized locals' response to warnings of the approaching danger: "These days big bombings on Padova, Verona, Bologna, and Florence. Here the night alarms started again, but we don't even notice them" (March 22, 1944). By the summer, war would strike hard in her area, though. With intensified shelling, she and fellow villagers abandoned their houses and fled to more secure refuges.

Gnawing hunger

Unsatisfied yearnings for peace were accompanied by an equally unmet need for physical sustenance. Being hungry was a stable feature of the war experience, and many a diarist obsessively listed details of the escalating costs of food as evidence of the immeasurable distance separating the current exceptional situation from the normalcy of the past.[13] Bread, sugar, and eggs were now prohibitive items, not to mention meat. With a soaring black market, few could even afford the basics.[14] South of Milan, Don Luigi Serravalle highlighted the predicament while hinting at the hiatus between people's priorities and war developments: "One hears much contradictory news. Instead, people seem more worried about food and think about the future" (September 11, 1943). The days ahead looked bleak. By the end of the year, Leone Fioravanti described the people of Schio as "gradually falling prey to apathy," and ever more so because of the persistent food problem (December 15, 1943).

Not simply responsible for undermining physical survival, hunger represented an existential condition that impacted one's relationship to life. It was an inescapable daily reality. As Paolisso saw it, "Hunger is becoming the common affliction. It nestles in every pore of our body and occupies all the spaces of our brain, it is the thought of thoughts, a fearful specter unknown until now" (September 12, 1943). Hunger was an obsessive, ravaging evil that Irene combated by chewing carobs, abundant in the area. Whereas only donkeys and horses used to feed on them, at present nothing else was left for the evacuees to consume: "Meanwhile we only chew carobs, from morning to evening, we only chew carobs. Even in the dark one can hear the teeth chewing in an attempt to tamper the pangs of hunger" (November 4, 1943). At the end of March 1944, close to starvation, Irene's family initiated a desperate march towards Rome. Six days into their trip, exhausted and helpless in the middle of the countryside, they willingly consigned their fate to oncoming German trucks. As Irene revealed, "We didn't hide, we didn't want to think of the worst, only pushed by the urgent need to be taken where one could finally eat, at whatever cost" (April 5, 1944). The family had long passed the limit of human endurance and dignity.[15]

---

[13] Emanuele Baldi, the grandson of Leo Baldi, has drawn from his grandfather's diary a summary description of the difficulties of surviving during the biennium 1943–45. A very precise account, he has condensed it in a privately printed booklet, "Quando un uovo costava un euro. Le condizioni di vita di una famiglia romana dall'occupazione alla fine della guerra (settembre 1943–maggio 1945)." I am grateful to him and his family for sharing that material with me.

[14] The black market was a reality both in the North and in the South. On its role in Rome in terms of its social consequences see Toto Lombardo, "Il mercato nero a Roma," in Gallerano ed., *L'altro dopoguerra*, pp. 181–90.

[15] It should be pointed out that the food situation varied across the Italian territory. It was much worse in the South, even if liberated, as all goods were much less available there. Nicola Gallerano talks of "terrible winters for liberated Italy" in 1944 and 1945, with the population "kept well below the bare minimum for survival." Conditions were worse in the cities, and in liberated Rome more than in Naples. Compared with the occupied North, cost of living in August 1944 increased tenfold in Milan but twenty-nine times in Rome. The middle classes were especially hit. See Gallerano ed., *L'altro dopoguerra*, pp. 39, 40. In his diary, Chevallard comments on the better situation in Turin than in Naples. See "Diario di Carlo Chevallard 1942–1945," pp. 60, 177–8.

Hunger was a daily nightmare, and the lack of bread, almost religiously chronicled by diarists, was particularly felt. In the fall of 1944, Caterina Gaggero Viale began to keep count: "Today is the third day that we have no bread." Then switching from her informational stance, she emphatically added, "We do not even realize it, but in general, we are so hungry!" (October 10, 1944). The material and psychological uncertainty that had become the trademark of daily life impressed consciences even beyond the immediate. Once the pandemonium ended, for many the traumatic singularity of their suffering was difficult to overcome or even share. In liberated Florence, Michelina Michelini wrote about this predicament in the last page of her diary. A young mother of three separated from her husband by his job in Southern Italy, she had lived the war by relying mostly on her own strength. By early fall 1944, with the Germans definitively gone, she was pondering how to reach her spouse, a challenging enterprise complicated by having small children in tow. In the entry addressed to her husband, she brought up one unforgettable incident she had experienced in her desperate attempt to procure food for their ailing baby daughter:

> I'm happy that you were never in danger. Perhaps in your case there will remain few marks of this long separation, but my soul is deeply affected. I remember an episode during the emergency, when our area had not been liberated yet. Tettina was ill, we needed rice porridge, I go out at eight and I'm in line for two hours at the Pollastri store, I can't manage to get anything, it's all gone. I go to the baker's; they take three stickers, three rations of bread for two hectograms of rice porridge! I leave the store, there is less bread for us, but we need to think of Tettolina. I see another line, they give out rice porridge, I am in line again it's already noon, I manage to get a little package of porridge, I leave the store, I'm about to take that first precious little packet that cost me three stickers of the ration, I can't find it any longer, they stole it from me in the crowd. I lean against the wall and cry.
> (Late September/early October 1944)

Vaguely resentful, although not directly acknowledging it, Michelina focused on the gap between her husband's experience and hers—she did not expect him to comprehend her suffering: "Who can understand if they did not live through this hell?" Hard to communicate, unspeakable trauma drove a wedge between this couple no matter their closeness. At least, that is how Michelina perceived the state of their relationship.

Practical matters dramatically defined everyday living in wartime. The transformation and dehumanization of personhood transpired from the habits and gestures of everyday life, the practices of normal coexistence. Afterwards, any return to normalcy was tested against the implementation of material improvements. Observable changes provided a shield against flights into fantasy, a tangible proof that matters had moved forward. Hence, the prospect of a reliable water supply offered Marisa Corsellini hope that pre-war life in liberated Florence would be restored, despite a still rampant black market and exceedingly scarce resources (September 3, 1944). Readjusting to life meant the resumption of daily rhythms and tempos in a sequence of expected regularities that followed familiar patterns. Normalcy was the antidote to despair; it constituted a reassuring realm from which one could weather the uncontrollable forces of sweeping historical changes.

To Italians, a return to normalcy especially equated with peace—it meant not being distraught by incoming air raids, not being forced to evacuate, and not being made to withstand the German occupiers' depredations. Even if life had not stopped its course during the war—factories kept running, though at a slower pace, shops were still open, cinema halls continued to play feature shows—the perversity of the apparent regularity inhered in the fact that the more common routines had been wiped out or greatly distorted by the war's happenstances.[16] In a disorienting reality that amplified people's sense of loss, the newly organized daily life brought to the surface questions about relationships of power and authority. Despite their desire to turn inward, Italians were squarely entangled with litigating their role as historical subjects.

History, Power, Authority

For many diarists, the combined focus on the everyday and personal matters provided one way to resist grand narratives—a form of protest, albeit often unconscious, against the anonymous march of History. For doubtlessly events often bypassed ordinary people's understanding—a realization that resonated vividly with Maria Alemanno. When she challenged the accusation of betrayal

---

[16] The sense of discomfort that derived from "perverse" regularity is registered by Concetta Bucciano with reference to her going to the movies (see entry of November 5, 1943). Maria Carazzolo similarly wrote that she "felt truly ill at ease" in a cinema hall. See *Più forte della paura. Diario di guerra e dopoguerra (1938–1947)* (Caselle di Sommacampagna: Cierre edizioni, 2007), p. 205 (entry of September 5, 1944).

being floated in the aftermath of the armistice, she lucidly acknowledged her powerlessness and subjection: "And who knows anything: only history will be able to tell us, and who knows if we will be there to listen to it" (September 9, 1943). As for the Germans, she held the same perspective: "Nobody will tell us whether or not they were betrayed because who knows where the truth is" (September 12, 1943). Insisting on the idea that people were being left in the dark, she kept raising the same question: "What is the truth?" Not only was the answer to that question difficult to ascertain, Alemanno maintained, but even if there was an answer, she doubted that people like her would have access to it.

The armistice laid bare the distance between those holding the strings of authority and the ones on the receiving end. While Alemanno's skepticism demonstrated that the fascist dictatorship had not managed to eradicate people's ability to question the veracity of official narratives, at the same time that distrust signaled Alemanno's cognizance of not being part of the privileged circle that controlled knowledge. Power relations are defined by exclusion—they impose hierarchical differences and reflect the distance between personal histories and History, a fact Alemanno alluded to when discussing Mussolini's liberation: "I would also be curious to hear how history will tell us about these episodes in the future and what light will be shed on this man who has upended the world" (September 23, 1943). She seemed to understand that historical judgments are a result of interpretation, although she could not but concede her need for guidance. She deferred to History a final verdict on Mussolini and his fascist creation.

Diarists invoked history to sanction their point of view; they also did it to deflect evaluations. In all cases, history constituted a source of authority to which they appealed. After lamenting Italy's betrayal in the armistice, for example, the self-proclaimed fascist Carlo Ciseri called on history to validate his negative assessment about the country and fellow Italians. Opposite his perspective, twenty-year-old Danilo Durando, who had reluctantly enrolled in the Fascist Republican army, offered a rather cynical evaluation of authoritative narratives. By denouncing the volatile nature of competing legitimacy claims, he exposed the irony of assertions of truth when checked against their self-referential ideological content. Opposite high-sounding declarations, he praised the authenticity of ordinary folks, genuine people like the Alpine Mountaineers: "Not the big words. Fatherland, Duty, Sacrifice, Victory, and other tales. […] Fatherland? What they defend is their home, is their girlfriend. It's their flock, their life that they defend" (June 10, 1944). By emphasizing the level of the material and the personal, Durando brought idealistic pretensions down to earth. Within his framework, reasons for fighting lost their abstract aura and pointed instead to dependability. The concrete contribution of real groups and individuals took center stage and replaced rhetorical posturing and ideological misconceptions.

The war had cracked open people's perennial disconnection from power. It had also deepened that fissure in the face of the Allied forces' seemingly incomprehensible tactics. For, besides the extreme slowness of their advance, the Anglo-Americans were bombing with an ostensibly blatant carelessness. After a terrible shelling killed and maimed several people in the Nomentano neighborhood, including a few Romans waiting to collect water at a fountain, Corrado Di Pompeo was exasperated: "The area where I was lacks any sort of military target, therefore I was wondering what do the English and Americans want from us. They surely know that we, or at least most of us, support them more than the Germans" (March 14, 1944).[17] For Di Pompeo, who helped carry the wounded until he felt sick to the stomach by the "terrifying" spectacle, it was hard to accept strategic choices of which people were the unwilling victims and whose consequences were so crudely tragic—a perspective many of his fellow citizens shared. Most especially, Di Pompeo could not reconcile the image of an ordinary activity such as fetching water with the horrible devastation of exploding bombs. That disconnection increased his pain. With the thought of torn limbs continuing to haunt him, he persisted in feeling ill the next day, understandably unable to erase the experience of the carnage. In his meditations about the future, about life and what was valuable, he ultimately recognized his own helplessness: "But destiny or American bombs will make of us what they want, for we don't have any means of defending ourselves from the one or the other" (March 15, 1944). The distance between those who made decisions and those who had to accept them felt unbridgeable to him. Fatalism aside, he lamented that the little people's sentiments were ignored.[18] Irene Paolisso agreed. As she commented with reference to the Anglo-Americans' slow pace, "what a mockery when the Big guys are wasting time

---

[17] Similarly, Paolisso wrote, "Even last evening invisible airplanes dropped bombs on the coast. We wonder if these isolated actions make any sense. The Allies must know that there are only a few Germans here, that therefore they could land without suffering too many losses, that the population is waiting for them ready to join forces. [...] The reasons for war remain obscure and incontestable" (October 2, 1943). Also see Maria Carazzolo who started to doubt the positive image of the English after witnessing their continuous bombings on civilian targets, including in nearby Padua. She wondered if they were "enemies at home." *Più forte della paura*, p. 149 (entry of February 16, 1944).

[18] Di Pompeo drew this conclusion after lamenting the lack of agreement by the two fighting fronts on the issue of allowing contacts between the separate jurisdictions, including the circulation of news, which would have allowed him to receive updates about his evacuated family on the opposite coast (April 9, 1944). Complaints about lack of news from family members and relatives was recurrent among all diarists.

trying to find an agreement among themselves and don't care about the agony of the Little guys, that is, those with no name nor right to survival" (October 2, 1943).

Although popular understandings of power were most often accompanied by a sense of resignation, the sobering awareness of one's impotence could also spur a critical impetus. For Concetta Bucciano the tipping factor leading her to contest authorities was realizing she could not keep up with the black market's skyrocketing prices: "The day will come when we will succumb to starvation; it is not possible to resist. And these leaders that command, these great captains, do not think of the people" (May 6, 1944). Bucciano questioned the wisdom of those in charge. Despite being a faithful Christian by her own admission, she also doubted the Church's preaching that appeared to ignore the issue of accountability: "Priests say that this is God's punishment, but why should innocent people suffer while the guilty ones, those responsible for such scourge, continue in their nefarious work and keep sowing abundant misfortune and misery?" Similarly, the pious E.R. (she attended Mass every morning) demanded a sort of popular justice: "If reason, justice, honesty, the good law is on our side, why doesn't it triumph? And why are those who provoked such mayhem allowed to act, speak up, take shelter behind the honor and love of the Fatherland?........." (October 2, 1943). Her feeling of being overpowered by evil forces was palpable.

In the unfolding drama of war and occupation and as confusion overcame Italians and disoriented them, some ended up flirting with perplexity. That was their response to the elusiveness of History. Manilio Tartarini fit that ticket. As a town clerk in charge of distributing food supplies, he felt more tortured by the decisions he needed to make about his own situation than by the dilemma of inadequate resources. Expected to enlist in the new Fascist Republican Party, he hesitated, mostly for reasons of opportunism rather than of conscience. Then, as pressure to conform mounted, he considered his options. Ultimately, he kept his possibilities open. Aware that his intentions as well as actions could be seen as contradictory, he admitted to be following a very coherent logic—the logic of an apolitical man:

> My politics can be summarized in the following words: work, family. The rest does not concern me. I'm apolitical in the broadest sense of the word and I will not enroll in political parties of whatever spirit and nature.
>
> The Fascist Republican Party was born and it even scared me. I follow it because it's the party of the day, but I will not enroll.

I'm sure of its vindictiveness and retaliations but I'm ready to endure. With serene mind and the conscience of doing my duty I will endure all consequences.   (November 22, 1943)

Tartarini assumed a heroic stance. And he insisted on his intent not to join the fascist party despite the negative consequences he might suffer (he was eventually transferred). One wonders where he found the strength for such a position considering the inconsistencies of his declared neutrality.[19] Regardless of the reason (but we know that his family encouraged him in this direction), Tartarini ultimately refused to commit to anything that did not specifically address his own declared apolitical leanings and individual concerns. For him, the personal and the political stood at opposite ends and he maintained this view throughout a challenging time. His focus on daily life and the private realm, even when decidedly arduous, helped him contain further pain and face up to history's intractable dilemmas.

Whether in a simple manner or more elaborately, if fully aware or unconsciously, in a tentative mode or assertively, diarists appeared to distrust the traditional holders of authority and manifestly displayed their detachment from the official truth. Even among those classes that comprised the regime's core constituents, the petty bourgeoisie, skepticism of institutions burst with a vengeance once Mussolini's rule collapsed.[20] Day-to-day reality forced people to recognize the malfunctioning of the administrations that were supposed to govern them. Feeling subjected to the ruses of power, many elected to counter its effects by fleeing into the private and refusing involvement in public affairs. Diaries offered the ideal venue for retreating into one's own personal sphere.

Styling Objectivity

The elimination of the subjective point of view stood as one of the principal devices that diarists used to challenge prevailing narratives. In a sort of self-effacement, scribes expressed dispassionate stances, even if in some cases,

---

[19] Just a few days earlier, for example, he had praised the fascist Republican government for having mitigated the negative effects of the German occupation.
[20] On public employees as a constitutive section of the petty bourgeoisie and their support for the regime see Mariuccia Salvati, *Il regime e gli impiegati. La nazionalizzazione piccolo-borghese nel ventennio fascista* (Rome-Bari: Laterza, 1992).

and paradoxically, they accompanied their neutral posturing with personal appeals to a particular individual, namely a loved one. In an unusual story format for a writing practice that is in principle private, even secretive, several authors had an imagined addressee to whom they directed their intimate entries and from whom they drew inspiration. The need to communicate with a family member away at war or away because of the war indeed sparked many diarists' initial impulse to the practice of journaling. Establishing contact with the missed person, no matter how vicariously, was one preferred way to keep that person alive in spirit, if not in actuality.

Depending on one's particular circumstances, sons, spouses, and brothers played the role of favorite interlocutors. For Caterina Gaggeri Viale, her prisoner-of-war son became the exclusive addressee of her daily accounts. Lacking regular updates about his fate, she appeared to gain emotional strength by simply maintaining a mental connection with him. In the case of Corrado Di Pompeo, his habit of writing daily to wife Antonietta helped assuage his neurotic relationship with the historical situation, while allowing him to unload deeply felt despair and frustrations. Needing a space for venting, Wanda Africano-Marabini "fought" with her husband in the pages of her journal as if they were having a regular in-person interaction. Fedora Brenta Brcic, instead, confided to her spouse about the "injustices" she suffered in wartime Rome. Absent any concrete channel of communication, and in defiance of all odds, private journals offered a crucial opportunity for keeping sentimental relationships alive.

In this uneven exchange, the "recipient" of messages, the addressee, played the role of mediator, or better arbitrator, of the ongoing communication and exerted a transformative effect on the nature of the written text.[21] No longer closed off and self-referential, diaries approximated the contextual situation of oral speech, where interlocutors typically engage in dialogue. Only, in the case of diaries, the absence of actual interaction between "speakers" did not allow for the adaptations and changes typically part of the dialogic relation. In contrast, the univocality to which the diarists/writers were constrained reinforced their tendency to avoid subjective reflections. Instead of being pliable and responsive to their dialogic partners, following the norm in conversational exchanges, journal writers took the rigid position of objective observers striving to remain accountable to their nonreciprocating recipients. Granted, diarists still relied on the conative function of language, which aims

---

[21] On the role of the addressee see Roland Barthes and Eric Marty, "Orale/scritto," in *Enciclopedia Einaudi* (Turin: Einaudi, 1980), vol. 10, p. 74.

at persuasion (minus its correlative of manipulation). However, they did so not to influence the behavior of their addressees, whom they were obviously unable to reach, but in order to come across as credible sources (and eventually be deemed as such by their addressees upon their return). Absorbed in this emotional rapprochement, journal writers conjured their "dialogic" partners as unaware co-conspirators in the enterprise of keeping track of history. In this imagined exchange, diarists did not expect any answer back from their absent interlocutors. Lack of response, however, was exactly what inspired them to push their self-mandated mission of recording facts and speaking as objective observers. Guided by a sense of obligation to accountability and reliability, and in the name of preserving history for their spouses and siblings, diarists assumed the viewpoint of a chronicler.[22]

Caterina Gaggero Viale was totally committed to playing the role of impartial reporter. Positioning herself from the perspective of an outsider looking in, she recounted the events that marked wartime in her seaside town of Ventimiglia, in Liguria. By downplaying her subjective impressions, she separated personal experience from historical commentary even as she drew from both. Thus, in one entry, she combined news, reflections, and observations in the same paragraph and in that order: "Rumor circulates that the Allies have taken Montone. I think with horror about what will happen to us and wonder whether we'll be able to save our skin. The fascists are almost all dressed in civilian clothes, but keep insisting that '*where they have been, they will return*'" (September 11, 1944).[23] Gaggero Viale displayed a refusal to be overtaken by the shifts and turns of events. She abstained from remarking on the war news, of which she wrote every day, and instead treated information with the same matter-of-fact approach she adopted in reporting her tavern's business. Her determination to maintain a supposedly dispassionate stance helps explain the chilling effect of the entry she wrote on December 18, 1944:

> This day was worse than yesterday. Ships shot *shrapnel* projectiles and one can mourn several dead and several wounded today too, among them Lea. We went home and spent the day picking olives with the usual brigade.

---

[22] On the relationship between selfhood and narration see Adriana Cavarero, *Relating Narratives: Storytelling and Selfhood* (London: Routledge, 2000). Cavarero advances the theory of identity as the result of a relational practice.

[23] Gaggero Viale mimics the RSI's propaganda slogan "Ritorneremo" (We will return). The slogan emphasized the idea of retaking the colonies as well as the occupied territories Italy had lost in the current war so to re-establish fascism's hold. The catchphrase "Ritorneremo" replaced "Vinceremo" (We will win), initially the refrain at the core of the regime's war campaign.

We are having a big bother because we haven't found a place to stay in Bordighera yet and we left the little stuff we have in four different places.

Yesterday, in Peidaigo, the Germans killed Giuseppina for having wanted to go pick some cauliflowers in her property which is a forbidden area.

(December 18, 1944)

The absence of dramatic tones or words and the non sequitur character of the report do not diminish the gravity of its content or the ability of the narrative to convey the brutal reality of people's everyday experiences. For, as disturbing as some of the conveyed facts were, Gaggero Viale enumerated the death of a neighbor among the usual activities occurring in the besieged community. Taking everything in stride, she implied that along with tending to the land and finding a more secure shelter, killing as well as wounding were normal happenings—they were part of one's daily reality and could result from as simple an act as harvesting a vegetable.[24]

In a twisted way, the "impartial" approach taken by Gaggero Viale and other diarists allowed them to build a screen behind which to take cover against the raw nature of the incidents they were witnessing. By assuming an impersonal role and eschewing emotions, diarists combated the overwhelming sense of smallness in the face of history's vagaries; they escaped their de facto subjection to the arbitrariness of existence. Like magicians pulling a trick out of their hats, they actively rejected their own diminutive position and momentarily denied their dependence on powerful forces, be they the state, the military, or the occupying army. Through their decision to write as observers, they exercised a measure of control, albeit limited. Ultimately, emotional detachment perhaps helped them increase their confidence in their writing ability too; it made organizing the narrative a less involving and cumbersome operation. This might explain the quirky manner with which Ada Vita concluded her entry of September 8, 1943. After describing the reactions at the momentous announcement of the armistice and hinting at the potential drama to follow, she plainly reported on her daily repast: "Everybody is in the street and screams with joy, but who knows what will happen here?!! The Germans will revolt!! At dinner I ate polenta and bran."

Reliance on objectivity does not imply that diarists eliminated personal involvement (and even among diarists there were obvious differences). To the contrary, subjective participation surfaced in full force at the formal level

---

[24] From the way Gaggero Viale wrote her sentence, it is unclear whether Lea was wounded or died, although it is plausible to infer that she was only wounded.

where authors' stylistic choices became part and parcel of their reservoir of expressive means—critical additional devices on which they drew in order to deliver thoughts, reflections, and sentiments otherwise left unspoken. The freedom journal writers took with language structure and formal rules, a liberty that countered the rigidity with which they handled their self-appointed role as senders of "messages," affected the content and tone of their speech. It contributed to creating integrated, cohesive stories. Even among the less literate diarists, recourse to rhetorical strategies and punctuation helped assign meaning to their tales, whether authors followed the rules of conventional speech and typography or arbitrarily manipulated them.

In the case of Cesarina Brugnara, the events she chronicled in the few pages that comprise her journal were written with a matter-of-fact style common among diarists at the time. Her "objectivity" notwithstanding, she seamlessly intertwined personal stories with historical occurrences, if without much fanfare. In her first diary entry of "September 1943" titled "Dates worth mentioning," for example, she moved from noting the details of her brother's drafting in August of that year to reporting Mussolini's resignations of July 25, addressing the consequences unleashed by the fall of the regime locally and nationally, and finally recounting the aftermath of the armistice. Seemingly arbitrary, though in many ways a standard summary of the previous two months, Brugnara's mixture of news was far from random. Once one reads her entry's final sentences, where she recounts the Germans' reactions to Badoglio's announcement of the armistice, it is noticeable how Cesarina's ending mirrors her beginning paragraph through reference to her brother. Under an ostensibly detached list of facts, Cesarina exposed deeply felt personal associations that guided the compositional logic of her narrative: "At that point, the Germans became contrarian to us, enraged for the part Italy played on them. They took prisoners our military as far as Rome and led them to Germany. Those who could escaped and returned home and my brother too had the good fortune of returning." Led by her common-sense wisdom, and in a seemingly unemotional tone, Cesarina ably connected a series of events: the Germans were angry, they captured Italian soldiers and sent them to Germany, some of the soldiers managed to flee and make it home, finally, her brother was among those lucky ones. The political, as the last link in the narrative chain shows, was personal.

National events affected local realities and one's small circle too, and it was through that connection that Cesarina understood historical phenomena. By injecting personal details into the anonymous theater of world news, she established an intimate, meaningful relation with distant and opaque facts—this was her way to live History. Hence, when she narrated the Anglo-Americans' landing in Sicily, she added that as a consequence of the invasion three or four of her fellow villagers were taken prisoners. Even if Sicily was the furthest Italian point from where she lived in Trentino, the fates of the people in the two regions were linked through their common sacrifice in the defense of the Italian nation. Similarly, after reporting on the bombing of several Italian cities, she lingered on her municipality of Trento and specifically addressed the number of dead and other damages suffered there. Or when she wrote about July 25, she stated that with Mussolini "all fascism has fallen, the Piccole italiane and the Balilla," oddly identifying fascism with the two youth organizations for girls and boys between eight and fourteen that were run by the regime and most certainly affected Cesarina firsthand—she was only twenty-one in 1943. Ultimately, an intriguing interaction between official perspectives and popular ones transpires in her diary. Cesarina's remarks on the announcement of the armistice are especially telling. Although she summarized Badoglio's broadcast message in a few simple words, her linguistic plainness reveals the paradoxical aspects of the pact even more caustically: "On the day of September 8, Badoglio gave the following speech: I signed the armistice with the Anglo-American with no conditions and they have willingly accepted."[25] Avoiding verbatim quotations, Cesarina freely paraphrased Badoglio's consequential statement, all the while seemingly reversing roles and misusing terms. Contrary to what her report suggested, Italy was forced to unconditional surrender and had to agree to the terms dictated by the Anglo-Americans.

Diarists' pursuit of dispassionate accounts attempted to minimize personal involvement. However, depending on the details included in the narratives, straightforward descriptions left a few openings for individual interpolations. When covering bombings, for example, complementary "facts" such as the count of victims added gravity to the reported news. Reference to numerical figures offered a tangible measure of the events' shocking nature—quantities made real something ostensibly unspeakable. Luigia Visintainer, who wrote her journal at the venerable age of sixty-eight, adopted an almost obsessive, bulletin-like style that allowed her to list bombardments along with their destructive results.[26] In her case, it was the punctiliousness of the notes she drafted that contributed to expose the dramatic magnitude of the facts she

---

[25] She wrote "con l'Anglo-Americano" in the original, using the singular noun.
[26] Her chronicle of bombings in her village of Calliano constitutes an important documentary source for local history.

was supposedly simply relaying. In another sleight of hand, her enticing use of adjectives added a subjective element that influenced the overall tenor of her reports. When citing the 10,000 victims that died in the bombing of Rome on July 10, 1943, for instance, she appended that the air raid "frighteningly" caused 10,000 dead. In other entries, her ample use of modifiers suggestively revealed her own reactions to events, as when she commented on Mussolini's resignation on July 25. She used expressions such as "very great astonishment" and "immense jubilation" to describe the general atmosphere. In the end, Visintainer's personalized approach did not undermine her overall efforts to play the role of witness as opposed to involved protagonist, and she insisted on approaching the subject from a distance, indirectly. In some instances, she even felt compelled to supply documentation for her stories—proofs to support facts in case anybody (but who?) would ever doubt her accounts. Hence, the day following the purging of Mussolini, she transcribed in its entirety a proclamation that filled two whole pages of her journal. Compiled by five political parties that would soon converge in the Committee of National Liberation (CLN), and confirming her own description of the regime, this "official" indictment addressed fascism as "the painful nightmare," "a monstrous faction that turned all ideal values upside down [...] frightening consciences," and ultimately led the country to an "improvised" war that was "not felt" (July 26, 1943). Although Visintainer shared the views she was conveying, a hidden, invisible interlocutor seemed to loom behind her efforts at playing the role of chronicler—an imagined court of opinion in charge of evaluating the veracity and reliability of her own "impartial" reporting.

An elliptical feast

Beyond vocabulary, a creative use of punctuation helped diarists give tone to their tales. Wanda Affricano-Marabini addressed her husband by combining double question marks with an exclamation point: "And you, what are you thinking at this moment??!" (October 2, 1943). Or she simply juxtaposed the two: "Don't we have two enemies at home?!" (October 21, 1943). Similarly, Vitruvio Giorni asked on the day of the armistice, "War is over!?!?!?" Maria Alemanno used either two question marks and an exclamation point (??!) or combined one question mark and two exclamation points (?!!), sometimes just one of each (?!), and occasionally also two question marks (??). (See her previously cited entry of September 9, 1943.) Roberto Cohen, in contrast, resorted to a double exclamation point along with suspension points to emphasize incredulity, as in his comments about Mussolini's surprising exit on July 25, 1943: "If I retreat kill me are his words......!! Mussolini handing his resignations to the king!!" In the case of Marisa Corsellini, she resorted to double exclamation points to highlight gravity, while Aldo Lanzoni and E.R. employed three exclamation points. "They still make us cry: Savoy!!!" was Lanzoni's protest against the obligation that the military hail the monarchy (June 13, 1944). E.R. instead used the typographical device to announce Mussolini's killing: "<u>Mussolini and company have been executed</u>!!!" (On underlining see discussion below.) Don Luigi Serravalle added five periods to one exclamation point, such as in his entry of September 8, 1943: "Armistice!...." Manilio Tartarini, in turn, combined a single exclamation point with an ellipsis to emphasize his own amazement, such as when he addressed the fate of the Italian army's soldiers scrambling to escape from both the Germans and the new Republican fascists: "They have all gone into hiding!..." (October 15, 1943). E.R. and Maria Fenoglio even marked memorable dates with an exclamation point ("September 8, 1943!"), while Bruna Talluri freely placed question marks between suspension points as when she wondered about the post-fascist future: "but what will happen afterwards.?." (July 28, 1943).

Defying traditional rules, these budding writers exercised expressive freedom through a liberal use of conventional signs and typographical devices, including spacing, capitalization, and underlining. Traumatized by the bombing on Bologna in fall 1943, for example, A.M. highlighted the date: "Yesterday, SEPTEMBER 25 is a date that will have to remain forever impressed in the memory of many." Giovanni Collina Graziani, who held strongly negative feelings about the armistice, commemorated it in 1944: "8 September—ANNIVERSARY OF ITALY'S DEBACLE." On that date, Lucio Macchiarella similarly noted, "Sad anniversary of the ARMISTICE!" Capitalization allowed writers to enhance meaning. Through exaggeration and the shunning of all restraints, it overcompensated for any eventual literary opacity. Indeed, several diarists combined typographical devices to amplify their thoughts and emotions. Ada Vita copiously employed both bolding and underlining to remark on circumstances she felt were particularly notable (such as the bombing of Bolzano on September 2, 1943 or Badoglio's announcement of the armistice, which she mistakenly interpreted as signaling the end of the war). Even more striking was E.R.'s extensive adoption of underlining. At times covering entire paragraphs, recourse to this expedient allowed her to manifest her feelings more emphatically and more assuredly, in obvious contrast to her habitual list-like style. Following the fashion of traditional books of bills, and aside from short notes on mundane daily tasks, E.R.'s typical journaling consisted of reports on the cost of purchased items.

Typographical devices granted diarists a high degree of independence and allowed them to manipulate words and meanings. Generously adopted, these expedients offered writers a chance to overcome the disadvantages due to educational imbalances, while helping them bridge the gap between spoken language (often dialect-based) and written one. As literacy levels and mastery of formal expression varied widely among authors, writing presented challenges. By emphasizing the natural, familiar rhythm of colloquial fluency, typographical devices helped scribes circumvent formalistic approaches to composition.[27] Punctuation and other conventional signs worked to compensate for linguistic deficiencies that threatened to restrict diarists' eloquence. Of course, the operation of selecting what to report that diarists were forced to undertake also reveals the limits that journaling imposes on the potentialities of expressivity. As Wanda Affricano-Marabini confessed to her husband, "I'm realizing that while I thought I would be able to let off some steam by writing, when push comes to shove, I'm unable to say more than half of all the thoughts crowding my head! One thing is to talk and another one is to write, especially for me!" (October 7, 1943).

Closing In: A Roman Duet (In Place of an Epilogue)

Under conditions of indubitable exceptionality, diarists shared a similarly idiosyncratic relation with the quotidian. Relished for its promise of normalcy and at the same time dreaded for the unsparing suffering it delivered, life's daily rhythm constituted the springboard from which diarists negotiated their connection with historical time. Although they all lived in the everyday and needed to navigate it, not all lives were the same, however. "Ordinariness" takes different shades, and class positions, among other factors, invariably set diarists apart. Concetta Bucciano and Fedora Brenta Brcic offer a vivid example of the distance dividing two women living in the same locale—the city of Rome. While both kept a diary into which they vented their miseries and through which they relieved their pain, the ways in which they experienced history and viewed the world could not be further apart.

---

[27] Barthes and Marty, however, understand writing as not necessarily linked to orality—writing exists before being "phoneticized." See "Orale/scritto," in particular p. 66.

A lesson in class status and human relations, the diary of Brenta Brcic combined a compulsive and at times paradoxical tale of scarcity with a socialite's account of mundane matters. In page upon page, Brenta Brcic chronicled her continuous struggle to sustain a sense of normalcy in life. The social activities she pursued, from tea parties to aperitifs, were reminders of a past privileged existence that she refused to surrender. Social engagements helped her maintain the illusion that, despite the mayhem, things were still the same (at least for her). In contrast, any impediment to her daily routine constituted a personal affront. She felt like a victim, if not the victim. Movement restrictions, such as curfews, were an annoyance that detracted her from worldly habits so critical to her mental health. An active life was necessary to her in order to avoid pain. Indeed, Fedora's days were filled with all sorts of happenings: meeting friends at cafés, going to the theater, and even dealing with the stock market. She also followed the course of the war, no doubt, but since she evaluated everything according to how it affected her personal life, the essence of her comments is hard to decipher. For example, was her proclaimed unhappiness about the Anglo-Americans' advance based on a political viewpoint or mere fear of inconvenience?

After Rome was liberated, the summer of 1944 proceeded pleasantly for Fedora, with a busy social schedule that included sun tanning among other pleasurable activities. Still, she was desperate for a return to normalcy—however exclusively she defined it—and wished for the war to come to an end. With competition for scarce resources rising, the military conflict exacerbated social relations. Fedora's discomfort with the lower classes seemingly grew—she perceived them as a threat, a lawlessness "rabble" that forecast the coming of communism. She could not feel any solidarity with them. Her encounter with a young shoeshine in early December 1944 is telling:

> I came back from Mass walking through Villa Borghese. Near the riding tracks I saw a little shoeshine (one of the thousands) that was crying holding a bloody handkerchief under his knee. He told me that a man had kicked him. Indeed, I saw a large jagged wound. Against his will I took him to [...] the "Red Cross American Club" for treatment. I found an Italian medic and delivered the boy to him. Poor little one, he was probably seven!
> (December 3, 1944)

At first struck by the child's woeful state, Fedora was aggrieved by his misery. Soon after, however, her resentment and sense of superiority prevailed: "On the other hand, today the class of shoeshine is a well-to-do class. I heard they make four to five thousand liras a day, while their sisters… much more!" Her disdain was tangible, evident in her slanted references to the shoeshines' sisters' supposed prostitution. Although not generalizable, her bitterness was unabashedly rooted in her class position. Hence, while describing the desolate situation in the city, with stores semi-closed for fear of a takeover by despondent "thugs," the so-called "hunger army," Fedora angrily commented, "These are troublemakers and not hungry people. The latter suffer in silence and they belong to the bourgeoisie." Taking stock of all the good things displayed on shop windows for the holidays, she also accused, "Those who buy these treats are black marketeers and people from the lower classes. The others are left watching" (December 8, 1944). To her mind, the dignity and superiority of the higher social echelons transpired from their stoic attitude, their quiescent behavior. Alternatively, she saw no legitimate room for those who loudly asserted their right to be fed in order not to starve.

In truth, she was not even sympathetic to her own upper-class friends. Obsession with material well-being and an ingrained sense of entitlement defeated her best intentions. Hence, she criticized the case of a war widow who received government aid, including food from the supply store. In Fedora's opinion, she was "doing very well" (October 9, 1944). Completely ignoring the woman's personal loss, Fedora focused on the widow's practical benefits. In a time of scarcity, the woman's access to basic necessities might have looked enviable, even if obtained under the unfortunate circumstance of her military husband fallen in the line of duty. Not that Fedora was callous or superficial. Rather, an established elite orientation provided her with mental resources for tackling an incredibly hard and wearing time. Fedora's class habitus steered her attention toward material goods as the sign of success and stability, something to hang on to when despair and anxiety struck. She exemplified the classic split personality of Dr. Jekyll, caught as she was between a genuine civic sense and a selfish attachment to wealth: "The situation in Italy is serious, though, and I'm very worried about the future. They are only sowing hatred and playing off party against party while neglecting the welfare of the Fatherland. I am terrorized thinking of the disorders that will ensue and I'm almost tempted to take some of the silver to the safety box" (November 3, 1944). As chaos unleashed and her fears of left-leaning movements grew over time, Fedora calculated how to best protect her possessions, even as she marveled with pain at the collapse of a familiar (and advantageous) status quo. Cognizant of the political and historical circumstances ripping Italy apart, her way of coping depended on a personal point of view totally determined by her understanding of where she fit in the picture. When the country was finally liberated in 1945, she did not rejoice at the prospect because she had no news of her husband. Her intimate, undeniable suffering built a lasting distance between private and public—personal story and history—even when they were evidently interdependent. As with Maria Alemanno, Corrado Di Pompeo, and others, family and love relationships remained her holdout, the anchor that guaranteed authentic bliss. And she kept contrasting the positive events of world history with the sad status of her longed-for husband—any satisfaction about the war's resolution was neutered in her case by the reality of her imprisoned spouse. She only heard about his liberation on July 27. On October 8, the day she finally expected to reunite with her husband, she ended her diary.

Almost the opposite of Brenta Brcic's self-centered narrative, Concetta Bucciano's diary offers a view into the hard conditions of a lower-middle-class couple deprived by the bombings of their only precious possession: a "little house." In a few, mostly short, entries, Bucciano conveyed her personal pain while eschewing self-commiseration. She expressed her thoughts in plain, soft-spoken lines: "Our house was hit. Italico went to via Casilina and came back heartbroken, poor Italico, seeing the house destroyed, our poor things dispersed in the street. He brings me back the photo of poor father, all beaten and torn, that he found among the tram tracks" (August 14, 1943). Compared to Brenta Brcic, Concetta's tone is humbler, almost resigned, and showcases generosity of spirit through mourning her husband's pain more than her own: "My dear Italico, so passionate about our beautiful little house that he never wanted to go out. He felt so happy at home, so proud, of his house, and now seeing it destroyed. As I watch him cry, I get all stirred up inside" (August 14, 1943). Despite the great personal misfortune of losing her apartment, Concetta seldom showed any self-pity, even if she hated her new rental accommodation: "What to do? What can be accomplished by despairing? My deepest concern is for this situation that is painful for all humanity; I wish I could lose whatever I have left so long as peace returned, so long as I could see families return to their homes" (August 20, 1943).

Owning a house was of critical importance to her—it sustained her sense of personal dignity. Yet in considering her misfortune she focused on the larger picture and the overall sorrow brought about by the war's devastating effects. Religious faith might have fueled her generosity—deeply devout, she at times invoked God. Nevertheless, her social compassion was all-embracing—she cared for those around her even as she absorbed the trauma of her bombed-out apartment: "We don't have our cute little house any longer, but still, we have a roof over our heads, and thinking about the many cases that are more woeful than ours, we must take comfort" (August 14, 1943).[28] When two months later she finally made it back to the site of destruction, she grieved for the whole community: "What an agony to see all those ruins, on the via Casilina, and at Pigneto, and on via Macerata. What a wasteland in those streets. The few remaining people look like grave keepers. [...] what an agony to think of who knows how many victims among those ruins, people we knew" (October 2, 1943). Concetta's description of the scarred landscape where her "little house" used to stand is poignant in its portrayal of the all-around despondency brought about by the bombardments.

Basic in content, as well as in style and language, Bucciano's diary brings to the fore the dreary reality of those who lacked the resources for countering the deleterious consequences of a violent war. Even when she wrote of simple daily things (the weather, outings, or the mail) and avoided all drama, the "normalcy" evoked in her raw tales exposes the dreadfulness of her experience. Ten days after they lost their apartment, for example, she described her husband's routine: "Italico goes home every morning" (August 25, 1943). Elementary in its structure and informational substance, the sentence straightforwardly described Italico's daily activity. And yet how tragically sad and overloaded with meaning that statement was. One can only imagine Italico's deep suffering as he engaged in the repetitive action of going "home" when there was no home left to go to, only the bombed-out site of what used to be a neighborhood. Concetta did not indulge in despair and rather focused on practical matters. She never even complained about her taciturn companion, who, affected by psychological problems (eventually he also lost his job as a marshal), could not provide much comfort to her. With economic troubles mounting and food resources dwindling, she continued to write with poise and humility. Equipped with a strong sense of decorum and honesty, she seemed to resent moral wounds more than material hardships. "Oh, it was better, better to die crushed by the rubble," she cried after learning that her landlord suspected her of theft (November 16, 1943). She could not quite absorb the shock.

Resilient under the hardships of the era, Concetta reached a critical point in March 1944, a few weeks into her job as door-to-door salesperson. Of weak constitution, she wondered, "Will I be able to endure? Many a time I think that it would be better to die, end it, not to know anything any longer" (March

---

[28] As time passed, she continued to feel that, as long as they were still alive, they were blessed: "One lives only with anxiety and trepidation. Still, in so much ruin, we are among the most fortunate, at least so far" (January 1, 1944).

29, 1944). Overwhelmed as she so evidently felt, she immediately counteracted her introspective concerns with a mindfulness for others, both loved ones as well as the larger national community. Despair had not numbed her yet. Although the war haunted her and she often cursed it for its horrors and torments, she still cared. But if at the start of the diary her comments on historical events were timid, her language took on a more aggressive tone as the war progressed. The news of Mussolini's resignation back in July 1943 had only elicited a neutral or tentative remark from her, not unlike other Italians—practical realism encouraged her to be cautious, even if she certainly did not regret the events. On the occasion of the armistice too, the uncertainty of the situation pushed Concetta to mitigate her enthusiasm—she did not easily fall prey to false optimism, no matter how anxiously she yearned for peace. With the liberation of Rome behind, however, Concetta relented her circumspect approach. Her writing came unleashed:

> It has been about a month since I last wrote on this page; how many things happened over this time; how many events for us, for all and for future history. We were waiting for the liberation of Rome and in fact it happened on the evening of the fourth. What days; it was a true delirium of joy, not to see the Germans in Rome any longer, the abhorred enemy that in these nine months of oppression has done nothing else than enact the most wicked means in order to dishearten us in every way thus attracting on themselves even more of the innate hatred we always had for that race. However, the fascists too, who still are our brothers, proved to be inveterate scoundrels, so it is with great relief now that we see this despotic, and bully, and liar government gone forever (at least we hope). (June 20, 1944)

Although her harshest words were directed at the Germans, she denounced the fascist regime not merely for being dysfunctional or corrupt, but also for its despotism. Her brother was one of the victims of the Fosse Ardeatine massacre. She characterized that carnage as "the heinous work of fascists and Germans" (July 19, 1944).

Concetta's political awareness grew as she lived in time. In the dynamic relationship she held with the unforgiving historical circumstances, her processual understanding of events unfolded while bringing to the surface unarticulated sentiments and meanings, structures of feeling, in fact, that in the summer of 1944 coagulated into an assertive stance. Whether the practice of writing a journal helped her reach this level of consciousness would be hard to determine. Like most ordinary diarists, Concetta exercised little self-analysis in the entries she composed. Nevertheless, all the ordinary diarists examined here, and especially those who started annotating during the challenging biennium of 1943–45, made recourse to journaling as a way to navigate complicated times and ascertain their own role in them. Writing is after all an elucidating medium of communication. It helps "vocalize" thoughts, no matter how unreflexively. Even if the constraints of reporting on the day might take away from considerations of the larger context, they also make possible to root otherwise-hard-to-grasp events into one's immediate experience, the concrete plane of the everyday. Although diaries do not guarantee that darkness would be lifted from the day's anarchic meshing of good and bad, they can illuminate the prosaic and still so powerfully consequential world of mundane activities.

In this chapter we have explored the realm of the everyday in wartime Italy as both a cluster of undertakings that helped individuals define their place in the world and the central notion driving the practice of keeping a journal. While the first two chapters focused on Italians' reactions to the political and historical events of the biennium 1943–45, here we have moved to examine ordinary daily routines with particular attention to the ways one's habitual practices were affected by the disruptive consequences of the military conflict. The incongruous connection between the exceptional war circumstances and the regular day-to-day existence has served to highlight the situational complexities people faced as they struggled to survive the painful effects of the Allied forces' invasion and the Germans' occupation (in addition to a resurgent fascism and the ensuing civil war). Diarists' own tales give us a sense of the ordeals suffered and the physical and psychological tribulations experienced as people adjusted to difficult conditions and longed for a return to an unglorified normalcy defined by the basic right to survival. Food and security at home were paramount desires predicated upon the end of the conflict and the re-establishment of peace—an objective that many realistically, though regretfully, recognized was out of their control. The sense of being under the grip of superior powers, and one's own impotence in the face of those same forces, weighed heavily on Italians' resilience and ability to overcome. Diaries gave journal writers the opportunity to bring back order in a life subjected to the arbitrariness of outside forces and occurrences. By filling in daily accounts, authors proved the persistence of habits and sentiments as well as the lasting life of relationships and the strength of family bonds (especially when they dialogued with a significant other). Writing confirmed that old ways of being were still possible, indeed the only path forward once the madness was over.

Furthermore, writing was an affirmation of subjecthood that counteracted the obliterating march of history. It challenged the legitimacy of power and provided ordinary individuals with a space to cast their own understandings of the war through tales of travails and horrors.

By journaling, authors exercised a limited form of control over the events and emotions that were brutalizing their existence. And while submissive to the genre's rules, and obviously abiding by the constraints of objectivity, they also made a creative use of style for expressive ends, thus adding balance to the timidity of their reporting, which relied on neutrality as a mark of accuracy. In their double role of refuge and arbitrator, diaries reflected and conveyed the chiaroscuro reality of daily life made starker by both the arbitrariness of war and a presentist tendency that was oblivious to the past. Although diarists revolted against the current reality by carving a space for themselves whose intimacy could not be violated or coopted, in so doing they limited their historical understanding of the ongoing public drama and the role they played in it. Trapped in the oppressive atmosphere of the war, they retreated into the private and immersed themselves in the phenomenology of everydayness, ultimately sidelining fascism and the regime. Absorbed in the desperate struggle to survive and recreate some semblancy of normal security, love, and well-being, they sacrificed their capacity to reflect on the broader historical reality and the bygone dictatorship. Whether or not diarists realized it, their narratives brought to the surface the inevitable contradictions of the everyday.

The next two chapters will compare the analysis of ordinary diarists with the journals composed by a different set of authors—affirmed artists and professionals—whose relationship with writing was nothing occasional or amateurish. The purpose of the comparison is twofold: on the one hand, it probes the level of engagement with fascism and gauges reactions to the events of 1943–45 outside the orbit of ordinary Italians. On the other hand, it indirectly tests the perspectives of ordinary Italians by ascertaining the impact of writing skills on diarists' reflexivity and on their ability to convey judgments at a very unsettling time. Did a higher degree of literacy facilitate self-examination and expose one's contradictions? Keeping in mind that the diaries analyzed in the next chapters constitute the main specimens of what was eventually published from this period, did the authors' intention to reach a public influence the content and style of their texts? What role did objectivity play in their commentaries as compared to the self-imposed task of reporting claimed by ordinary diarists? Furthermore, how did everyday experience help intellectual diarists articulate a response to the historical drama whose predicament they shared with fellow Italians? While chapter 5 will deal with the latter question, the next chapter lays out intellectual diarists' struggles to confront the crisis provoked by the events of summer 1943. By measuring them against the structures of feeling of ordinary Italians, the chapter reviews intellectual diarists' attempts to resolve their own ambiguities, past and present.

4
The Diary as Alibi

> Only the murmuring rises, but it is wind.
> (June 7, 1943)*

I jotted down *Memories of the grandfather* for my little grandchild who is not even one year old yet and loves me *angrily*, screaming as soon as he sees me because he wants to come into my arms. In these memories I sketched a diagnosis of fascism, which I see as a petty-bourgeois malady. Perhaps their publication might be good in order to begin discussing the point of view I advance. My son-in-law finds them very interesting and I will engage in doing the work of rereading them and filling in the inevitable lacunae. Later, I will decide whether or not to leave them in the drawer.

Thus, the lawyer Giulio Pierangeli wrote in a letter to the journalist and politician Oliviero Zuccarini on October 3, 1944.[1] He had begun the *Memories* just a year earlier, laying them out as a collection of diary entries in the form of epistolary addressed to his infant grandson.[2] With an interlocutor admittedly unable to read, Pierangeli conceived the document as testimonial for future generations. Far from gathering intimate details or providing a mere chronicle of events, the diary constituted a forum through which Pierangeli wished to engage in serious reflection on the significance of fascism—a phenomenon

---

* From the diary of Andrea Damiano, *Rosso e grigio* (Bologna: il Mulino, 2000).

[1] The letter is cited in Antonella Lignani and Alvaro Tacchini eds., *Giulio Pierangeli. Scritti politici e memorie di guerra* (Città di Castello: Petruzzi editore, 2003), pp. 229–30, footnote 1. It is held at the Archivio della Domus Mazziniana, Pisa, "Fondo Zuccarini."
Of socialist ideas, Giulio Pierangeli (1884–1952) translated works by Proudhon and Marx and published them in the early 1920s with a printing house he founded in Città di Castello. He also wrote on and circulated works by Russian Marxists and promoted texts of political philosophy. Oliviero Zuccarini (1883–1971) was an active member of the Italian Republican Party, which he rejoined in the postwar period after the end of fascism.

[2] The grandson, Pier Giorgio Lignani, was born on October 31, 1943. Pierangeli filled up four copybooks with his daily reflections. The first three were put in a box and buried by his son-in-law and never found again, probably mistaken as treasure and stolen. The dates of those first three diaries are unknown, but according to Pierangeli's interpreters and heirs, the earliest he began his diary is probably spring 1943 (personal communication). The fourth copybook has been published as "Memorie del nonno per Pier Giorgio Lignani. 4° quaderno," in Lignani and Tacchini eds., *Giulio Pierangeli*, pp. 229–54.

that had radically altered the country's history as well as Pierangeli's own life and that of his fellow citizens in the Umbrian town of Città di Castello.

Not unusual in its narrative format modeled after letter writing and directed to a specific recipient, the diary compiled by Pierangeli differed notably from those of Corrado Di Pompeo or Wanda Affricano-Marabini, who also composed their journals in ideal dialogue with an absent interlocutor—their spouse. In Pierangeli's case, the quiet despair that transpires from the hopelessly solitary annotations of Di Pompeo and Affricano-Marabini is counteracted by the obvious intention to reach a larger audience. He ostensibly wrote with the awareness that the public he wished to involve would eventually be able to respond. Publishing the document, even if still a hypothetical, was part of Pierangeli's vision—a goal that signaled his conviction that the fascist reality must be confronted. That determination motivated his notes, guided his choice of topics, and influenced his style of argumentation.

In truth, most of the diarists discussed in this chapter kept a journal believing that the observations they logged in daily would eventually be printed. That assumption affected the selection of what and how they wrote, albeit it did not necessarily make their concerns less genuine when compared to ordinary diarists. Different degrees of reflexivity characterized all journal writers, no matter their social origins and professions. In the case of intellectual diarists, however, the prospect of publication enhanced their sense of moral duty and often led them to focus closely on the question of fascism's significance in Italian history. More than a summary of facts, in their hands the diary rose to the role of moral compass—a tool for national self-examination. In addition, close attention to stylistic issues helped them add pathos to their descriptions of daily experiences and intimate feelings.[3] Ultimately, one challenge the journals of intellectual diarists present for the analyst is their editing a posteriori—authors often reworked their notes before publication (as testified by Pierangeli's intent in the letter to Zuccarini). Caesuras, gaps, and losses signal the reality of diarists' interventions into their texts. Although willing to open up their personal world, diarists also wished to hide sensitive documents from the scrutinizing eye of the public. Positioning themselves in anticipation of readers' reactions, not lost in their minds were the implications of past thoughts and actions once the larger community would become privy to them.

---

[3] The issue of language differentials in unified Italy is a long-standing one, flagged by Antonio Gramsci and addressed by a vast literature. See among others, Tullio De Mauro, *Storia linguistica dell'Italia unita* (Bari: Laterza, 1963). On a unified language and schools, see the 1960s milestone publication Scuola di Barbiana, *Lettera a una professoressa* (Florence: Libreria editrice fiorentina, 1967).

The diaries considered here under the broad umbrella of "intellectual" belonged to individuals with disparate identities and backgrounds. They can be grouped under two loosely defined categories: on the one hand, journals of novelists and artists; on the other, those of humanist professionals, inclusive of jurists, philosophers, administrators, and journalists. This distinction reflects the type of journal composed. While the first group is literary oriented and more actively engaged in daily events, moral and political considerations typically characterize the diaries of professionals. Both groups, however, share a common feature: their diaries were mainly started during the war years (especially 1943 and 1944) and ended during the final phases of liberation. For most, the extracts they published focused on those specific months. Leonetta Cecchi Pieraccini (1882–1977), Bonaventura Tecchi (1896–1968), Corrado Alvaro (1895–1956), Ardengo Soffici (1879–1964) and Giovanni Papini (1881–1956) comprise the diarists in the first group. The second cluster is composed of Benedetto Croce (1866–1952), Piero Calamandrei (1889–1956), Giulio Pierangeli (1884–1952), Gaetano Casoni (1879–1962), Venanzio Gabriotti (1883–1944), Andrea Damiano (1900–63), Carlo Trabucco (1898–1979), and Elena Carandini Albertini (1902–90).[4] Here follows a brief introduction to the scribes (minus the already mentioned Pierangeli).

Why Write a Diary?

A jurist and university professor, the Florentine Piero Calamandrei began his diary on April 1, 1939, only five months before the outbreak of the Second World War. Although the impending war only looked like a possibility at the time, its mere threat dominated Calamandrei's initial entries—armed conflict was a reality he feared, a specter waiting incarnation. Many a sign seemingly confirmed that ominous presage, including the Italian government's unexpected summoning of military personnel. With a massive mobilization unfolding, new geopolitical events added more concerns to the inevitable prospect of a conflict. "Draft cards are pouring," Calamandrei warned.[5] Powerless at the "systematic murder of civilization," he disconsolately watched as the Germans "invaded" Italy: "Night and day, from the Campo di Marte

---

[4] Elena Carandini Albertini is an odd case since her reputation was built on the diaries she wrote.
[5] Piero Calamandrei, *Diario 1939–1945* (Florence: La Nuova Italia, 1982 and 1997), 2 vols., vol. I, p. 7 (entry of April 4).

station, one hears trains going by whistling, one after another: I imagine them loaded with German soldiers: they give me the impression, almost physical, of carriers of infection penetrating our country: *poussées* of spirochetes in our poor veins."[6] Comparing Hitler's armies to bacteria attacking the bodies of Italians, Calamandrei accused Mussolini of complicity in Europe's destruction. Even more damning, he found him guilty of destroying the Risorgimento—that sacred period in national history marked by the Italians' fight for unification and independence from foreign domination.[7] It was the final straw, the forbidden line one should not have crossed. Never a supporter of the regime, Calamandrei judged the latest developments of Mussolini's politics as devastatingly tragic.

Come fall 1939, the war started. Although Italy would only join the conflict in June of the following year, the sober tone of Calamandrei's comments in those April days of 1939 stands out as a prescient warning—an alarm sounded amidst a climate of apparent obliviousness. Filling pages with notes that denounced Mussolini's irresponsible government, Calamandrei asked himself, "But why do I write all these observations that, if they reached the hands of some relevant authority, at the very least would be sufficient to send me to confinement?"[8] He listed two reasons, both of which emphasized the historical value of the diary as a source of information and testimonial. For Calamandrei, keeping a daily chronicle constituted an expression of civic duty and a future point of reference. Once the regime would fall, as he hoped, then the scenes of daily happenings, vignettes, and conversations evoked in his often-long entries might help "reconstruct the atmosphere in which we are suffocating today" and offer poignant examples of people's current moods and beliefs. Ultimately, an ethical motivation guided Calamandrei's efforts at journaling: "And then, then I write just to protest, just to let myself know, by rereading what I wrote, that there is at least one person who does not want to be an accomplice!"[9] A sense of moral responsibility ran through the more than five years of daily notes Calamandrei jotted down (his diary ended in May 1945). While generational conflicts heightened his sentiment of civic obligation (he feared his son, and youth in general, did not perceive the criminal nature of fascism's politics), his diary highlighted the personal struggle

---

[6] Calamandrei, *Diario*, vol. I, p. 9 (entry of April 8, 1939).
[7] One of the first scholarly interventions on the Risorgimento and its myth is *Il mito del Risorgimento nell'Italia unita. Atti del convegno: Milano 9–12 novembre 1993* (Milan: Edizioni del comune di Milano, 1995). For a more recent overview see Massimo Baioni, "Un mito per gli italiani: Il Risorgimento tra ricerca storica e discorso pubblico," *Italian Culture* vol. 30, no. 1 (2012): pp. 7–20.
[8] Calamandrei, *Diario*, vol. I, p. 28 (entry of May 4, 1939).
[9] Calamandrei, *Diario*, vol. I, p. 29 (entry of May 4, 1939).

that people of conscience experienced as their principles were tested and their intentions challenged in the day-to-day dealings with the regime.[10] Extricating oneself from the far-reaching tentacles that Mussolini had extended deep into the organization of everyday life was not an easily achievable undertaking.

Paradoxically, although diaries were supposed to soothe their authors, they also lay bare the contradictions that vexed even those, like Calamandrei, who had declaredly refused to endorse the regime.[11] For in truth the question of complicity was thornier than could be resolved by avowing an antifascist stance in the pages of one's journal. By writing, Calamandrei looked for reassurance about his own integrity, cognizant of the fact that, in spite of all good intentions, his struggle to be on the morally right side was exactly that: a struggle. Besides, fascism could not be compartmentalized or isolated from the realm of social networks and family relations in which one was embedded. The fluidity of human interactions—be it at work, at home, or in the larger public sphere—made it impossible to draw a clear-cut distinction between oneself and the regime, let alone between oneself and fascism's followers. At the level of the lifeworld—in the course of daily encounters or when dealing with mundane matters—one was inevitably and continuously negotiating disparate beliefs and practices that put community relations to the test.

Although not all the thirteen diaries examined were as comprehensive and focused as the one composed by Calamandrei, the mixed nature of the "commerce" taking place in everyday exchanges emerges in full colors in the journal of Leonetta Cecchi Pieraccini. Covering approximately the same time period as Calamandrei, the diary was begun in August 1939 and ended with

---

[10] For a testimonial about the conflict between son and father, see Franco Calamandrei, "Piero Calamandrei mio padre" in Piero Calamandrei, *Diario*, vol. I, pp. vii–xxi. In 1943, Franco Calamandrei renounced fascism and joined the Resistance (most famously, he was part of the group that attacked German military on via Rasella in Rome, to which the Nazi responded with the massacre at the Ardeatine Caves). After the liberation, he became an active member of the Italian Communist Party.

[11] Calamandrei was among the signatories of Croce's 1925 *Manifesto of the Anti-Fascist Intellectuals*, compiled in response to the *Manifesto of the Fascist Intellectuals* written by the philosopher Giovanni Gentile. On the two manifestos see Emilio R. Papa, *Storia di due manifesti. Il fascismo e la cultura italiana* (Milan: Feltrinelli, 1958). In 1941, Calamandrei joined the antifascist movement Giustizia e Libertà and was among the founders of the Action Party (Partito d'Azione) in 1942. The bibliography on the Action Party is extensive. For a synthetic history see Giovanni De Luna, *Storia del Partito d'Azione. 1942–1947* (Milan: Feltrinelli, 1982). On intellectuals and the Action Party see David Ward, *Antifascisms: Cultural Politics in Italy, 1943–46. Benedetto Croce and the Liberals, Carlo Levi and the "Actionists"* (Madison: Fairleigh Dickinson University Press, 1996), chapter 5 "The Action Party: Fascism as Italy's Autobiography." Mariuccia Salvati discusses the partisan groups operating under the direction of the Action Party as an original aspect of the Italian Resistance. This is because they were inspired by the value of freedom before equality and solidarity. See Salvati, *Passaggi. Italiani dal fascismo alla Repubblica* (Rome: Carocci editore, 2016), p. 153.

the liberation of Rome on June 5, 1944.[12] A painter, Cecchi Pieraccini belonged to an intellectual circle whose political sympathies tended to align with the regime. Her own husband, noted art and literary critic Emilio Cecchi, had received the highest honor fascism bequeathed on intellectuals when he was elected member of the Accademia d'Italia—an institution founded by Mussolini in 1929.[13] Official ties with the regime notwithstanding, intellectuals of all ideological leanings crisscrossed Cecchi Pieraccini's salon and socialized together. Not new to writing a journal, a habit she took up in 1911, Cecchi Pieraccini published two books based on the "little agendas" kept over the years.[14] The diary covering the Second World War is one of those books. Lacking Calamandrei's moral awareness or ethical standing, her journal brings to the surface the political hybridity and connivance of the intelligentsia class. It also illustrates the normalcy of adaptive practices under the dictatorship. More a portrait of situations and characters than a factual annotation or reflective exercise, Cecchi Pieraccini's diary refracted the free-floating nature of intellectuals' personal positions as painters and *littérateurs* confronted the new dilemmas raised by the regime's ill-advised involvement in a disastrous war.[15]

Propelled by a sensitive political conscience, the personal notes that Elena Carandini Albertini wrote after Mussolini's fall reveal her desire to chronicle the country's vicissitudes. The daughter of a prominent newspaper director who had been forced to renounce his post after refusing to participate in the regime, she was married to a man active in liberal political circles.[16] As a member of Italy's enlightened bourgeoisie unsupportive of Mussolini, she followed the historical unfurling of national and international events with the expectation that the country would eventually regain its path toward democracy. Amidst the commotion of regime change and the intensifying terror of the world conflict, Carandini Albertini took diary writing as an act

[12] See Leonetta Cecchi Pieraccini, *Agendina di guerra (1939–1944)* (Milan: Longanesi, 1964).
[13] Cecchi was nominated for the Accademia in 1940. He also won the Premio Mussolini for literature in 1936. Previously, he was among the forty original signatories of Croce's 1925 *Manifesto of the Anti-Fascist Intellectuals* (a first list of names was published on May 1, 1925 and two more lists were published between May 10 and 22).
[14] The first diary was published as *Vecchie agendine (1911–1929)* (Florence: Sansoni, 1960), reprinted in a version more faithful to the original as *Agendine 1911–1929* (Palermo: Sellerio, 2015), edited by Cecchi Pieraccini's great-granddaughter Isabella D'Amico.
[15] Cecchi Pieraccini's diaries are also among the most reworked of all those examined here. See D'Amico's note in *Agendine*, pp. 19–21. I have checked the passages I quote from her diary against the original manuscripts housed at the Archivio Contemporaneo "Alessandro Bonsanti" in Florence.
[16] Her father, Luigi Albertini, had been director of *Il Corriere della Sera* from 1900 to 1925. Her husband, Count Nicolò Carandini, became the first ambassador to Great Britain of post-fascist Italy. He was dispatched to London in 1944 by the government of Ivanoe Bonomi, who after the liberation of Rome had succeeded Badoglio as the country's prime minister.

of testimonial, even if at first directed solely to her family. While she started journaling at a very young age, she later reviewed and reassessed for publication only the diaries from 1943 onwards.[17] Already in an entry of summer 1943, she chastised her previous writing efforts as "unreflective and sentimental" and vouched from then on to be closer to "*reality*" while holding on to this "vice." Keeping a diary had become a compulsion, "a little mania" that defied any reasonable assessment of risk.[18] Undeterred by the fear of consequences, Carandini Albertini resorted to hiding her journals rather than giving up the habit, at times writing notes on little pieces of paper soon to be tucked away.[19] Although she continued journaling, she did not, however, stop questioning the legitimacy of her own role as narrator. She persistently doubted her lack of gravitas: "What is the purpose of continuing the diary if it is unable to convey the relentlessly painful reality and our own reactions to it?"[20]

In the case of the philosopher Benedetto Croce too, journal writing was a long-standing practice, and only political urgency convinced him to publish sections of his diary that covered the period immediately following Mussolini's resignation. Initially printed in two separate installments, the notes appeared in *Quaderni della "Critica"* in 1946 and 1947 and covered the period from July 25, 1943 to early June 1944.[21] In the original preface, Croce stated that their publication was motivated by the need to correct the narratives circulating after the war.[22] Even more relevant, Croce explained that his habit of writing a diary over the course of four decades, either at the beginning or end of the day, was originally meant to record the pace at which he engaged in his literary work. The events following the regime's fall, however, "vehemently" pushed their way into the diary, forcing him to include "many news concerning political matters." At first making their entrance "almost involuntarily," those political notes eventually reached a substantial number and came to

---

[17] See Elena Carandini Albertini, *Dal terrazzo. Diario 1943–1944* (Bologna: il Mulino, 1997); *Passata la stagione…Diari 1944–1947* (Florence: Passigli, 1989); and *Le case, le cose, le carte. Diari 1948–1950* (Padova: Il Poligrafo, 2007). On Carandini Albertini's early journaling and her work of revision on the later diaries see Andrea Carandini, "Presentazione," in *Dal terrazzo*, pp. i–ix. Also see Serenella Baggio, "*Niente retorica.*" *Liberalismo linguistico nei diari di una signora del Novecento* (Trento: Università degli Studi di Trento, 2012), chapter III, "Una piccola operazione editoriale" (A small editorial intervention).

[18] Carandini Albertini *Dal terrazzo*, p. 7 (initial entry, no date).

[19] Carandini Albertini *Dal terrazzo*, p. 21 (entry of August 31, 1943). Throughout the diary Carandini Albertini mentions that she hid her little pieces of papers.

[20] Carandini Albertini, *Dal terrazzo*, p. 42 (entry of September 25, 1943).

[21] They can be found in Benedetto Croce, *Taccuini di guerra, 1943–1945* (Milan: Adelphi, 2004). Croce had originally planned for the extract to cover the period through December 1945.

[22] See Appendix in Croce, *Taccuini di guerra*, pp. 387–8.

constitute the bulk of the extracts Croce selected for publication.[23] A sense of moral responsibility weighed heavily on this editorial decision—Croce's intention was to contribute to the public debate that, with the war over, was taking place in those momentous months. No longer a device to monitor the direction of his own intellectual agenda, the diary became an outward means for recounting in an orderly manner political developments that, albeit confusing, were about to transform Italy's course after twenty years of fascism.[24] Leaving literary and private matters aside, the philosopher withdrew behind the more compelling civic duty (to which he felt obliged) of making transparent the mechanisms and deliberations of the country's new liberal direction.

The private journals of Giovanni Papini and Ardengo Soffici offer a different scenario. Both literary figures had publicly supported fascism at points in their lives and remained decidedly close to its ideals after the regime's fall. Guided by a missionary sense of art and a mystical belief in tradition, both upheld a spiritual approach to existence that emphasized nationalism and patriotism. Their diaries reflected the torments they endured in navigating the field of politics while relying on moral and aesthetic values. Papini initiated his diary early in 1916 with a few scattered notes that included lists of books and practical reminders. His level of engagement with journal writing remained low for several years, and on Christmas day of 1925 he even confessed, "I have started the diary five or six times and I have always quit it, sooner or later."[25] In 1937, however, in a major reversal, Papini began penning entries on a daily basis. Filling up several notebooks, he continued this habit throughout the difficult times of the war and until his death in 1956.[26] When first published in 1962, his diary was not changed from its original manuscript version.[27] Curiously, though, a whole notebook on the critical period from late February to early November 1943 is missing and presumed lost.[28]

---

[23] Appendix in Croce, *Taccuini di guerra*, pp. 387–8. However, politics was not absent from Croce's notes prior to the 1943 events. On this issue see Fabio Fernardo Rizi, *Benedetto Croce and Italian Fascism* (Toronto: University of Toronto Press, 2003). Rizi examines Croce in terms of his political personality. On impressions of Croce as a politician from the time of the armistice to June 1944 (when the Bonomi government was established) see Filippo Caracciolo di Castagneto, '43–'44. *Diario di Napoli*. Florence: Vallecchi, 1964.

[24] See comments by Piero Craveri, "Postfazione," in *Taccuini di guerra*, pp. 437–54.

[25] Giovanni Papini, *Diario* (Florence: Vallecchi, 1962), p. 42.

[26] See "Notizia" in Papini, *Diario*, p. x (editor's note). Obviously emotionally attached to his journal, Papini even thought of hiding it during his peregrinations as an evacuee in the summer of 1944. See *Diario*, p. 195 (entries of June 16 and 17, 1944).

[27] The original version presents only minimal corrections by the author. See Papini, *Diario*, p. xi (editor's note).

[28] Papini, *Diario*, p. x (editor's note).

This gap finds a similar counterpart in Soffici's diary, even if in this case caused by the author's expressed will to restrict publication to specific sections.[29] As Soffici wrote in the foreword to the printed edition of the diary:

> This is certainly not the time to make public a part, and by far the largest, of the diary. Too many are still the sorrows, resentments, and partisan hatred generated by the military and civil wars for us to risk reigniting them. I therefore limit myself to selecting those parts that without running this type of risks can nonetheless offer some interest, not only in terms of chronicle, but possibly of history, due to their authenticity and accuracy, in their role as documents of a certain era.[30]

Aware of his own "compromised" reputation in post-fascist Italy, Soffici supposedly eliminated sensitive portions from the diary's published version and only maintained segments he considered of "documentary" value. His aim was to offer a portrayal of the years 1939–43 that could be perceived as objective and devoid of polemics—goals that did not stop him from injecting his own voice into the discussion. Far from merely stating facts, Soffici's journal registered his travails—the crisis of a conscience moved by fascist ideals but whose evolutionary transformations were not intended to be shared with readers. For, as it turns out, the narration stops at a pivotal moment in the history of Italy's participation in the war: The eve of the armistice with the Allied forces and the subsequent declaration of war on Germany by the Badoglio government.[31]

While silences and omissions add gravity to Papini's and Soffici's personal torment, the diary of the journalist Andrea Damiano elevates moral anguish to a national crisis.[32] Probably reworked before its publication in 1947, Damiano's journal does not advance any claims to truthful facts and objectivity. In contrast, it makes spiritual matters the thread weaving through the wartime tales the author aims to recount. With reflexivity pushed to an

---

[29] See Francesco Perfetti, "Prefazione," in Ardengo Soffici, Sull'orlo dell'abisso. Diario 1939-1943 (Milan: Luni, 2000), p. 10. The diary was originally published in a volume also containing Giuseppe Prezzolini's journal. See Ardengo Soffici and Giuseppe Prezzolini, Diari 1939-1945 (Milan: Il Borghese, 1962).

[30] Soffici, Sull'orlo dell'abisso, p. 13.

[31] Soffici was not new to the genre of diary writing. As a combatant in the First World War, he published several collections related to that time. Some are included in Ardengo Soffici, I diari della Grande Guerra. Kobilek. La ritirata del Friuli, edited by Maria Bartoletti Poggi and Marino Biondi (Florence: Vallecchi, 1986).

[32] Andrea Damiano, Rosso e grigio (Bologna: il Mulino, 2000), originally published in 1947 by Muggiani Editore.

utmost degree, Damiano carries out a self-examination that rises to the level of general soul-searching, a sort of denunciation of the country's ills made more dramatic by recourse to literary devices. In his first diary entry of November 15, 1942, Damiano confessed that in the thirty months since Italy entered the war, he had told himself more than once, "this is the time for diaries."[33] However, he finally made the decision to start a journal only as the war seemed to be reaching a critical point. Amidst bombings, ruins, and deaths, and with the country becoming a major physical site of the conflict, Damiano put all Italians on trial.

A Germanist and later a university professor, Bonaventura Tecchi began his career as novelist with a collection of short stories published in 1924. Focusing on questions of existential and moral import, he continued to engage in diverse genres of narrative throughout his life, eventually gaining considerable recognition for his work. The diary he published in 1945 covered the summer and fall of 1943 and represented a small section of a fifty-year-long secret journal that mostly remained unpublished. Printed with the suggestively idyllic and almost counterintuitive title *Un'estate in campagna* (A Summer in the Country) and displaying a considerable literary sensibility, the short autobiographical tale chronicles the events that changed Italy's historical course over the span of a few critical months.[34] More than a descriptive account or an introspective analysis focused on subjective experience, Tecchi's daily notes promote the particular case of a small countryside outpost in the middle of the peninsula to a general template for reflecting on people's sense of morality, the dignity of existence, and the relation of political matters to the human condition. Moving beyond the level of observation, the diary becomes a platform for assessing the lyric potential of life exactly when existence seems to be at its lowest point. Tecchi's aim was not to pursue forms of absolution, however. Rather, and against all triumphalism, he revealed personal vulnerabilities and fears as well as the frailty and weaknesses of the nation, all of which, he admonished, required acknowledgment and reckoning in the spirit of Christian morality.[35]

---

[33] Damiano, *Rosso e grigio*, p. 27.

[34] Bonaventura Tecchi, *Un'estate in campagna (Diario 1943)* (Florence: Sansoni, 1945). The extract spans the time period from July 1 to mid-November. An abbreviated version of the book was also published by Sansoni in 1971, with a preface by Filiberto Mazzoleni. In 1946, Tecchi also published *Vigilia di guerra 1940* (Milan: Bompiani, 1946).

[35] On August 12, 1943, Tecchi wrote that, if ever published, his "secret diary" could be entitled *Heautontimoroumenos*, from the Greek the self-tormentor, so much was he trying to dig deep into his own weaknesses. Tecchi added that "this sort of spiritual 'masochism'" needed as its counterpart "a true purification," otherwise it risked turning into mere "modern morbidity." See Tecchi, *Un'estate in campagna*, p. 40.

A heightened sense of Christian faith also subtended the "witness" accounts left by Gaetano Casoni, Venanzio Gabriotti, and Carlo Trabucco. Respectively a lawyer, a military veteran administrator, and a journalist, and all at risk of persecution by the regime, they approached their diaries through a factual approach that blended analysis of Italy's political situation with detailed descriptions of specific local experiences. In Florence, Casoni recounted the frantic months prior to the liberation of the city and focused on the antifascists' efforts to save Florence's artistic patrimony from the Germans' ignominious reaping.[36] Arrested by the local authorities and then released, he wrote of his personal ordeal too. He ultimately hoped that his military son, whose fate as prisoner of the Germans remained uncertain, would be able to access those memories upon returning. Casoni was convinced that knowledge of all the misery his family and fellow citizens suffered in those days would deeply impress the young man and "touch his soul."[37]

In the instance of Carlo Trabucco, his diary retells the 268 days of German occupation in Rome between the armistice of September 8 and the liberation of the capital on June 4 and 5, 1944.[38] Living underground during that time span, Trabucco annotated everything he observed and heard. Filtered through his own journalistic sense, and aware that "[t]his is nothing more than a diary. It is not a literary work and not even a historical work," the information Trabucco gathered was meant to offer a testimony of that harrowing experience, no matter the inexactitudes it was bound to contain.[39] Diaries might not stand the test of accuracy, Trabucco realized, but as living documents they powerfully register the atmosphere of an era—that era's truths as well as its fables.[40]

If documenting was a paramount preoccupation for Trabucco, the diary of Venanzio Gabriotti, begun on September 14, 1943 and ended on May 4, 1944, equally aimed at gathering "the most interesting news of this sad and grave period for our Italy."[41] From his native town of Città di Castello, Gabriotti

---

[36] Gaetano Casoni, *Diario fiorentino (giugno-agosto 1944)* (Florence: G. Civelli, 1946), reprinted by Edizioni Polistampa in 2015.

[37] Casoni, *Diario fiorentino*, prefatory note of October 1944, no page number.

[38] Carlo Trabucco, *La prigionia di Roma. Diario dei 268 giorni dell'occupazione tedesca* (Rome: Editrice S.E.L.I., 1945).

[39] See "Premessa" in Trabucco, *La prigionia di Roma*, p. 7.

[40] The book is credited with being the first to report on the massacre of the Ardeatine in Rome using the term "fosse" (pits or ditches) when they were in fact caves. That appellation has withstood the test of time. See Robert Katz, *Death in Rome* (New York: Macmillan, 1967), translated into Italian as *Morte a Roma. La storia ancora sconosciuta del massacro delle Fosse Ardeatine* (Rome: Editori Riuniti, 1967).

[41] Venanzio Gabriotti, *Diario 25 luglio 1943-4 maggio 1944* (Città di Castello: Petruzzi editore, 1998), edited by Alvaro Tacchini, preface by Mario Tosti, p. 45 (entry of September 14, 1943).

examined the evolution of the country's political situation and reflected on its consequences at the local level, where his beloved community faced the urgency of adjusting to a rapidly moving reality, including the return of fascism. Committed to liberal ideals, Gabriotti made the decision to resist the German occupation. Eventually forced into hiding, he continued to monitor his fellow citizens' reactions to the Germans' presence—a military takeover that turned the life of his provincial town upside down. Captured and imprisoned by the Germans, Gabriotti was executed on May 9, 1944.[42]

Of all the diarists examined here, Corrado Alvaro constitutes a hybrid case: he was both a writer and a journalist and throughout his life actively engaged in both practices. Following a trend typical among the *littérateurs*, Alvaro kept a diary for several decades. In a demonstration of journalistic sensibility, however, and with a keen eye for reporting news and moods, he considered the diary a form of testimonial more than a confessional. He obviously struggled with the genre. Started in 1927 and covering the period up to 1947, Alvaro's journal was published in its entirety in 1950 with the title *Quasi una vita* (Almost a Life), though an extract from July 25 to September 8, 1943 appeared in the review *Mercurio* in December 1944—a sign of Alvaro's desire to bear witness. In its format, the diary lacked the classic structure of daily entries aimed at summarizing one's experiences. In contrast, it featured scattered notes ranging from observations and reflections to occasional aphorisms and vignettes, all gathered under yearly headings and with only rare references to months or days. Indeed, although the book was originally subtitled *A Writer's Journal*, Alvaro reneged on its diaristic nature, mostly citing its lack of exemplarity as a reason. "People like me, of my generation, do not have a fable of a life"—he wrote in the note preceding the 1950 volume—"Therefore, this book is not a diary or an autobiography. It was a compilation of notes meant to be of use to me, to my stories, the essays, the works that I would write one day."[43]

Aware of his own personal flaws, and cognizant of the compromised nature of most Italians' relationship to fascism, Alvaro did not consider himself a model of virtue. This acknowledgment notwithstanding, or maybe exactly because of it, a moral imperative governed Alvaro's impulse to communicate his travails. As a writer, he was driven by the desire to maintain a record of

---

[42] He had been arrested a few days earlier on May 5.
[43] See Corrado Alvaro, *Quasi una vita. Giornale di uno scrittore* (Milan: Bompiani, 1950), p. 5. "Mine is not an exemplary biography," he continued a few lines later, adding that the volume was "the opposite of a Goethe biography in the sense of a life committed to an increasingly higher perfection," p. 6.

how he had approached a "hard and tiring and suffered" life, so as to offer a vivid example of the tortuous and difficult experiences many Italians withstood in the shade of the regime.[44] "Like all my contemporaries, I have tried to salvage my existence physically and morally through an epoch we all know. [...] I tried to survive," he stated as he listed prison, death, and exile as the other available options.[45] Countering fascism head-on required enormous sacrifices. Admittedly, Alvaro was not up to it: "I don't have what it takes to be a martyr, unless I'm forced to."[46] Being unwilling to become a hero left him with no other choice but to participate in the regime, even as he strove to "remain faithful to the best of himself" and tried "not to receive official honors, remaining an irregular, nonclassified, non-card-carrying."[47] One could either be in or out, though, and Alvaro was aware of his own contradictions. As he conceded at the conclusion of the prefatory note to *Quasi una vita*, "At this point I realize that I shouldn't even dare speak. But that's my profession, and it is too late to change life and job."[48] A signatory of Croce's *Manifesto of the Anti-Fascist Intellectuals*, Alvaro successfully continued his writing career under Mussolini's dictatorship and received major awards by the regime.[49] He survived indeed—almost a life.

The diarists examined here wrote about their historical present in order to provide a source of information for the future.[50] They wished to offer a

---

[44] Alvaro, *Quasi una vita*, p. 6.
[45] Alvaro, *Quasi una vita*, pp. 5 and 6. He also thought that "one day I might be able to say something useful, if not necessary, in accordance with the eternal illusion harbored by writers," p. 6.
[46] Alvaro, *Quasi una vita*, p. 6.   [47] Alvaro, *Quasi una vita*, p. 6.
[48] Alvaro, *Quasi una vita*, p. 7.
[49] He won an award for *Gente in Aspromonte* in 1931 and was the recipient of the Accademia d'Italia award for *L'uomo è forte* in 1940. On Alvaro and fascism see among others Ruth Ben-Ghiat, *Fascist Modernities: Italy, 1922–1945* (Berkeley: University of California Press, 2001).
[50] There are two notable diaries written during the period that I am not considering in this study. One was published by the writer Sibilla Aleramo (*Un amore insolito. Diario 1940–1944* [Milan: Feltrinelli, 1979]). Mostly focused on the author's love story with the younger poet Franco Matacotta, it was heavily reworked with savage edits and massive cuts when first published in 1945 by the Tumminelli press. Matacotta contributed to the editing and especially excised those sections that dealt with the details of their relationship, although the diary fundamentally remained an account of the couple's tempestuous affair. Guided by literary and commercial ambitions (the latter testified by its swift publication), the journal is mostly filled with reflections on Aleramo's and Matacotta's romance, even if between the lines the misery Aleramo suffered under German occupation also transpires. The book was originally titled *Dal mio diario (1940–1944)*. The excised parts were reintegrated in the version of the diary published a few decades later. Aleramo continued to keep a journal after 1944 (see *Diario di una donna. Inediti 1945–1960* [Milan: Feltrinelli, 1978]). She was a signatory of Croce's *Manifesto of the Anti-Fascist Intellectuals*, but like Emilio Cecchi and others she later subscribed to the regime.
The other diary is *War in Val d'Orcia: A Diary* (London: Jonathan Cape, 1947), by Iris Origo, an English-born writer who lived at a country estate near Montepulciano, Tuscany with her Italian husband. Conceived for a British audience, the diary adheres to the principles of impartial observer and the proclaimed aim for objectivity pursued by the intellectual diarists examined here. In her preface to the book, Origo emphasized the value she placed on firsthand knowledge and even cautioned her

testament of experience at a critical juncture in the country's transition to a post-fascist period. Not all the authors were concerned with affirming their political conscience or adhered strictly to their purported role of reporter. A few followed the call of moral responsibility, tried to balance political and ethical values, and wished to mount a denunciation of Italy's spiritual weaknesses. In some cases, the tension between the personal and the political was scarcely resolved, while in others little-exercised reflexivity went hand in hand with ideological hybridity. In general, the desire for bearing witness through journaling presented intellectuals with several epistemological challenges ranging from not being able to represent and convey the nature of reality to needing to correct the prevailing narrative and reassess the truth, as well as feeling the chasm between the loftiness of authenticity and the baseness of documenting. Silences and omissions went side by side with a self-proclaimed veracity, while accuracy was applied to the uneventful and the common as well as the local. All rejected the model of journaling as confessional and affirmed the value of testifying, however problematically. Driven by that demonstrative ambition, intellectual diarists evaluated the events of summer/fall 1943 and revisited fascism, although they mostly failed to appraise their own response to the country's political and moral crisis. Hiding behind the veneer of objectivity, they reported on the experience of the period as external observers.

"It all ended too suddenly, too simply."[51]

The disenchanted tone with which Alvaro described his diary in the preface to *Quasi una vita* infused the spirit with which he jotted down his entries, whether he was simply recounting scenes of life in Berlin during his travels in 1929, voicing general ideas about the future of Europe in the following years, or more basically reporting humorous stories and political jokes. Out of an array of notes, his comments on the events that beginning with July 1943 marked a novel course in Italian history are especially notable. As his

---

audience that the events portrayed in the diary were "singularly undramatic and unheroic," p. 11. They reflected commonly lived experiences, instead—a feature she seemingly believed would reassure readers about the relevance and reliability of her account. Writing was not a new experience for Origo, however. As much as she might have wished to pass for an accidental diarist who adopted this practice with a sense of duty under grave circumstances, she had already published two well-received biographies during the 1930s, one on Giacomo Leopardi (1935) and the other on Cola di Rienzo (1938), in addition to a biography of Byron's daughter.

[51] Alvaro, *Quasi una vita*, p. 300 (September 1943).

dispassionate words suggest, "It all ended too suddenly, too simply." Stationed in Rome during that summer, Alvaro gathered his impressions of people's responses to the fall of Mussolini. Anything but exultant, his remarks were measured and almost cynical in their realism. His penetrating eye dwelled on the less blatant manifestations, the subtleties of individual behaviors, the moods emerging from the ranks of party functionaries and the popular classes as well. Far from displaying any triumphalism, Alvaro emphasized the inconsequentiality of the regime's collapse on the Italians' civic conscience. The frenzy of the destruction in the aftermath of Mussolini's dismissal was not necessarily a good predictor of Italy's political maturity or future well-being, he cautioned.

Even in the days prior to the Grand Council's historic decision to disempower Mussolini, Alvaro was negatively struck by a sort of disconnection he noted in people's reactions to the devastating Anglo-Americans' bombing of Rome on July 19. With the curious and occasional voyeurs flocking to the destroyed sites, he dryly commented, "A large number of onlookers visited the hit neighborhoods in order 'to see the bombing.' In San Lorenzo, cars were full of girls touring the ruins as if on a field trip. Following the fashion, they were wearing elegant foulards tied under their neck, in the peasant manner." And he continued, "What an extraordinary gift we have of always focusing on particulars, seizing the detail, and ignoring general facts and ideas."[52] Single episodes of destruction shocked the populace and attracted their attention, Alvaro remarked with not some degree of contempt for the stylish girls on a sightseeing mission. The same people, however, failed to link those extraordinary incidents to the country's overall political ruin. They failed to identify the conditions that had led to the unfortunate events. Most of all, they failed to take action against those responsible for such a state of affairs. "Inertia," Alvaro called it, arguing that Italians only counteracted indolence in their imagination: "they narrate legends of events that happened elsewhere, acts of courage, inscriptions on walls, over there, in another neighborhood, nobody knows where, but someplace where one imagines that people are still alive and have the will and ability to react."[53]

Not unlike other diarists, Alvaro evaluated individuals' behavior by assuming the role of distant observer, his scrutinizing gaze unforgiving as he pierced through the state of mind of fellow Italians. Poetically oriented, he summed

---

[52] Alvaro, *Quasi una vita*, p. 294.
[53] Alvaro, *Quasi una vita*, p. 295. Meanwhile, Alvaro lamented, Italians kept "'watching the spectacle'" (in quotation marks in the original).

up his impassive picture of Italy by citing the country's lack of a sustained sense of tragic.[54] In Alvaro's assessment, people's common-sense approach to daily existence risked trivializing the gravity of exceptional historical instances. Habitual conduct and inclinations deprived Italians of the ability to evaluate the moral magnitude of the extraordinary reality they were facing. Even the clamor of July 25 was deceptive in his estimation: "The crowd, in the same way it had acclaimed its idols for twenty years, now insulted them."[55] Statues that people were strewing around, vestiges of the old regime, might just serve for cashing in on the bronze, he cynically insinuated, whereas street disorders merely offered incensed youth occasions to steal.

Admittedly, Alvaro detected a spark of hope amidst all the opportunism. From the unbridled chaos, the genuineness of the sense of relief at the fall of Mussolini shed light on the deep wounds that fascism had inflicted on ordinary citizens:

> On July 25, lots of bad youth in the streets, devastations of offices, thefts of typewriters in offices and of watches and handles on buses. But there were women of the people, those that suffer their whole life, alive and truly happy for one day. One of them, at Campo dei Fiori, with a big tricolor flag, was screaming, and it was truly freedom, something luminous that arose from her suffering as a poor woman. A mother was carrying her infant child in the street, saying, "I want him to breathe this air too."[56]

For Alvaro, the brutality of fascism had deeply affected the little people, the commoners. The others, in contrast, the well to do, party supporters, and executives, had revealed their unscrupulousness—one could not expect them to acquire a political conscience or be enlightened all of a sudden. At the most, a sense of fear vexed them after years of enjoying the privileges the regime had dispensed to followers and loyalists. Uncertainty about the future,

---

[54] "The catastrophe happened in the well-known Italian atmosphere, which is incapable of drama. Italian life has a little drama every day, never tragedy." Alvaro, *Quasi una vita*, p. 298.

[55] Alvaro, *Quasi una vita*, p. 298. Sibilla Aleramo and Leonetta Cecchi Pieraccini also showed disdain for Italians' two-faced behavior. After the fall of Mussolini, Aleramo marveled at the change in people's spirit and dwelled on the swift nature of the perplexing transformation. Her attention was especially directed at the difference between the Italians' seeming submission to the regime for years upon years and their sudden euphoric condemnation of that same regime. See Aleramo, *Un amore insolito*, p. 262 (entry of July 26, 1943). For Cecchi Pieraccini's reaction see *Agendina di guerra*, pp. 222–3 (entry of July 26, 1943).

[56] Alvaro, *Quasi una vita*, p. 298.

it turns out, also motivated the regime's devotees to escape towards safer destinations, concerned as they were only with saving their skin.[57]

Although Alvaro's impressions were jaded and disenchanted, the tone of his narration never reached bellicose levels. It rather remained neutral, almost muted, as he strove to maintain an objective sensibility (if one can conceive of such an oxymoron). Not that Alvaro avoided engaging with the issues at hand. Later in the summer of 1943, having taken over the reins of the daily *Il Popolo di Roma*, he realized that the transition from fascism to Badoglio's government had not been as seamless as one might have initially hoped. His diary highlights the predicaments arising from this abrupt shift. In one specific instance, he cited letters of complaint about local issues that ordinary citizens were seemingly feeling free to send his paper. It so happens, those letters featured fake signatures—Italians were still wary of institutions and did not have confidence in the new system:

> Everybody is scared to sign even the simplest grievance about water or public transportation. Having decided to answer all letters of our readers, almost all our letters are being returned by the post office because the addressee is unknown. This is a sign that almost everybody uses aliases. The country doesn't trust. The country fears the worst.[58]

In light of twenty years of dictatorship, who could blame Italians for suspecting that surveillance practices were being continued by the newly established government? After all, in his role as director of a major newspaper, Alvaro witnessed firsthand the continuity of power's strictures in the new Badoglio government. The same executives at the same Ministry of Popular Culture that had been a staple of the dictatorship still controlled and censored the news—every evening they sent phonograms to newspapers to set the tone.[59] Change indeed appeared ephemeral.

When the armistice was announced on September 8, Alvaro's qualms about Italy's change of guard failed to be assuaged. Not only did he doubt Italians' commitment to a more democratic course, but he soberly recognized the

---

[57] Alvaro had already noted this tendency a few days prior to July 25: "Some well-born girls have numerous lovers. They say they don't know what will happen to them. Bourgeois and aristocrats hold big lunches and receptions, maybe for the same reason. Functionaries and newspaper directors discuss whether it might be better to send their families to Biella or Verona. Health resorts in Northern Italy are filling up with wealthy bourgeois fugitives." Alvaro, *Quasi una vita*, p. 295 (undated but probably July 22).

[58] Alvaro, *Quasi una vita*, p. 300.

[59] Alvaro, *Quasi una vita*, p. 301.

contradictions marring the new government. "Formalism in tragedy," he commented when Badoglio asked that the news of the armistice be published between two black stripes in sign of mourning.[60] The following day, the marshal fled the city along with the king. Alvaro's last diary entry for the month of September capped an already somber picture of the nation in that momentous summer: "A bersagliere, near the station, a poor bersagliere, went on a shooting spree from an overturned Italian tank, like a madman, alone, standing. He was easily killed by the Germans."[61] An army in disarray, let loose and abandoned by its leaders, epitomized the true tragedy the country was living amidst events of immense proportions. The next two years would test the resilience of the whole population caught between the flames of opposing forces. With the Germans taking over the capital on September 10, Alvaro too vacated the premises. His directorship at the helm of *Il Popolo di Roma* had lasted less than two months.[62]

Keeping a diary offered Alvaro a way to dig deep into his feelings. It also allowed him to hide those same feelings behind a veneer of objectivity. By focusing on others, the diary provided him with a sort of alibi, literally removing him from the reality he was describing.[63] And yet he was fully involved in the events he recounted, especially if one considers his position of responsibility as director of a newspaper in the new era of (supposedly) a free press. The reprimands he received for his responses to the censors' requests in the days following the fall of the regime reveal his active role. Granted, he obeyed the new orders. However, he also alerted readers to the presence of a censoring hand by printing blank spaces in lieu of excised sentences (Figure 4).[64] His gesture openly exposed the contradictions at the core of the new government's political course—a disclosure that was certainly not appreciated by those imposing the directives.[65]

Despite forays into symbolic protest, something remained unarticulated in Alvaro's diary: the disorientation, the sense of void he appeared to feel at the abrupt ending of fascism. For he was doubtlessly right that it all happened too

---

[60] Alvaro, *Quasi una vita*, p. 302. Several newspapers followed that move, although it is unclear whether there was an actual directive from Badoglio.

[61] Alvaro, *Quasi una vita*, p. 303.

[62] Alvaro started working at the newspaper on July 25, 1943; he left the directorship after September 8. In March 1945, Alvaro became the first director of national radio news for RAI. He resigned after three weeks in the name of journalism's independence. On this episode see Guido Crainz, "Fra Eiar e Rai," in Nicola Gallerano ed., *L'altro dopoguerra. Roma e il Sud 1943–1945* (Milan: Franco Angeli, 1985), especially pp. 514–15.

[63] From its Latin etymological roots, alibi means elsewhere.

[64] Alvaro, *Quasi una vita*, p. 299.

[65] Censors accused his action of being "demagogic." Alvaro, *Quasi una vita*, p. 302.

suddenly and too simply. The country was running the risk that the hard years of dictatorship would be swept aside and left unaccounted. Indications of unresolved questions were aplenty, as Alvaro hinted when contrasting the continuity of ministry functionaries to the swift removal of Mussolini's portraits in public offices. In an environment such as fascism, obsessed with visual power and the primacy of style, images conveyed the oppressive reach of political authority. The establishment of a new scopic regime by the Badoglio government doubtlessly signaled an alteration meant to cancel the past, even if merely symbolically. Yet could two decades of fascism be wiped out by a single, though highly emblematic, gesture? Alvaro worried about the danger of a shallow turn of events. The darker shadows left on office walls by the discarded pictures of Mussolini stood as reminders of an era that had left undeniable marks. The deletion of fascist signs from public buildings, ordered by the new government as one of its first legislative acts, was not sufficient to address the deposed dictatorship. Like Anna Menestrina, Alvaro wondered about confusing form with substance and failing to learn lessons. Having found that the picture with the king replaced the one of Mussolini in his office, his comment was unforgiving: "It appears then impossible to get used to living without portraits on the walls."[66]

Contained in a few critical observations, the moral, if not political, question of fascism loomed behind Alvaro's apparently casual remarks in the aftermath of July 25. He was not alone in raising the ethical issue. Slowly emerging as a recurring theme from intellectual diarists' tales was the need to make sense of the long-standing fascist phenomenon. The regime's collapse in 1943 brought this question to the forefront. It was high time for a reckoning.

In Solidarity: Fatherland Reconsidered

Alvaro's reactions to July 25 and September 8 condensed his fears about Italy's political immaturity and the negative feeling he held about the population's unpreparedness for a democratic turn. In his assessment, the Italians' passivity, but also their lack of understanding of the fascist phenomenon, were worrisome signs of the predicament the country faced in its new institutional phase. Although Alvaro left his contradictory positions unarticulated, all the while evaluating fellow citizens with the presumed objectivity of a distant observer, he advocated the need for moral responsibility in order to confront

[66] Alvaro, *Quasi una vita*, p. 298.

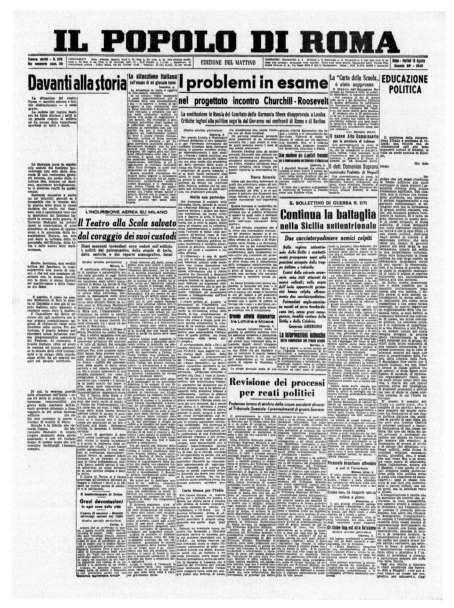

Figure 4. Front page of *Il Popolo di Roma*, August 10, 1943 (with censored excisions).

fascism's past and present. The notes he wrote in the days and months following the collapse of the regime indicate the strong ethical impetus driving his reflections in spite of his own supposed lack of exemplarity. The diary offered him a critical means to address the depraved nature of a twenty-year-long authoritarian government.

Piero Calamandrei pushed the examination of conscience to the utmost point. His journal constitutes a lesson in analytical depth and honesty. By reporting on the incredible happenings that turned Italy's current history upside down, Calamandrei reviewed the regime's failings and deconstructed its logic. In a denunciatory style that was as systematic as it was unforgiving, he condemned the fundamentally aberrant nature of Mussolini's movement.

Calamandrei had been wrestling with the immorality of fascist politics for quite an extended time when late in the evening of July 25 he heard the broadcast news of Mussolini's resignation. "God, God! Is it possible? We cannot believe it. At first, we are unable to realize the magnitude of the news. The end of fascism? There is no more duce?... The shame of these twenty years is about to crumble?..."[67] Incredulity, as well as hilarity, overwhelmed Calamandrei at first, though joy soon gained the upper hand. Such was the commotion all around him that he even stopped annotating his diary for a few days. Then on August 1 he resumed his account by laying out his understanding of the historic event:

> Truly, what we felt these days can be summarized, without being rhetorical, in this sentence: we recovered the fatherland. The fatherland as the sense of cordiality and human understanding that exists among those who, born in the same country, can communicate with a glance, a smile, an allusion. The fatherland as the sense of closeness and intimacy that at times allows for trust and friendship among people who do not know each other, whose upbringing and profession differ, but who nonetheless acknowledge each other based on something deep inside that they share and that unifies them.[68]

Enthusiastically celebrating the end of an era, Calamandrei reclaimed ownership of a concept that had been co-opted by fascist rhetoric: the fatherland. And he did so by completely recasting the meaning of the term. While the regime emphasized the cult of grandeur and promoted pompous self-importance through territorial expansion, Calamandrei saw "fatherland" as meaning affinity and brotherhood—a sense of community that one could savor even among strangers. "What a sigh of relief! We can talk with one another; we can express our true views," he exulted.[69] Fascism implied divi-

---

[67] Calamandrei, *Diario*, vol. II, p. 153.
[68] Calamandrei, *Diario*, vol. II, p. 154.
[69] Calamandrei, *Diario*, vol. II, p. 154. On revisiting the notion of fatherland after the regime see, Claudio Pavone, *Una guerra civile. Saggio storico sulla moralità nella Resistenza* (Turin: Bollati Boringhieri, 1991), chapter 4, "La guerra patriottica."

sion; it separated Italians into two camps that deemed cooperation impossible and where one side experienced oppression by the other as if under foreign occupation. In contrast, the solidarity Italians felt after July 25 signaled their ability to share thoughts without fear, including when they hurled banal catchphrases at the regime: "Finally! These assassins! This coward! This buffoon!"[70] Calamandrei detected a sort of "tenderness" in those utterances. They revealed a collective sentiment of belonging, a commonality of spirit—they expressed the power of retaking possession of one's own country not only in political but also in mental terms. "We found each other again. We are human too... One of the gravest faults of fascism was exactly this: killing the sense of fatherland," Calamandrei insisted. Mussolini's regime had turned "fatherland" into a "disgusting" word.[71]

Calamandrei's original approach to the question of fatherland was the result of years of political and civic engagement that he poured into the pages of his diary starting in 1939. Through continuous reflection over the significance of fascism and the power of its appeal, Calamandrei gradually built a counter-narrative that unmasked the moral and political claims of the regime and challenged its ideological framework. By focusing on the notion of fatherland, he evaluated fascism's aberrant path and stated his absolute refusal to be co-opted. Also, by maintaining the values of liberalism and democracy against any territorial understanding of fatherland, he opposed the regime's vainglorious dreams and abused patriotism. A provocative note of April 11, 1940, written as he followed the news of Hitler's warmongering, is revealing. Calamandrei proclaimed that "the English and the French and the Norwegians who are defending freedom are now my fatherland."[72] Explicitly renouncing soil-centered notions of citizenship, he asserted his refusal to identify with Mussolini's Italy—a belief he more forcefully advocated after the fall of the dictator: "These Italian fascists that encamped on our land were foreigners: if they were Italian, then we were not Italian."[73] Anticipating an issue that would become central to the Resistance, Calamandrei interpreted the whole *ventennio* in terms of the gulf between those who supported fascism and those who had to bear the burden of its yoke silently.[74] That cleavage was now bursting open. Badoglio's eventual declaration of war against Germany, and the

---

[70] Calamandrei, *Diario*, vol. II, pp. 154–5.
[71] Calamandrei, *Diario*, vol. II, p. 155 ("Questo nome di patria per venti anni ha fatto schifo").
[72] Calamandrei, *Diario*, vol. I, p. 147.
[73] Calamandrei, *Diario*, vol. II, p. 155 (entry of August 1, 1943).
[74] On this issue see Claudio Pavone, *Una guerra civile*, chapter 1, "La scelta" and chapter 5, "La guerra civile."

consequent lining up of Italian fascists alongside Hitler, only exasperated the already existing rift by adding to it the drama of armed confrontation. In a true assault against the Risorgimento ideals, fascism had been steadily squashing national solidarity. In Calamandrei's view, there could be no worse consequence of these actions than the specter of Italy's potential submission to foreign powers once again.

Memory of the nineteenth-century war for national independence was fresh among people of the older generation, whose parents valiantly represented the Risorgimento tradition of civic duty and patriotism—they had been steeped in those ideals. In addition, the First World War had intensified Italians' negative disposition towards Germany as they fought to reclaim lands from Prussia in a conflict whose brutality appeared to undermine the whole idea of "civilization." Within this background, the sight of Germans roaming the peninsula could not but feel as an anathema to Calamandrei. Equally disconcerting to him, their invasion confirmed the reality of Italy's internal divide. Already at the beginning of the Second World War, as Hitler's troops invaded Poland, Calamandrei addressed the conundrum, his sense of morality crushed by the prospect of fighting alongside Germany—the opposite outcome of what he felt ethically right.[75] A few weeks before Italy entered the conflict, he confided:

> If there was a remnant of good will and intelligence left in Italy, we would all unite, fascists and antifascists, and only work, night and day, to prepare resisting the *flagellum Dei*. This is the only danger: the Germans. In the dark future ahead, I see a German governor in Florence and our departures for concentration camps as real possibilities.[76]

Calamandrei's state of despair was aggravated by the absence of any protest against Hitler's aggressions and by the realization of Italy's own obliviousness to the risk of being invaded.[77] The nightmare scenario that featured the country's return to dependency on foreign powers obsessed him as a shameful and unfathomable probability—his worst nightmare. Mussolini's cowardly, indecisive behavior further contributed to Calamandrei's sense of dishonor.

---

[75] See his entry of September 2, 1939, where he compared the situation to the First World War: "If we will be fighting the war alongside Germany, our Fatherland will be on that other side." Calamandrei, *Diario*, vol. I, p. 71.

[76] Calamandrei, *Diario*, vol. I, p. 153 (entry of April 27, 1940).

[77] Calamandrei, *Diario*, vol. I, p. 161 (entry of May 13, 1940). "This indifference of Italy to the Germans' attack against Belgium and Holland marks the end of Italy as an independent people."

Italy's deficient ethical stance, her "indifference," and likelihood of entering the conflict increased his consternation to the point of "agony, a continuous suffering, also physical, this continuous sense of enervation in the stomach and the heart. [...] To wake up, to wake up, to chase away this horrible dream."[78] Alas, the nightmare did not stop. On June 10, Italy declared war against France. If ever there was an idealistic force within fascism, Calamandrei painfully concluded, it was now over, done with.[79] The only remaining and meager consolation was that "nothing worse than this could happen: nor ever more shame than this."[80] It was an abysmal comfort. By betraying France, Italy had not merely demonstrated cowardice and callousness, she had also proved her willingness to renounce all the values France represented: "civilization, humanity, dignity, the fatherland."[81] Infused with a sense of powerlessness and inevitability in the face of such catastrophic loss, Calamandrei's ever bleaker entries culminated in an ultimately dramatic claim: to save Italy one had to be against Italy, one had to wish she would lose the war.[82] This position, an almost schizophrenic split, characterized true patriotism:

> The widening phenomenon around us, which would seem horrible with the criteria used thirty years ago, is that people are terrified at the eventual joint victory of Germany and Italy and hope with all their heart for the defeat of this Italy that is fighting today. Those who think along these lines are the most honest and exemplary persons, those with whom we would like to be friends, those with whom one feels the kind of moral and cultural solidarity that constitutes the true fatherland...[83]

---

[78] Calamandrei, *Diario*, vol. I, p. 176 (entry of June 1, 1940).
[79] See entry of June 10, 1940. Calamandrei wrote, "From today on, whatever happens, fascism is finished." Calamandrei, *Diario*, vol. I, p. 182.
[80] Calamandrei, *Diario*, vol. I, p. 183 (entry of June 14, 1940).
[81] On June 13, the Germans had occupied Paris, which prompted Calamandrei's entry of June 14. See Calamandrei, *Diario*, vol. I, p. 186.
[82] Claudio Pavone discusses the dilemma that caught many Italians at the time of the country's declaration of war on France on June 10, 1940. He interprets people's wish for Italy's defeat as critical for shaping the relations between antifascists and young generations in the Resistance movement that formed later. See Pavone, *Una guerra civile*, chapter 2, "L'eredità della guerra fascista."
[83] Calamandrei, *Diario*, vol. I, p. 222 (entry of August 25, 1940). Papini took the opposite stance and indicted Italians with lack of moral unity. Writing on January 26, 1943, and seeing the war taking a bad direction for Italy, he commented, "Everybody feels deeply sad, I mean, every Italian that sincerely believed in a grander destiny for our people, including politically. The others, the majority, are almost happy with the enemy's victories and hope that, from a defeat, good will come for them and the country. Love of fatherland has not succeeded in ending and surpassing partisan hatred. This is a sign that the nation has yet to reach a true moral unity after eighty years of political unity." Papini, *Diario*, p. 104.

Wishing to rescue the concept of fatherland from the manipulative narrative of the regime, Calamandrei called for a larger and more active brotherly community.

Idealism aside, few Italians answered his call. Having withstood years of fascism, people were far from being able to shake off the passivity encouraged by the regime.[84] With a pessimistic stance, Calamandrei pronounced an undesirable reality: "The great strength of Mussolini is that all Italians are more coward than he is (who doesn't kid when it comes to cowardice)."[85] Despairing over his countrymen and women's ability to arise morally, Calamandrei particularly denounced the indifference of the middle classes, which he saw as inclined to accept evil in exchange for promises of conquests and for the equally tantalizing prospect of profit. Lacking any sense of justice, the bourgeoisie seemed happy to proclaim, "If Germany wins, we will have everything back. 'Everything,' that is, the land. These are people who conceive 'everything' in terms of material goods, of territorial possession. And they don't know that 'everything' is dignity, is freedom..."[86] For many, fatherland, territorialism, and victory went together, and it was hard to give up that combination.

In view of the several moral impasses the country faced, Calamandrei raised a tragic dilemma that left him prostrated: how could one distinguish Italy from fascism and separate the one from the other, especially if the country was going to fall under German domination? This was the crux of the matter, the "heartbreaking tragedy":

> Until now, this Italian collapse might have merely looked like the collapse of fascism, and that's all. Now, starting with Trieste, the collapse of Italy begins. And if we have to fight to defend our land [...], how will we be able to fight wishing for victory, when we know that Europe will be confronted with injustice, and how will we be able to wish for defeat if it will lead us to lose our independence?[87]

A drama enveloped the country and even appeared to undermine the achievements of the Risorgimento. Weakened by fascism's ethical emptiness, Italy

---

[84] Although not a practicing Catholic, Calamandrei believed religion could help reignite a moral standing among the people. See his entry of May 13, 1940: "What happens today in Italy, this absolute passivity in the face of injustice, is the result not only of the personal work of Mussolini and fascism, but also of all the work of anticlerical materialism stupidly pursued in Italy during the previous decades." Calamandrei, *Diario*, vol. I, p. 163.

[85] Calamandrei, *Diario*, vol. I, p. 307 (entry of February 22, 1941).

[86] Calamandrei, *Diario*, vol. I, p. 324 (entry of April 4, 1941).

[87] Calamandrei, *Diario*, vol. I, p. 327 (entry of April 7, 1941).

risked subjugation by the German ally.[88] That menace became a certainty following the September 8, 1943 armistice. By then, with the illusion of an end to war ever dimming, the identification of Italy with fascism's goals threatened to become the perverse outcome of the twisted historical events. Responses to that eventuality were equally disturbing—rooting for defeat, if justifiable when the regime was in force, felt more agonizing now that it implicated the country's sovereignty. Whereas extricating Italy from the mark of infamy branded by the regime could not be easily accomplished, ethical coherence dictated that one needed to renounce national interests. It was an intractable dilemma, indeed, and one that showed the durability of the knot fascism had tied around Italians.

Fascism, Fascism Not

Traveling by train two days after the proclamation of armistice, Calamandrei became involved in a skirmish with another passenger, an officer in the Marines, who, horrified at the recent news, found disgraceful Calamandrei's opinion that the war was worse than the armistice. Bitter and mortified, Calamandrei tried to unravel the false logic guiding the officer's perspective. He realized, however, and this was most upsetting to him, that the officer's opinion had a persuasive force able to exercise enormous power on many Italians; he found himself "surprised at hearing how strong the shame of the armistice is, even among humble people."[89] Worse still, fascism seemed to be re-emerging unscathed from the infelicitous turn of September 8, and Calamandrei sensed the dangers associated with the seamlessly smooth way the regime had fallen. The mere celebratory rituals of symbolic destruction with which Italians had saluted the dictator's resignation were not sufficient to adjudicate Mussolini's long tenure. It was Calamandrei's hope that the armistice, while helping to solidify hatred for the Germans, would offer the public a chance to settle accounts with the regime. One needed to consider that the fundamental elements of fascism's brutality had remained unchallenged after the dictatorship's fall, including the continuation of a predatory war that the country was now inheriting. It was time to redraw the lines.

---

[88] On November 2, 1941 Calamandrei wrote, "Here in Italy, we are approaching the occupation, even official and declared, by the Germans. We'll endure raids, impounds of radios, concentration camps, hunger and revolts." Calamandrei, *Diario*, vol. I, pp. 395–6.

[89] Calamandrei, *Diario*, vol. II, p. 189 (entry of September 10, 1943).

Probably due to the surprising circumstances under which the regime had collapsed, the critical issue of the Italians' past and future relationship to fascism had been left aside or, more accurately, evaded. Not that it was an easy question to address, Calamandrei recognized. Like others, he too did not feel immune to the predicament caused by the dictatorship. If, on the one hand, those who acted inside fascism with the hope of being able to bring change from within were deluded, on the other hand, being actively antifascist meant either exile or commitment to violence. Calamandrei could not subscribe to either option. How to oppose fascism then? The alternatives seemed both dire and ineffective and, like Alvaro, Calamandrei wished for a better way to be useful while "remaining spiritually outside."[90] In the past, he had succeeded in maintaining distance from the regime's worldview, although he accepted compromises when it came to his professional duties. In the current circumstances, however, being outside was no longer an acceptable alternative. One way or another, the whole of Italy needed to come to terms with the historical experience of fascism, especially in light of the latter's recrudescence in the newly constituted Italian Social Republic. Under this new incarnation, the fundamentally immoral nature of fascism was brought into even starker relief. Calamandrei felt particular repulsion for these "Republican" fascists—vengeful, cruel, and shameful—whose profound wickedness was showcased during the January 1944 prosecution of the members of the Grand Council accused of betraying Mussolini at the meeting of July 25, 1943.[91] As the special tribunal of the RSI delivered a death sentence to five of the six defendants present at the hearing, the judges exhibited no regard for the rule of law, nor did they show respect for the administration of justice.[92] The court instead operated as a political tool aimed at revenge and assassination.[93] To Calamandrei, the whole trial was a symptom of fascism's worst instincts—it was a concerning sign of its future direction. Absent liberation by Allied forces, Calamandrei despaired, Italy would fall back into the hands of ignoble criminals.

---

[90] Calamandrei, *Diario*, vol. I, p. 37 (entry of May 15, 1939).
[91] See his entry of December 12, 1943 in *Diario*, vol. II, p. 279–81.
[92] There were nineteen original signatories of the document that demanded Mussolini's resignations at the meeting of the Grand Council of July 1943. With the exception of the six sentenced in January 1944, none of the other members of the Grand Council were ever captured by the authorities of the RSI. They all survived the war.
[93] On the occasion of the trial, Calamandrei wrote, "Every week that goes by one can see that everything we ever said or thought about fascism in our hatred and our indignation has always been too lax, too weak in the face of reality. They are true street bandits, common delinquents, bloody mad lunatics, and, moreover, cowards and thieves." See Calamandrei, *Diario*, vol. II, p. 313 (entry of January 12, 1944). The trial was a true shocker for many Italians.

Whereas the collapse of Mussolini on July 25 had lifted the spirit of countless Italians, it was becoming ever more apparent that the magnitude of fascism's scope, its long-lasting dominance, and the extent of its effects could not be easily liquidated. Despite the population's desire to simply move on, the fascist nightmare was not over. On the contrary, it had transmogrified into a two-headed Hydra powered by an ever-more despondent Nazi army deployed throughout the country. In Central Italy, where Calamandrei was located, the reality of the occupation forced people to confront fascism's persistence well into 1944. Further north, Italians would have to wait until April 1945 for the fascist grip to end. Only in the South the political situation turned more auspicious as Allied forces gained the upper hand. Although Naples was the second most bombarded Italian city and suffered enormous destruction, by late September 1943 its people had successfully pushed back the German occupiers, eventually easing the arrival of Anglo-American forces on October 1.[94] One of the most notable residents of the city, Benedetto Croce, became involved in organizing the government of the freed Kingdom of the South, his paramount intent being to prepare the return of liberal democracy in Italy. How did Croce address the concern over fascism's endurance raised by Alvaro and Calamandrei? And how did other intellectual diarists relate to this conundrum? As it turns out, the range of responses varied. Nevertheless, and in spite of the moral impulse that underlay the analyses of intellectual diarists, a perplexing trend toward evading core questions unified the different perspectives. Guilt became the notion at the center of litigation, though its assignment took surprising, if maybe not unexpected, turns. Fascism was not necessarily on trial.

Voiding fascism: The pure and the impure

After first hearing the news of Mussolini's resignations on July 25, Croce exultingly wrote, "The feeling I have is of liberation from an evil which weighed upon the heart's core; derivative evils and dangers remain, but that evil will not return."[95] Unable to rest for the next few nights, Croce was highly

---

[94] On the so-called "quattro giornate di Napoli" (four days of Naples) the bibliography is extensive. Some accounts were published soon after the event in 1943 and 1944.

[95] See *Croce, the King and the Allies: Extracts from a Diary by Benedetto Croce July 1943-June 1944* (New York: Norton, 1950), translated by Sylvia Sprigge, p. 9. I will be quoting from this source, when available, but will add the corresponding page numbers of the Italian original version published in *Taccuini di guerra*. On the specific passage cited here, see p. 13 of *Taccuini di guerra*.

apprehensive about the country's future: "Fascism seems already a thing of the past to me, a cycle that is closed, and I have no taste for the pleasures of vendetta. But Italy is still a painful problem."[96] Wishing to look ahead, Croce avowed the need to leave fascism behind, enshrined in a cloud of fog characteristic of all things past, faded and nebulous. To him, the long span of history inhabited by the regime constituted a sort of aberration—it could not, by any means, provide resources for moving the country forward. On the contrary, the fascist phenomenon only represented an obstacle. Hence, Croce championed the need to step back in time, prior to the two decades of Mussolini's rule, and tap into the old liberal tradition.[97] In his perspective, ignoring fascism essentially amounted to a sweeping condemnation; it was a radical form of criticism.

With summer unfolding, the philosopher found himself completely involved in the behind-the-scenes negotiations between Badoglio and the Anglo-Americans. Foreign officers in charge of the occupied southern territories considered Croce a major point of reference, a central figure in what they envisaged as the reorganization of Italian politics. Representatives of Allied forces paid continuous visits to the philosopher during the month of September, and even transported him and his family away from their residence in Sorrento fearing that the Germans would take him hostage. Cognizant of Italy's fragile conditions and unfortunate state of dependency, Croce shed his scholarly mantle and focused on fulfilling civic responsibilities. Instead of a writing routine, his daily schedule was filled with immediate political issues, regardless of his declared ineptness in that realm—politics was not Croce's vocation and did not figure among his natural dispositions either (or so he claimed). Nevertheless, he felt obliged to offer unequivocal commitment to the final defeat of Nazi-fascism.[98] Like Calamandrei, he believed that Hitler's delirious design of conquest threatened to enslave the entire European continent. Like Calamandrei, he could only wish for Italy's military loss.[99]

---

[96] Croce, *The King and the Allies*, p. 9 (*Taccuini di guerra*, p. 14) (entry of July 27, 1943).

[97] In 1932 Croce wrote a book on the crisis of liberalism and its relationship to history in *Storia d'Europa nel secolo decimonono* (Bari: Laterza, 1932) translated as *History of Europe in the Nineteenth Century*. For a commentary in English, see Hayden White, "The Abiding Relevance of Croce's Idea of History," *Journal of Modern History* vol. 35, no. 2 (June 1963): pp. 109–24. Also see Rizi, *Benedetto Croce and Italian Fascism*, chapter 10.

[98] See entry of November 13, 1943, in *Croce, the King and the Allies*, p. 38 (*Taccuini di guerra*, p. 44).

[99] See entry of July 27, 1943: "And yet, once at the cross-roads, there never was but one course for Italians, to choose defeat rather than apparent victory by the side of the kind of allies whom Mussolini had inflicted on Italy, when he sold Italy and its future and co-operated in enslaving every one in Europe." *Croce, the King and the Allies*, p. 10 (*Taccuini di guerra*, p. 14).

While a moral imperative compelled Croce to evaluate the regime and denounce its evils, he maintained that fascism was inexorably finished. He also expressed skepticism about fascism's long-term effects, in contrast proclaiming its historical obsolescence. Aligning with the sentiments of many Italians, Croce believed it was time to move on despite the fact that fascism kept creeping back both phenomenally, through its reactivation, and in Croce's own reflections and work, no matter his best attempts at ignoring it. Having agreed to contribute an opinion piece on the topic for *The New York Times*, Croce noted in his diary that he "could not get on with it. I find is so repellent and wearisome still to be talking of Fascism."[100] The next day he finally managed to accomplish the task, but could not help restating his profound exhaustion at entertaining the subject:

> I shall not say what the life of Italy has been like in the period which opened then and which lasted more than twenty years, because those who lived it, and consequently had to observe it and talk about it, even though merely in order to oppose it, now only wish not to think of it and not to speak any more about it.[101]

Croce expressed an absolute sense of disgust towards the whole fascist phenomenon. After living under the authoritarian regime for so many years, he could not bear dealing with it any longer. It was "a subject which is highly disagreeable and repugnant to me," he confessed, and the only reason he decided to write about it was his conviction that fascism constituted a danger for any society. The attraction Mussolini exercised over statesmen all over the world especially alerted Croce to the need of sounding the alarm. Fascism was a "contemporary sickness" not merely a "*morbus Italicus*" (an Italian disease), he insisted, and it should not be underestimated.[102] Ultimately, Croce found consolation in the fact that even if Italy had to perish, it would not be by fascist hand.[103] Fascism was absolutely an anomaly, and, moreover, one that needed to be avoided unconditionally.

---

[100] *Croce, the King and the Allies*, p. 26 (*Taccuini di guerra*, p. 31) (entry of October 13, 1943).

[101] Croce, "The Fascist Germ Still Lives," *The New York Times* (November 28, 1943), p. 44. As already noted in the Introduction, the second part of the sentence starting with "because" did not appear in the version published in *The New York Times*. See original version "Il fascismo come pericolo mondiale" in Croce, *Scritti e discorsi politici* (Bari: Laterza, 1963), vol. 1, p. 12.

[102] *The New York Times* (November 28, 1943), p. 45 (quotation marks in the original). On Croce's notion of fascism as an infection see Pier Giorgio Zunino, *Interpretazione e memoria del fascismo. Gli anni del regime* (Rome-Bari: Laterza, 1991), pp. 132–9 and David Ward, *Antifascisms*, pp. 70–5.

[103] "And now Italy is free of the fascist infection. Although still in grave danger, she can die any kind of death but no longer that death," *The New York Times* (November 28, 1943), p. 44.

There was a sort of contradiction in Croce's austere view of fascism, almost a double entendre. On the one hand, he was convinced that as a historical phenomenon fascism constituted a generalized threat with the potential to reverberate globally. On the other hand, he appeared to trust that Italy, after bearing fascism's brunt for over two decades, had become freed of its malignancy—a particularly jarring assertion considering that the crumbling of fascism was not instigated by the will of the people and that only war had made possible the end of Italy's tragic spell.[104] Since external circumstances precipitated the regime's collapse, how could one be assured that the body politic was cleared of the disease or immunized against its resurgence? Total cleansing could not be expected when many in the body's legs and arms refused inoculation (to continue with the physiological metaphor). Complicating things further, Croce focused attention on the body mass, that is, those ordinary people who had supposedly been the passive recipients of the "disease." He appeared to discount the degree of their actual involvement in the regime to the point that, in what will become a central feature of his perspective on political purging, he argued that their rehabilitation should not be hindered. When the chief of British police in Capri (Croce's temporary residence in the fall of 1943) asked him if he was protecting local fascists, the philosopher denied it, soon after reporting in his diary:

> Then I told him my feeling that, since many Italians in order to live, out of fear, through vanity or through laziness, had accepted Fascism, it would be impossible to reduce Italy to a place in which a small number of the pure, or the alleged pure, would accuse and condemn the majority of their fellow citizens, and that therefore not only justice but indulgence and forgiveness must be brought into play.[105]

Taking on the question of fascism's legacy, Croce dwelled on a dichotomy of his own construction that divided Italians between "pure" and "impure"—a distinction that was supposed to widen the circle of innocents while seemingly believing in the innocuous nature of people's passive acceptance of the dictatorship. Croce also left aside the question of fascism's true believers as

---

[104] Elena Carandini Albertini was well aware of this reality. In considering the aftermath of Mussolini's fall, she referred to "the impure origin of our liberation on July 25." See *Dal terrazzo*, p. 12 (entry of August 12, 1943). Also see entry of September 11, after the announcement of the armistice: "The fall of fascism did not come from the Italians' act of conscience," p. 32.
[105] Croce, *the King and the Allies*, p. 35 (*Taccuini di guerra*, p. 41) (entry of October 13, 1943).

well as the problem of fascism's lasting impact on governmental practices and institutions. An entry he wrote on Mussolini confirms this orientation, as the philosopher again downplayed the significance of the phenomenon, this time by declaring the current irrelevance of the dictator. No discussion of Mussolini's political effectiveness was entertained. Instead, Croce emphasized his dishonesty:

> This morning I thought how practically no one now talks of Mussolini, not even to rant against him. The very rumour which occasionally goes about, that he is dead, proves that he is really dead in everybody's mind. Even I seldom find feelings rising up in me against him at the thought of the ruin to which he has brought Italy and the profound corruption which he has left in every branch of public life.[106]

A contaminating immorality flowed from the figure of Mussolini—a man that Croce wanted to designate as unmemorable and unworthy of consideration and, even more consequentially, not central for explaining the terrible course of recent Italian history. In a long meditative entry, Croce warned future scholars against falling prey to the temptation of focusing merely on Mussolini in their interpretative accounts of the period, potentially making recourse to superlative features as justifications for the dictator's success. In his opinion, that would be a mistake: "The only problem worth of inquiry and of meditation does not concern his personality, which is null, but Italian and European history, in which the trend of ideas and sentiments crowned the fortunes of such a man."[107] Seeing Mussolini as irreparably deflated, "a cardboard figure which has lost its wooden framework and hangs limp and folds up floppily," Croce suggested broader lines of inquiry to make sense of what he interpreted as a European crisis more than an Italian one.[108] His orientation toward reducing Mussolini's legacy to mere corruption scarcely comes across as a wise one, though, even if countless Italians seemed to agree with him. In its

---

[106] Croce, the King and the Allies, p. 43 (Taccuini di guerra, p. 49) (entry of December 2, 1943).
[107] Croce, the King and the Allies, p. 44 (Taccuini di guerra, p. 50) (entry of December 2, 1943).
[108] Croce, the King and the Allies, p. 44 (Taccuini di guerra, p. 50). In the original, a different simile is used, "the figure of a stuffed dummy that has lost the sawdust that filled it." There might not be a connection here, but in 1935 the journalist George Seldes published a book on Mussolini by the title Sawdust Caesar: The Untold History of Mussolini and Fascism (New York: Harper and Brothers, 1935). The book had been ready since 1931 but was not released because of Mussolini's persistent popularity. See Henry R. Spencer's review of the book in American Political Science Review vol. 30, no. 2 (April 1936): pp. 384–5. Spencer writes that Mussolini had been "a figure for journalistic adulation, a perfect 'headliner'," p. 384.

extended rule, fascism had implanted more than dishonesty in the country. And as much as one might have found the regime superficial and empty, its ability to penetrate under the epidermal layers of people's beliefs and practices could not be discounted. Aberrations leave their marks once normalcy resumes, and diseases cause scars, even when cured. Why would the *morbus* of fascism be any different?

Croce's profound aversion for fascism translated into a distinctive critique that, unlike Calamandrei's cultural and ethical evaluation, left unresolved a host of intractable problems about the status of Mussolini and his movement. When Calamandrei welcomed the regime's fall on July 25, he addressed the ideological power and legacy of fascism, its distorted appropriation of "fatherland," the question of fascists as foreign, the unethical status of Germany's war, and the issue of patriotism. Although focused on the dilemma of how to separate Italy from fascism, Calamandrei advocated the definite need to reckon with a phenomenon that had kept the country under its grip for twenty years. Croce, in contrast, opted to relegate fascism to the dustbin of history—it was an anomaly that did not deserve to be considered, and one that would be better left alone and silenced. To Croce, fascism was gone, Mussolini appeared inconsequential, and his power was but an extreme form of corruption. Italians, in turn, had responded to the dictatorship with a passive attitude rather than genuine involvement and could not be blamed or held responsible. In spite of his antifascist stance, Croce ultimately advocated ignoring the entire fascist experience as irrelevant for determining the future of the country. His infamous idea of parenthesis, according to which fascism was only a temporary break in the long course of Italy's liberal history, justified demoting twenty years of abused freedom. Fascism definitively took a backseat in his analysis, even if one can deduce that the strategic motivation of safeguarding the country's future stood behind his move.[109] A similar trend can be observed in other intellectual diarists whose commentaries, though still driven by equally moral motivations as Croce, simply adjusted the course and moved their target of culpability.

---

[109] Eugenio Di Rienzo affirms the political rationale of Croce's thesis. See Di Rienzo, *Benedetto Croce. Gli anni dello scontento (1943–1948)* (Soveria Mannelli: Rubbettino, 2019). For a critical discussion of the parenthesis thesis see Pier Giorgio Zunino, *La Repubblica e il suo passato. Il fascismo dopo il fascismo, il comunismo, la democrazia: le origini dell'Italia contemporanea* (Bologna: il Mulino, 2003), chapter 5, "Mito della 'parentesi' e realtà dell'Italia fascista in Benedetto Croce." Zunino also supports the argument that political reasons underlie Croce's parenthesis thesis. See chapter 6, "Verso 'un mondo violento, oscuro e barbarico'."

We are all guilty

Differently from Croce, Andrea Damiano was particularly sensitive to the issue of Italians' complicity with the regime. Well ahead of fascism's collapse, he pointed the finger at those who evaded the question of personal connivance. Motivated by a Christian sense of guilt, he focused on individual responsibility:

> I am not fond of the common vituperation against fascism. It's too easy! In the majority of cases universal imprecations betray a concern that is all practical and scarcely noble: the age-old need to blame others for the inevitable disaster. And it so happens, the louder the complaints or worse the damages, the more they reveal people's effort at passing the buck and identifying themselves as victims, never co-responsible. For twenty years Italians endured fascism. Countless of them were pleased with it. Now this is a sin in need of atonement.[110]

Damiano's scorching denunciation of Italians was unrelenting, and he advocated reviewing one's past actions critically: "The day will surely come when these last twenty years will be on trial [...]. That day the Italian people will finally have to find the strength to look deep into themselves with patience, resolve, and an inflexible thirst for truth."[111] According to Damiano, no excuses would be acceptable or defensible. Indeed, he rejected them outright. Conversely, he maintained the importance of self-reflection so that Italians would be able to recognize their responsibility for fascism's thriving.[112] Already sensing the end of the regime's tenure some eight months ahead of its actual expiration, Damiano questioned the significance of fascism's tenacity across two decades. He feared, while resenting it, the Italians' disorientation and detected no hopeful sign for the near future. Italians were guilty of following unquestioningly even when skeptical. "What a useless people of sluggards we are," he lamented.[113] In his view, those compromised with the regime were looking for an alibi and wished for a free pass. The others, instead,

---

[110] Damiano, *Rosso e grigio*, pp. 29–30 (entry of November 22, 1942). I am not dwelling on issues of rhetorical style in the case of intellectual diarists, but Damiano was certainly among the most highflown of them.

[111] Damiano, *Rosso e grigio*, p. 33 (entry of November 25, 1942).

[112] "But the Italian that today shrugs, and that to justify himself almost claims to having been a slave—without realizing [...] that fascism was born because he allowed it—this Italian wants to elude his original responsibility," *Rosso e grigio*, p. 34 (entry of November 25, 1942).

[113] Damiano, *Rosso e grigio*, p. 33.

remained mute and submissive, not even offering a hint of passive resistance.[114] Aware of his own moral weaknesses, Damiano projected personal discontent onto fellow citizens and extended to them the severity with which he evaluated his own conduct. Within the complex historical situation in which Europe and Italy found themselves, people's lack of direction put Damiano in a bind, deepening his pessimism and mortification while heightening his "anxiety over not knowing how to live in a free world any longer."[115] Since Italians appeared to be waiting out the regime, would they eventually be ready to engage in public life and abandon skepticism, as well as spiritual corruption, after years of enslavement? That was the question: "When the corpse called fascism will be removed, then, we say and think, we'll begin to live again. But *how*, exactly, will life be then?"[116] In Damiano's eyes, the degree to which fascism had altered people's critical abilities was disheartening; it was a symptom of the moral crisis afflicting the country.

When on July 25 news arrived of Mussolini's arrest, Damiano's reactions were mixed. Still putting the Italians on trial, he showed contempt for the popular euphoria that welcomed the announcement. "The slaves rejoice," he wrote—a corrosive statement.[117] Although he immediately recognized that to be happy in such circumstances "is human," he obviously resented his fellow citizens' enthusiasm, finding it both naïve and misdirected: "People don't think, they don't want to think, they are satisfied with this only fundamental thought: fascism is over. But the war? The new government has proclaimed that 'the war continues.' Who believes that? Today it suffices that the regime is finished."[118] From the height of his self-righteousness, Damiano expressed impatience with ordinary people's joyous reactions. He reproached them for failing to grasp the reality of the situation and for falsely identifying the end of fascism with peace. The "crowd" did not understand that "the worst is yet to come and twenty years of fascism cannot be liquidated with forty-eight hours of partying."[119] Surely, Damiano conceded, one could empathize with popular abandonment, but he saw another troubling sign in festive reactions. Almost blasé in their attitudes, Italians were looking back at fascism as "already far: an anachronism [...], as if after all there was not much to it: wasn't fascism already dead long ago?" True, Damiano admitted, fascism "had fallen softly,

---

[114] To those thoughts, Damiano added, "Only the murmuring rises, but it is wind." Damiano, *Rosso e grigio*, p. 60 (entry of June 7, 1943).
[115] Damiano, *Rosso e grigio*, p. 62 (entry of June 21, 1943).
[116] Damiano, *Rosso e grigio*, p. 61 (entry of June 21, 1943).
[117] Damiano, *Rosso e grigio*, p. 70 (entry of July 27, 1943).
[118] Damiano, *Rosso e grigio*, p. 70 (entry of July 27, 1943).
[119] Damiano, *Rosso e grigio*, p. 71 (entry of July 27, 1943).

with no resistance, like an overripe fruit," but what did it all really mean to the people?[120] The question was not irrelevant. Absent a popular insurrection, the Italians' relationship to the regime remained to be assessed. For Damiano, this was a priority.

Highly perspicacious, Damiano's stern posture was slightly tempered by sanguine descriptions of popular responses to the news of the regime's fall. On his way back to Milan from a mountain retreat, he ran into cheerful groups: "The crowd seemed inebriated by that sun, that blue sky, a new sense of life: free, free! I didn't notice any arrogance, or anything threatening or raucous. It was a street joy, simple." A sensation of lightheartedness struck him too: "In the afternoon the trams stopped. Not having a bike, I had to run on foot right and left. How many kilometers did I travel? I did not feel any tiredness: that wave, that jubilation, that fever."[121] Caught in the collective enthusiasm, Damiano shared the communal fervor and felt genuinely involved in people's emotional passion. Not much time passed, however, before he lapsed back into affliction, powerless at the dramatic unfolding of events and still regretful over the Italians' lack of initiative. He bitterly commented, "If we waited for the populace, who knows how much longer fascism would have lasted." While the fall of Mussolini had only been made possible by the king's maneuvers, Italy's future remained uncertain. Would the country be fighting against Germany or not? "Doubts, resentments, repulsions. You can't get out of the tangle. Everything is murky, sour, ominous. There is a horrendous feeling of being ensnared, a physical sense of strangulation. We brood our grief and our impotence with a stony heart and a bruised soul. Suffocating days. This anguish."[122]

To Damiano, the picture was dire. In his excessive zeal, almost a religious fanatic in pursuit of purity, he continued to indict Italians for having enabled fascism. The lack of moral standing that had caused the regime to rise remained at the center of his invective till the end of the diary in 1945, and he scarcely took up the issue of the actual costs the dictatorship inflicted on the country for over two decades. Nor did he address the pain that people experienced on a daily basis or the question of the regime's institutional legacy. Ultimately sidelining fascism in favor of promoting individual guilt, he ironically obtained the same result of ignoring the regime's historical significance for which he reproached fellow citizens. Damiano had rightly identified the

---

[120] Damiano, *Rosso e grigio*, p. 71 (entry of July 27, 1943).
[121] Damiano, *Rosso e grigio*, pp. 72, 73 (entry of July 27, 1943).
[122] Damiano, *Rosso e grigio*, pp. 76–7 (entry of August 6, 1943).

critical issue of Italians' collusion with the regime as central to an explanation of the fascist phenomenon. His offended moral sensibility, however, drove him to downplay the other side of the equation. Beyond vague assertions of unaccountability and laziness, he failed to account for the causes of people's complicity.

Fascism's imago

While intellectuals such as Damiano struggled with the ethics of responsibility, Ardengo Soffici projected his sense of morality onto fascism. He genuinely believed in the necessity of its ethical existence and firmly accepted the premises of the movement as originally developed by Mussolini. Disconcerted by the outbreak of the war in September 1939, and wishing to bring back spiritual and political stability to Europe, Soffici placed all his hopes in fascism's virtue. He trusted that Mussolini would hold on to high-principled standards (according to Soffici's own worldview), even though one could not ignore the regime's dysfunctions. Fascist Italy "has a foot in chaos. Actually, it has many heads in it, those of the many superficial, easy going, vulgar individuals that have every finger in the pie and operate without having an inkling of the thought and great vision proclaimed by the Leader."[123]

Soffici's critique was aimed at separating fascism's pure followers from the opportunists and Pharisees. Although he did not doubt fascism's superior ideals, he saw a gap between principles and reality and was skeptical about the degree to which those professing to be fascist believers approximated the movement's original intent. As Italy entered the world conflict amidst fears of losing the war, personal failures appeared to Soffici more blatantly consequential. He bitterly pointed to the shifting stances of the so-called loyalists, who loudly acclaimed Mussolini when he triumphed, but fell silent and appeared reluctant to support his military engagement in the currently less favorable circumstances.[124] To Soffici, fluctuations in the degree of displayed support were a sign of naked opportunism. And he had no qualms denouncing the alleged fascists who were spoiling the movement—they made a mock-

---

[123] Soffici, *Sull'orlo dell'abisso*, p. 34 (entry of November 6, 1939).
[124] See his entry of February 4, 1941: "As already in September 1939, the glorious gerarchi of official fascism, the 'fedelissimi' of Mussolini when he was in vogue, don't show up, remain silent, are nowhere to be found; they do not exist any longer. At very grave and important moments, these good people, who were so content to warble, to wave flags, to indulge in parades, have nothing to say." Soffici, *Sull'orlo dell'abisso*, p. 64.

ery of it. Moreover, because of their administrative ineptitude and inability to govern, they would end up provoking popular revolts. In this potential scenario, one should not interpret as antifascist the Italians' protests against the lack of basic provisions such as bread. On the contrary, eventual disorders were a sign of true fascism in that they opposed "*this* fascism of the incompetent, careerist, idiotic and selfish rhetoricians, unscrupulous braggarts."[125] Dejectedly pessimistic, Soffici proclaimed his own confusion in the face of "a defeatist, dishonest, lackadaisical fascism, the negation of what it was meant to be."[126]

Painstakingly registering his distress throughout the diary, Soffici lamented the current state of affairs but continued to trust Mussolini and wondered how to bring those dysfunctions to the leader's attention, since certainly Mussolini must have been kept in the dark. Nothing short of the spirit and soul of the movement were at stake, and only deep devotion to fascism's ideals stopped Soffici from giving up his beliefs. "I am spending atrocious days, even though still animated by my faith of an ancient and new Italian. Mystical faith," he wrote on December 1, 1942.[127] Relentlessly anguished at the sight of "the betrayed and dishonored fascist idea," he was unable to contain a sense of horror at the malfeasance of local governments, which he saw as the main culprit of Italians' ill feelings toward the regime.[128] In essence, the problem boiled down to one basic truth for Soffici: Italians were good people brought to exasperation by corrupt politicians—not a very original conclusion.

After witnessing the discredit caused by this "false" fascism among the population, an overwhelmed Soffici was tempted to stop writing his journal altogether.[129] As the course of events was not favoring the regime, on May 27, 1943 he fittingly began his entry, "My repugnance at continuing these sad notes persists and is getting worse."[130] Two months later, with the facts of July 25 barely behind, he was ready to give up entirely: "The enormity of the errors and recklessness of that degenerated fascism having reached a tragic point, I was not feeling the courage to continue this anguished and depressing diary any longer."[131] One could almost sense the shock Soffici suffered at the news of the regime's collapse. Equally painful must have been acknowledging the Italians' reactions at the happening: "Today we learn that Mussolini fell and

---

[125] Soffici, *Sull'orlo dell'abisso*, p. 71 (entry of May 31, 1941).
[126] Soffici, *Sull'orlo dell'abisso*, p. 76 (entry of September 20, 1941).
[127] Soffici, *Sull'orlo dell'abisso*, p. 110.
[128] Soffici, *Sull'orlo dell'abisso*, p. 118 (entry of January 22, 1943).
[129] On false fascism, see, for example, entry of April 8, 1943, *Sull'orlo dell'abisso*, pp. 122–3.
[130] Soffici, *Sull'orlo dell'abisso*, p. 123.
[131] Soffici, *Sull'orlo dell'abisso*, p. 125 (entry of July 26, 1943).

the king put himself at the head of the nation at war. All throughout, Italy brims with joy."[132] It was a debacle.

As deep as his desolation was, Soffici continued to defend the ideals represented by Mussolini. And while he despaired over the infelicitous turn of events in that momentous summer of 1943, he still salvaged fascism in an operation that denounced its internal liabilities—nothing else was the source of the disrepute. Soffici focused on the several levels of responsibilities that had led to the deterioration of fascism and conceded that Mussolini had inadequately addressed a long-standing simmering issue.[133] In the end, however, Soffici's seemingly measured approach foundered, and he lashed out his anger at all Italians. He demoted them to a morally degenerate horde guilty of mindlessly celebrating the fall of the dictator: "The crowd unleashes its raucousness; the subversive mob rises up and stews."[134] Steadily attached to an image of fascism founded on "a generous, great, heroic, fundamentally Italian idea" as pursued by Mussolini, Soffici insisted that mediocrities had caused the experiment to fail, triggering fascism's ruin and jeopardizing Italy's grandeur.[135] Unable to fulfill a "beautiful and grand destiny," Italy was then doomed to die in a tragic end.[136] There could be no worse outcome than the country's descent into historical and political irrelevance. A perspective on the fascist movement from within, Soffici's analysis became more pessimistic as the regime's declining spiral accelerated. From an initial emphasis on internal corruption, his critique ultimately moved to indict the whole Italian people—they had done nothing to stop fascism's fall.

Not as explicit as Soffici's, Giovanni Papini's evaluation of fascism was moot, and the hole in his diary covering the crucial months from the end of February to mid-November 1943 surely contributes to the opacity of his sparse declarations. In Papini's case, silence speaks. Certainly, the horizons of his thought were expansive, and more than an assessment of political matters his diary combined pseudo-philosophical views with references to current events, such as when he appealed to a vague notion of "old European civilization" against American and Soviet formulas. Already anticipating a culture war of sorts, Papini aspired to compose grandiose all-encompassing works

---

[132] Soffici, *Sull'orlo dell'abisso*, p. 125 (entry of July 26, 1943).
[133] "That unfortunate Leader, in many other ways great, by the fact that he kept misunderstanding the true state of things and tolerating the worst misdeeds of many false fascists—his true enemies—had been losing his old prestige for some time and making his regime unpopular and grotesque too," Soffici, *Sull'orlo dell'abisso*, p. 125 (entry of July 26, 1943).
[134] Soffici, *Sull'orlo dell'abisso*, p. 126 (entry of July 29, 1943).
[135] Soffici, *Sull'orlo dell'abisso*, p. 130 (entry of August 21, 1943).
[136] Soffici, *Sull'orlo dell'abisso*, p. 130 (entry of August 26, 1943).

that defied confines and limits, including a treatise he called *Universal Judgment*. Early in 1943, he alluded to his vision for it: "Will I be able to give an idea of *all* the forms, *all* the problems, *all* the greatness and *all* the misery of human existence?"[137] Led by totalizing ambitions, Papini's desire to ponder the human condition by appealing to a Christian vision led him to pronouncements about fellow Italians that were as wide-ranging as they were ahistorical—a mixture of anthropological and generic evaluations thrown into a big cauldron of prophetic divinations. Especially once the whole fascist castle crumbled, he could not spare critical assessments of his compatriots. Sometimes benevolent and at other times harsher, his criticisms shifted attention away from the regime with the presumption that fascism was only guilty of having "made mistakes."[138] In not so many words, he continued to uphold his faith in the movement while exonerating himself of any moral liability: "I made many mistakes in my life, as a person and as a writer, but always because driven by imagination and sentiment, naïveté and haste, never, NEVER, because of calculation, interest, or hatred, or wickedness."[139] Dismayed at the regime's collapse—a downturn that he interpreted as marking the defeat of any claims of superiority Italy might assert—Papini eventually blamed Italians' gullibility, laziness, and self-interest for fascism's faltering.[140] No longer hiding behind a semblance of neutrality, he declared to have definitively lost any trust in his fellow citizens: "The Italian people have so painfully and radically disappointed and refuted my hopes that I am now necessarily muted."[141] Dumbfounded, and in the name of the fatherland, he decided not to inveigh.[142]

As it turns out, he was silent on more than just his compatriots. Echoes of the events ripping the country apart registered in his journal with almost no comments. It was hard to talk and write "when the heart is oppressed and the mind is troubled," he justified.[143] Fitting his uncommunicative stance, he

---

[137] Papini, *Diario*, p. 109 (entry of February 10, 1943), italicized in the original. *Giudizio universale* was published in 1957. Another encompassing work was the *Report on Men* published as *Rapporto sugli uomini* in 1978.

[138] Papini, *Diario*, p. 116 (entry of November 20, 1943).

[139] Papini, *Diario*, pp. 195–6 (entry of June 18, 1944), capitalized in the original.

[140] Papini, *Diario*, pp. 140–1 (entry of January 12, 1944).

[141] Papini, *Diario*, p. 158 (entry of March 2, 1944). Also see entry of April 30, 1944: "From a letter of Soffici I understand that he is also beginning to realize of what material the Italians are made—those Italians in whom we placed so many, indeed too many, hopes. He has realized that most people are just plebs." Papini, *Diario*, p. 180. On the correspondence between Papini and Soffici see Giovanni Papini and Ardengo Soffici, *Carteggio*. Vol. IV, *1919–1956. Dal primo al secondo dopoguerra*. Edited by Mario Richter (Rome: Edizioni di storia e letteratura, 2002). For a discussion of the commonalities between Papini and Soffici see Zunino, *La Repubblica e il suo passato*, pp. 557–77.

[142] On August 12, 1944, he continued to advocate silence. Papini, *Diario*, p. 216.

[143] Papini, *Diario*, p. 125 (entry of December 13, 1943).

spent the last few months of the German occupation at a monastery.[144] Despite his professed anguish, however, he was able to draft four chapters of *Universal Judgment* by the summer of 1944.[145] It appears that all he wanted to escape thinking about was historical reality. As he admitted in early October of that year, writing actually helped him chase away the anguish of the current situation: "Only work—and work that takes me outside of the present time— lets me forget for a few hours Italy's matters, that are always so very sad."[146] Maybe Papini identified with the figure of the intellectual whose contours he had vaguely outlined months earlier. In an apparent protest against all censorship, including of the fascist kind, Papini argued that nonpartisanship was the intellectual's only route.[147] Papini distanced himself from the fray and held firm to his individual pains and maladies (of which he had a few). After all, he rationalized, he was not responsible—he had never been an active participant. Realizing that he might suffer consequences in post-fascist Italy, he concluded that others should be reproached for their lassitude.[148] For his part, he could not be compared to the plebs. Like his friend Soffici, Papini regretted the turn of events that had unexpectedly swept fascism away. And like Soffici, he blamed ordinary Italians for their inability to serve the movement's supposedly higher cause.

Redemption

If Soffici and Papini looked at the fall of fascism as a tragic instance of Italians' moral failure and a stain on the history of Italy, Bonaventura Tecchi considered the end of the regime a release from two long decades of bondage—a time for redemption. Religious faith, even of a secular kind, can only thrive on conditions of freedom, and fascism's dictatorial system had all but killed the foundations from which spiritual ideals emerge.[149] The regime's sudden

---

[144] He was at the monastery of La Verna from June 27 to September 8, 1944.
[145] See his entry of August 24, 1944 in Papini, *Diario*, p. 221. Already on May 26, he listed many more accomplishments over just one year: "I wrote one hundred chapters of my book; a poem of one hundred lines; reflections on Michelangelo; some hundred pages of notes and reflections; some hundred letters. I would have accomplished much more if the unfortunate events in Italy did not take away from me concentration, strength, and peace of mind." Papini, *Diario*, p. 188.
[146] Papini, *Diario*, p. 238 (entry of October 3, 1944).
[147] "The drama of intellectuals is the most painful of all. Having more awareness, they can't embrace any party with the required faith," Papini, *Diario*, p. 131 (entry of December 27, 1943).
[148] He began to express concerns about his fate on October 11, 1944 upon his return to Florence. See Papini, *Diario*, p. 242 and following.
[149] See for example his discussion of de Tocqueville on August 28, 1943 in *Un'estate in campagna*, pp. 50–5.

disintegration fortunately allowed for a glimpse of hope. To Tecchi, it was an auspicious sign of Italy's moral resurgence and a chance to reinstate the ground on which ethical principles would grow again. The future definitively appeared less bleak.

Similar to innumerable other Italians, Tecchi reacted with incredulity when he first heard the news of Mussolini's resignation on July 25. It all began around midnight, when he was awakened by a drunkard singing loudly in the street: "We praise the God [...], we praise the God who is our father, we praise the God who is our king"—a sort of premonition.[150] Shortly thereafter, Tecchi's brother burst into his bedroom. Holding a flashlight in his hand to navigate the darkness, he told him, "Mussolini is gone, fascism is over. There is a proclamation of the king and one of Badoglio, the new head of government."[151] Finding it hard to fall asleep again after that astonishing announcement, Tecchi began to doubt having ever experienced the odd intrusion. In the blackness of the night, he kept wondering, "Did my brother really come or was it a dream?"[152] Such was his surprise at the unfathomable happening that the sensation of hallucinating accompanied him throughout the early morning. Then at 7:15 a.m. the national radio confirmed the veracity of the event and "joy exploded uncontrollable."[153] The end of fascism was real.

As soon as he tasted the intense elation stemming from this unexpected turn of events, Tecchi was overtaken by another less blissful sentiment: anguish: "What will happen to Italy? What will the future bring?"[154] The grim reality of the current historical situation dictated caution even to those like him who had never aligned with fascism and long wished to see it vanish. Unable to separate the felicitousness of the outcome from the drama of war, Tecchi's sense of relief was cut short. By July 27, his merriness had dissipated. After wandering through the streets of his village all decked in tricolor and in full festive mood, he confessed, "But in truth I was not happy. Concern over the tremendous, tragic political and military situation in which we find ourselves [...] in the end suffocated all joy, and by the evening that concern turned into anguish. I fled the festivities and hid at home."[155] Tecchi agonized over the intractable situation that in a sudden twist had made the burden of the war fall onto the shoulders of the whole country. The fascist government,

---

[150] Tecchi, Un'estate in campagna, p. 21 (Tecchi added that the original religious hymn said "we want" not "we praise").
[151] Tecchi, Un'estate in campagna, p. 22.
[152] Tecchi, Un'estate in campagna, p. 22.
[153] Tecchi, Un'estate in campagna, p. 23.
[154] Tecchi, Un'estate in campagna, p. 23.
[155] Tecchi, Un'estate in campagna, p. 24.

guilty of entering the conflict, had dissolved, and Italy was inheriting its warmongering legacy. It was a catastrophe.

Throughout the previous two-and-a-half decades, Tecchi's assured, stalwart opposition to fascism and his undying belief in the value of liberty had helped him preserve a moral compass. With the country now cursed by a war marked by ethical and strategic wrongs—a war that was fascist through and through—Tecchi's own ethical standing was in the balance. Whereas in the past he found comfort in the idea that an eventual war loss would be merely the fascist regime's loss (like Calamandrei), the current collapse of the regime recast the entire Italy into a liable role. In this situation, the predicament confronting Tecchi appeared tragically insurmountable and a somber feeling continued to haunt him in the days following the regime's tumble. Obsessed with the dilemma, he found objectionable the plethora of analyses of fascism that filled newspapers and radio waves. The war constituted a much more impelling actuality and one that needed to be taken on with urgency. Italy's moral and physical survival was at stake:

> For a long time now it's not the phenomenon "fascism" that is (or has been) in the forefront in Italy, but the war, which was generated by fascism. […] It's absolutely true that fascism is its father, the guilty one, and that, given fascism, the result could not be but war, and *this wa*r, this unjust and disastrous war. But the reality now (August 8, 1943) is the war more than fascism.[156]

Like other diarists' reactions in the aftermath of the July 25 event, Tecchi's inclination was to turn away from the past regime and shift attention to the world conflagration—a conflict he definitely condemned for its destructive potential but also feared it might turn the new Badoglio government into an accomplice of fascism: "This is the equivocation: we should not forget that the nation (and I mean, individuals, populace, everybody) was not as much waiting for the end of fascism as for the end of the war, that is, the end of the most terrible (and also logical, consequential) fruit of fascism: war."[157] In the everyday experience of Italians, war had replaced fascism as an existential threat—it had acquired a life of its own independent of the regime. Due to these historical contingencies, Tecchi advocated leaving aside the question of fascism,

---

[156] Tecchi, *Un'estate in campagna*, pp. 37–8 (entry of August 9, 1943).
[157] Tecchi, *Un'estate in campagna*, p. 38 (entry of August 9, 1943). On Tecchi's perspective on the war also see *Vigilia di guerra, 1940*, especially pp. 31–5 (entry of June 1, 1940).

even if he recognized that people's attitudes towards the past regime were ambivalent at best. After all, wasn't he arguing that Italians were looking forward to the end of the war more than of fascism? On this issue he was in accord with Damiano, who worryingly exposed the Italians' blasé reactions at the news of Mussolini's resignation.

Both Tecchi and Damiano fundamentally realized the Gordian knot facing Italians, caught as they were between two lines of fires, both metaphorically and literally. At the figurative level, worries over the country's legacy of connivance with fascism clashed with anxieties over the ongoing war. At the concrete, experiential level, Italians were under attack on the one side by both Germans and (eventually) die-hard fascists and on the other by the Allied forces. Considering the systematic destruction of Europe inflicted by Hitler's armies since 1939, the war especially carried deep connotations of immorality. Just on the eve of Italy's entry into war, Tecchi had despaired at the news of Belgium, Holland, and France all falling under German yoke. Christian ideals—that Tecchi considered the repository of good inasmuch as they constituted the opposite of violence—were being unabashedly refuted by a Germany that imposed its might indiscriminately while championing abhorrent notions of race and blood. How would Europe and the world be able to surmount this obliteration of spiritual values and parallel suppression of true freedom?[158] Haunted by the question, Tecchi could not but plunge into a gloomy mood when Mussolini announced Italy's participation in the conflict. His own country was now participating in that monstrous enterprise, a war that was "totally, essentially, irreparably wrong," an "unjust and disastrous" war.[159] Deeply opposed to the violent pursuit of power, Tecchi wished to distance Italy from the fighting. This explains why, once Mussolini's government fell and the war was not a mere fascist war any longer, he turned impatient at "theoretical discussions" about the future and the hypothetical role of freedom in it. He insisted, "Today there is another reality: that reality is war. All the rest seems academic to me."[160] Unfortunately for Tecchi, Badoglio's government's response to the conundrum was a confusing armistice—a pact unable to lift the country from its dire conditions. Even more ominously, the pact could not ensure Italy's withdrawal from the conflict.

---

[158] On freedom see Tecchi, *Vigilia di guerra*, p. 18 (entry of May 14, 1940). Tecchi returned to the idea of freedom as linked to religion in *Un'estate in campagna*.
[159] Tecchi, *Un'estate in campagna*, pp. 25, 38 (entries of July 30 and August 9, 1943).
[160] Tecchi, *Un'estate in campagna*, p. 58 (entry of September 1, 1943).

Tecchi's intense preoccupation with the morality of war did not necessarily blind him to fascism. Similar to Damiano, however, he addressed the phenomenon through a focus on individual responsibility, almost anthropological in nature:

> It is too easy *today* to go after fascism and attribute to it all the defects of Italians. One needs to be more severe and less sectarian. We need to realize that some of the wrongs pertaining to the Italians' character preexist fascism, and we should indeed understand that it is because of these preexisting defects that fascism was able to easily break through the Italian people, or at least not find great resistance among them.[161]

In Tecchi's analysis, Italians were doubly at fault. Not only did they fall for fascism, but inherent flaws facilitated their participation in the regime. Merely accusing fascism of all wrongdoing was, therefore, an insufficient, albeit undoubtedly easy, response to the jeopardy the country had endured for years. The characteristic evils of the regime, listed by Tecchi as "servility, thievery, and camorra," preceded Mussolini's movement and were rather trademarks of Italians' moral weakness.[162] They should not be ignored.

Although Tecchi's evaluation avoided all sentimentality and aggressively demanded that the country face collective responsibility, he seemed to believe that the evils he enumerated (whether preexisting or not) were sufficient to define the entirety of the fascist phenomenon—they accounted for its endurance as well. Could one then equate fascism with corruption, as many wished? Even Tecchi's advocacy for the need "to defeat the fascism in ourselves" in order to eradicate it, while in theory acknowledging Italians' involvement and complicity with the regime, failed to address the historical specificity of fascism, its genesis, and duration.[163] In the end, Tecchi's insistence on war as the central wrongdoing of the regime effaced other crucial dimensions of fascism, including its principles, beliefs, values, and goals. It also neglected fascism's institutional effects and legacy. Sidelined, fascism remained misunderstood, almost a thing of the past, in fact, passé.

To be sure, in contrast to Soffici and Papini who supported the regime and felt a strong sentimental affinity for it, Tecchi, as well as Damiano, were unequivocally critical of Mussolini's dictatorship and held the regime in high

---

[161] Tecchi, *Un'estate in campagna*, pp. 59–60 (entry of September 3, 1943).
[162] Tecchi, *Un'estate in campagna*, p. 60 (entry of September 3, 1943).
[163] Tecchi, *Un'estate in campagna*, p. 61 (entry of September 3, 1943).

contempt. And yet despite ideological differences, the four ended up similarly discounting fascism's responsibilities. By sharing contempt for the Italians, whether because they failed the fascist project or because of their collusion with it, Soffici, Papini, Tecchi, and Damiano put their fellow citizens on trial. With vague allegations of Italians' moral weakness, they absolved fascism from scrutiny, blamed others for its shortcomings, and de facto moved analytical attention away from the regime. In the case of Tecchi, the urgent reality of the war particularly complicated his perspective. Since the conflict widened the range of ethical guilt, and due to the fact that war was no longer under fascism's aegis, the question of how to separate Italy from fascism became Tecchi's preeminent concern and affected his reception of the armistice too. Aware of the intractability of Italy's anomalous situation, he realized that a price had to be paid. His reaction of simultaneous "joy and sadness" at the news of September 8 is indicative of both his lucid understanding of the historical reality at hand and his sense of humiliation at the conditions imposed by the Allied forces.[164] It is notable that, although he found the armistice truly shameful and mortifying, he did not evaluate it through the lens of betrayal. In contrast, he judged the armistice as the logical, though unfortunate, result of Mussolini's ill-advised decision to join Germany in the conflict.[165]

In this chapter we have examined intellectual diarists' responses to the eventful summer and fall of 1943 and the different structures of feeling that emerged from their daily contemplation of the shifting state of affairs in Italy. Compared to the journals of ordinary people, a deeper level of reflexivity transpires from the notes written by this group of scribes, an inclination in part facilitated by the authors' more or less explicit intent to publish, but also due to their familiarity with the genre as well as their established fluency in the art of writing. More than occasional references, the topics intellectual diarists addressed were treated recurrently and in long entries that illustrated the significance of the issues covered and their relevance in the eyes of the individual diarist. Preeminent among the concerns raised were the fascist nature of the current war, its impact on the idea of fatherland, and the Italians' connivance with the regime. Especially after the fall of Mussolini, which they

---

[164] Tecchi, *Un'estate in campagna*, p. 64 (entry of September 8, 1943). He continued, "But it is the logical, fatal conclusion of June 10, 1940."
[165] Tecchi, *Un'estate in campagna* (entry of September 21, 1943). Tecchi wrote, "The 'about-face' was not nice and I believe no one among the noncynical Italians could be happy about the way it unfolded. But isn't the about-face (and let's also say the words: defection, betrayal) the terrible, wretched consequence of the monstrous tyranny?" pp. 71–2. Also see entry of September 30, pp. 80–1.

saluted with enthusiasm (at least those not aligned with the regime), intellectual diarists focused on the moral dilemmas that engulfed the country. Decidedly disgusted by fascism's hideousness, they were not willing to compromise—redemption had to come with some costs. One of the most consequential predicaments they faced was the difficulty of separating Italy from fascism in the face of a war that, initiated by the regime against the will of the people, was now inherited by the Badoglio government. Judged fundamentally immoral in its intents and objectives, the military conflict confronted intellectual diarists with the unfortunate but necessary decision to wish for Italy's defeat in the name of vanquishing the Nazi-fascist alliance. But if that choice felt less cumbersome when the regime was in charge of the country, it now prostrated its proponents. Losing the war evoked the specter of foreign powers and images of dependency—fears that were at odds with memories of the Risorgimento struggles for independence and the nationalistic sentiments of honor and dignity. Clashing realities complicated intellectual diarists' feelings about the country's integrity and rectitude, no matter that Italy eventually joined the antifascist coalition. Past bonds could not be erased.

The intellectual diarists' urge to regain ethical standing also guided their analysis of fascism and led them to focus on individual responsibilities. Much more inclined than ordinary diarists to examine people's compromises with the regime, several of them tended to eschew historical specificity as well as political analysis and ended up formulating generic critiques of Italian defects that shifted the bulk of the blame onto fellow citizens. Their crusade of moral denunciation, combined with a limited analytical attention, resulted in the questionable erasure of the dictatorship and its ills. Even when releasing Italians from all blame, as in the case of Croce, fascism continued to be sidelined. By setting the political question aside, the ethical orientation of intellectual diarists ultimately drove them to decline any personal responsibility, a tendency facilitated by their posture of objective reporters. Their declared desire to bear witness and inform the public became an alibi to exclude oneself from judgment—they acted as observers looking in. Posturing as recorders of facts gave these diarists the excuse to hide behind the self-assigned duty of testifying. Even for those who did not subscribe to the task of documenting, diaries were far from leading to self-analysis. Ultimately, a paramount concern with the ongoing war unified ordinary and intellectual diarists and heightened their distance from fascism.

The next chapter will dig deeper into the themes illustrated above and especially emphasize how intellectual diarists shaped their understanding of fascism past and present in light of the historical developments that followed the regime's end. By zooming in on the level of the everyday, the chapter highlights the relevance of social interaction and relationships for the diarists' political positions. It also takes the everyday as the prism through which to lay bare intellectual diarists' vulnerabilities in their efforts to allocate responsibility and assign guilt from an assortment of liable candidates. Ultimately, attention to the everyday exposes the chiaroscuro ambivalences that marked intellectual diarists' reckoning with their own role as historical subjects involved in simultaneously living the events they recounted and struggling to survive the indignities of wartime.

5
The Personal and the Political

> It's such a mixture of banality and drama
> what we are living at present.
> (May 31, 1944)*

Due to its generic nature, the moral indictment that intellectual diarists directed at Italians for their role during the regime diluted the distinctively pernicious features of fascism. Because atemporal and unconditional, moral flaws, when taken as explanation for people's failure to act, are applicable to any political arrangement regardless of specific governmental formations or power structures—ethical explanations cancel out the context to which they supposedly relate. If, as Iris Origo claimed, apathy and fatalism were a perennial feature of the Italians' tendency to "*tira a campare*," then those attributes operated indefinitely, no matter the circumstances.[1] In a perverse fashion, the intellectual diarists' denunciation of Italians' shortcomings annulled the singularity of the fascist experience and neglected its actuality—their criticism ignored the effects the dictatorship exerted routinely on people's lives under the normalized condition of authoritarian rule.

Once we move attention to the processes of social interaction and interpersonal relationships, however, a more concrete picture of how Italians navigated ideological divisions and ethical matters comes to light. Especially in the period following July 25, the realm of daily experience reveals the continued influence of past habits and traditions on Italians. The everyday exposes several of the interpretive quandaries intellectual diarists confronted as they tried to determine their own moral and political standing against the fuzziness of the present historical context. Most prominently, the question of separating friends from enemies presented writers with a plethora of possibilities that

---

* From the diary of Elena Carandini Albertini, *Dal terrazzo. Diario 1943–1944* (Bologna: il Mulino, 1997).

[1] Origo wrote that "the great mass of the Italian people [...] '*tira a compare*.' Profoundly disillusioned, cynical, tired, fully conscious that more suffering and privations still lie ahead, they are a defeated nation—and the only remaining universal incentive is that of self-preservation." *War in Val d'Orcia: A Diary* (London: Jonathan Cape, 1947), p. 98 (entry of October 15, 1943). *Tira a campare* is translated by Origo as "just rubs along" in footnote 1, p. 98.

extended from the "good" fascists to the "bad" ones as well as the "evil" Germans and the more generic figure of the "foreign" invader. In part because more actively engaged in the oppositional movement than their ordinary counterparts, in part because personally involved in the episodes they recounted, intellectual diarists addressed the undeniable issue of fellow Italians on the "other" side, signaling the significance of the matter for their personal world and for the fate of the larger community as well.

Sentimental Fascism

Despite the lack of an organized opposition to the twenty-year-long regime, not all Italians willingly embraced fascism. Those more politically engaged went into exile (the so-called *fuoriusciti*), others were imprisoned or sent to *confino*, and many more adapted to the system, accepting some of its demands and skirting others, at times exposing themselves to grave risks, but mostly getting by and carrying on with their daily routines.[2] Once far from the clamor of parades, and having dutifully observed official events, people conducted their lives the way they would under any government: working, socializing, raising families, and basically surviving. In the everyday commerce of life in common, and considering the often-atavistic origins of social networks in villages and small towns, interactions between true "fascists" and less politically engaged Italians were matters of normal occurrence. When the dictatorship crumbled in the wake of Mussolini's forced resignation, this intermingling of individuals who subscribed to contrasting ideological orientations did not come to a halt. Built on professional commonalities, family ties, and childhood friendships, social relations continued to connect disparate people at times of uncertainty. While old habits and practices kept crashing down, a semblance of normalcy could be maintained by holding on to the ongoing flow of human contacts and time-honored connections. Fellowship ignored political differences, though the amicable status of social relations

[2] For a general history of the *fuoriusciti* see Aldo Garosci, *Storia dei fuoriusciti* (Bari: Laterza, 1953). Also see C.F. Delzell, "The Italian Anti-Fascist Emigration 1922–1943," *Journal of Central European Affairs* vol. XII, no. 1 (1952): pp. 20–55; Simonetta Tombaccini, *Storia dei fuoriusciti italiani in Francia* (Milan: Mursia, 1988); Raffaella Castagnola, Fabrizio Panzera, and Massimiliano Spiga eds., *Spiriti liberi in Svizzera: la presenza di fuoriusciti italiani nella Confederazione negli anni del fascismo e del nazismo, 1922–1945* (Florence: Franco Cesati Editore, 2006). On *confino* there is a vast literature. For a recent contribution, see Piero Garofalo, Elizabeth Leake, and Dana Renga, *Internal Exile in Fascist Italy: History and Representations of Confino* (Manchester: Manchester University Press, 2019). Also see Michael Ebner, *Ordinary Violence in Mussolini's Italy* (Cambridge: Cambridge University Press, 2010).

admittedly changed as the fascists regrouped in the Italian Social Republic (RSI) and continued to collaborate with the Germans.

For Leonetta Cecchi Pieraccini, political hybridity was a defining feature of her extended family. From one end of the spectrum to the other, her kin covered opposed ideological stances, none of which she appeared to question or find divisive. When she heard about the consequences of July 25 for one high-ranking fascist member of her family, for example, she made light of the situation and focused on its comic aspects. It so happened that this relative of hers, who held the office of *podestà* in Poggibonsi, was traveling at the time of the regime's fall. Now in transit in Rome, "He is about to return home and will find his *podestà* position gone and the regime outright replaced. We ended up laughing together about it."[3] As she emphasized the incongruous effects of the recent political upheaval on her relative's life, Cecchi Pieraccini registered the ironic reverberations of the turnaround. Whereas antifascists used to go underground during Mussolini's reign, the situation in Italy had changed so dramatically that it was the turn of the oppressors to look for places to hide: "Now he too might be better off in the wind."[4]

An upside-down shake-up reminiscent of a carnival ritual had subverted the dominant social order and its established norms. As folk humor suggested, it was a situation ripe for laughter, and there were doubtlessly humorous elements in the story evoked by Cecchi Pieraccini. Here was a man who, over the space of only a few days and while away on a trip, found himself dispossessed of his power and long-standing governing post and forced to face an unexpected reversal of fortune. How not to find comedy in this tragedy? Remarkably, and any hilarity aside, Cecchi Pieraccini refrained from advancing any judgments of political or ideological nature on the incident, nor did she focus on the political crisis that was causing the mayhem. In contrast, she addressed the supposedly "comic" situation of the *podestà* from the perspective of her affective ties to him. Seeing his life completely upended by the sudden crash of the regime, she expressed solidarity and support.

In a similarly neutral political stance, Cecchi Pieraccini sentimentally celebrated her seventy-nine-year-old brother's newly acquired freedom in the aftermath of the dictatorship's collapse. A longtime socialist and opponent of the regime, the elder Gaetano Pieraccini had suffered years of ostracism

---

[3] Leonetta Cecchi Pieraccini, *Agendina di guerra (1939–1944)* (Milan: Longanesi, 1964), p. 227 (entry of August 1, 1943).
[4] Cecchi Pieraccini, *Agendina di guerra*, p. 227.

and forced clandestinity under Mussolini.[5] With the end of fascism, he was now afforded the chance to pick up the pieces of his career as a physician while regaining the right to engage in the political process—an enormous enhancement in the quality of his life.[6] Leonetta could not but rejoice at her brother's changed fortunes and was proud to report positive comments on him:

> My son-in-law D'Amico was at dinner with us. He talked of my brother Gaetano Pieraccini [...]. The fall of fascism has restored Gaetano's prominence in Florence, and his house has become again the center of workers' political activities in the region. Recalling his goodness and that miraculous vitality that makes him find faith and joy of living as if he had a whole life ahead of him, D'Amico concluded, "But that man is forty not eighty."[7]

In the same nonjudgmental way in which Leonetta had considered the doomed fate of her fascist relative, she did not express any evaluation of her brother's socialist affiliation. Nor did she comment on the turn of events that in Gaetano's case, as opposed to the *podestà*, made possible an auspicious outcome. She instead focused on human interest through the personal ties that linked her to her brother. Even the seemingly accidental manner in which she mentioned his story (while recounting a dinner conversation) seemed to minimize the causes of Gaetano's past suffering—it downplayed the historically monumental nature of the current institutional shake-up. Whether or

---

[5] Gaetano Pieraccini was among the signatories of Croce's *Manifesto of the Anti-Fascist Intellectuals*. Leonetta's other two brothers were also antifascist and had often risked their lives during the dictatorship. Already in 1926, she shared her worries about them: "With the assassination attempt of Mussolini by Anteo Zaniboni on October 31, and the related political recrudescence, I have been concerned for my three brothers and nephews as well, all socialist and antifascist for life. Guido in Poggibonsi is less exposed, but Gaetano in Florence and Arnaldo in Arezzo are right in the middle of hot spots." See Leonetta Cecchi Pieraccini, *Vecchie agendine (1911-1929)* (Florence: Sansoni, 1960), p. 204 (entry of mid-November 1926).

[6] After the liberation of Florence from the Germans, Gaetano Pieraccini was acclaimed mayor in September 1944, the first post-fascism mayor of the city. Piero Calamandrei had also been proposed for the same position, but declined the invitation. See Calamandrei, *Diario 1939-1945* (Florence: La Nuova Italia, 1982 and 1997), 2 vols., Vol. II (entries of late July through early October 1944). Gaetano Casoni's name was also in the mix of potential candidates for mayor.

[7] Cecchi Pieraccini, *Agendina di guerra*, p. 230 (entry of August 6, 1943). Fedele D'Amico, a music critic, was a member of the Roman Catholic left. An antifascist, he went into hiding during the war and lived in a house he shared with Gaetano Pieraccini in Leonetta's native Poggibonsi. On the Catholic-Communists see Carlo Felice Casula, *Cattolici comunisti e sinistra cristiana 1938-1945* (Bologna: il Mulino, 1976). Also see Francesco Malgeri, *La sinistra cristiana (1937-1945)* (Brescia: Morcelliana, 1982).

not Leonetta had opinions on fascism, she did not let politics affect her relation with family and kin.[8]

There was a sort of lightheartedness in the way Cecchi Pieraccini handled political matters of undeniable gravity—she was not willing to enter a terrain that was full of emotional risks should she be forced to take a position. Even a private diary was not to be trusted as holder of intimate feelings, despite the fact that Cecchi Pieraccini did not hesitate to use her journal to express personal opinions on a variety of subjects and showed no reluctance recounting the views and sentiments of friends. When it came to fascism, however, she had little to say. After a friend phoned her on July 25 with the news of Mussolini's downfall, for instance, she limited herself to reporting the shouts coming from the street, the hails to freedom, and popular denunciations of fascists. She hid behind her role of chronicler even as she infused her report with inferential assertions. One can sense her veiled contempt for fellow Italians' response in her account of the feverish destruction of fascist symbols pursued by many volunteers in the streets and piazzas of Rome. "A waste of tricolor," she called it, suggesting that this was not a national celebration.[9] Also, her caustic observations about the new national government that was taking shape indicate that her neutrality often remained an aspiration.[10] Nevertheless, by allowing her to play reporter, the diary eased Cecchi Pieraccini's noninvolvement in the events that shook the country; journaling helped her smooth over political idiosyncrasies and naturalize them, all the while bringing their importance to the surface. At the concrete level of everyday life, though, how was one to deal with allies and adversaries in flesh and blood?

The good fascists

Gaetano Casoni highlighted the peculiar role of ideological differences in the relationship he held with friends and acquaintances in his native Florence, a city considered a notorious fascist hub due to the presence of both hard-core militants among its citizens and a local fascist party that consistently

---

[8] One should add that Cecchi Pieraccini's son Dario (born in 1918) went into hiding in the fall of 1943, after deserting his barrack in Rome. Leonetta did not write explicitly about his situation, but in a few entries of September and October 1943 she mentioned his case. See *Agendina di guerra*.

[9] Cecchi Pieraccini, *Agendina di guerra*, p. 223 (entry of July 26, 1943).

[10] See Cecchi Pieraccini, *Agendina di guerra*, p. 235 (entry of August 18, 1943). In truth, the political shake-up perturbed her: "In whichever way these facts originated, we are all quite unsettled and feel a vague sense of distress." Cecchi Pieraccini, *Agendina di guerra*, p. 224 (entry of July 27).

governed with a heavy hand. Standing at odds with the reality of political divisions, Casoni's accounts show that habitual patterns of social exchanges in post-regime Florence followed an almost counterintuitive fashion. People on opposite ideological sides came into regular contact and interacted based on long-standing practices of associative life, be it professional, cultural, or merely recreational. The relevance of personal connections played a particularly critical part during the summer months of 1944, when, in view of the imminent liberation of the city by the Allied forces, the civic sense of the Florentines (or claims to it) appeared to prevail over contrasting political allegiances. Casoni's diary provides a window onto the web of crisscrossing interests that influenced the fate of Florence in the days from early June to late August 1944, when the Germans were set to vacate the premises and local fascist Republicans pondered their next moves. While Florence lived through a nightmarish scenario of bombardments and destructions, Casoni narrated a tale of human solidarity—a surprising story of communal unity in which he happened to play a leading role.

It all began on June 12, when he received a surprise visit by the prominent Florentine lawyer Uberto Puccioni, who also happened to be a loyal supporter of the regime and one among the "first" fascists (fascisti della prima ora). Purportedly wishing to make the transition from occupation to liberation easier for his fellow citizens, the lawyer offered to volunteer as liaison between the city's high fascist representatives and the Tuscan Committee of National Liberation—an enticing proposal that Casoni promised to convey to the right authorities within the CLN.[11] The prospect that negotiations with outgoing Republican fascists would ensure a positive outcome for those antifascists currently imprisoned (so that they would not be shipped to concentration camps, for example) was tantalizing, as was the possibility that concessions might be obtained from the Germans toward preserving Florence's artistic patrimony (which the occupiers seemed keen on plundering).[12] After reporting the meeting in his diary, Casoni weighed the reasons for considering Puccioni's offer of collaboration:

> I know this colleague quite well as the son of my friend, the lawyer Mario Puccioni, who died several years ago. But more than Uberto, I had the chance to frequent his brother, the lawyer Bruno, ardent fascist but in good

---

[11] The Comitato di Liberazione Nazionale (CLN) also had regional committees, one of which was headquartered in Florence.

[12] Another factor Casoni considered was the issue of avoiding bloody revenges in the future. See *Diario fiorentino (giugno–agosto 1944)* (Florence: G. Civelli, 1946), p. 7 (entry of June 12, 1944).

faith, fervent Italian that largely paid a personal cost by fighting in Somalia and then in Tripolitania, earning well-deserved medals of honor and being gravely wounded and maimed in the leg.[13]

In his deliberations on the proposal offered by Puccioni, Casoni first considered his own personal ties to Uberto, describing him as the son of a friend, the brother of Bruno, and a professional colleague—all factors that inspired trust. He then dwelled on Bruno, with whom he was better acquainted, and proceeded to praise his patriotism and spirit of sacrifice. Particularly noteworthy in Casoni's judgment were Bruno's actions on behalf of Florence in the aftermath of the armistice—harbingers of Uberto's current efforts to ensure the town's welfare. Having remained in good rapport with high-ranking German officers after his military mission in Africa, Bruno used those relations to spare Florence and the Florentines numerous abuses from their occupiers. Casoni emphasized the positive part Bruno played in civic life—a merit that rightly gained him "large sympathies" from the city's inhabitants.[14] Finally, Casoni evaluated both brothers on the basis of a general ethical standpoint that effectively underplayed their role as zealous supporters of the regime. He insulated Uberto and Bruno from the evils of fascism and applied to them a dichotomous Manichean interpretation that, although predicated on the corrupted nature of Mussolini's dictatorship, still allowed him to separate the "good" fascists from the "bad" ones. Thus, Bruno was above all "a fervent Italian," and Casoni added that, yes, he was "an ardent fascist but in good faith." His and Uberto's contributions to the well-being of Florence ultimately demonstrated remarkable generosity. Irrespective of their ideological creed, their selfless love for the city represented undeniable proof of their moral rectitude.[15]

To be sure, Casoni did not ignore that both brothers had applied for membership in the reincarnated Fascist Republican Party—an obvious sign of their true status as die-hard believers. Nevertheless, they had accompanied their application with a critical letter that exposed the party's past mistakes and demanded a new course. The fact that their membership was denied, Casoni reasoned, only served to confirm their inner goodness, a further proof of their standing as "good" fascists.[16] Their high sense of devotion and

---

[13] Casoni, *Diario fiorentino*, p. 8.   [14] Casoni, *Diario fiorentino*, p. 8.
[15] Fearing the consequences of the Allied forces' arrival and the defeat of the fascists, Bruno had left Florence and headed north with his family. Uberto, in contrast, decided to remain.
[16] "The two brothers had asked to enroll in the Republican Party in a letter in which they explicitly addressed the mistakes of the past. As a condition for their membership, they proposed that those

genuine beliefs in fascism's original transformative mission were guarantees for trusting them—ideological purity constituted an evidentiary credential and added further validation to Casoni's direct knowledge of the brothers' character. Personal connection definitively allowed Casoni to profess confidence in Uberto Puccioni despite, or because of, his supposedly authentic and honest fascist faith.[17] Indeed, successful collaboration between opposing sides, as pursued by prominent figures of Florentine politics during the months that led to the liberation of the city, could not have happened without the protagonists' familiarity with each other. Personal and ancestral links connected the past with the present in unforeseen potential relations of reciprocity that challenged the actuality of divergent philosophical positions. Fascism might have disrupted the natural flow of associations and upset traditional ties; it had not, however, eliminated them.

Casoni's own bond with the family of Giovanni Gentile, fascism's foremost philosopher, is illustrative of this pattern. Their relationship was not built on shared political beliefs. Rather, it grew out of normal circumstances related to a particular phase in their life course: parenthood. In his entry of July 17, 1944, Casoni illuminates this point while mourning the loss of the philosopher's youngest son (three months after the elder Gentile's assassination):

> Today Fortunato Gentile passed away. He was the youngest son of Giovanni Gentile.
>
> I was best man at Fortunato's wedding last October 1 [...].
>
> I got to know the Gentile family several years ago in Forte dei Marmi, where I was spending the summer with my wife and children in a little cottage next to the "Villa Erminia" of the Gentiles. From then on, my sons Giorgio and Ugo became friends with Federigo and Fortunato Gentile and our families continued to maintain cordial relations.[18]

Living in the same resort town and frequenting each other as parents of children of the same age cemented the connection between the heads of the two households and fortified the ties between their families. As a matter of fact,

---

mistakes not be repeated. Naturally their application was rejected," Casoni reported. See *Diario fiorentino*, p. 9. Casoni added that a periodical the two brothers had founded as a forum for expressing their ideas was suppressed after only two issues by order of the head of the Fascist Republican Party, Alessandro Pavolini.

[17] In an attempt to gain Casoni's trust, Uberto Puccioni cited his own moral integrity as a guarantee. Although he would not renege his past beliefs, he argued that he had not committed any violence or injustices under the fascist mantle. Casoni, *Diario fiorentino*, p. 5.

[18] Casoni, *Diario fiorentino*, p. 147. Giovanni Gentile was assassinated on April 15, 1944.

the friendly relationship became so warm that Casoni was asked to be best man at Fortunato's wedding—quite an honor. In the familiar setting of everyday interaction, albeit under the special leisurely circumstance of summer holidays, Casoni developed enormous respect for the philosopher. Direct knowledge of Gentile the person, as opposed merely to his intellectual work, moved Casoni to appreciate his integrity and sense of the fatherland, irrespective of the ideological differences separating them: "I learned to admire Giovanni Gentile more than for the excellence of his mind, commonly acknowledged, also for the nobility of his spirit and the strong patriotism that animated him."[19] Despite Gentile's indubitable loyalty to the regime, personal acquaintance with him helped Casoni elevate the philosopher to a position above all negative judgments. A "good" fascist, in Casoni's schema, Gentile was mortified at the sight of the evil caused by the dictatorship he so faithfully supported. He also fought against injustice and denounced fascism's minions responsible for torturing political opponents. If people realized all the behind-the-scenes work that Gentile had done to correct fascism's wrongful direction, Casoni pleaded, nobody would have dared assassinate him.[20]

Casoni's defense of Gentile was unconditional. He even supported the hypothesis that the same fascists who might have felt threatened by the philosopher's accusations were responsible for murdering him.[21] Evidently, his trust in Gentile was boundless, sealed by the personal nature of their relationship—he even donated a sum in Gentile's memory to benefit displaced people and disaster victims.[22] Inspired by "a sentiment of devotion and warm

---

[19] Casoni, *Diario fiorentino*, p. 148.

[20] Casoni wrote, "How much he must have suffered, before his noble heart was ravaged by murderous strokes, as he witnessed the damage created by the regime he had unfortunately sustained with his important name! But if everybody knew how he used his high authority to protect those who were persecuted, Jews or antifascists, whose life he knew was honest and the spirit deserving; how he fought openly and directly the Leader in whom he believed against the emergent indecency, arrogance, and violence of the big and little *ras*, there wouldn't have certainly been anybody daring to hit him." Casoni, *Diario fiorentino*, p. 148.

[21] Florence had an unfortunate fame with regards to a special political police corps (Reparto dei Servizi Speciali) headed by Mario Carità, who instituted it in 1943 under the RSI. The corps, also known as the "Banda Carità," was responsible for numerous crimes, especially the torturing of prisoners. Gentile was among the critics of the Banda's brutal methods, and when he was assassinated, many believed the Banda to be responsible. See Francesco Perfetti, *Assassinio di un filosofo* (Florence: Le Lettere, 2004). On the Banda see Riccardo Caporale, *La "Banda Carità." Storia del Reparto Servizi Speciali (1943–1945)* (Lucca: Edizioni S. Marco Litotipo, 2004). The Banda also operated in the Veneto region, where it moved in July 1944 after the Allied forces' advance in Tuscany. It remained in Padua until the end of the war. Some of the Banda's deeds in the area are recounted in Maria Carazzolo, *Più forte della paura. Diario di guerra e dopoguerra (1938–1947)* (Caselle di Sommacampagna: Cierre edizioni, 2007).

[22] In July 1943 (but before Mussolini's resignation), Casoni offered Gentile his house in Troghi, a small village outside Florence. Gentile remained there until the end of October. See Gabriele Turi, *Giovanni Gentile. Una biografia* (Florence: Giunti, 1995), pp. 500–8.

friendship," Casoni's gesture raised suspicions about the supposedly apolitical nature of his intentions, ultimately earning him accusations of subscribing to fascism.[23] To Casoni, however, issues of conscience took priority over every other matter—politics and friendship were not mutually dependable. A strong believer in God's justice and politically a moderate, Casoni exemplified the hope that revenge should not further bloody a country already marked by unspeakable pain and horrendous destruction.

The sacrality of human relations stood at the center of Casoni's ethical world, as evident in the supplementary entry he added to his diary on October 22, almost two months after ending the journal following Florence's liberation: "I resume my diary because I want to conclude it with some news that, later obtained, gives completion to what I narrated earlier and offers further comments."[24] Casoni reported on the fate of one of his cellmates (he had been briefly incarcerated in July), who turned out to be a traitor and a spy and was shot by the partisans. He detailed the miserable status of Florence's art patrimony whose fate under the German occupation had been at the center of his concerns throughout the diary. Ultimately, he informed on the situation of Uberto Puccioni, the lawyer of fascist beliefs whose offer to mediate between the governing Republican fascists and the Committee of National Liberation had given impetus to Casoni's own decision to initiate a journal. As it turns out, Puccioni's story presented a few intriguing twists. Although the people of Florence held him in strong regard and seemed aware of his efforts on behalf of the city, British military had resolved to send him to a concentration camp in Southern Italy, cognizant of the fact that he had been the president of the city's Institute for Studies of Judaism.[25] Pressed by the family of Puccioni to intervene, Casoni complied with that wish "very willingly as an act of dutiful justice in hope that this will come to some advantage to him."[26] The personal relationship he had established with Uberto only a few months earlier helped smooth over the deep ideological chasm that otherwise divided them. On the basis of the trust built working together, Casoni was ready to forgive and redeem the fascist man who unexpectedly contacted him in those early June

---

[23] Casoni reacted to these accusations by citing his distance from political programs: "I never was and never considered myself a *political animal*." Casoni, *Diario fiorentino*, p. 151. He had already mentioned his distance from party politics at the beginning of his diary (entry of June 12, 1944, p. 7). Also, he never enrolled in the fascist party. After the war, Casoni was active in the Liberal Party (Partito Liberale Italiano).

[24] Casoni, *Diario fiorentino*, p. 309.

[25] On the camps see Carlo Capogreco, *I campi del duce. L'internamento civile nell'Italia fascista* (Turin: Einaudi, 2004).

[26] Casoni, *Diario fiorentino*, p. 310.

days of 1944, when Florence was fighting to withstand the last months of the Germans' stranglehold.[27]

To Casoni and many Italians who did not actively support the regime, a "fascist" was not merely a government functionary or a local party representative to be treated with distance and a bit of annoyance if not altogether contempt. "Fascists" were also neighbors, acquaintances, friends, and one judged them on the basis of sentimental features separately from the person's active politics or ideological inclinations. In the case of the older generation, that is, people who had reached adult age by the time Mussolini became prime minister, the attribute of "fascist" was a late addition to an individual's overall makeup—it supplemented other long-standing characteristics. For the young, instead, "fascist" might not particularly distinguish one person from another in a society supposedly defined by Mussolini's new doctrine—fascism was a currency that circulated freely and in abundance. Within this contextual environment, the commerce of social relations knew few borders during the regime. All jobs and professions, as well as daily interactions, required diverse types of exchanges that connected people of divergent political creed and put them into contact with one another. Rather than blanket judgments, one had to evaluate the individual person on the basis of their singular attributes. For Casoni and others, that meant sorting out the good fascists from the bad ones.

Fascist Who?

In his role of eminent jurist, Piero Calamandrei faced several hybrid situations, most notably in the late 1930s, when he was summoned to be part of a commission in charge of reforming the Civil Code. The newly appointed Minister of Justice, Dino Grandi, asked for Calamandrei's collaboration despite the latter's lack of fascist credentials. After meeting with the minister in December 1939, Calamandrei wrote of Grandi, "I immediately had a favorable impression of him. He seems like a 'civilized' man, courteous, respectful of scholars, and wishing to work on purifying justice—a substantively liberal temperament, in which it seems to me a native Bolognese candor, humanity, and frankness is fused with the urbanity and poise he

---

[27] Calamandrei was much less generous in his mentions of the Puccioni brothers, and especially Uberto, although he mainly talked about them before the fall of the regime. On March 1, 1942, for example, he recounted how Uberto Puccioni proposed to have him (Calamandrei) canceled from the bar association for "political indignity" (indegnità politica). He also reported on Puccioni's antisemitism on December 12, 1942, and defined him as an incompetent careerist on December 13, 1942. See Calamandrei, *Diario*, vol. II, pp. 9, 92, 93.

learned in England."[28] Struck by Grandi's openness, and considering him one of the better minds in the regime, Calamandrei remarked favorably on the fact that the minister had not greeted him with a Roman salute but instead shook his hand, nor did he address him with the *voi*.[29] Later on, when one of his friends admonished him for collaborating with a fascist minister, Calamandrei recognized the merits of the criticism, but wondered how he could not offer his expertise when it might help Italians obtain a better code.[30] Compromises of all sorts, depending on their scope and objective, were to be contemplated as a necessity, Calamandrei suggested, although there were limits to how far he would go. Hence, he absolutely rejected the idea of becoming a member of the fascist party and worried obsessively over the possibility of being assigned an honorary card—it would be a "humiliation."[31] Symbolism had its importance, and if the enlightened pragmatism of a political actor such as Grandi was acceptable to Calamandrei, he felt less generous when it came to figures such as Giovanni Gentile. In obvious divergence from fellow Florentine Casoni, his reactions at the news of the philosopher's attempted assassination (he only heard the confirmation a few days later) showed no mercy:

> To enslave high culture to a regime of legalized brigandage, to justify with his philosophy the fait accompli, to benefit with wealth and honors from this enslavement, these have been Gentile's true faults. And if the news is true, history here pays him back with his same medicine, and it is precisely his philosophy that justifies his murder.[32]

In Calamandrei's view, continuous support for fascism even in its latest Republican version was not Gentile's worst crime, although many seemed to hold that opinion. In contrast, it was in his capacity as the official philosopher of the regime that Gentile had ruinously failed all Italians. His death was the historical consequence of the "general horror" unchained by a movement that Gentile's actualist doctrine justified and promoted via a solipsistic view of the

---

[28] Calamandrei, *Diario*, vol. I, p. 117 (entry of December 22). Grandi had been ambassador to Great Britain from 1932 to 1939. Also see Calamandrei's comments of October 28, 1939, in which he counted Grandi among the "thinking heads of the party" for siding against the war launched by Germany. Calamandrei, *Diario*, vol. I, p. 104. Previously, on May 30, 1939, however, Calamandrei had written a negative note about Grandi. See Calamandrei, *Diario*, vol. I, p. 43.

[29] Calamandrei had heard from friends that Grandi did not consider his lack of party membership a hindrance when it came to collaborating on the Civil Code. Supposedly, Grandi was "not looking for cards but brains," *Diario*, vol. I, p. 112 (entry of November 30, 1939). Later on, Calamandrei continued to value Grandi positively. On September 5, 1940, fearing Grandi was gravely ill, he wrote, "Is it fate that the best ones are always eliminated?" *Diario*, vol. I, p. 227.

[30] Calamandrei, *Diario*, vol. I, p. 139 (entry of March 14, 1940).

[31] Calamandrei, *Diario*, vol. I, p. 144 (entry of April 9, 1940).

[32] Calamandrei, *Diario*, vol. II, p. 407 (entry of April 17, 1944).

world.[33] Calamandrei's blunt, unforgiving judgment only relented once he considered the human side of the tragedy by way of his acquaintance with those left behind: "Above all, I think of that poor Mrs. Erminia, already struck by the death of her son; the tragedy at their doorsteps, the sudden event that in an instant took that family from the atmosphere of bourgeois normalcy, peaceful and pleasure-seeking, to the drama of blood."[34] With empathetic thoughts, Calamandrei imagined the pain of Gentile's spouse and could identify with her emotional strain especially because she was a familiar figure in the scholarly circle to which both Gentile and he belonged.[35] They shared a common universe of human relations.

Calamandrei applied degrees of culpability in his evaluation of opponents and judged their shade of fascism according to criteria that, though often inflexible, were at the same time colored by personal experience. According to his assessment, being a fascist did not necessarily coincide perfectly with fascism; on the contrary, a hiatus separated people from their ideological convictions. In the process of seeking to identify the good from the bad that Calamandrei and others pursued, however, a whole mechanism was put in motion that by untying fascists from fascism focused on individual responsibilities and sidelined fascism' overall significance. Personalizing the regime and its RSI continuation resulted in added immunity for the historical experience of fascism. A game of assigning guilt ensued.

Guilty, not guilty

Although considerate of the personal nature of social relations, Casoni and Calamandrei were still wary of the dictatorship's abhorrent nature and

---

[33] Calamandrei, *Diario*, vol. II, p. 407. Calamandrei also condemned Croce's philosophy in relation to fascism, even though Croce expressed strong reservations about Gentile's actualism. Considering the past friendship of the two philosophers, Calamandrei wondered about Croce's reactions to Gentile's assassination. From Croce's diary we know that when he heard the news, he wished Gentile had been spared such harsh punishment. Croce, however, still condemned Gentile's philosophical system and equated it to the lowering of morality. Indeed, the entry Croce wrote when he heard of Gentile's assassination focused more on Gentile's philosophical shortcomings than his death. Croce, *Croce, the King and the Allies: Extracts from a Diary by Benedetto Croce, July 1943–June 1944*, translated by Sylvia Sprigge (New York: Norton, 1950), pp. 111–12 (*Taccuini di guerra, 1943–1945* [Milan: Adelphi, 2004], edited by Cinzia Cassani, pp. 121–2) (entry of April 17, 1944). With regard to Gentile's death, Fabio Fernardo Rizi claims that Croce wrote "three slightly different accounts of this incident for his diaries." See Rizi, *Benedetto Croce and Italian Fascism* (Toronto: University of Toronto Press, 2003), p. 252.

[34] Calamandrei, *Diario*, vol. II, p. 407. Gentile was shot as he was returning home. One of Gentile's sons, also named Giovanni, died of sepsis on March 30, 1942, at the age of thirty-five. See Turi, *Giovanni Gentile*, p. 490.

[35] Erminia Gentile was also a friend of friends, in particular of the academic and literary critic Luigi Russo.

approached people's ideological standings with caution. Other Italians navigated less circumspectly their interactions with fellow citizens. Judging from Leonetta Cecchi Pieraccini's account, in the case of artists, as well as intellectuals and cultural circles in general, there was much fluidity and openness in deciding whom to include in their networks.[36] Cecchi Pieraccini, for example, maintained the same social ties and connections throughout the decades of her life, whether it was before Mussolini's ascent to power, during the regime, or afterwards. Especially in large cities such as Rome and Milan, intellectuals frequented the same circuits and shared friendships regardless of one's political views. Cultural work, more than ideological inclinations, brought them close together.[37] Admittedly, assessing the consequences of professional practices on one's social engagement or moral integrity constitutes a challenging task. However, one might take as symptomatic a comment by Elena Carandini Albertini, who, writing about a literary friend days after the fall of Mussolini, pondered the difference separating her from him: "In my time, in my circle, politics is a serious thing that rests on conscience and morality the more severe the situation is."[38] Deeply concerned about the country's current predicament, Carandini Albertini feared that many writers and artists had become habituated to life under the regime and were hostile to change. In not so many words, she addressed the issue of their political ambivalence.[39] Considering the regime's lengthy duration, her concerns were legitimately founded. Cohabitation with fascism necessarily implied a degree of compromise and acceptance, although not everybody agreed about the malignancy of the regime's effects. Who was truly guilty? And what was their culpability relative to the rest?

For Carlo Trabucco, whose diary retells the 268 days of German occupation in Rome, Italians had enrolled in the fascist party out of necessity, not out of conviction. People had been complicit because pressed by the need to support their families, but they "were never for fascism." Instead, Mussolini was

---

[36] For one perspective on intellectuals and fascism see Angelo Ventura, *Intellettuali. Cultura e politica tra fascismo e antifascismo* (Rome: Donzelli, 2017), introduction by Emilio Gentile.

[37] The inclusiveness of artistic and intellectual circles can vary depending on different factors. For an analysis of poets in secularizing Turkey see Barış Büyükokutan, *Bound Together: The Secularization of Turkey's Literary Fields and the Western Promise of Freedom* (Ann Arbor: University of Michigan Press, 2021).

[38] Elena Carandini Albertini, *Dal terrazzo. Diario 1943–1944* (Bologna: il Mulino, 1997), p. 7 (entry of August 5, 1943).

[39] In that same note, Carandini Albertini explicitly referred to Cecchi Pieraccini's husband, Emilio Cecchi, and their poet friend, Antonio Baldini: "The incorrigible homme de lettres asks me: 'What will happen to people like Cecchi and Baldini?' I frown at him. Who cares about them? Maybe we'll find them again one day with their Feluca cap in a born-again academy, but for now let us believe in a different future." Carandini Albertini, *Dal terrazzo*, p. 8.

"uniquely responsible for Italy's ruin."[40] Trabucco identified fascism with the leader and drew a line between the regime and Italy, thus redeeming the country from any blame. In this evaluative operation, he also managed to shift fascism's guilt from the previous twenty years to the current situation dominated by war and foreign invasion. With the fascists reorganizing after Mussolini's liberation, and the Germans promptly occupying Rome, two new inimical figures emerged from his critical analysis: Germans and their domestic collaborators. A clandestine pamphlet he happened to find and then recirculated instructed the Roman population to "hate the German, drive out the German, hate traitors, kill traitors."[41]

Leaving aside the Germans for the moment, in Trabucco's taxonomy not just any fascist but rather current Republican fascists—those unmistakably associated with the Germans—were the enemy, despite the fact that most RSI followers were not newcomers to activism and simply continued the militancy previously exerted under the dictatorship. Doubtlessly, it was their current association with the occupiers in an ignominious fight against fellow Italians that made Trabucco condemn them to their negative status. He classified them as "domestic traitors," a most abject qualification. Through this symbolic name calling, the old-time "fascists" were replaced by the "repubblichini," whose main fault was linked to the current civil war. Overshadowing their organic link to the now defunct regime, the "bad" fascists were isolated from the original sin, so as not to spoil Italy's potential path to rehabilitation. If the country was fundamentally good and its citizens fair at heart, Trabucco believed, one only needed to identify and discard from the whole those that ignored the will of the people and continued to cause harm. Inoculated against evil compatriots, Italians would be able to leave fascism behind.

Trabucco's rationalization of the ways the country could overcome its recent history was based on a desire for appeasement partly derived from his Christian faith. A wish for forgiveness guided his attempt to review the past in order to set it aside and begin anew. That wish, however, also implied minimizing fascism's legacy and significance. Trabucco's interpretation of popular reactions at the liberation of Rome on June 5 illustrates his disregard for

---

[40] Carlo Trabucco, *La prigionia di Roma. Diario dei 268 giorni dell'occupazione tedesca* (Rome: S.E.L.I., 1945), p. 26 (entry of September 17, 1943). Trabucco stated that, pressed by need, people enrolled "while cursing" because they had no other choice if they wished to support their families. Playing with the party acronym, PNF, he argued that Italians were motivated by "the urgency to translate at the level of reality the three initials: Party of Needs of Families" (Partito Necessita' Famigliari).

[41] Trabucco, *La prigionia di Roma*, p. 44 (entry of September 25, 1943). This sentence concluded an otherwise lengthy pamphlet that aimed at explicating the current situation. Trabucco transcribed the whole pamphlet in his diary.

the past: "The spectacle offered this morning in the center of Rome was something unimaginable. The parade of Allied troops [...] took place among an enthusiasm that one should say was truly indescribable. [...] July 25 was a pale imitation of carnival. In contrast, June 5 is a date that no Roman will ever be able to forget."[42] In Trabucco's account, people welcomed the Anglo-Americans' arrival more joyously than they had celebrated the regime's end a few months earlier. Whether or not his assessment was accurate, it displayed his conviction of the dictatorship's irrelevance in light of contemporary developments.

Trabucco looked ahead. Fascism had been a bitter experience for the country, it went without saying, but it had now exhausted its life. It might be better to "forget the past," as a Neapolitan song of the time suggested, and think of reconciliation.[43] If popular responses to the trial and execution of the Grand Council's members that had voted down Mussolini were any indication, the Italians' revulsion at the regime's abjections indicated a desire for justice, not vengeance. No matter how hateful and despicable the sentenced fascist leaders were, Trabucco reasoned, Italians stood shocked at a verdict that blatantly and viciously indicated retaliation—they did not wish for such a harsh punishment. Their empathetic ethical stance suggested that a balanced approach was applicable in Italy and that negative passions could be overcome.

Giulio Pierangeli, a resident of Città di Castello, shared Trabucco's opinion. In the name of the country's "resurrection," Pierangeli advised Italians to move forward by trusting the power of social solidarity. As he wrote in a letter of May 21, 1944 to his daughter, one needed "to answer evil with good."[44] Throughout the long summer before the liberation of Città di Castello, and while in hiding, Pierangeli advocated "reconciliation" and "peaceful coexistence" in the best Christian tradition.[45] Arbitrary persecution against fascists ought to be avoided in favor of lawful punishments, he maintained. Also, vengeance should not be an answer nor be considered a remedy either:

---

[42] Trabucco, *La prigionia di Roma*, p. 255 (written at 8 p.m.).
[43] "Simmo 'e Napule, paisà," written by Peppino Fiorelli in 1944, sported the refrain based on a popular proverb: "Who had, had, had, who gave, gave, gave, let's forget the past." The song was criticized by some for purportedly downplaying recent history, although others believed the song communicated a message of hope. See Pietro Gargano, "Simmo 'e Napule, paisà," *Il Mattino* (February 11, 2007); Raffaele Cossentino, *La canzone napoletana dalle origini ai nostri giorni. Storia e protagonisti* (Naples: Rogiosi, 2015); Vittorio Paliotti, *Storia della canzone napoletana* (Rome: Newton Compton, 1992).
[44] See Antonella Lignani and Alvaro Tacchini eds., *Giulio Pierangeli. Scritti politici e memorie di guerra* (Città di Castello: Petruzzi editore, 2003), "Lettere alla figlia," p. 259.
[45] See "Memorie del nonno per Pier Giorgio Lignani. 4° quaderno," in Lignani and Tacchini eds., *Giulio Pierangeli*, p. 246 (entry of June 11, 1944).

No matter how hard these nine months of suffering and oppression have been, and following the example of July 25, there shouldn't be indiscriminate retaliatory attacks. Those responsible for executions and arrests, men who put themselves at the service of the Germans for repressions and roundups and who indeed used the Germans to give vent to their own hatred, cannot escape the deserved punishment [...] but these punishments should not be impulsively applied in a savage reaction that would lead to acts of revenge as a consequence. It is preferable that a guilty person be spared punishment than to condemn a man in good faith who followed his conviction.[46]

Pierangeli believed that the period of Republican fascism brought out the worst in Italians. Nevertheless, he separated from among his fascist countrymen those who followed their beliefs and those "responsible for executions and arrests." This second group had no excuses for their brutality and subservience to the Germans. Since they chose to betray their fellow citizens and persecute them, they deserved to be castigated.

To be sure, Pierangeli went beyond a mere assessment of the current reality and claimed that to make sense of the present predicament a serious analysis of the regime and its long duration was needed. He lamented the absence of popular resistance, refused to justify Italians, and, although he did not conjure atavistic defects, concluded that "we all have to atone for our sins and mistakes."[47] He also insisted that one needed "to prosecute fascism, not the fascists. Responsibilities are not individual but collective."[48] Pierangeli was much more aware than Trabucco of the pitfalls inherent in indicting individuals as opposed to the system. Nevertheless, he still had to deal with real people, those fascists (including the repubblichini) that had operated in town and would not magically disappear from the scene once the Allied forces finally arrived.

In truth, although Pierangeli did not mean to forget, he was willing to forgive. After British troops liberated Castello on July 22, he wrote to his

---

[46] "Memorie del nonno," in Lignani and Tacchini eds., *Giulio Pierangeli*, p. 246. Venanzio Gabriotti also thought along those lines. See for example his entry of October 17 in *Diario 25 luglio 1943–4 maggio 1944* (Città di Castello: Petruzzi editore, 1998) (edited by Alvaro Tacchini, preface by Mario Tosti), p. 108.

[47] Lignani and Tacchini eds., *Giulio Pierangeli*, p. 270 (letter of July 2, 1944 to daughter Giuliana). A month earlier Pierangeli had penned in his diary, "To assign all the blame to fascism would be an unforgivable mistake; one enormous fault falls on the whole Italian people" (entry of June 4, 1944), p. 231.

[48] "Memorie del nonno," in Lignani and Tacchini eds., *Giulio Pierangeli*, p. 250 (entry of June 22, 1944).

daughter, "I am a man of peace, maybe too inclined to forgiveness, and I only wish for the ex-fascists not to be in positions of command and be decent enough not to come forward."[49] Relying on tolerance, even if he still preferred for Mussolini's men not to play leading roles in Italy's rebuilding, he did not advocate any legal repercussions. Similar to Trabucco, Pierangeli's analysis of fascism was guided by one critical quandary: If in the end all Italians were guilty, how could the country effectively emerge from the political and moral crisis? A way out of this impasse was necessary. Pierangeli proposed that punishment be limited to those who, under German instigation, had cruelly persecuted their fellow citizens. He devised a solution that was meant to have it both ways, in a manner of speaking. Doubtlessly, the issue presented no easy alternatives.

Defascistization

Trabucco and Pierangeli raised the question of guilt at the time of liberation of their cities and in the context of Republican fascism. However, the dilemma of "epuration," as it came to be called, confronted the interim government of Marshal Badoglio immediately after July 25.[50] How deeply should the purging of fascists go, or better, how aggressively did the country need to hound those that had been active in the dictatorship? Such interrogatives were critical and required an urgent establishment of responsibilities—a delicate, complicated task that entangled both governmental leadership and the Italian public at large, as well as the Allied forces in charge of Sicily after they occupied it in July 1943.

Scholarship on Italy's handling of fascist crimes describes a tortuous history characterized by several phases that not only shifted over time but were also marred by internal contradictions. In the heydays of Mussolini's ousting, few reprisals were registered among civilians, and very limited episodes of

---

[49] Lignani and Tacchini eds., *Giulio Pierangeli*, pp. 288-9 (letter of July 27, 1944). Città di Castello was liberated by two Indian divisions of the eighth British Army corps. Although also composed by British military, the infantrymen of the two divisions were mostly professional military from the British colonies.

[50] On epuration see Roy Palmer Domenico, *Italian Fascists on Trial, 1943-1948* (Chapel Hill: University of North Carolina Press, 1991); Hans Woller, *I conti con il fascismo. L'epurazione in Italia, 1943-1948* (Bologna: il Mulino, 1997); Romano Canosa, *Storia dell'epurazione in Italia. Le sanzioni contro il fascismo (1943-1948)* (Milan: Baldini and Castoldi, 1999); Andrea Martini, *Dopo Mussolini. I processi ai fascisti e ai collaborazionisti (1944-1953)* (Rome: Viella, 2019); and Cecilia Nubola, Paolo Pezzino, and Toni Rovatti eds., *Giustizia straordinaria tra fascismo e democrazia. I processi presso le Corti d'assise e nei tribunali militari* (Bologna: il Mulino, 2019).

physical violence occurred between opponents (in Rome, for example, no fascist supporter died, although the situation turned tenser in Northern Italy).[51] Despite the scarce number of direct confrontations, the issue of epuration was taken seriously at the governmental level, where measures were promptly adopted with the goal of beginning to dismantle the regime's institutional structures. Thus, scrutiny and removal of public administrators were carried out (though only partially), symbolic erasures of fascist testimonials took place, newspapers saw a change of helm, and university professors with a fascist past were fired.[52] These critical steps were deemed necessary to ensure legitimacy for Badoglio, both domestically and in the eyes of the Allied forces.[53] Once Badoglio's government moved to Brindisi in the aftermath of the armistice, however, the initially active approach underwent a few changes. Decisions became more fractured, since the government merely oversaw a limited territory in the Kingdom of the South. The American military, in turn, were in charge of epuration in Sicily but, as it advanced up to Naples, found it could not apply the same methods in the two areas. Only after June 1944, when Bonomi replaced Badoglio as head of government following the liberation of Rome, was the issue of epuration in public offices taken up again and its range extended with a decree issued on July 27.[54] The experiences of the German occupation and the RSI administration demanded a more coherent policy, also in view of a growing popular resentment that was leading to individual settlings of scores—a phenomenon exasperated by the atrocities that marked the period of liberation.[55] After the war, state intervention in the process of "defascistization" remained embroiled in contradictions. Sanctions in the realm of public administration were still applied, but with difficulties, and punishment for fascist crimes attracted even more controversies.[56]

[51] See Woller, *I conti con il fascismo*, p. 22. In his diary, Carlo Chevallard reported that Turin had not seen much violence, but he was aware of graver disorders in Milan. See his entries of July 26 and 27, 1943 in "Diario di Carlo Chevallard 1942–1945," edited by Riccardo Marchis, in *Torino in guerra tra cronaca e memoria*, edited by Rosanna Roccia and Giorgio Vaccarino, with a Preface by Alessandro Galante Garrone (Turin: Archivio Storico della Città di Torino, 1975), p. 73.

[52] For example, Calamandrei became the new rector at the University of Florence. His regency only lasted until the armistice of September 8.

[53] Obviously, one main obstacle to epuration was that many in the new government, including the king and Badoglio, had been involved in the regime.

[54] Legislative decree 159 "Sanzioni contro il fascismo." Bonomi was prime minister until June 1945.

[55] This more popular side of the epuration has been called "wild" epuration (epurazione selvaggia).

[56] For many Italian commentators, the epuration was a failure. See for example Alessandro Galante Garrone's preface to Roy Domenico, *Italian Fascists on Trial*, pp. vii–xiv. According to Angelo Michele Imbriani, failure to enact epuration laws bred people's distrust towards the new government. See *Vento del Sud. Moderati, reazionari, qualunquisti (1943–1948)* (Bologna: il Mulino, 1996), p. 34. The idea of a "failed" epuration held by several Italian historians is contested by Woller, who cites, among other accomplishments of the program, the number of trials up to 30,000 that took place in Italy between 1945 and 1946. As for the deaths due to summary justice between 1944 and 1946,

Meanwhile, individual pursuits of justice resulted in victims numbering in the thousands. Indisputable perpetrators of horrific crimes in villages and towns, RSI fascists and collaborationists had broken the covenant—they had crucified their own brothers and sisters. They were now being made to pay—a popular form of epuration. Against the background of the Resistance to Nazifascism, it was easy to identify the repubblichini as culprits in the dramatic battle that pitted Italians against Italians.[57] But as the brief history of epuration illustrates, the attempt to ascertain and categorize degrees of individual responsibilities in the regime, as opposed to the RSI period, was much more fraught with ambiguities. The two fascist incarnations were seemingly treated as separate entities, and evaluations of the former appeared shakier and more uncertain. Initially, as some of the intellectuals' diaries reveal, there was a certain discomfort at any sweeping measure that would indict Italians for their past involvement in Mussolini's dictatorship. Ontological and epistemological issues also complicated the inquiry on culpability: What defines a fascist and how to recognize one?

Benedetto Croce was among those who felt uneasy about the whole matter of epuration and continued to do so throughout 1944. As one of the leaders of the Liberal party, he was implicated in the political process in charge of postregime Italy and formulated advice on the policies for cleansing the country of its fascist past. But, as his earlier difficulty to distinguish pure from impure fascists anticipated, his reluctance to purge remained firm. While recommending lenience, he pleaded for a thoughtful, restrained program. "Friends in Naples have asked me for a letter setting down the criteria to be followed in the 'epuration' which is about to begin and which we Liberals wish to see conducted in the most temporary and indulgent way," he wrote in early January 1944.[58] A complex matter of nonnegligible proportions, the issue of epuration occupied Croce's mind for months, although he never ceased to maintain that moderation should prevail over vengeful impulses. "Defascistization"—which

---

Woller cites the figure of 12,000. See Woller, *I conti con il fascismo*, pp. 8, 573. Christopher Duggan mentions 20,000 deaths in the two years following April 1945. See *Fascist Voices: An Intimate History of Mussolini's Italy* (Oxford: Oxford University Press, 2013), p. 418. Canosa cites 10,000 as "prudent governmental estimates" between 1945 and 1946. See *Storia dell'epurazione in Italia*, p. 386. Canosa also shares Woller's opinion that epuration in Italy was not a failure.

[57] From here one can understand the more exacerbated nature of the problem in the North as opposed both to the South, where the RSI never ruled, and Central Italy, which was spared the final eight to nine months of the German occupation and the RSI administration.

[58] Croce, *The King and the Allies*, p. 65 (*Taccuini di guerra*, p. 74) (entry of January 12, 1944). The letter to the Liberal Party mentioned by Croce was published as a small pamphlet in 1944 with the title "Intorno ai criteri dell' 'epurazione," now in Croce, *Scritti e discorsi politici (1943–1947)* (Bari: Laterza, 1963), 2 vols., vol. 1, pp. 44–9.

he found to be an inherently "fascistic" word—was not an easy undertaking.[59] It required separating those who belonged to the high hierarchies of the regime from the millions of Italians who had followed and obeyed—supposedly a straightforward distinction that was not, however, as neat as one would have hoped. How to discriminate fairly among forms of participation and subjection? Croce especially insisted on the need to be "indulgent with the large multitude of those belonging to the subordinate and humble ranks."[60] Entire Italian families would face complete chaos and disruption if the men of the house were to be identified as responsible for fascist crimes. Ultimately, Croce feared that, were any strong measures to be applied, a popular revolt would ensue, with the added risk of Mussolini's potential resurgence—all signs pointing to Italy's inherent fragility.[61]

In Croce's opinion, the mere fact that he, a man of letters, was being pressured to take on the reins of the country was symptomatic of Italy's weakness. It indicated the Italians' continued faith in the value of the exceptional man, even if a "miraculous" leader was being identified in his case with "an eighty-year-old man who has been a philosopher and humanist his whole life and never thought of governing his country or did any preparation for it."[62] The hope that one person could resolve the country's myriad problems was an anachronism, Croce believed; it was the sign of a lesson not learned. Ultimately, the priority of defending Italy from other potential political crises motivated Croce to advocate softening all interventions against fascism and its past ordeals.[63] Less familiar with the RSI brutalities, Croce focused on the cruxes created by the regime while claiming that the "disease" of fascism was a matter of "sentiment, imagination, and generically human will."[64]

---

[59] See his comments after attending a Cabinet meeting in Salerno on May 23, 1944: "At Omodeo's request several corrections were made in the 'defascistization' decree (an ugly word which, although anti-Fascist, has a Fascistic sound)." *Croce, the King and the Allies*, p. 131 (*Taccuini di guerra*, p. 143).

[60] See "Intorno ai criteri dell' 'epurazione,'" in Croce, *Scritti e discorsi politici*, p. 46.

[61] See entry of December 17, 1944 in *Taccuini di guerra*, p. 255. Also see entry of August 4, 1944 in Croce, *Taccuini di guerra*, p. 193.

[62] *Taccuini di guerra*, p. 251 (entry of December 10, 1944).

[63] On this issue see Eugenio Di Rienzo, *Benedetto Croce. Gli anni dello scontento (1943–1948)* (Soveria Mannelli: Rubbettino, 2019).

[64] Croce, "Chi è 'fascista'?" in *Scritti e discorsi politici*, vol. 2, p. 48. The article was first published in Naples' *Giornale* on October 29, 1944 and also in Rome's *Risorgimento liberale*. Croce was not optimistic about the future. A sense of gloom transpires from his diaries, and he dismissed any illusion of things returning to the way they once were. Those sorts of expectations were only a fantasy: "We must resolutely detach ourselves from such hopes, and get accustomed to the idea of living a life with no stability, upon which we can no longer weave the old individual and socially ordered activities; it will be a day-to-day life, so repugnant to us." Croce, *Croce, the King and the Allies*, pp. 89–90 (*Taccuini di guerra*, p. 99) (entry of March 1, 1944).

"The Germans, the Germans, the Germans!"

The association of Mussolini's Social Republic with Nazi Germany, especially in Northern and Central Italy, heightened the evilness of Republican fascists and helped dig a deeper gulf in people's minds between the past regime and the RSI. Within this new scenario, the repubblichini filled the villain's role, even though the ex-ally still constituted a haunting inimical force that contributed to deflecting attention from fascism's responsibilities. As Elena Carandini Albertini perceptively protested in early September 1943, fear of the "eternal enemy" dominated the population even before the start of the occupation: "The Germans, the Germans, the Germans! This obsession, this threat always present and ever growing. Let them come, exterminate us, take away everything, but let's stop talking about them."[65] The trope of the eternal enemy as well as the historical legacy of the association of Germans with barbarians, both already in long-standing circulation, came to play a preponderant role in the way intellectual diarists perceived the ex-ally. And in the same way that ordinary Italians made the Germans compete with local fascists for blame, so did intellectual diarists. In occupied Rome, although the wicked deeds and corrupt actions of fascists had re-emerged with all their viciousness after the short break of the forty-five days, Trabucco reserved his harshest words for the "barbarian" Germans, who appeared as duly befitting followers of their ancestor Attila. The Germans' practice of murdering hostages in response to killings of their own soldiers especially magnified the savagery with which they treated the Italian population. The massacre of the Ardeatine Caves on March 24, 1944, about which we know Trabucco provided one of the first historical accounts, only confirmed to him the extent of the horror Hitler's military could unleash.

While Trabucco did not waver in his opinion about the Germans, other intellectual diarists did. In some cases, such as for Giulio Pierangeli and Gaetano Casoni, initially nuanced approaches gave way to escalating negative excoriations of the "eternal enemy"—a trend similarly observed among ordinary diarists. Hence, Pierangeli at first identified with those Italians that feared the Germans but were impressed by their organizational skills and discipline and did not generally pronounce negative judgments on them: "There is no hatred against the Germans. One understands that they pursue their interests carelessly. They have no sense of boundaries and of the future,

---

[65] Carandini Albertini, *Dal terrazzo*, p. 22 (entry of September 2, 1943).

but this is not surprising. It is their way of thinking and behaving."[66] By the time Città di Castello was liberated, however, Pierangeli could not justify the disproportionate amount and degree of destruction the Germans gratuitously inflicted on the local population. As more than a century of civic and economic life was obliterated, he concluded that "the German army behaved like the most irreconcilable of enemies."[67]

In a similar manner, Gaetano Casoni's assessment of the Germans, though restrained until a few weeks before Florence's liberation, worsened at the end of the occupation. With Nazi actions becoming increasingly merciless, Casoni cited the Germans' lineage and barbarism in order to warn about their constitutional evilness: "Let God protect and free us as soon as possible from this oppressive kind!"[68] By identifying Germans with an "oppressive kind" (*opprimente genìa*)—a bloodline dating back to unknown, distant times—he underscored their indelible guilt. Reference to their "kind" exposed the irredeemable nature of their ignobility. Ultimately, despite his earlier tolerance, Casoni expressed an almost tribalist opinion of the Germans, whose horrifying behavior had decidedly put on display their worst instincts and truly dishonorable essence. Calling them "barbarians" helped him express his utmost outrage. "It is an entire people of vandals, officers and soldiers, with rare exceptions, that has passed throughout our lovely regions causing destruction. As enemy of civilization, they have plundered everything of most value created by our genius," he wrote in his final diary entry two months after the liberation of Florence.[69] Reiterating his belief in the abject character of the Germans, Casoni unfavorably compared them to Italians.

Although unforgiving, Casoni was far from advocating revenge. Also, he did not absolve all his compatriots of responsibility either. Instead, he called on God's justice, hoping that the Almighty would award the right punishment to Germans and, along with them, their "Italian imitators."[70] The brutality of Hitler's army had pushed Casoni's Christian sense of tolerance to the limit— his indictment of fellow Italians signaled the gravitas of the moment. But would

---

[66] "Memorie del nonno," in Lignani and Tacchini eds., *Giulio Pierangeli*, p. 248 (entry of June 17, 1944). Also see his letter to Giuliana of July 12, 1944, p. 278: "The German army is still formidable. Not only it must have good leadership, but it is compact, disciplined, and determined to fight to the bitter end."

[67] "Memorie del nonno," in Lignani and Tacchini eds., *Giulio Pierangeli*, p. 253 (undated entry). On the damages inflicted by the Germans also see Pierangeli's detailed description in "Dal 25 luglio al 22 agosto 1944. Cronaca di Città di Castello," section on "Il mese del martirio," in Lignani and Tacchini eds., *Giulio Pierangeli*, pp. 208–13, and his letters to Giuliana, in particular the one of June 20, 1944, pp. 263–5.

[68] Casoni, *Diario fiorentino*, p. 85 (entry of July 4, 1944).
[69] Casoni, *Diario fiorentino*, p. 312 (entry of October 22, 1944).
[70] Casoni, *Diario fiorentino*, p. 312 (entry of October 22, 1944).

God's justice actually be fulfilled? And should one consider the Italians' vile behavior a mere imitation of the Germans? Piero Calamandrei, for one, did not think the issue could be, nor should be, so easily solved. Differently from Casoni, he reserved his most severe judgment for fellow citizens, those he called "the servants": "To paraphrase the saying of he who stated that the more he knew humans the more he loved dogs, I can say that the more I know the fascists the more I love the Germans."[71] A statement *ad absurdum*, he recognized, but that was obviously meant to magnify fascist Italians' wicked actions as they hid behind the Germans' might to carry out "their cold vengeance against the weak and the helpless, little bloodthirsty people they are."[72]

Calamandrei was not in Florence when he composed those reflections, having evacuated to Umbria in mid-October 1943.[73] He was thus partially spared the misery suffered by the Florentines during the occupation. One could speculate that he might have been less inclined to "love" the Germans had he experienced more directly their behavior in the city. Yet it is evident that his declaration of "love" was meant to underline the profound dislike he felt for Italy's fascists. His scrutinizing eye continued to remain fixed on the repubblichini—his compatriots.

The historicity of one's lived world structured individual diarists' responses to the present as they confronted the issues of how to categorize the fascists, identify enemies, adjudicate guilt, and assign blame. With a range of candidates from which to select the most despicable ones, the decision process appeared not only difficult, but also unresolvable once and for all—in contrast, it challenged assumptions and defied previously held positions on a continuous basis. Fluctuating as circumstances allowed, choices were vulnerable to reconsideration. Although the Germans provided a temporary smokescreen that obviated the task of evaluating fellow Italians, the options between good and bad fascists, old guard or repubblichini, guilty or not guilty still puzzled intellectual diarists. Despite partaking in a will to explain fascism's origins and endurance, they were caught in the currency of the moment, a situation that, while leading them to focus on local realities and relationships,

---

[71] Calamandrei, *Diario*, vol. II, p. 279 (entry of December 12).

[72] Calamandrei, *Diario*, vol. II, p. 280 (entry of December 12). However, Calamandrei had expressed negative judgments on the Germans in earlier entries (see chapter 4). For example, on December 26, 1942, he wrote, "They are a people that obviously lacks the sense of humanity of civilized people; they lack compassion. Their feeling of racial superiority is so insane that massacring other people is for them equivalent to what killing a fly would be for us." Calamandrei, *Diario*, vol. II, p. 98.

[73] Calamandrei moved to Colcello, near Amelia (he called the village "Colcello" in his diary, but its actual name is Collicello Umbro). He kept up to date about events in Florence through friends, newspapers, and other outlets.

at the same time moved their attention away from the past. Fascism, as a system of government and authoritarian power that had yoked Italy for more than two decades, was archived and began to fade away behind the horrors of the biennium 1943–45. At the same time, intellectual diarists' concerns about Italy's future promoted ideals of forgiveness and reconciliation, while ties of friendship encouraged them to overcome the limits of ideological intolerance. Political hybridity and compromises were part of the familiar world, a recognizable feature of everyday interactions—people were molded by the experience of a historical reality they shared in common.

The story of Venanzio Gabriotti recounted below summarizes, and in many ways exemplifies, the complex situations faced by intellectual diarists as they lived through the misery unleashed by the war, foreign occupation, and the resurgent fascism of the RSI. Filled with quirky occurrences and a dramatic outcome, Gabriotti's tale illustrates the reverberations of micropolitics in the setting of a small Umbrian center caught in the country's uneven fate between July 25, 1943 and the end of the war in early May 1945. With an active citizenry responsive to historical changes, local events mirrored the larger national trends, including the eventual organized resistance against the German occupier. A participant in the opposition, and sensitive to the cultural resonance of Risorgimento values and patriotic ideals, Gabriotti operated in an environment that was embedded in traditional networks and personal ties, split between old-time loyalties and new inimical forces, attuned to the virtues of community, and sensitive to Christian morals. His story reflects the effects of those factors on the version of history that unfolded in his home town of Città di Castello, about a hundred and twenty-five kilometers further north from the village of Colcello, where Calamandrei had evacuated. The mental (but also physical) strains Gabriotti endured typify the experience of many who, even if antifascist, were pulled by contradictory forces that, on the one hand, alerted them to the reprobate infamies of Nazi-fascism and, on the other hand, encouraged them to appeal for peace and concord in the name of national rebirth.

Micropolitics: Glory and Misery of the Local

With a population of 12,260, the tightly knit nature of social relations influenced the political dynamics of Città di Castello more than in larger urban centers such as Florence.[74] Not surprising, when Mussolini's government fell

---

[74] The population figure is for the town only. As for the territory under the jurisdiction of Città di Castello, the total amounted to 35,625 (Archivio comunale di Città di Castello).

in July 1943, the reconstituted oppositional forces in town decided not to pursue reprisal against their fascist citizens. In a place where everybody knew everybody else, concerted efforts were made on both sides to avoid violent confrontations.[75] Once the Germans occupied the area after September 8, however, local fascists who joined the newly constituted Social Republic found themselves in a peculiar situation; eventually, they surrendered their initially good intentions.[76] Mounting resistance by several groups of "rebels," including youth, Italian military on the run, and Slav and Anglo-American ex-prisoners, required the assistance of German troops—the fascist Milizia was unable to contain the incessant armed incursions of the resisters.[77] A quickly forming collaboration between Germans and Republican fascists in Città di Castello ensued, producing novel political configurations that upset more established ties. Venanzio Gabriotti fell victim to this infelicitous turn.

Immediately following July 25, Gabriotti had published a "rushed" periodical that celebrated Italians' return to freedom. Called *Rinascita* (Rebirth) and produced in collaboration with a small circle of friends, the "flier" augured the continuation of the prospected process of renewal—all the suffering of the previous twenty years was to be converted into, and lead towards, the "general uplifting" of the nation (Figure 5).[78] Most importantly, this "periodical of free men," as it was subtitled, affirmed its initiators' desire for "diligent unity" (*concordia operosa*). Social collaboration and ideological tolerance were among its stated priorities, along with respect for the person and for rules. A short paragraph at the bottom of page one reinforced the genuineness of these proclaimed intents by urging citizens not to pursue individual actions of revenge. People should place their trust in the regular course of justice instead.

With all its idealistic expectations of a "radiant" future to come, the periodical's short life was harbinger of Italy's grim times ahead. Six weeks after the fall of the regime, Gabriotti was deeply troubled by the armistice of September 8 and its aftermath. Immersed in his memories as a volunteer in the First World War, he felt appalled watching the millenarian enemy overtake the

---

[75] See Alvaro Tacchini, *Il fascismo a Città di Castello* (Città di Castello: Petruzzi Editore, 2004), p. 76 and notes on p. 179.
[76] According to Tacchini, 325 citizens of Città di Castello enrolled in the RSI fascist party. See *Il fascismo a Città di Castello*, p. 76.
[77] On war prisoners who fled the internment camp of nearby Anghiari after September 8, see Giovannino Fiori, *La memoria della gente comune. Nel cinquantesimo anniversario della Liberazione di Caprese Michelangelo* (Anghiari: I.T.E.A., 1994).
[78] On its first page, as well as in Gabriotti's diary, the periodical was referred to as "foglio volante" or "foglio." Only the issue of July 27 was printed. One hour after it went on sale, the periodical was confiscated by the police for lacking an authorized permit, but even within that one hour, according to Gabriotti, it had "an unexpected success." See Gabriotti, *Diario*, p. 47. Giulio Pierangeli was among those involved in the periodical. See Lignani and Tacchini eds., *Giulio Pierangeli*, p. 37.

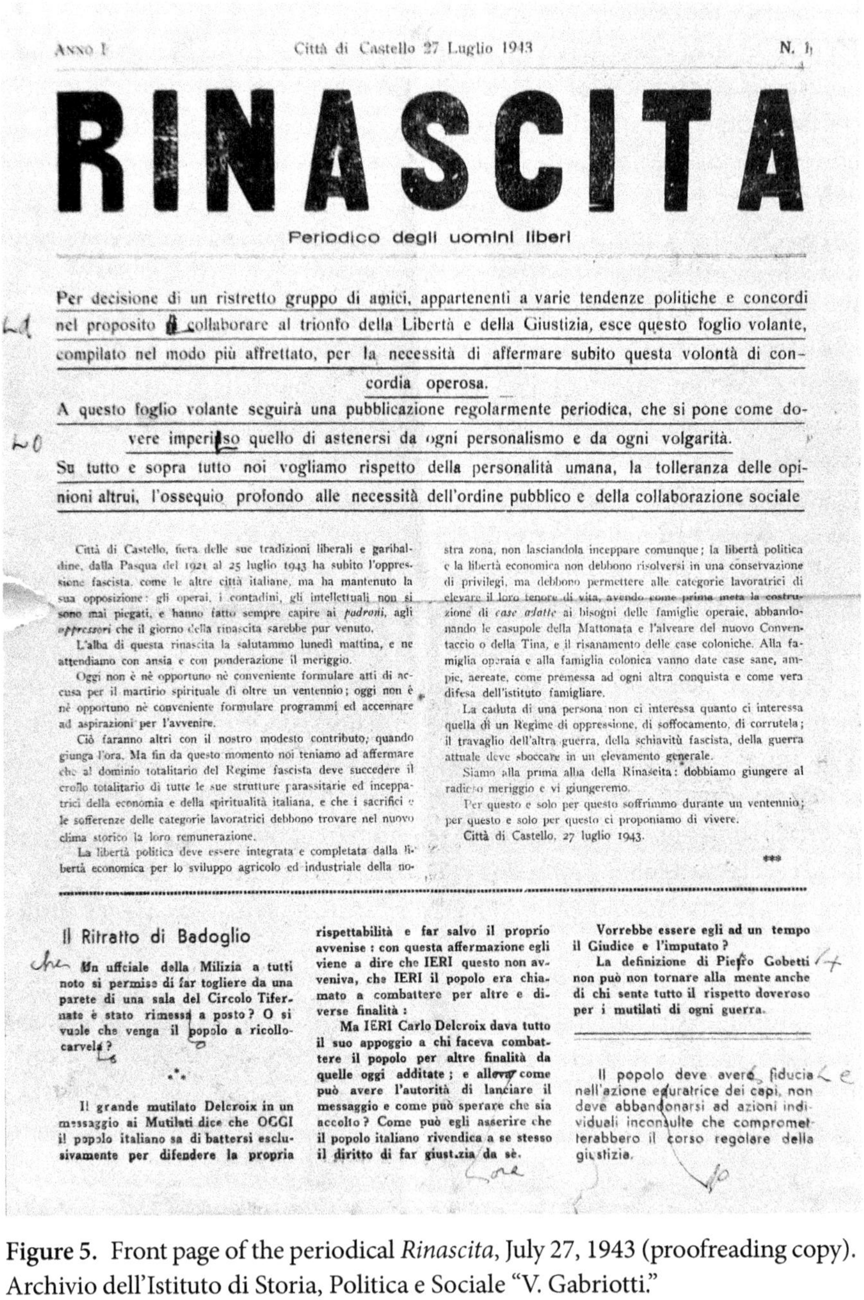

Anno I — Città di Castello 27 Luglio 1943 — N. 1

RINASCITA

Periodico degli uomini liberi

Per decisione di un ristretto gruppo di amici, appartenenti a varie tendenze politiche e concordi nel proposito di collaborare al trionfo della Libertà e della Giustizia, esce questo foglio volante, compilato nel modo più affrettato, per la necessità di affermare subito questa volontà di concordia operosa.

A questo foglio volante seguirà una pubblicazione regolarmente periodica, che si pone come dovere imperioso quello di astenersi da ogni personalismo e da ogni volgarità.

Su tutto e sopra tutto noi vogliamo rispetto della personalità umana, la tolleranza delle opinioni altrui, l'ossequio profondo alle necessità dell'ordine pubblico e della collaborazione sociale

Città di Castello, fiera delle sue tradizioni liberali e garibaldine, dalla Pasqua del 1921 al 25 luglio 1943 ha subito l'oppressione fascista, come le altre città italiane, ma ha mantenuto la sua opposizione: gli operai, i contadini, gli intellettuali non si sono mai piegati, e hanno fatto sempre capire ai *padroni*, agli *oppressori* che il giorno della rinascita sarebbe pur venuto.

L'alba di questa rinascita la salutammo lunedì mattina, e ne attendiamo con ansia e con ponderazione il meriggio.

Oggi non è nè opportuno nè conveniente formulare atti di accusa per il martirio spirituale di oltre un ventennio; oggi non è nè opportuno nè conveniente formulare programmi ed accennare ad aspirazioni per l'avvenire.

Ciò faranno altri con il nostro modesto contributo, quando giunga l'ora. Ma fin da questo momento noi teniamo ad affermare che al dominio totalitario del Regime fascista deve succedere il crollo totalitario di tutte le sue strutture parassitarie ed inceppatrici della economia e della spiritualità italiana, e che i sacrifici e le sofferenze delle categorie lavoratrici debbono trovare nel nuovo clima storico la loro remunerazione.

La libertà politica deve essere integrata e completata dalla libertà economica per lo sviluppo agricolo ed industriale della nostra zona, non lasciandola inceppare comunque; la libertà politica e la libertà economica non debbono risolversi in una conservazione di privilegi, ma debbono permettere alle categorie lavoratrici di elevare il loro tenore di vita, avendo come prima meta la costruzione di *case adatte* ai bisogni delle famiglie operaie, abbandonando le casupole della Mattonata e l'alveare del nuovo Conventaccio o della Tina, e il risanamento delle case coloniche. Alla famiglia operaia e alla famiglia colonica vanno date case sane, ampie, aereate, come premessa ad ogni altra conquista e come vera difesa dell'istituto famigliare.

La caduta di una persona non ci interessa quanto ci interessa quella di un Regime di oppressione, di soffocamento, di corrutela; il travaglio dell'altra guerra, della schiavitù fascista, della guerra attuale deve sboccare in un elevamento generale.

Siamo alla prima alba della Rinascita: dobbiamo giungere al radioso meriggio e vi giungeremo.

Per questo e solo per questo soffrimmo durante un ventennio; per questo e solo per questo ci proponiamo di vivere.

Città di Castello, 27 luglio 1943.

***

Il Ritratto di Badoglio

Un ufficiale della Milizia a tutti noto si permise di far togliere da una parete di una sala del Circolo Tifernate è stato rimessa a posto? O si vuole che venga il popolo a ricollocarvela?

***

Il grande mutilato Delcroix in un messaggio ai Mutilati dice che OGGI il popolo italiano sa di battersi esclusivamente per difendere la propria rispettabilità e far salvo il proprio avvenise: con questa affermazione egli viene a dire che IERI questo non avveniva, che IERI il popolo era chiamato a combattere per altre e diverse finalità:

Ma IERI Carlo Delcroix dava tutto il suo appoggio a chi faceva combattere il popolo per altre finalità da quelle oggi additate; e allora come può avere l'autorità di lanciare il messaggio e come può sperare che sia accolto? Come può egli asserire che il popolo italiano rivendica a se stesso il diritto di far giust.zia da sè.

Vorrebbe essere egli ad un tempo il Giudice e l'imputato?

La definizione di Pietro Gobetti non può non tornare alla mente anche di chi sente tutto il rispetto doveroso per i mutilati di ogni guerra.

Il popolo deve avere fiducia nell'azione equatrice dei capi, non deve abbandonarsi ad azioni individuali inconsulte che comprometterabbero il corso regolare della giustizia.

Figure 5. Front page of the periodical *Rinascita*, July 27, 1943 (proofreading copy). Archivio dell'Istituto di Storia, Politica e Sociale "V. Gabriotti."

country—he could not fathom how all the efforts he had undertaken with his compatriots during the Great War now risked being wasted. In a language reminiscent of the Risorgimento battles, Gabriotti vowed to push back "the foreigner" (*lo straniero*) and "continue the fight against the eternal invader."[79] The subjugation by the Germans struck him as a historical anachronism that was reopening Italy's old wound as a divided country subject to foreign domination. That past haunted Gabriotti not merely because of his experience in the First World War, but also in light of the nineteenth-century fight for national independence led by an older generation represented by his father. In a tragic twist and as in one's worst nightmare, the accomplishments of that whole era were now being challenged by a new wave of invaders. Nor were the Germans the only guilty protagonists in this drama. Although supportive of the Allied forces, Gabriotti gloomily considered the implications for the country of the Anglo-Americans' conquering role. It was a baffling but all too sobering reality. And the irony was that he could not but hope for those foreigners' prompt arrival as he watched the fate of local parents who were threatened with arrest if their sons did not enroll in the RSI army: "Poor Italy: after so many struggles for freedom, we are left with only the freedom to desire a dominator less ferocious than another?! What would my father say who fought twelve years for the unification of the Fatherland? What would the many martyrs of the Risorgimento say?"[80] The enormous weight that foreign dominance would impose on the country could not be downplayed, for invaders were still invaders no matter their geographical provenance.

Italians faced an impossible conundrum, although young people offered Gabriotti reason for hope in redemption. He particularly admired the courage of those going into hiding to escape the military call—fully engaged in the fight against the occupier, fugitives were ready to defend the nation. Gabriotti found in those rebels an echo of his own patriotic ardor when, at thirty-two, he had enrolled as volunteer in the Great War. The stakes, indeed, could not be higher—the soul and body of the nation were on the line. Seeing that

---

[79] Gabriotti, *Diario*, p. 77 (entry of September 20). Gabriotti cited a speech by Badoglio from Radio Algiers aired on that same date of September 20: "After the speech, the song of the Piave re-evoked the sad days of the Fatherland and reawakened my youth spirit and the desire to take again my place among the soldiers in order to continue fighting against the eternal invader." The song of the Piave was a patriotic hymn commemorating the Battle of the Piave River in the First World War. After the fall of Mussolini, the song was selected to be Italy's new national anthem. One of the most memorable lines of the song goes, "The foreigner shall not pass!"

[80] Gabriotti, *Diario*, p. 94 (entry of October 2, 1943). Gabriotti's father had fought with Garibaldi's troops.

Italians, in the guise of the youngest, were responding to the call for action reassured Gabriotti—the fatherland could be saved both materially and spiritually.

Gabriotti was not so naïve as to believe that all Italians were headed on a path to salvation. In fact, he denounced homegrown betrayal and pointed his finger at those who collaborated with the Germans. Their behavior was nothing short of "ignominious."[81] But if Italians' duplicity disturbed Gabriotti no less than the Germans' intimidating attitude, he understood the constraints people felt in the face of a superior subjugating force. Also, his personal relations and interactions with local fascist functionaries softened his judgment about those whose ideas he opposed. In addition, and most consequentially, traditions of friendship and respect in Città di Castello helped smooth contrasts between conflicting factions. Already on September 13, 1943, a group of citizens of divergent political persuasions had gathered in the town hall to prepare a document that would "demonstrate unity in the name of civic interest."[82] The manifesto advocated forgetting past divisions and renouncing any projects of reprisal. It also encouraged "doing everything one can so that our Town will not be injured by deaths and ruins."[83] The future of Città di Castello was a priority. As events evolved (and the Germans were about to take charge of the area), the document was never made public. It, however, presaged a continuous desire for solidarity shared by individuals of different orientations in the name of the inhabitants' common interests. The network of personal relations that constituted the social fabric of the town remained strong amidst the chaos of the occupation.[84] And it came to play a central role in the local political dynamics that engulfed Gabriotti and eventually determined his fortune late in the spring of 1944.

After Italy declared war against Germany on October 13, Gabriotti knew his personal situation was critical considering that he was an opponent of the past regime in a territory currently under German occupation.[85] By November 4,

---

[81] On October 17, anniversary of his father's death, Gabriotti wrote, "If he was alive today, he would have to realize that all his work and ardor combating the Germans for twelve years have been frustrated! Today the Germans are once again dominating our Italy, bullies as ever, and the worst news is that this is the result of the ignominious behavior of a section of Italians." Gabriotti, *Diario*, p. 106. Also see entry of October 1, 1943, where Gabriotti addressed the issue of homegrown betrayal while discussing the Germans' retreat and pillaging in Southern Italy, *Diario*, p. 93.

[82] Gabriotti, *Diario*, p. 61 (entry of September 13, 1943).

[83] The text of the manifesto was transcribed by Gabriotti. See *Diario*, p. 61.

[84] For a case study of small-town relations in wartime see Bruno Cartosio, "Memoria e storia: una famiglia tortonese nella guerra (1940–1945)," *Quaderno di storia contemporanea* 8 (1990): pp. 57–81.

[85] See entry of October 13, 1943 in Gabriotti, *Diario*, p. 104: "We are now in a more serious situation in this area, and reactions, reprisals, and arrests are to be expected...Naturally, I am among those the most at risk."

he received communication of an arrest warrant. The news sent shockwaves around. "I know that in town my situation makes an impression and provokes discussions," he wrote on November 9.[86] After all, he was a well-regarded figure in Castello. Fugitive and hiding at his sister's house, Gabriotti prepared his last will and testament. Although friends advised him to leave town to avoid capture, he could not stand the thought.[87] Meanwhile, on the evening of November 21 he went to see the head of the area's fascist party, whom he referred to as "more than anything else my personal friend."[88] One can gather that in spite of his suspicious political activities Gabriotti received special treatment from the town's authorities. The fascist party leader had actually requested they meet. "He expressed his regrets for what happened, and assured me that, within the limits of his power, he will try to support me. Friendship surpasses partisan differences," Gabriotti acknowledged. Adding a twist to the story, his friend also invited him to dine together, a proposal that was full of dangers for both, but that Gabriotti ultimately accepted. Later, at the restaurant, where another fascist leader also joined them, they addressed the issue of their unusual commingling and joked about the risk of being executed by the Germans for it. And yet those same fascist leaders asked Gabriotti to return in a few days for a meal of Castello's signature dish. "Thursday night they want that...I return to Castello to go eat the...cappelletti! Life comedies...When will we be able to tell these stories?" Gabriotti commented.[89] Continuously alerted by the town's authorities of any potential actions against him, in mid-December Gabriotti was exonerated of all suspicions.

While local politics temporarily allowed Gabriotti reprieve through favorable decisions that spared him the worst, he was not deterred from pursuing his avowed moral mission of resisting the Germans. Despite the risks, and against all friendly warnings to stay put, he continued to support the rebel movement until he was arrested. It was May 5, 1944. A series of circumstances, including the successful intensification of activities by local resistance groups, had presented the fascist leadership of Castello with challenges they could not adequately meet. After German troops were assigned to assist the town's fight against partisan forces, Gabriotti's fate was sealed. The occupiers saw in him a leader of the Resistance whose punishment might serve as

---

[86] Gabriotti, *Diario*, p. 118.
[87] "I don't feel like it. I can't bear the idea of leaving town," Gabriotti, *Diario*, p. 121 (entry of November 16).
[88] Gabriotti, *Diario*, p. 128 (entry of November 22, 1943).
[89] Gabriotti, *Diario*, p. 128. Gabriotti did not, however, reveal his hiding place to his hosts. In contrast, he told them made-up stories of his peregrinations as a fugitive away from town.

exemplary to the population. Even if the fascist citizens of Castello continued to labor to save his life (affective ties guiding their actions), on May 9 Gabriotti was executed. In the chronicle of his fellow citizen Giulio Pierangeli, "That day was a day of deep mourning for the town. Even the fascists seemed to participate in mourning, as they fully realized the enormity of what had happened and were anxious not to be considered responsible: everybody wanted to claim they had done the impossible to save his life."[90]

An episode that shook the town to its core, the execution of Gabriotti left a deep wound in the people of Castello. He doubtlessly enjoyed great standing in the community, as Pierangeli's comments highlight, and the murderous act to which he fell victim was unanimously resented, no matter one's political stance. Indeed, because of the close personal ties that linked the town's citizens, Gabriotti had managed to avoid troubles for months. His relationship with local fascist leaders exposed sentimental layers that were stronger than any ideological position, making it hard to maintain strict divisions between camps of opposing faiths. In an environment of tightly knit connections, the interweaving of personal and political elements colored one's perspectives of the "other," even if it did not necessarily eliminate critical evaluation. In principle, if nothing else, Gabriotti denounced those Italians who collaborated with the Germans. Scarce popular participation in the new Fascist Republican Party, however, gave him reassurance that one should look ahead.[91] Although Gabriotti did not live to see what the future would bring to Città di Castello, his disposition aligned with that of fellow diarists who wished to overcome past conflicts and fascism's dark times through a process of national reconciliation.[92]

Banality and Drama: Enduring Instability

While intellectual diarists struggled to define their relationship with fascism old and new, war was the experiential environment within which they lived

---

[90] See "Dal 25 luglio 1943 al 22 agosto 1944. Cronaca di Città di Castello," in Lignani and Tacchini eds., *Giulio Pierangeli*, p. 203.

[91] Gabriotti also recognized that fellow Castellani were moved by hostile sentiments against him based on local dynamics. On December 19, 1943, for example, he cited jealousy: "In town, the usual jealousy is starting anew among the fascists, who disapprove how people greet me and compliment me. I've been told to stay quiet!!" Gabriotti, *Diario*, p. 144.

[92] No revengeful killing of fascists occurred after Italy's liberation in Città di Castello, and the same applies for the entire territory of the Umbrian Upper-Tiber Valley. Only two locals were executed by partisans in 1944 (three more were killed by Slav partisans). For information on the dead in Città di Castello in the months leading to and around liberation see Alvaro Tacchini, *Guerra e Resistenza nell'Alta Valle del Tevere (1943–1944)* (Città di Castello: Petruzzi Editore, 2015), third part, chapter 2.

their political conflicts in the aftermath of July 25, 1943. The fall of the fascist regime did not occur in a historical void, a standstill time of dictatorial inertia and corrosion. In contrast, the simultaneity of different temporalities, as well as the sedimented presence of past histories, complicated Italians' relationship to Mussolini's past government and made that relationship far from linear.[93] Inexorably, Italy's misguided participation in the war forced people to confront the contingency of their own historical entanglements. Whereas the abrupt implosion of the regime on that infamous July night "perversely" helped dissipate Mussolini's dictatorship from Italians' immediate consciousness, intensified bombings by the Allied forces, as well as the hardship imposed by the German occupation, contributed to the parenthetical oblivion of fascism. War ruled over the Italians' existences and homogenized their experience; it dominated their daily reality and caused their misery. Depending on where on Italy's map one was located, war as the more tangible and immediately physical terror—inclusive of destruction, hunger, and displacement—affected individuals of any class and age, common folks and well-to-do alike. For those who lived in Central and Northern Italy, the war especially signified the pain of leaving home and the agony of waiting for the arrival of the Allied forces, in addition to continuous efforts to procure food and escape bombardments. The day-to-day dealings with existence in the constraining conditions of wartime structured the lived world of intellectual diarists and marked their relationship to history in the same way that daily struggles affected ordinary diarists. Whereas the fettering effects of normalcy mostly worked to dampen intellectual diarists' civic engagement, those same chains also opened up occasional spaces of brightness that helped them challenge the accepted order of things. The inevitable reality of the daily grind offered them the chance to reflect on the country's past and present.

The morality of daily struggles

Although ordinary diarists suffered the disruption of daily existence as much as did intellectual diarists, the latter especially tended to emphasize the moral degradation of everyday experience—the overturning of life as one knew it. To many of them, war had pushed the boundaries of what it meant to be human; it exposed the extreme effect of material constraints on one's spirit,

---

[93] On history as repetition and duration see Reinhart Koselleck, *Sediments of Time: On Possible Histories* (Palo Alto: Stanford University Press, 2018).

for the reality was that one could not flourish without first surviving. In late 1942, Calamandrei wrote a somber analysis forecasting the insidiously gradual transformations of everyday life about to unfold:

> It happens little by little: one plunges into it slowly. Food restrictions, darkness, decline in travel, lines, ration cards, points, requisitions... And then come the faraway bombings, then those nearer, the first news of fires and collapses, the danger that draws closer, displacements, escapes... Boxes of linen and books start being shipped. [...] vacating becomes contagious. And then, what will happen to us... At some point even personal hygiene will suffer: we will have no baths or hot water any longer. Degradation will start. And yet we will continue to live, attached to life. Alas![94]

Calamandrei anticipated a dangerous spiral of misery even ahead of Italy's switch in military alliances in September 1943. His prediction turned out to be ominously accurate, including his own escape from Florence (and country home), in fear of political persecution. At first taking refuge in the Tuscan hills of Montepulciano, Calamandrei punctiliously registered his daily deadening as survival became his primary source of concern:

> Here, in the satisfaction of the most animalistic physical needs, that is, eating and sleeping, we feel as if we were living in peace, unscathed by the drama. We try to forget. I realize that the most unbearable sufferings are physical. Once these needs are appeased, and although this might sound unbelievable, the dangers and dejections that have struck us or are threatening us leave one almost indifferent.[95]

Critical of his own lulling, Calamandrei saw the enjoyment of basic comforts as inexorably leading to the obliteration of conscience and of the surrounding reality, even if he soon acknowledged the inconsistency of such a conclusion. With the Gestapo active in the area, fear of their roundups was tangible. As he prepared to flee to yet another location, this time in Umbria, Calamandrei despaired that one could ever overcome the trauma.[96] By early 1944, he was convinced life could never be the same: "When we think of the end of the war

---

[94] Calamandrei, *Diario*, vol. I, p. 94 (entry of December 13, 1942).
[95] Calamandrei, *Diario*, vol. II, p. 220 (entry of October 5, 1943 written in Montepulciano).
[96] "Here too everybody's life is made of these fears, of these anxieties that consume us and leave a mark from which we will never recover," Calamandrei, *Diario*, vol. II, p. 229 (entry of October 13, 1943).

as that which will bring us back to our homes, our jobs, the beach, the countryside, books and friends…we are deluded."[97] Wartime changes had been deeply transformative and could not be easily dismissed. Irrevocable, they quashed all illusions of reacquiring past normalcy—one's reliance on the regular life course made up of simple activities such as working, vacationing, and enjoying pastimes.

Having been torn from home and forced to leave as an evacuee was a circumstance that exerted negative psychological effects on Calamandrei. It also brought him closer to fellow Italians. Not that original class differences disappeared, nor were privileges and advantages eliminated, but the shared tragedy of displacement helped smooth out distinctions. Cecchi Pieraccini noted a similar leveling when she reflected on her unexpected engagement with housework—she had become like any other housewife:

> This morning, while I felt pain on my hands and arms for the weight of the stuff I carried, I spotted near me a pregnant, nice, delicate young newlywed. She was burdened by a load of vegetables that made her doubly bulky. Without knowing each other we exchanged a nodding smile, to which a third lady, quite elegant, also ended up participating. She was carrying a pot and a pan in the place where in the past she might have held a big bunch of flowers.[98]

War served as an equalizer, not so much in terms of social ranking but of experience. For Calamandrei, the occasion of his personal misfortune as an escapee led him to reflect on the inanity of his privileged status. Thinking of his own villa in the countryside raided by the Germans, he felt that "maybe it's the right punishment—we were too proud. For four years, unintentionally, we pleased ourselves with the beauty of that panorama, the beautiful furnishing, the paintings: sin of pride, while the world was crumbling…" He began to question his old assumptions and habits, the advantages he enjoyed as a person of means. Ultimately, he came to recognize the futility of those benefits in the face of his new standing as a person on the run: "Now it's our turn."[99] More and more entrenched in his newly acquired identity of "sfollato," Calamandrei pondered over the senselessness of his old sources of

---

[97] Calamandrei, *Diario*, vol. II, p. 342 (entry of February 15, 1944).
[98] Cecchi Pieraccini, *Agendina di guerra*, p. 277 (entry of December 28, 1943).
[99] Calamandrei, *Diario*, vol. II, p. 224 (entry of October 9, 1943).

satisfaction and the comforts he derived from them. In April 1944, he wrote in his diary:

> This condition of evacuees is an unsurpassable school in humility. Everything that in the past gave us the illusion of a certain social distinction, affluence, culture, academic titles, a certain professional notoriety, is gone. [...] Here nobody knows who I am, or my profession. [...] I am a displaced person, inserted in this situation of human equality, on the same level as everybody else.[100]

Moral degradation canceled all differences and flattened distinctions in the face of the mere necessity to survive—a basic human need.

The order of things

Giovanni Papini was among those for whom evacuating became a necessity, an unavoidable outcome that felt spiritually and physically debilitating. His journal entries reported on the peregrinations he and his wife undertook in the Tuscan countryside of the Upper Tiber Valley after leaving their primary residence in Florence in May 1943. By the time the diary resumed on November 12, 1943 (the notes from the previous nine months were supposedly lost), the couple was at their house in the little mountain hamlet of Bulciano. Come summer 1944, they would be on the move again as the entire area became unsafe—it was hard to escape the actuality of war. First headed to a nearby village, the two eventually settled at the monastery of La Verna. Papini was devastated: "We abandon our house where I have worked and was happy, the house that for thirty years I thought was the safest and most inaccessible refuge! Immense pain, atrocious, unimaginable. Maybe I'll never see it again—or I will find a pile of rubble."[101] Continuously obsessing over the fate of "my" house, he particularly regretted abandoning his books, which he estimated at four thousand volumes, although many more were scattered at his other residences. Would they survive? Mindful of Christian ethics,

---

[100] Calamandrei, *Diario*, vol. II, pp. 415–16 (entry of April 24, 1944). Calamandrei continued, "One wanders around with a sense of mortification, looking at [...] the peasants who work, and one almost feels the need, by greeting them first, to make them forgive our uselessness, our idleness, our petulance of beggars in city clothes, beggars, if not for a piece of bread, for a couple of eggs, a pigeon, one kilo of flour."

[101] Papini, *Diario* (Florence: Vallecchi, 1962), p. 197 (entry of June 22, 1944).

THE PERSONAL AND THE POLITICAL 273

Papini refused to get attached to earthly things, and yet it was hard for him to let go. No matter how much he tried, those material possessions, those books, helped him define his place in the world and his mission in life, they gave meaning to his existence. If nothing else, the thousands of volumes he had lovingly collected were critical for his work of thinking and writing. In early January 1945, after his return to liberated Florence, he received news from the Upper Tiber Valley: "I'm being told that the German soldiers who were camping at my house in Bulciano used to light fires with my books—and it was summer."[102]

Giulio Pierangeli also had to vacate his primary residence during the months of German occupation. Settled in the countryside near Città di Castello, he tried to reorganize his daily activities while looking to establish a degree of normalcy within an environment that, though familiar, was hardly regular. Whereas writing became his primary means for occupying time, the agony of waiting for an end to the suffering imposed by the war often defeated his best intentions—it was hard to remain calm and weather the storm. Lack of information on the progress of the Allied forces, as well as on the evolving events in Castello, particularly prostrated him. But like countless of his compatriots, and despite his own privileged position having secured a safe shelter, Pierangeli mostly longed to be able to exercise control over his life again. The account he wrote in mid-June 1944 of German lootings in the peasant community in which he temporarily resided underlines the issue in poignant terms. The incapacity to salvage at least the appearance (if nothing else) of mastering one's own existence was a source of profound psychological distress: "These episodes spread a real terror that breaks the spirit. Any certainty over one's belongings and life disappears. Everybody tries to hide objects of some value or stocked-up food or head of cattle that eluded the official requisitioning."[103]

Material possessions in a society already characterized by scarcity provided a claim to security, a way of holding on to life—they were a guarantee of survival. Even a pair of socks or underwear constituted precious goods.[104] As Henri Lefebvre theorizes about our relationship to things, "To be attached

---

[102] Papini, *Diario*, p. 275 (entry of January 10, 1945). He uttered no judgments on the Germans. Their defeat was the defeat of a fascist world in which he had put his faith.

[103] Lignani and Tacchini eds., *Giulio Pierangeli*, pp. 247–8 (entry of June 17, 1944).

[104] Socks and underwear featured among the items Pierangeli listed in his account of the Germans' raid at his country residence: "They poked around and rummaged in all the trunks and all the suitcases in the lower bedroom, and they took whatever they found that could be of use: buttons, spools, etc. They did not neglect to pick up also a pair of socks and a pair of underwear of Annetta." See letter to Giuliana of July 13 in Lignani and Tacchini eds., *Giulio Pierangeli*, p. 280.

to objects, to privilege them affectively, is today, as in the past, to create a shell or a bubble—that is to say, a protective layer against the assaults of a hostile world. [...] The more threatening the outside world becomes, the greater the importance and continuity of the interior—that which surrounds or protects subjective interiority."[105] Maintaining the center of one's self is a relational endeavor that requires interaction with the external environment as confirmation of one's presence. When basic belongings happen to be confiscated, as in the instance mentioned by Pierangeli, resilience weakens. The particular timing of the episodes described by Pierangeli heightens their dramatic character. With the Anglo-Americans closing in, the Germans had turned into a rampaging and ever more frightening destructive force, so much so that Pierangeli believed it would be impossible for the local population to bear that terror much longer: "Only one hope remains: that this tormented period lasts one week, or two, or three at the most, and that one can then return to a life that, if not normal, is orderly and protected."[106] Desire for predictability, knowing where things stand and being in control, albeit in a limited way, are millenarian features that ensure the stability of personhood. Disorder can be barely tolerated.[107]

Waiting for liberation from the Germans had become an ordeal, and the more so because expectations of the event were invariably mistaken. Already in November 1943, Venanzio Gabriotti lamented, "If only the Allies would come soon! [...]. How long must this agony last? Sadness overtakes me for this stupid inaction."[108] Città di Castello had to wait eight more months for Gabriotti's wish to be fulfilled. The hiatus between the anticipated arrival and its actual occurrence turned out to be disconsolately wide, and even in the days preceding that final event the Anglo-Americans' lack of speed remained

---

[105] Henri Lefebvre, *Critique of Everyday Life*. The One-Volume Edition (London: Verso, 2014), vol. III, p. 734. On materiality and the everyday during the war see Sarah De Nardi, *The Poetics of Conflict Experience: Materiality and Embodiment in Second World War Italy* (London: Routledge, 2018).

[106] Lignani and Tacchini eds., *Giulio Pierangeli*, p. 248 (entry of June 17, 1944).

[107] On the historical production of the unified subject and individuation as a historical process that defines our being in the world see Ernesto de Martino, *Il mondo magico. Prolegomeni a una storia del magismo* (Turin: Boringhieri, 1973). To de Martino, the unity of the person (the person's "presence") is fragile and risks being undermined during situations of crisis. Also see the classic study of Mary Douglas, *Purity and Danger: An Analysis of Concepts of Pollution and Taboo* (London: Routledge and Kegan Paul, 1966) for an anthropological perspective on order as the way through which we organize our environment. According to Douglas, rituals of purity serve to create meaning by ensuring unity in experience. The need for order is a reaction to ambiguity and anomaly and is related to the question of being versus nonbeing.

[108] Gabriotti, *Diario*, p. 124 (entry of November 19, 1943). A few weeks later, on December 12, Gabriotti wrote, "The Allies move slowly and this creates a sense of malaise in all because we wish to be freed from this pain as soon as possible," p. 139. Gabriotti held that the Germans "know how to fight a war," the implication being that the Allies did not (see entries of December 11, 1943, p. 138 and February 10, 1944, p. 164).

unnerving. Pierangeli experienced that agony firsthand: "English slowness is exasperating. Since yesterday they have been one kilometer away from our house. They have nobody seriously posing resistance to them, but twelve hours have passed without them moving not even one bit."[109] (One is reminded of Irene Paolisso's reflections here.) Although what the future reserved was hard to foresee (and it certainly did not look bright), people hoped that liberation from both the Germans and the Republican fascists would re-establish a more predictable state of normalcy that would allow one to reconnect with dispersed family members and achieve the long-sought-after return home. The ongoing efforts to coexist with the new reality of war on domestic soil had affected Italians ever since the Anglo-Americans' landing in Sicily in July 1943. Shifts in war dynamics, however, were adding more miseries to one's daily experience, and the German occupation surely deteriorated living conditions even more. Attempts at leading a normal existence became a form of reassurance; it implicitly suggested that not everything was lost despite the exceptional circumstances.[110]

"Bloody 'food'"

With mounting challenges, and as the issue of physical safety complemented that of psychological insecurity, the already severe problem of food scarcity remained people's top concern during wartime, including for the intellectual diarists examined here. Corrado Alvaro highlighted the essential and comforting role of food in a terse but moving note written on July 1943: "Lunch at N. with everything in abundance and hard to find. P. was crying in front of an enormous serving of pasta."[111] While war on the home front expanded, normalcy acquired an extraordinary value—it became an object of longing. Procurement of food, once a routine activity in one's daily schedule (particularly for women), presented an ever more demanding task.

Leonetta Cecchi Pieraccini began lamenting the hardship of finding provisions early in the war years. Besides reporting on the uncontrollable expansion of the black market, she wrote of the fatigue entailed by the foraging for

---

[109] Letter of July 12, 1944 written to daughter Giuliana from his countryside shelter, in Lignani and Tacchini eds., *Giulio Pierangeli*, pp. 278–9.

[110] Here is how Giovanni Papini's approached the dominant disorder: "Singular, even incredible life. Not too far, bombs are falling, artilleries thunder, airplanes pound, machine guns crackle, and I, almost all day long, think, write, and talk of theological problems and divine matters. I am astonished of myself." Papini, *Diario* (Florence: Vallecchi, 1962), p. 205 (entry of July 12, 1944).

[111] Corrado Alvaro, *Quasi una vita. Giornale di uno scrittore* (Milan: Bompiani, 1950), p. 294.

primary necessities. Walking long distances, waiting in line, competing with others for scarce goods had become the norm. "Between the groceries one can't find and those available at exorbitant costs, domestic traffic for provisions has become very tiring, besides expensive," she observed on July 26, 1942.[112] Mostly, she suffered from exhaustion, a feeling of being worn out, a sense of enervation. While all energy was funneled into survival, basic needs overwhelmingly structured her relationship to daytime, and the situation only worsened as months went on. Cecchi Pieraccini's comments escalated accordingly. In late October 1943, following a practice quite common among ordinary diarists, she began to list the prices of goods: "One quintal of potatoes costs one thousand and five hundred lire. In contrast, until two years ago it cost six. I repeat, *SIX*."[113] A recurrent obsession, price listings became a staple feature of her diary entries as did the alimentary situation in general:

> You go to the haberdashery and from under the counter sugar turns up; you go the greengrocer and spinach appear or silk stockings. The trafficking of works of art, in contrast, is on the decline. A year ago, those who owned a small painting with original signature believed themselves among the very rich. These days, even a Raphael could possibly be exchanged for some hams and a sack of grains.[114]

Come 1944, Cecchi Pieraccini was reaching the brink, both physically and mentally. After hearing about the tragic end of two acquaintances and their maid under heavy bombing, she alarmingly described her inability to welcome a friend's visit: "I'm almost unable to talk. /They say that stuttering, forgetting, and difficulty of expression originate from lack of fats in one's diet. Today, between the lack of fats and abundance of sorrows, I find myself dumbfounded."[115] When the friend asked Cecchi Pieraccini to see some of her paintings, she had a catatonic reaction: "I have nothing to show her. I don't paint, I don't take care of my work and I find it fantastically absurd that somebody has even any memory of it. Of concrete, I only see my daily

---

[112] Cecchi Pieraccini, *Agendina di guerra*, p. 164.
[113] Cecchi Pieraccini, *Agendina di guerra*, p. 268 (entry of October 29, 1943), capitalized and italicized in the original.
[114] Cecchi Pieraccini, *Agendina di guerra*, pp. 271–2 (entry of November 21, 1943).
[115] Cecchi Pieraccini, *Agendina di guerra*, pp. 285–6 (entry of January 7, 1944). The bombing that killed the three women occurred in the Tuscan countryside where Cecchi Pieraccini was born. It destroyed the old palazzo in which the three lived, which was owned by one of Cecchi Pieraccini's sisters, already deceased. One of the victims was her sister's daughter-in-law.

trafficking as a housewife. There is no servant that can sweep better than me."[116] An aggravated Cecchi Pieraccini found pride in activities that in better times she would have delegated to helpers.[117] Her status as an artist, whether of means or not, had previously separated her from the average woman. The current reality, however, could not but assign her the role of housewife. And while in the past she might have detested that condition along with the tedium of daily chores associated with it, she now welcomed physical labor: "In the present state of mind, I only feel an irresistible desire to throw myself into hard work that will tire me out and stop me from thinking and remembering."[118]

As challenging as it was, the struggle to satisfy material needs distracted her from mental fatigue, although that diversion did not make her daily tasks less onerous. Searching for food required constant attention. For example, a sunny day in usually cold January became the occasion for "wandering around trying to scrape together some provisions."[119] Attending an art exhibit offered her the opportunity to buy vegetables from a peasant she fortuitously encountered in the street: "I immediately grabbed a bunch of broccolini and held it in my arms as if I was carrying a bunch of roses."[120] Cecchi Pieraccini even turned into a seller herself, bartering her own artwork for a provision of oil.[121] With a tough attitude, she continued to tramp onward in the following months, even if by early March, when gas and water services came to a halt due to recent bombardments, she was unable to maintain her tough composure. Household duties were becoming unbearably difficult, and women, who had the responsibility of taking care of their families, felt the hardship intensely. "It makes one cry," she penned.[122] Eventually, she highlighted the comic side of it all: "Sometimes I really burst out laughing considering the worries

---

[116] Cecchi Pieraccini, *Agendina di guerra*, p. 286.

[117] Her notes often reveal an imperceptible bias in the way she related to the lower classes. After describing the "nouveau riche" status of a young man, for example, she commented, "In the streets one finds many beggars, mostly women, children and the elderly, but often also able-bodied men. However, if you are looking for a maid or a porter for special services at home, you will not find any." Cecchi Pieraccini, *Agendina di guerra*, p. 323 (entry of June 1, 1944).

[118] Cecchi Pieraccini, *Agendina di guerra*, p. 286 (entry of January 7, 1944).

[119] Cecchi Pieraccini, *Agendina di guerra*, p. 288 (entry of January 15, 1944). She continued by listing the rising prices of sugar, potatoes, butter, oil, and vegetables.

[120] Cecchi Pieraccini, *Agendina di guerra*, p. 299 (entry of February 13, 1944).

[121] "I also meet a guy who traffics in art works and asks me if I'm willing to sell a small painting he is interested in. I ask for two flasks of oil in exchange. He thought I was excessively demanding—oil, salt, and sugar have become as precious as gold," Cecchi Pieraccini, *Agendina di guerra*, p. 299.

[122] Cecchi Pieraccini, *Agendina di guerra*, p. 303 (entry of March 8, 1944). Bad news kept compounding, and at the end of March the bread ration was lowered to 100 grams (see entry of March 29, 1944, p. 310). A few days later, Pieraccini wrote about the welcomed exceptional gift of 150 grams of bread that Italians received on the occasion of Easter (entry of April 9, 1944), p. 313.

and the trafficking that pester us because of this bloody 'food' (benedetto 'mangiare')."[123] Particularly humorous she found the involvement of upper-class people in food foraging and distribution, with some of them even turning their houses into destination centers for provisions from their country estates: "It was just today, when I was collecting my rustic package of flour and beans from the hands of my writer friend (who was elegantly dressed in a cyclamen-colored silk pajama with her raven hair down on her shoulders) that I realized once again the funny oddity of our daily situations."[124]

As a surrealist composition, the juxtaposition of normally conflicting images (silk and sacks) created a laughable moment. Bloody food indeed, as a somber Papini also observed with consternation:

> Everywhere, in barbers' shops, in living rooms, in the street, all we hear about is stuff to eat and ways to find it and the exorbitant prices as well as the unforeseen bartering for obtaining it. We are returning to an animal status: the belly is the highest god one needs to satiate; hunger is the great enemy one needs to vanquish every day. Mortification derived from this fixation on the abdomen.[125]

Seemingly detached from the everyday reality of material necessities, Papini missed the dramatic nature of people's obsession with food. Imbued with spiritualism, his comments were a castigation of the body in favor of the superior prominence of the mind.

Be that as it may, regular procurement of food, as Papini's passage highlights, was a day-long enterprise embedded in a never-ending cycle—a draining activity with which people of all classes and statuses were forced to engage. In Rome, Elena Carandini Albertini's relationship to food, whether consumed or merely sought after, became central to her daily experience in wartime. On an August day in 1943, she fondly wrote of an excursion to the beach with her mother and children. Conjuring images of the "blond sand" and "blue sea," the swimming and "indifferent nature," she concluded by describing the

---

[123] Cecchi Pieraccini, *Agendina di guerra*, pp. 318–19 (entry of May 3, 1944).
[124] Cecchi Pieraccini, *Agendina di guerra*, p. 319. Curiously, in the same passage Cecchi Pieraccini mentioned Bonaventura Tecchi as one of the original providers: "The very cultured professor Niccolò Gallo is about to head to the estate of the distinguished writer Bonaventura Tecchi in Bagnoregio to pick up some amounts of flour, cheese, and legumes for several friends at very reduced prices." Noticeable is Cecchi Pieraccini's use of the adjectives "very cultured" and "distinguished" next to the description of the mundane activity of food foraging. She also reported other cases of upper-class people engaged in trafficking. See for example entry of March 13, 1944 in Cecchi Pieraccini, *Agendina di guerra*, pp. 304–5.
[125] Papini, *Diario*, p. 247 (entry of October 22, 1944).

idyllic meal that capped the day: "On our return we had an exceptional breakfast with fried fish and cream pie. That's how one still fakes normalcy."[126] The whole outing was extraordinary in that it contradicted the harsh actuality of the ongoing military conflict as well as the uncertainty created by the recent fall of the regime. But what made the trip especially memorable was its evocation of a past normality, with the lunch highlighting an endearing routine now missed—the regular rhythm of life before the latest historical drama. By late September, even the memory of the past, and how things used to be, felt far away to Carandini Albertini. She found herself involved fulltime in the role of managing food and ensuring her family's survival:

> In the past, because of my privileged position, I was not aware of the single elements that make up our meals. Now everything goes through my hands, tallied, weighed. I learn the value of minimal things: how much a cauliflower or a bunch of herbs cost. Actually, I must admit that I didn't use to know "herbs" because I almost never stepped in the kitchen or was near the stove.[127]

Being forced to learn how to be a housewife, Carandini Albertini became indistinguishable from the many women she encountered in the street or at the market during her numerous shopping expeditions, although she still felt embarrassed by her relative advantage. After all, she could still afford to invite friends over and offer them a decent meal—those opportunities were highly valued.[128]

With the military and political situation remaining stalled, winter 1944 provided no relief to Romans.[129] The arrival in the capital of displaced people hoping to escape war's ravages magnified the individual problem of food foraging. In her volunteer work of assistance to those in need, Carandini Albertini confronted the most extreme cases of misery. There, hunger truly caused "torment."[130] Watching others suffer made her feel a deeper pain, and

---

[126] Carandini Albertini, *Dal terrazzo*, p. 16 (entry of August 18, 1943).
[127] Carandini Albertini, *Dal terrazzo*, p. 43 (entry of September 30, 1943).
[128] See for example her entry of December 7, 1943: "We are noticing that everybody appreciates our invitations very much and the healthy and genuine food, even though we are not rolling in abundance. Bread, and pasta, and meat, they are well below what is sufficient and we are suffering the consequences. Other things compensate though: sweets, chestnuts, ricotta, etc. /The matter of food is ever more problematic and important." Carandini Albertini, *Dal terrazzo*, p. 69.
[129] In her entry of early February, 1944, Carandini Albertini wrote, "By now the nightmare of hunger is growing for everyone. I do not say much about it, but even for us privileged it is a daily problem, and we can't manage to feed the children as adequately as we'd wish." Carandini Albertini, *Dal terrazzo*, p. 91.
[130] Carandini Albertini, *Dal terrazzo*, p. 94 (entry of February 12, 1944).

she remained resolute in her will to help while facing a situation of bread shortages that could hardly be overcome.[131] By early May, with her family now seriously confronting inadequate amounts of food, she began to engage in the litany of listing available items.[132] Her housewife abilities could only go so far.

Sleepwalkers opening their eyes

If Carandini Albertini was particularly skilled at communicating the nightmarish reality of the struggle for food in occupied Rome, she addressed equally well logistical and psychological elements that disrupted daily life in wartime. Her community engagement, inherited from her father's civic commitment, but also linked to her husband's involvement in political affairs, led her to be always abreast of the events affecting the country.[133] Thus, her diary reflected a whole range of experiences, from the material to the spiritual, that impinged upon her existence and refracted her personal dealings with the inexorable reality of a changing world. A struggle to mediate between the exceptional and the normal, the past and the present, the old and the new emerges from her reflections. If, on the one hand, she felt helpless at the worsening of Italy's situation in the aftermath of the armistice, on the other hand, she found solace in rethinking her intellectual presuppositions as well as class privileges. "Another healthy reaction: I feel ashamed of having been preoccupied over the last few days with saving our things. It is necessary to save one's spirit in moments such as these," she confessed on September 14, 1943.[134] Over the next weeks, she continued to be in agony and demanded of herself a

---

[131] See entry of March 11, 1944: "Every day gets harder. There never is any gas and how can one cook the little food one has? There is no water at home, and there is little at the fountains too. [...] /But the most severe problem in the city is bread." Also see entry of February 12, 1944: "The pain I felt in via in Arcione follows me at home and gives me no rest. I'll do everything I can to increase milk and general aid." Carandini Albertini, *Dal terrazzo*, pp. 101, 95.

[132] See entry of May 8, 1944 in Carandini Albertini, *Dal terrazzo*, pp. 116–17.

[133] Carandini Albertini followed historical developments attentively and was part of the elite group that would shortly assume a central role in the reconstitution of Italy's democratic government. Her husband, Nicolò Carandini, in hiding as a member of the underground Committee of National Liberation (CLN), was a rising star of the liberal current and actively involved in discussions of the new democratic government held within the circle of Croce. In June 1944, he became a Minister Without Portfolio in the Bonomi government, replacing Croce, and in November 1944 began to serve as ambassador to Great Britain until late 1947. An innovative mind, Carandini was eventually sidelined for his radical ideas by the more conservative members of the Liberal Party (including Croce) and broke with them in 1948 (although not definitively).

[134] Carandini Albertini, *Dal terrazzo*, p. 38.

genuine recognition of the "pressing painful reality" all around.[135] What would a diary be good for, if it did not contain more serious thoughts? She asked. Meanwhile, she identified the mechanisms that were permitting Italians to continue to live a regular life even amidst the worst adversity: normalcy (or the appearance of it) within the state of exceptionality.[136] For Carandini Albertini, the mere enjoyment of a sunset helped displace the sense of loss—attachment to the natural surroundings was "a way to maintain a sort of obstinate normalcy for as long as possible."[137] Conversely, she found it striking that "one ends up finding normal the most abnormal and most terrible things," such as people's disappearance.[138] One way or another, she continued to appeal to habits. Everyday practices saved her from feeling despair, even if at times she realized that her efforts to stick to routine were proof that normalcy was artificial: "At home we continue our daily rituals, and the children instinctively advise us to keep faith and trust in petty normality."[139] Times were hard, but hadn't the previous two decades been worse? Their memory shamed her: "The grip is getting tighter and what is happening now seems unbelievable if we think of it with the spirit of the past. [...]. More disheartening is the fact of having accepted the apparent normalcy of fascism for so many years."[140] Fascism's version of life had been a fake, and, unfortunately, everybody had fallen for it, Carandini Albertini concluded. There could be no worse offence.

By focusing on daily life Carandini Albertini developed a critical analysis—a reflexive understanding of the different ways in which day-to-day activities opened up to historical repercussions and helped structure one's own relationship to the future. She struggled to maintain the divide between past and present and experienced guilty feelings when memories of past well-being made her yearn for the old days. Eventually, she realized that discomfort and gloom helped her defy normality and regain some vestige of historical and social conscience. After an outing with a friend that was complemented by a modest shopping spree, she professed:

---

[135] Carandini Albertini, *Dal terrazzo*, p. 42 (entry of September 25, 1943).
[136] She wrote, "Maybe it is important to observe that internal defenses allow us to resume, or continue almost automatically, a certain normality even if it is only exterior." Carandini Albertini, *Dal terrazzo*, p. 42 (entry of September 25, 1943).
[137] Carandini Albertini, *Dal terrazzo*, p. 63 (entry of November 18, 1943).
[138] "Everyday somebody disappears," Carandini Albertini wrote. See *Dal terrazzo*, p. 64 (entry of November 21, 1943). In October 1943, she also began to write frantic notes on the roundup of Jews in Rome. To her eyes, it was the first signal of the deteriorating situation. Carandini Albertini, *Dal terrazzo*, pp. 51–2 (entries of October 15 and 16).
[139] Carandini Albertini, *Dal terrazzo*, p. 70 (entry of December 11, 1943).
[140] Carandini Albertini, *Dal terrazzo*, p. 70 (entry of December 11, 1943).

I come back home loaded with small purchases, but tired and also sad. Sometimes one needs to succumb to fatigue in order to better put up with it. How to explain that I suffer not for me or for those that are dear to me, for this person or that one, but for all and as much and more for those I don't know than for those I know. But, then, why do I allow my personal nostalgia for happiness to mix with similar sentiments? The past is dead. We are, or better we will be, different persons.[141]

Caught between past and present, a dichotomy that she recognized might be false, she found the former more appealing, covered as it was in the patina of memory. Nevertheless, and although her personal background of privilege pulled her back to older times, she wished to look at the world from a new vantage point, fully aware that the decision of where to stand presented challenges. In the end, reality clashed with intellectualization and became overbearing to the point of being indescribable. Even writing a diary felt like a futile endeavor:

Oh, enough with saying who I see, what I do, the little events of everyday together with the big ones of History. I wish I was able to convey here the spirit with which we live this tragedy—a little like sleepwalkers that occasionally open their eyes. Each one of us, in their own little way, connected to the events and ashamed of our own impotence.[142]

The sense of guilt and powerlessness was tremendous, and yet Carandini Albertini knew that even an appearance of normality could save her from being completely overwhelmed by the horror of the present situation. After attending a concert set up to support struggling musicians, she recognized, "Yes, it seems incredible: a concert." Did such an activity make sense amidst the misery of a raging war? In truth, she was surprised at the positive effect it had on her.[143] Although she was still practicing piano (rarely and a bit reluctantly), it was almost in defiance of writing—an activity she clearly

---

[141] Carandini Albertini, *Dal terrazzo*, pp. 72–3 (entry of December 14, 1943). Also see her entry of early January 1944, written after hearing of the destruction at their estate in Torre in Pietra: "They burned all the legs of the beautiful dining table. They also burned the sides of the billiard table. They destroyed or stole much more furniture. But I don't want to keep thinking of these matters." Carandini Albertini, *Dal terrazzo*, p. 83.

[142] Carandini Albertini, *Dal terrazzo*, p. 83 (entry of January 15, 1944). Here is Croce's reaction to routine daily occurrences: "The way ordinary and private annoyances, great and small, intrude into the tragedy of the nation and of civilization! [...] all this exasperates me." *Croce, the King and the Allies*, p. 59 (*Taccuini di guerra*, p. 68) (entry of January 4, 1944).

[143] Carandini Albertini, *Dal terrazzo*, p. 85 (entry of January 20, 1944). She wrote, "Music gives me great relief, which I didn't think was at all possible at present."

equated with commitment. In the end, even if music seemed out of place in the hard reality of war and foreign occupation, it offered a degree of solace: "Playing lets me vent more than writing these shabby words."[144] When nothing seemed to change, when one had to repeat the same things over and over, when all hope was continuously crushed, writing a journal felt like a senseless exercise. Carandini Albertini especially lamented her inadequacy at expressing the depth of the drama the country was experiencing: "What to say anymore? That life becomes more difficult and scarier by the day?"[145] As Italians continued to struggle with an overbearing daily life filled with gas shortages and insufficient food, she feared that writing only achieved the banal: "I always say the same things and not the ones I would love to put in."[146] At loss for words, and failing to render the traumatic consequences of an oxymoronic long-lasting emergency, Carandini Albertini dismissed her narrative efforts. She called them "diarizing."[147] At the same time, in many ways, the diary continuously reminded her of the surrounding stasis. The moment she wrote it down and registered it, that immutability became more present to her consciousness; it acquired a concrete physiognomy. Maybe that is why she decided to keep writing, even as she remained conflicted about it. At the minimum, journals provided testimonials.[148] A few days before the liberation of Rome, with the overall situation reaching an emotional crescendo, Carandini Albertini candidly exposed her sense of inadequacy in the face of a reality seemingly fleeting and mystifying: "*Fata trahunt*. I don't know what to write, we are not realizing what is about to happen. It's such a mixture of banality and drama what we are living at present."[149] She recognized her own limits. Yet by allowing repetition of the same prosaic realities no matter how ugly, writing invariably delivered a comforting sensation to her, and she did not give up embracing the ordinary. Driven by the duty to testify, she chronicled people's daily misery even as she lost the desire to keep journaling.[150]

---

[144] Carandini Albertini, *Dal terrazzo*, p. 91 (entry of first days of February, 1944).

[145] Carandini Albertini, *Dal terrazzo*, p. 91.

[146] Carandini Albertini, *Dal terrazzo*, p. 116 (entry of May 8, 1944).

[147] Carandini Albertini, *Dal terrazzo*, p. 116 (entry of May 8, 1944). She wrote, "Apathetic about diarizing." On Carandini's references to her journaling as "diareggiare," a somewhat dismissive designation, see Serenella Baggio, *"Niente retorica." Liberalismo linguistico nei diari di una signora del Novecento* (Trento: Università degli Studi di Trento, 2012), chapter 2, "*Diareggiare.*" As Baggio notes, this frequentative verb is not to be found in Italian dictionaries.

[148] As she had written in early February, "I will not however stop the diary that at best will preserve these days." Carandini Albertini, *Dal terrazzo*, p. 91.

[149] Carandini Albertini, *Dal terrazzo*, p. 125 (entry of May 31, 1944). "Fata trahunt," from Latin, expresses the idea that fate leads.

[150] Carandini Albertini's peculiar relationship with journaling continued even as the political situation improved. On April 12, 1945, she repeated her sense of inadequacy at fulfilling what she conceived as the higher role of a diary: "Dear diary, I report the quotidian always too much in a hurry,

Once Rome was liberated, Carandini Albertini continued to write her daily entries. Now focused on the political reorganization of the country, she could not but be aware of the drama still afflicting more than half of Italy. War and German occupation had not disappeared, and her newfound normalcy became a point of reference for attesting to this idiosyncratic actuality. It was a reminder of the nation's dissonant perversity—a platform for denouncing the apparent lightheartedness of those who had been lucky enough to be able to reclaim partial control over their lives. As she penned at the end of 1944, "And here we are, now safe, conducting life as if nothing happened. Sometimes I feel horrified by our insensibility."[151] With Christmas festivities approaching and shoppers filling the streets of Rome, she was especially dismayed at human obliviousness and the "garish and shameful materialism."[152] In the end, even the most conspicuous, ghastly manifestations of people's return to mundane habits signaled the end of exception, and Carandini Albertini had to admit, "It is doubtlessly extraordinary how normal life resumes around us."[153] Whereas, only months earlier, claims to the everyday had helped Carandini Albertini challenge the horrors of war, her current acknowledgment of the return to normalcy seemed to suggest a more disconsolate truth: Nothing had changed in spite of all the horror.

While liberation and the end of war were a relief, the toll the conflict had taken seemed unmeasurable. What people saw, heard, or felt, even when not directly involved in the most atrocious episodes of the final two years of the war, had all the characteristics of trauma. Aside from shocking experiences, pressing political issues posed further challenges to the path of normalization. That the country was emerging from the mayhem in a state of dependency was obvious to anybody who cared to check, and one could not but feel the enormity of the present hardship and the complexity of the task ahead. Might this explain Calamandrei's sense of disorientation as he joined Florentine crowds ready to celebrate the announced end of the war in May 1945? "Thus, it's over: we arrived, alive, to peace. PEACE: I feel like I am not understanding the meaning of this word any longer, as if it was in another language. I'm not sure if this heartache, this sense of emptiness that almost paralyzes me,

---

treating everything too lightly: our own issues and bigger events. Alas, it's an inevitable sloppiness also because I write in a hurry." Carandini Albertini, *Passata la stagione…Diari, 1944–1947* (Firenze: Passigli Editori, 1989), p. 104.
[151] Carandini Albertini, *Passata la stagione*, p. 77 (entry of December 1944).
[152] Carandini Albertini, *Passata la stagione*, p. 82 (entry of December 21–4, 1944).
[153] Carandini Albertini, *Passata la stagione*, p. 86 (entry of January 1, 1945).

is joy or pain: incurable pain."[154] Calamandrei's experience conveyed the untranslatability of emotions and previewed the complexities of a return to life as it once was. After five years of war, normalcy had acquired a whole new significance. One needed to adapt to it anew.

Against the situational background of wartime emergency, this chapter has taken the everyday dimension of the lived world as the interpretive lens through which to examine intellectual diarists' relationship to fascism. Pointing to the sentimental layers that structured social interactions, it has highlighted the hybrid nature of diarists' political positions. Scribes bridged the gulf separating fascists from nonfascists via feelings based on timeless values that were made to supersede more mundane distinctions; family ties and bonds of friendship effaced ideological differences and overcame divisions. Personalized, fascism was turned into a game of guilt that in the dramatic conditions of 1943–45 led to place most responsibilities onto the fascists of the RSI—the resurrected government established by Mussolini in September 1943—rather than the two-decades-long dictatorship. Another element of deflection was provided by the trope of the "eternal enemy," barbarian and irredeemable, that in a crescendo re-emerged as the intellectual diarists' dominant perception of the Germans. Although fascism was at the center of these diarists' concerns, especially in regard to the country's future, its comprehensive evaluation often fell to the sidelines in the face of more contingent and concrete situations. Reconciling the dictatorial system with its representatives, or even with the reality of an impassive population that had cohabitated with the regime for twenty years, presented epistemological challenges that marred diarists' analytical efforts. Defascistization proved to be a perplexing quandary that risked undermining the imagined covenant deemed necessary for the future reconstruction of the country.

While the willingness of intellectual diarists to set the "good" fascists apart from the "bad" ones does not find a parallel in the journals of ordinary diarists, nor did the latter report significantly on personal relationships with the "other" side, there were commonalities between the two groups. In particular, both sets of diarists shared the experience of schizophrenic disorientation in the face of a wartime exceptionality that had become the new normal and where everyday routines had turned into major hurdles. Scarcity of food,

---

[154] Calamandrei, *Diario*, vol. II, p. 561 (entry of May 1945). Here is Croce's not very dissimilar reaction: "Announcement of Germany's surrender. Although it should be an announcement of peace, it has a lugubrious sound, because it opens the way to an uncertain period of hard labor towards a future that threatens us with servitude and barbarism." See *Taccuini di guerra*, p. 291 (entry of May 7, 1945).

forced displacement, and overall lack of basic comforts, which had prostrated ordinary diarists, engaged intellectual diarists (particularly women) at an incessant rhythm. These inevitable afflictions pushed a few authors to question their status and privileges, challenge their nostalgic yearnings for the past, and defy their old assumptions. Writing especially helped intellectual diarists confront the sorrows they faced; it elevated those sorrows to an existential and moral interrogation of one's historical role and responsibilities. Although intellectual diarists, not unlike ordinary ones, insisted on playing objective reporters and posed as impartial witnesses, the compelling reality of everydayness, as opposed to the grander import of political developments and historical changes, pierced through their armor of detachment. The inevitability of daily life forced them to question and revisit the normalcy by which they had been previously lulled. In the process, they even doubted the practice of journaling, if unable to communicate the sense of gravity that the years of occupation had imposed on one's lived experience. Writing helped intellectual diarists shed light on the darkness of the quotidian.

In comparing the journals of intellectual diarists to those of ordinary Italians, motivation to publish emerges as a significant discriminating feature separating the two. Less certain is whether the prospect of publication impacted intellectual diarists' portrayal of fascism, past and present, or their analysis of the current political situation. Their impetus to reach the public—a desire to bear witness—also raises the issue of what defines a testimonial and whether the rules of objectivity by which ordinary diarists appeared to be constrained were similarly felt by intellectual diarists and shaped their texts. Could detachment and impartiality be weaved in the drive to inform and mold people's minds? Also, with an eye kept on the future of the country, what did an ethics of responsibility require? A jumble of often contradictory impulses presided over intellectual diarists' composition of their journals, and a wide array of formats ensued. Despite differences, however, by providing space for reflection diaries helped authors clarify their assumptions. They also exposed the limits of scribes' evaluations as well as the ambiguities that marred their relationship to history.

Conclusions

> How much we longed for it and now it came.
> (May 7, 1945)*

Gina Traverso began keeping a school journal in October 1942 as part of her third-grade language assignment. Exuding fascist teachings, the entries she penned demonstrated her ability to master grammatical rules while engaging in essay composition. In short reflections on mundane topics and everyday activities, this seven-year-old expressed the typical worldview of a schoolchild her age. When she entered fourth grade the following year, however, momentous events in the summer of 1943 had altered the historical situation in Italy and her personal one as well. An evacuee in the countryside village of Vobbia, not far from her hometown of Genoa, Gina had to adjust to new life and habits. With Italy in full war-mode against Germany, she appeared to have a good understanding of the transformations happening around her. A child, she obviously took cues from the adults, probably listening in to their conversations. Only a month into the school year, she undramatically summarized the new state of things: "We cannot go back to the city so many are the bombings, the destroyed buildings, and the dead. I pray a lot for peace. They told us that the Duce is gone, but the war is still on because there are the Germans. Maybe the Americans will come to liberate us" (November 8, 1943).

An involuntary witness to a complicated historical reality, Gina registered facts (not always accurately for, as we know, the duce had returned) by translating them into simple digestible sentences that helped her make sense of the new living environment. Dutifully fulfilling her student responsibility, she kept updating her journal with the main goal of accomplishing the task prescribed by the teacher, though she demonstrably chose to focus on what felt compelling to her. With a measure of naïveté and at the same time full awareness of the dramas unfolding right in front of her eyes, Gina touched on peace, the Germans, and the partisans, revealing hidden secrets of the little village and making the reader wonder about the risks her innocence might

---

* From the diary of Zelinda Marcucci.

Fascism, the War, and Structures of Feeling in Italy, 1943–1945: Tales in Chiaroscuro. Simonetta Falasca-Zamponi, Oxford University Press. © Simonetta Falasca-Zamponi 2023. DOI: 10.1093/oso/9780192887504.003.0007

have cost the rural community had some untrustworthy eyes ever scrutinized her diary. Gina talked about the children's anti-German sentiment as they sang against the occupiers in dialect (apparently to avoid being caught), and recounted the subversive ways in which the local population acted. Mentions of Resistance fighters began after a priest visited her class and encouraged pupils to help those in need: "As he spoke, I thought of the people that I see arrive at the village furtively and then disappear in the woods. Maybe they take shelter in the 'hotels,' the chestnut drying houses. They are called 'partisans'" (November 25, 1943). A schoolmate soon shared with her a secret about the villagers: "Ino, [...] who knows everything, told me that at night they go with the mules to bring stuff to the partisans and help them with sabotage. They have also blown bridges up. Ino told me this as a big secret because we are all in danger and urged me to keep quiet" (February 20, 1944).

It so happens, the Germans had become suspicious. One day they came to requisition several men: "Us kids we didn't eat today. The tears and sad faces of the grownups are still in our eyes. In our ears there is the long lamentation, the desperate sobbing. [...] It's a very sad day" (April 10, 1944). Supposedly, the men had been taken to work in Germany. One of them had fathered Luigino, a baby boy Gina often took care of to alleviate his young mother, Giovanna. Gina did not explicitly confess it, but the war was taking a toll on her. As she anxiously waited for peace, the disappearance of those villagers remained a haunting thought. Once the conflict ended, she was still wondering about the fate of the detained men (May 6, 1945). A few days later, the tragic news:

> The whole village is weeping because it was communicated that those taken prisoners by the Germans died in concentration camps. They were not taken to work camps but in extermination areas. Giovanna is very distressed, desperate, does not believe it. I often take Luigino to play in the meadows. Hidden, I cry a lot because I don't find it right that Luigino will never be able to know his father. Here is the cruelty of war! (May 10, 1945)

Although church bells were ringing all across the land and celebratory rituals were held in towns and villages, the pain Italians suffered during the occupation did not dissolve after peace was declared. Leo Baldi perspicaciously caught the somber reality: "May 7, 1945. The war is over! The announcement arrived with the sound of sirens and bells at 6 pm, but we Italians received the news with some bitterness. I was in a small truck with Alfredo, coming back from Primavalle, and some women next to me were crying. One of them had lost her son." With so many dead and with families still facing uncertainty about the status of captured soldiers, relief at the conclusion of the war seemed conditional—a sense of uncanniness accompanied it. An exasperated Emma Di Raimo questioned her own unhappy reaction to the incredible occurrence:

> One could at least appreciate knowing that the destruction, the plight, ended, that so much blood is not spilled senselessly any longer... but... joy does not come... I feel tremendously sad, oppressed to the point of suffocating. Why? These are questions I ask myself and to which I try to find an answer to no avail, no avail. (May 6, 1945)

In truth, besides being unable to forget all the war's deaths and destructions, Emma was anxious about her brothers, of whom she had no news.

Even the privileged Perla Cacciaguerra, whose family had emerged relatively unscathed from the war, was caught by an eerie feeling of uneasiness as she soberly considered the gravity of the turn of events: "Now that I think of it, it seems such a strange thing that from now on a peaceful era begins [...]. It seems to me such a beautiful thing that I still cannot believe it is true" (May 2, 1945). The magnitude of the change was overwhelming. Her peer A.G. deemed it undeserved, an unmerited reward: "Oh my God! We wished for this day so long that it almost seems unreal, I don't know, I feel so confused that I can't even make any sense. By now we had gotten so used to the war that peace seems like too good a thing, something of which we are not worthy" (May 2, 1945).[1] Maybe A.G. thought of all the horrors she had witnessed (she had reported on the massacre of Sant'Anna di Stazzema) or maybe she simply needed time to adjust. Trauma had left its marks.[2]

In liberated Milan, the elder Dino Villani was also struggling to forget the tremendous reality of the previous two years—those memories lived on in his mind and in the fabric of the city, where reminders appeared at every corner. Streets sported makeshift altars for those youth killed by the Nazi-fascists— the victims' photographs hanging on doorways framed with tricolored ribbons and flowers. One could count up to four victims on each street. The ugliness of what had been was hard to overcome, and Villani refused to accept any new version of violence, including the violence of revenge. The similarities linking presently armed young people to those who used to roam the

---

[1] At first, German forces surrendered unconditionally to the Allied armies only in Italy, effective May 2. Germany's definitive surrender to the Allied forces on May 7 ended the war in Europe. The diarists cited here refer to either events or both.

[2] All the diarists cited in the paragraphs above, but for young Gina, lived in areas that had been liberated in 1944 and were thus spared the latter part of the war's mayhem.

streets a week earlier, even wearing the same (requisitioned) military garb and driving the same (requisitioned) vehicles, struck him deeply. Uniforms and guns were mementos of the ghastly past, unmerciful triggers of a still recent ordeal—an open wound. How could one vanquish that nightmare when signs remained all around? The sheer sense of panic once provoked by the Nazi-fascists' oppressive measures was re-emerging:

> One needs to think hard in order to remember that Mussolini and his are buried in the German section of the cemetery of Musocco. One needs to think hard to feel that we do not need to fear the SS and the several Italian gangs any longer, that we can store in our pockets names and addresses of certain friends, that we can be seen reading the *Avanti* or *L'Unità* on the tram and in the street without hiding the title, that one can contradict the ideas of a friend or an acquaintance without fear of being reported. (April 30, 1945)

The climate of terror suffered under fascism, both during the dictatorial state and in the Italian Social Republic (RSI), was not lifting easily. Maybe that is why Villani was impressed by American soldiers patrolling the streets without bearing arms (May 4, 1945). He needed to see clear evidence of change in order to lower his guard, and even then, it was not simple.

As the war's end coincided with the liberation from Nazi-fascism, at least in the northern part of the country, Italians' responses to the events were entangled. What did they celebrate? A harrowing experience, the war had dominated people's existence especially during the years of Nazi occupation. Yet as Villani's testimony demonstrates, the scourge of fascism had not gone unheeded; it was resurfacing as an indelible scar exactly as the war reached its final gasp. The killing of Mussolini and his collaborators especially brought out the depth of Italians' sedimented feelings and emotions. At the news of those executions, Emma Di Raimo confessed, "The death of these individuals that dragged us to ruin leaves me indifferent… what is a shot compared to all the evil they did to us?!. They should have made them suffer, before executing them!…." (May 1, 1945).

When the bodies of Mussolini and his subordinates were displayed in Milan in the same piazza where a year earlier the Nazi-fascists had massacred fifteen civilians, accounts of the events were disturbing.[3] Initially struck by the

---

[3] Aligi Sassu painted the massacre of the fifteen in his work "La guerra civile," also known as "Martiri di Piazzale Loreto." See his autobiography, *Un grido di colore. Autobiografia* (Lugano: Todaro, 1998).

news, Mario Tutino concluded that it was the sad but "inevitable," necessary action: "It's the end. Justice" (April 29, 1945). As he ran into people coming from the scene, however, he became perturbed by the lightheartedness with which they laughed off the spectacle and made fun of the corpses. "And you, aren't you going to see?" somebody asked him. People showed no mercy. Magda Ceccarelli De Grada described "impenetrable" crowds watching: "Nobody is horrified, nobody is moved. [...] One woman returning from the scene says with a deep sigh of relief: 'How satisfying...they are really dead'" (April 29, 1945). Hardened emotions emerged, although a sense of liberation, both physical and mental, was reflected in genuine festive moods. While in Robecco Pavese and in San Casciano Val di Pesa locals celebrated at the sound of bells ringing, in the streets of Milan the processions of partisans and soldiers moved Mario Tutino: "I don't believe I've ever lived a more beautiful hour during my sixty years. I don't know if I'll ever live a similar one in the short time I have left" (May 6, 1945). For Tutino, liberation and the end of the war were cathartic moments, unrivalled experiences that became supreme markers of a lifetime. "It is all over, we can breathe," Magda Ceccarelli De Grada aptly expressed (May 6, 1945).

The corpses of fascism brought back the forlorn reality of the regime, almost a reawakening after the prolonged chilling experience of war and Nazi terror and the RSI aberration too. Fascism's ghost had remained lurking in the background—the cause of all the mayhem of the past years and the unacknowledged source of two decades of diminished existence. As its final defeat was announced on the front page of newspapers, gruesome pictures of dead fascists' bodies on display in shop windows provided further testimonial to the enormity of the recent past—twenty long years eclipsed by the lethal reality of the world conflict.[4] The end of the war conjured those old specters, reopened unhealed wounds, resurrected buried traumas. It was a reckoning of sorts, whether one had been an active participant in the fascist regime or an acquiescent bystander or even a firm believer. How to make sense of two

---

[4] Giovanni Collina Graziani described the situation in Faenza: "On the windows of some stores there appeared the photos of the big characters of fascism hanging... The events have led the public to look at them with indifference" (May 5, 1945). On the photographer who took some of the first pictures of the corpses and on the iconic importance of the event see Giovanni Scirocco, "Christian Schiefer: un fotografo a Piazzale Loreto," in Maurizio Guerri ed., *Le immagini delle guerre contemporanee* (Milan: Meltemi, 2017), pp. 35–54. At first, those photographs were not published. In view of their crude nature, the Swiss newspaper to which Schiefer sent the images declined to print them. On May 1, photos of the fascists' hung bodies appeared in *The New York Times* with the caption, "Inglorious End of a Dictator," p. 3. In Italy, the commercial circulation of images of the hanging bodies, taken by several local photographers, was banned. See Giovanni Scirocco, "Christian Schiefer."

decades of dictatorship? As Adorno warned in retrospect, it was necessary to work through the past, not just archive or master it.[5]

That chance was missed in the aftermath of July 25, 1943, seemingly buried beneath the understandably emotional reaction at the fall of the dictator and compounded by the illusion of an approaching peace that never materialized. Be that as it may, with German occupation and Allied bombings becoming the dominant reality in the subsequent months, the war absorbed the attention of ordinary families and individuals alike. The question of the past remained suspended or, better, enshrouded in a mist of obliviousness and misperception. Hence, when the armistice was announced on September 8, Italians agonized over the dilemma of betrayal and seemed to neglect the crucial fact that the armistice allowed the country to cut its ties to Nazi Germany—continuing the war contradicted Italy's newly acquired freedom from fascism. Similar quandaries characterized the few evaluations of the regime that circulated in the months following July 25. Malfeasance by office holders turned into the main weakness of Mussolini's government and transformed the millenarian sin of dishonesty into the sole fault of fascism, hence helping to dilute the gravity of the dictatorship's crimes. As the war raged on, a growing dislike for the Germans further deflected Italians' attention from their own responsibilities in the past regime. With unspeakable horrors marking the experience of occupation, the crises people confronted on a daily basis—hunger, impermanence, death—also left little room for self-reflection and examination. Meanwhile, sentimental bonds and personal relations built in the course of everyday interactions made it hard to accept the reality of the civil war. Confusion over who was the enemy (foreigners or nationals?) only exacerbated the difficulty of identifying the country's guilt.

At the conclusion of the conflict, as the appalling crimes of repubblichini piled up on top of the violent acts already committed by Mussolini's regime, a reassessment of the dictatorship appeared even more complicated. New issues came to the surface. While some advised against retaliation, others advocated pursuing those who fought alongside the Germans. The question whether justice could ever be restored loomed over the process of rebuilding the nation. A cautious position emerged represented at an early stage by Benedetto Croce, who advised against too severe an epuration. Impelling efforts at reconstruction further distracted from a deep soul-searching.[6] Eventually, claims of

---

[5] Theodor Adorno, "What Does Coming to Terms with the Past Mean?" in Geoffrey Hartman ed., *Bitburg in Moral and Political Perspective* (Bloomington: Indiana University Press, 1986), pp. 114–29.

[6] The same issue has been at the center of the debate in Germany. See in particular Alexander and Margarete Mitscherlich, *The Inability to Mourn: Principles of Collective Behavior* (New York: Grove

victimhood helped Italy absolve itself from the fascist perverseness. What moral and political costs that decision comported one can only speculate.

The current normalization of fascism suggests that a more severe approach would have been advisable, although we know that forms of populism and authoritarianism, in combination with fascist tendencies, have emerged worldwide regardless of precedents. History should teach us not to repeat past mistakes or, at the minimum, one should remain vigilant against potential recurrences. As a country that experienced the ugly reality of fascism, Italy (as well as Germany) should be well armed to fend off that danger, having firsthand knowledge of fascism's nature and its unbridgeable distance from democratic governance. That awareness, however, and the kind of civic education necessary to sustain it, remained severely deficient in postwar Italy and eventually defaulted. Admittedly, even the longest lasting democracy of our modern times, the United States, has shown that democratic principles can be elusive concepts whose meaning is hard to comprehend or appreciate. Living in a democracy does not imply loving it. Thus, although many have invoked the exceptionality of the Italians (or of the Germans for what matters), that uniqueness remains in question and the issue of how best to uphold democratically founded ideals and values appears equally unsettled.[7] Becoming acquainted with the Italians' perspectives during the critical years between 1943 and 1945—hearing their voices, listening to their stories, contemplating their life lessons—instead of just assuming knowledge of them, offers unique access to a historical understanding of fascism and the quandaries of the people who lived through it.

While one might argue against the idea that there is anything essentially Italian about fascism or irredeemable about Italy's disastrous dictatorial experience, equally relevant is recognizing that the relationship of citizens to politics is not a straightforward affair. To the contrary, it follows circuitous paths. Moreover, it is mostly embedded within the habitual rhythms of everyday life—people do not typically engage actively in politics, and especially not on a regular basis. That distance or disconnection can then have a lulling, even

---

Press, 1975). For a view of the Mitscherlichs' book as missing the issue of historical trauma, see Matt ffytche, "Psychoanalytic Sociology and the Traumas of History: Alexander Mitscherlich Between the Disciplines," *History of the Human Sciences* vol. 30, no. 5 (2017): pp. 3–29.

[7] On the challenges of Italy's democratic public sphere see the special issue of *Journal of Modern Italian Studies* vol. 18, no. 3 (June 2013), edited by Simonetta Falasca-Zamponi and Richard Kaplan. The contribution of Marco Revelli especially details the historical context of Italy's idiosyncratic relationship to democracy in "A Fragile Political Sphere," pp. 296–308. In his discussion of the "nation" Gian Enrico Rusconi confronts a similar issue by addressing the meaning of (democratic) "nation" and people's understanding of it. See Rusconi, *Se cessiamo di essere una nazione. Tra etnodemocrazie regionali e cittadinanza europea* (Bologna: il Mulino, 1993).

dulling effect. All the arguments advanced about those Italians who were compromised, ambivalent, or halfway-in (both under the fascist dictatorship and during the RSI) fail to capture the ordinariness of uncommitted behavior. They neglect the modalities through which we all tend to go along with life "as is," the normalcy, the homogeneous time that makes up most of our waking hours. This does not mean that the everyday is always the site of inglorious behavior, nor should its routine features be a justification for inaction. But it does point to the significance of the everyday in our relationship to the world—the everyday is truly where all our life takes place, where we interact with friends and neighbors, where we work and engage in pleasurable pursuits. Indeed, it is not by considering the everyday as a special oasis of magical surprises and hidden treasures—the "marvelous" everyday of "blue roses" extolled by the Surrealists—that we can begin to gauge the relevance of the quotidian.[8] In contrast, we are only able to comprehend the full potential of daily life by realizing the mediating role it plays in linking the particular and the universal. Going beyond the immediate details of a given moment, one needs to consider the repetitive acts that mark any day, while grasping the concrete ways in which everything (or "the socio-economic-political whole") rests upon daily life.[9] We cannot understand the macro level of historical variability without acknowledging its connection to the relentless regularity of everydayness.

Doubtlessly, by epitomizing our determined condition, daily life risks becoming a refuge from the tragic; with its unavoidable recurrence, the everyday helps us avoid or domesticate the violence of the unpredictable. As Henri Lefebvre claimed, "Above all else, people seek, and find, security there."[10] This redoubles the masking power that the certainty of the everyday contains. At the same time, however, the appeal of daily normalcy steers us toward recognizing the often undesirable nature of times of exception, whether one deals with political, cultural, or economic crises. Everydayness can then become a site of critique. Undeniable but sobering, the Janus-faced essence of the everyday, its fundamental "chiaroscuro" ambivalence, should not be dismissed.

A daily ritual and at the same time the actual reporting of one's day every day, journaling establishes a privileged rapport with the quotidian. It allows

---

[8] See André Breton's first "Manifesto of Surrealism," where he writes, "This summer the roses are blue; the wood is of glass." In *Manifestoes of Surrealism* (Ann Arbor: University of Michigan Press, 1969), p. 47, translated by Richard Seaver and Helen. R. Lane.
[9] That is how Henri Lefebvre dubbed it in *Critique of Everyday Life*. The One-Volume Edition, vol. III: *From Modernity to Modernism (Towards a Metaphilosophy of Daily Life)* (London: Verso, 2014), p. 731.
[10] Lefebvre, *Critique of Everyday Life*, vol. III, p. 841.

diarists to make sense of the experience they are living—a reality that in the case of wartime Italy was indubitably pregnant with tragicness. While the cyclical rhythm of time captured by diaries ensured forms of continuity and offered authors a solace of sorts, it also reminded them of what they were missing or of what had changed in their habitual routine—it evidenced the impermanence of one's sense of rootedness and embeddedness. The outcomes that ensued from that realization were by no means uniform or even predictable among the authors surveyed here. That instability nonetheless affected diarists' relation to the larger political environment. While home became the celebrated comfort for many—a symbol and mark of nostalgia, a hope for a better future—it inadequately responded to the unmet challenges of a nefarious past. As Alvin Gouldner remarks, "Ordinariness and stability are the ontological requirements of serenity. Or, more properly, of the sense of serenity, and of passivity and acquiescence also. To construct a social world that is ordinary and solid is to quiet doubts and anxieties, to relax and tranquillize; it is a world in which one can be at home, or rather, at Home."[11] Home, no matter if individually longed for or academically theorized, can only be achieved by eliminating the extraordinary and its effects.[12] Solely in that way can it manage "to quiet doubts" and tranquillize—home marks the triumph of the private, a retrenching away from public life. "Private," after all, is etymologically linked to privation. A life deprived implies exclusion from the surrounding happenings, a self-marginalization, which is also and at the same time an illusory move—it postulates a chasm between the lived and history, when in reality it is a way to live history.[13] The diaries examined here point to this paradox and show that even individual attempts at self-isolation are continuously being redefined by the outside world, which is an active social world

---

[11] Gouldner's statement was meant to address a positivistic-oriented "normal sociology" that depicts the social world's reality as an external, out-there entity independent of events and people. See "Sociology and the Everyday Life," in Lewis A. Coser ed., *The Idea of Social Structure: Papers in Honor of Robert K. Merton* (New York: Harcourt Brace Jovanovich Inc., 1975), p. 432. On home and dwelling see especially the work of Martin Heidegger and Gaston Bachelard. Adorno also warned that in today's world, "It is part of morality not to be at home in one's home." See *Minima Moralia: Reflections from Damaged Life* (London: Verso, 1974), p. 39.

[12] On a more nuanced view of "home" see Rita Felski, "The Invention of Everyday Life," in *Doing Time: Feminist Theory and Postmodern Culture* (New York: New York University Press, 2000), especially pp. 85–9.

[13] The Latin "privatus" has the meaning of "withdrawn from public life." It derives from the verb "privare," which means "to deprive." See Lefebvre's etymological discussion in *Critique of Everyday Life*, vol. I, p. 169, and vol. II, pp. 381–9. Also, Lefebvre distinguishes between "functional housing" (housing as an economic function) and the more poetic "dwelling." The convergence of thinking between Lefebvre and Gouldner deserves to be probed, along with the commonality of concerns in Lefebvre and Williams's thought (see for example Lefebvre's discussion of levels and of the conjuncture/structure relation, where by conjuncture he means the process of becoming [Lefebvre, *Critique of Everyday Life*, vol. II, pp. 412–19 and 458–9]).

and always in movement. Shifting moods are but the norm, even if patterns eventually emerge, structures of feeling that epitomize and define particular historical moments and display the making of one's political subjectivity.[14]

Whether Italians were trying to identify the "enemy," figure out the meaning of fatherland, or define their relationship to authority, their perspectives were fluid. While often diverging from official views, the heterogeneity of their opinions responded to the unforgiving relentlessness of historical contingencies—a situation that required continuous reassessment. Obliviousness about the past regime was a consequence of these challenging scenarios and became especially aggravated by concerns over the dreaded eventuality of a civil war.[15] Initially only a fear, the conflict between brothers (and sisters) soon arose as a reality against which the specter of fascism receded only to re-emerge at liberation. By then, however, it was engulfed in rationalizations and speculations of political expediency. Truly a hornet's nest, the country's process of reconstruction generated narratives refractory to self-examination.[16] In an apotheosis of salvation, and out of an amalgam of instability and sudden political alterations, beliefs and sentiments were channeled into a successful story of absolution.

Admittedly, revisiting the past does not guarantee against the return of an untoward precedent. Also, it can be an excruciating operation. Nevertheless, the idea that the restructuring of institutions—legal, economic, or educational—could be effectively conducted in postwar Italy without serious analysis of the fascist regime was a misplaced form of wishful thinking. As Bruna Talluri feared, continuity with the past was a threatening reality that extended beyond the institutional level.[17] Rising from the still burning ashes of fascism's ghastly experiment, a new movement founded late in 1944 was managing to turn political apathy, or "whateverism," into a legitimate position to be loudly defended—as if, by eliminating parties and politicking, one could start from scratch.[18] *Qualunquismo*, an attitude that fundamentally implies passive

---

[14] Here I am following Sadeq Rahimi's understanding of subjectivity as incorporating both the collective (that is, the political) and the temporal (by which Rahimi means the historical as well as the imaginary). See "Haunted Metaphor, Transmitted Affect: The Pantemporality of Subjective Experience," *Subjectivity* vol. 9, no. 1 (2016): p. 85.

[15] Rusconi's work is again helpful here as it encourages to consider how people actually understood terms and situations. Rusconi, *Se cessiamo di essere una nazione*.

[16] See Filippo Focardi, *Il cattivo tedesco e il bravo italiano. La rimozione delle colpe della seconda guerra mondiale* (Rome-Bari: Laterza, 2013).

[17] For an analysis of continuity with the regime in the field of operatic production see Harriet Boyd-Bennett, *Opera in Postwar Venice: Cultural Politics and the Avant-Garde* (Cambridge: Cambridge University Press, 2018).

[18] The party that sponsored "whateverism," the Fronte dell'Uomo Qualunque (Movement of the Common Man), was officially launched in February 1946. It was the offshoot of the homonymous

reliance on authorities to take care of things, helps reduce the hassle of evaluating and assessing—an incredible, almost anachronistic outcome in a country emerging out of two decades of dictatorial darkness. In Talluri's words, "Fascism authorizes one not to think, because there is always somebody who can think for us. That's why Giannini invented the Movement of the Common Man: the common man does not think, he loves order and delegates others to deliver it with whatever means" (December 28, 1945). The Movement of the Common Man conveyed the sense of uncertainty over the previous period, when fatigue, both mental and physical, overtook bombed-out city and country dwellers alike and when current compelling concerns drowned out past matters. The obsessive priority of the present and its brutality engaged the attention of most.

Personal daily narratives attest to the centrality of the here and now in people's existence, and this book has sought to assess the lived present of Italians during the biennium 1943–45 as filtered through their private writings—surely a demanding operation. For diaries are fraught with interpretive challenges, beginning with the authors' reticence and the often terse nature of their accounts—a problem compounded by the scribes' desire to be objective chroniclers. (In the period considered, we know that factuality in a state of exceptionality presided over writers' style.) Diaries' repetitive cadence also constitutes a potential obstacle to individual expression as it encourages list-like accounts of daily habits—a descriptive exercise that avoids more active types of engagement.

Hermeneutical difficulties notwithstanding, diaries offer unique access to historical experience. They constitute a venue from which to examine structures of feeling—meanings and understandings that, because of their temporal variability, often sit "at the very edge of semantic availability."[19] As Raymond Williams argued, structures of feeling illuminate the "forming and formative processes" of human cultural activity—they highlight the social embeddedness of one's singular and developing views and beliefs.[20] Journaling exposes the flexibility and changeability of people's perspectives. Moreover, like all kinds of writing, journaling can be meaningful and communicative

---

movement that developed around the periodical *L'Uomo qualunque*, founded by Guglielmo Giannini on December 27, 1944. In the administrative elections of 1946, the Fronte reached substantial success in the South—an achievement that soon fizzled. In 1949, the party was rescinded. See Sandro Setta, *L'uomo qualunque 1944–1948* (Rome-Bari: Laterza, 1975). Also see Maurizio Cocco, *Qualunquismo, una storia politica e culturale dell'uomo qualunque* (Florence: Edizioni Le Monnier, 2018).

[19] Raymond Williams, "Structures of Feeling," in *Marxism and Literature* (Oxford: Oxford University Press, 1977), p. 134.

[20] Williams, "Structures of Feeling," in *Marxism and Literature*, p. 128.

beyond its content. Formal elements contribute to signification by articulating "shared sounds and words,"[21] and the diarists presented here (especially the "ordinary" ones) took advantage of the several orthographical devices that complement the practice of writing. A liberal use of literary and topographical conventions enhanced their personal testimonials. Even the act of engaging in the practice of composing daily entries, one should add, constitutes a meaningful activity and manifests a whole host of motivations on the part of its protagonists.[22] A large number of the authors featured in the book began their journals during the 1943–45 period, suggesting that dramatic circumstances elicited their desire to serve as witness. Writing helped diarists process a perplexing present, often offering comfort and alternatively inspiring empowerment. Through writing, individuals navigated exceptional times and events; they confronted history and had the chance to evaluate their own role in it.

For some diarists, the first bombing of their hometown sparked a desire to chronicle. In a few cases, it was the fall of fascism that motivated individuals to begin documenting a time of uncertainty. Others started writing on September 8, whereas-imprisonment in camps led military men to engage in diary-keeping. Although several scribes continued a long-held habit dating to before the war, the variety of contextual circumstances that spurred journaling suggests we should not consider diaries as uniformly adhering to an abstract, general formula (the "intimate" diary) that ends up neutralizing their historical situatedness. Still part of a routine practice, diaries written between 1943 and 1945 (including those initiated prior to that time) responded to a condition of crisis, an existential state of emergency. And they need to be read against this backdrop, while keeping an eye on the cascade of events that affected authors' responses. For, again, although often documentary in intention, diaries are not static evidentiary texts, and writers' points of view are affected by external conditions and show shifts over time—dynamics of becoming that mark the constitutional essence of structures of feeling.

In the case of wartime Italy, personal journals shed light on the process through which Italians came to understand uncontrollable events that profoundly altered the rhythm of their lives and affected their political subjectivity. Faced with precarious situations and the shattering of their habitual sense of place, individuals had to renegotiate personal existence, all the while

---

[21] Williams, "Forms," in *Marxism and Literature*, p. 191.
[22] Although focused on reading rather than writing, Janice Radway famously evidenced the importance of people's activities in her classic study *Reading the Romance: Women, Patriarchy, and Popular Literature* (Chapel Hill: The University of North Carolina Press, 1984).

engaging in a work of interpretation amidst contrasting messages from competing official sources.[23] How to reduce complexities to manageable pieces of knowledge and how to apply that knowledge to one's particular circumstances became a recurrent trial. Diaries helped their scribes process troubled times, whether in the more enclosed and predictable environment of war camps or in the much more open and volatile setting of civic sociality. Unsurprisingly, many wrote the last page of their journals in the days or weeks following liberation or after the return of their loved ones from prison camps. The reestablishment of normalcy marked the end of an extraordinary experience of hardship (and of the need to account for it). As Maria Carazzolo stated one month after peace was announced, the diary "made sense as long as we lived in exceptional times, but if continued it would be a boring chronicle of insignificant things."[24] In keeping with her role as witness of incomparable occurrences, Carazzolo saw no meaning in journaling once the extraordinary experience she dedicated herself to recounting was over. Even if in many ways an account of the everyday, diaries written during the war conveyed an unparalleled reality.

To recapitulate: This book was never intended as a history of the period—indeed, much of what took place during 1943–45 is missing or treaded lightly in our account—nor is it a study about diaries. In contrast, the goal was to identify the Italians' relationship to fascism by excavating the sentiments with which they greeted the fall of the regime and reacted to the ongoing war, the Germans' occupation, and the struggle for liberation. Inspired by Raymond Williams's cultural approach, we began with the assumption that people's feelings most often remain unarticulated and one needs to detect them through an interpretive work that, moving beyond content, looks into interstices and through gaps and also considers formal dimensions. Diaries offered the ideal medium through which to detect Italians' emergent opinions and their changes, the evolving and variable status of their thinking. Granted, diaries cannot be taken at face value, and a host of issues intervene in the composition of daily notes, including one's ability to convey thoughts (which implies familiarity with the practice of writing and with journaling as a genre) as well as expectations about a diary's purpose. Nevertheless, and no matter the

---

[23] On this issue see Donald Sassoon, "Italy after Fascism: The Predicament of Dominant Narratives," in Richard Bessel and Dirk Schumann eds., *Life after Death: Approaches to a Cultural and Social History of Europe during the 1940s and 1950s* (Cambridge: Cambridge University Press, 2003), pp. 259–90.

[24] Maria Carazzolo, *Più forte della paura. Diario di guerra e dopoguerra (1938–1947)* (Caselle di Sommacampagna: Cierre edizioni, 2007), p. 277 (entry of mid-June 1945). (However, she continued her reportage until 1947 with accounts focused on returning soldiers.)

accuracy of the purported truths, private journals allow us to follow the dynamics of individuals' attitudes on a daily basis. Through their connection with the everyday, both as a referent and a source of content, diaries help move the analysis of fascism down to the level of lived experience. Far from approaching fascism as a political theorem, abstract and separate from one's practical world, the everyday let us hear and give prominence to people's voices. By measuring fascism against a world of things and relations, habits and traditions, networks of sociability and family interactions, the everyday makes it possible to approximate the concrete, albeit moving, meaning that Mussolini's regime held in Italians' lives. Via the everyday, fascism descends from the plane of historiographical question and turns into an issue of lived conflict between inner being and external reality, or personal history and History. The youngest among the diarists surveyed here especially stood out as remarkably outspoken participants in their historical present. Expressing their opinions with a commanding prose, lively and persuasive, a few even outsmarted their literary counterparts—Irene Paolisso being one exemplary case.

As for the results of the study, the portrayal of Italians' relationship to fascism that emerges from our analysis is doubtlessly variegated, and ordinary diarists present features that do not always appear among their intellectual counterpart. Beyond differences in style and vision, however, a significant commonality defines ordinary and intellectual diarists alike: Their accounts tend to sideline the many years of dictatorship, an almost casual reckoning with the past that flattens the latter into a faded reality detached from the pressing and vivid traumas of the biennium 1943–45. Even if intellectual diarists felt a more compelling duty to reflect on their current reality and leaned toward questioning Italians' past responsibilities in fascism, their seemingly deeper awareness did not stop them from falling prey to the confounding entrapments experienced by ordinary diarists, and they rarely questioned their own role in the regime. The wish to separate fascism from Italy and the Italians was especially alluring to them; the regime's disgrace weighing on many like a heavy coat. The analysis of intellectual diarists confirms the general sense of elusiveness presiding over ordinary diarists' relationship to fascism.

Having reached this conclusion, the question remains: How does the knowledge we have acquired through the examination of diaries help us understand the recurrence of fascism after the war, including more recent "flirtations" with it (to put it mildly)? Also, was the biennium 1943–45 a critical historical moment for defining the role of fascism in Italy or did the postwar period prove more consequential in terms of fascism's lasting effects on institutions and mentalities?[25] Is it even possible or wise to separate the two? Fascism's version in the guise of the Social Republic has certainly complicated the debate by further distancing Italians from the "original sin." An easily recognizable repository of hatred, the fascist repubblichini constituted a visible source of evil that deceptively moved the target of outrage from the regime's twenty years to the nineteen months of the RSI.[26] But a point worth making is that, granted the cognitive and semantic confusions of the war days, diarists' reactions to July 25 already signaled people's sense of closure vis-à-vis the experience of the past regime. It was as if, having reached the brim, the liquid had spilled in myriad (forgetful) directions, and one could not but expect it would eventually evaporate.

And yet those twenty years remain key for theorizing the Italians' relationship to fascism. Although freedom immediately, albeit vaguely, arose as a value hailed by Italians when Mussolini was deposed, the fact remains that the habituation people experienced during the regime proved scarcely conducive to challenging the system. A lack of gravitas defined the Italians' everyday living under the fascist regime—a superficiality that casts a shadow of grayness on people, not for their failure to act, however, but because they did not see the need to rise up. This might be the more pessimistic evaluation of Italians' perspectives on fascism during the twenty years of dictatorship and as fascism unashamedly continued into 1945 and is re-emerging at present. Mario Tutino's rage at friends' nonchalant assessment of life under Mussolini rings like a premonition. As he sensed, absent an ethical approach to politics, all sorts of excuses, smacking of "absolute barbarity," justified one's attachment to the old regime: "After all, they now say, what bad did fascism do to me personally?" (October 23, 1943). The dearth of a sustained sense of civic solidarity and shared community ideals, of beliefs in social justice and individual rights, inevitably sound the death knell of a true democratic future.

If, as Tutino speculated, questions of narrow-mindedness as well as connivance and pure self-interest had motivated the middle classes to support

---

[25] For an analysis of Italy's passage to democracy within the framework of critical liminal situations see Rosario Forlenza, *On the Edge of Democracy: Italy, 1943–1948* (Oxford: Oxford University Press, 2019). Defined as "periods of great uncertainty in which social identity and agency are highly fluid and political outcomes indeterminate," Forlenza sees liminality "as constitutive of social order by means of the emergence of new meanings, states of consciousness, and symbols," p. 221.

[26] Mariuccia Salvati cites an unsigned editorial of the newspaper *Il Tempo*, published on June 23, 1945, explicitly suggesting that one needed to punish not those Italians who had made the mistake of following the regime, but those who continued to make that mistake after July 25. See Salvati, *Passaggi. Italiani dal fascismo alla Repubblica* (Rome: Carocci editore, 2016), p. 74.

Mussolini's ghastly experiment, those reasons also blinded the same classes to the tyrannical nature of the dictatorship. The working classes might have had more reasons to contest the regime and not minimize its malignity. From what we know, their activism continued during the years of occupation, and many individual workers were deported to German camps for refusing to respond to the RSI draft calls. Little research is, however, available about them, which brings us to the issue of what is missing from the tales reported in this book. The absence of working-class diarists, especially from the Turin and Milan areas where the Resistance was fiercer and long-lasting, is notable.[27] Catalogues of diaries found at archives are not necessarily compiled according to the needs of historical researchers, unfortunately, and the selection of relevant diaries can only be partial. It is also true that focusing on activism would change the focus on "ordinariness" central to this study, no matter the complexity of the notion.

But returning to the central question of the Italians' reckoning with fascism, one wonders if, rather than the ill-advised forgetting of the past, the focus of concern should be people's failure to recognize the perniciousness of that past, in which case, two sets of processes would be necessary to deal with fascism. One requires understanding its anti-democratic nature and rejecting it on that basis; the other involves cultivating the memory of the fascist past as a safeguard for the future, so that it will not happen again.[28] Having originated the phenomenon, Italy should be in the forefront of rejecting that past forcefully. As Claudio Pavone persuasively argued in his work, this was the moral stance that guided the Resistance movement.[29] No matter the political rationale and strategies that presided over the Resistance, the partisans' sacrifice of their lives was an active gesture of atonement, an expression of the felt sense of obligation for Italy's undeniable responsibility. Even if they could

---

[27] Also significant is the fact that "class war," which Pavone considers a component of the Resistance, does not emerge as a main trope from the diaries examined here. See Claudio Pavone, *Una guerra civile. Saggio storico sulla moralità della Resistenza* (Turin: Bollati Boringhieri, 1991). Accounts of the peasantry are also missing, and in general the diaries consulted seldom address key experiences that might emerge from other documents, such as memoirs. Fear of German roundups, which could be severe, or the impact of the RSI's newly formed Black Brigades (Brigate nere) on the population rarely emerge from the narratives. Almost absent are also references to the Kingdom of the South and its vicissitudes (but for Croce).

[28] On this issue, see the important survey "Tra i giovani: fascismo, antifascismo e democrazia," a 2018 study conducted by Alvaro Tacchini, http://www.storiatifernate.it/pubblicazioni.php?cat=49&subcat=144&group=402. Similar initiatives are in dire need. For a discussion of the survey results see Simonetta Falasca-Zamponi, "Is Democracy in Italy Secure? Fascism's Appeal to Italian Youth is a Worrisome Trend," *Public Seminar* (2020), online https://publicseminar.org/essays/is-democracy-in-italy-secure/.

[29] Pavone, *Una guerra civile*. Also see Gian Enrico Rusconi, *Resistenza e postfascismo* (Bologna: il Mulino, 1995), chapters I and IX in particular.

have chosen to wait passively for liberation, members of the Resistance took upon themselves the guilt of the nation; though a minority, they acted in the country's name, selflessly, as representatives of the whole. An ethical stance defined their response to a period that felt like a shame, a true mortification. As Bruna Talluri expressed it in liberated Tuscany, "I went to the movies to watch 'The Dictator'—dictatorial power ridiculed by Charlie Chaplin, while Allies soldiers laughed with amusement in the theater. I could not laugh: the memory of our shame is too recent..." (December 27, 1944).

If, as Adorno hinted, the issue is how to bring the fascist era into consciousness, much of that reflective work obviously was and still remains undone in Italy after July 25.[30] Once the excruciating process of liberation came to a successful conclusion, that realization hit Piero Calamandrei hard. As he was lunching with friends at a trattoria in late April 1945, finally free to discuss politics without fears of repercussions, the radio's hourly time signal took him back to the era when everybody would stop their activities and listen to the news in silence. This time, however, the broadcast was announcing the liberation of Milan and the execution of fascist leaders listed by last and first names. A sobering mood overtook him:

> At the end of the broadcast there are some moments of silence, desolate and empty silence: not a comment, not a jubilation, not an expletive. For twenty years we anticipated, we waited for, we invoked this fatal end. Now that the conclusion comes, inexorable like the moral of a horrible fable, we find ourselves humiliated by disgust and shame, rather than consoled. It was all here: twenty years of appalling apocalypse concluded in this heap of bloody rags. And we were not able to stop it, and we waited twenty years to come to such simple reckoning.[31]

---

[30] In his brief introduction to Adorno's piece "What Does Coming to Terms with the Past Mean?" Geoffrey Hartman points to the inadequacy of translating "Aufarbeitung" as "coming to terms with" (the original German title of Adorno's essay is "Was bedeutet: Aufarbeitung der Vergangenheit"). Hartmann alludes to the psychoanalytic connotations of Aufarbeitung and emphasizes its underlying meaning of reprocessing, working through. The issue, he writes, is "how to take the Hitler's era into consciousness." See Geoffrey Hartman ed., *Bitburg in Moral and Political Perspective*, p. 114.

[31] Piero Calamandrei, *Diario 1939–1945* (Florence: La Nuova Italia, 1982), vol. II, pp. 560–1 (entry of April 1945). This was the only entry Calamandrei wrote for the month of April.

Methodological Appendix

The largest portion of this research is based on private diaries and correspondence housed at three small archival institutions in Italy: The Archivio della scrittura popolare (ASP) in Trento, the Archivio diaristico nazionale in Pieve Santo Stefano (ADN), and the Archivio Ligure della scrittura popolare (ALSP) in Genoa. At these sites (although considerably less at ALSP), I consulted a total of 150 personal documents relevant to the biennium 1943–45. The material was selected following a preliminary search (with fascism as a key word) conducted with the assistance of the archivists. After an initial scrutiny, out of 150 journals I chose ninety for closer analysis based on their pertinence to the topic of my study. The final list of authors whose journals and correspondence are cited in the book is annotated in the Table of Diaries along with demographic and other information.[1]

In examining personal writings, my main objective was to track individual and collective perspectives as they evolved during the two years considered. Although factual accuracy was not my central concern, I excluded retrospective analyses and personal memoirs from my sources. Invaluable works on the recent past have resorted to the study of memory for retracing people's perceptions and experiences. However, I found this approach inadequate for assessing the dynamic nature of the lived reality of the time. Memory concentrates on how people (witnesses) remember the past; it does not question—in contrast it implies—that a "real" finished product we label as the past is retrievable, even if it concedes there are different interpretations of it.[2] Furthermore, memory is a presentist operation that supposedly recovers moments we left dormant in our consciousness; it looks to explain those historical moments post facto by uncovering layers of sedimented emotions and feelings.

My analysis of post-fascist Italy relies on different ontological premises. It considers the past as emerging out of an array of lived experiences that helped produce it—what people felt and how they acted at the time affected their present and shaped their understanding of it. Determined not to frame diarists (especially "ordinary" ones) within a fixed category of interpretation, I paid close attention to the development of their perspectives.[3] Hence, I applied a double approach to my reading of texts. On the one hand, I surveyed authors' reactions to the main historical events: the fall of Mussolini on July 25, 1943, the armistice of September 8, 1943, and the declaration of war to Germany of October 13, 1943. Here

---

[1] One note: Because of the particular statute of the ADN, in some instances those who deposited their original diaries at this archive chose to divide up their journals. For example, in the case of Angelo Peroni, two separate diaries were filed.

[2] For another critical approach see Robin Wagner-Pacifici, "Reconceptualizing Memory as Event: From 'Difficult Pasts' to 'Restless Events'," in Anna Lisa Tota and Trevor Hagen eds., *Routledge International Handbook of Memory Studies* (New York: Routledge, 2016), pp. 22–7.

[3] Although embedded in a psychiatric tradition, Sadeq Rahimi's work illuminates these points particularly well. I found his approach on the "pantemporality" of subjective experience especially instructive. See Sadeq Rahimi, "Haunted Metaphor, Transmitted Affect: The Pantemporality of Subjective Experience," *Subjectivity* vol. 9, no. 1 (2016): pp. 83–105. By the same author also see *Meaning, Madness and Political Subjectivity: A Study of Schizophrenia and Culture in Turkey* (London: Routledge, 2016).

the number and array of responses was important, although equally significant were silences, or the absence of reactions. On the other hand, I conducted an in-depth analysis of individual views on a series of themes of grave political and existential implications. Due to diaries' constitutional link to the everyday, I especially focused on the "dragging" of time, or "what happens when nothing happens," as determinant of people's historical experiences during a particularly trying period.[4]

Because I regard diarists as authors in their own right (also in view of comparing "ordinary" with more "professional" diarists), I chose to report their texts verbatim (including punctuation) whenever possible, based on the conviction that how they wrote was as relevant as what they wrote. The tight relation between content and form can be particularly consequential in the case of "ordinary" diarists, whose complaints or dissatisfaction about their inability to express themselves often transpired in the pages of their journals. I also refrained from isolating single statements or detaching them from the context of the diarist's entry on a particular day and from the diary's overall structure as well. I deemed authors' continuities in expression, opinions, and interests as significant as discontinuities, also considering that in most cases we know very little about their background history.[5]

Although the majority of the "ordinary" diaries I examined are still unpublished, I did not pursue them for their testimonial value as historical scoops or "discoveries." I concentrated instead on what individual voices had in common and communicated about the different structures of feeling that were taking shape and eventually emerged out of the historical chaos in Italy between 1943 and 1945. As for the published diaries of the "ordinary" authors, a few are not in the public domain, since they have been printed for limited circulation and sometimes in abridged form.[6] When their content differed from the original manuscript, I abstained from citing them, unless I could identify and single out the differences and was given authorization to do so.[7]

Finally, throughout the book I refer to diarists with their full name. In the few instances when the copyrights owners did not answer my request for permission (there were a handful), I resorted to initials in place of the authors' first and last names.[8]

---

[4] On dragging time see Georges Perec, *An Attempt at Exhausting a Place in Paris* (Cambridge, Mass.: Wakefield Press, 2010), translated by Marc Lowenthal, p. 3. Also see Perec's essay on Robert Antelme's memories of the concentration camp, "Robert Antelme or the Truth of Literature," in *Species of Spaces and Other Pieces* (London: Penguin, 1997). Perec points out the lack of any "horror image" in Antelme's *L'Espèce humaine* and admires the book's focus on "time dragging itself out, […], a present moment that persists, hours that never end, moments of vacancy and unconsciousness, days without a date," p. 257.

[5] To the diarists located at the archives I added two more authors, Carlo Chevallard from Turin and Maria Carazzolo from Montagnana, near Padua, whose journals have been published but whose original copies are not at the institutions I visited. The significance of their diaries resides in the fact that they consistently cover the entire period studied and come from two locations in Northern Italy that are scarcely represented in my sample. Not being able to evaluate the accuracy of the published versions, however, I mostly cite the two diaries in footnotes as backup evidence. In the case of Carazzolo, we know that the editor corrected her original quirky punctuation, for example, whereas my study values the originality of diarists' expressive means.

[6] I list in the bibliography the diaries I was able to identify as published, even if they might not be available to the public and are often printed in an abridged or edited form.

[7] I should add that since my goal was to highlight diarists' common structures of feelings—those elements of unity that characterize the seemingly "subjective" nature of personal narratives—there follows the often repetitive nature of textual citations.

[8] The ADN requires obtaining citation permission from authors—a procedure that is at times unsuccessful. One needs to reach the diarists or, in view of the fact that most are deceased, either their inheritors or the people who originally deposited the manuscripts on their behalf.

Table of Diaries

Diarists	Birth dates	Gender	Education	Location	Start date
Wanda Affricano-Marabini (ADN)	2-14-1909 3-28-1948	F		Central Italy	10-2-1943
Francesco Agnello (ADN)	2-6-1890 1975	M	University degree	Southern Italy	5-2-1941
Giacomo Agnese (ADN)	9-26-1905 1974	M	High school degree	Northern Italy	Epistolary
Maria Alemanno (ADN)	12-26-1900 11-16-1988	F	High school degree	Central Italy	9-8-1943
Pompilio Aste (ASP)	8-9-1908 8-22-1985	M	University degree	Northern Italy	9-8-1943
Aldo Bacci (ADN)	1900 1977	M	Elementary school	Central Italy	7-22-1943
Leo Baldi (ADN)	11-27-1908 2005	M	University degree	Central Italy	9-1943
Michele Barile (ADN)	2-3-1919 1988	M	High school degree	Southern Italy	10-13-1943
Fedora Brenta Brcic (ADN)	3-23-1898 2-25-1988	F	High school degree	Central Italy	9-8-1943
Cesarina Brugnara (ASP)	12-22-1922	F	Post-elementary degree	Northern Italy	9-1943
Concetta Bucciano (ADN)	12-24-1895 2-22-1980	F	Elementary school	Central Italy	
Perla Cacciaguerra (ADN)	1926 2012	F	Student	Central Italy	10-4-1943
Massimo Campregher (ASP)	5-22-1911 9-18-1971	M		Northern Italy	9-24-1943
Ettore Castiglioni (ADN)	8-28-1908 3-12-1944	M	University degree	Northern Italy	12-5-1925
Magda Ceccarelli De Grada (ADN)	1892 1985	F	High school degree	Northern Italy	6-12-1940
Carlo Ciseri (ADN)	12-24-1896 1984	M	High school degree	Central Italy	1915
Roberto Cohen (ADN)	8-26-1902 1996	M		Northern Italy	1935

Continued

Diarists	Birth dates	Gender	Education	Location	Start date
Giovanni Collina Graziani (ADN)	1884 1967	M	University degree	Northern Italy	9-8-1943
Mario Corbolini (ASP)	9-15-1920	M		Northern Italy	6-1940
Marisa Corsellini (ADN)	1-4-1927	F		Central Italy	7-1944
Giorgio Crainz (ADN)	1915	M	University degree	Central Italy	9-12-1943
Agostino De Pedri (ASP)	8-7-1913	M		Northern Italy	9-9-1943
M. D. (ADN)	1919	M	High school degree	Southern Italy	9-8-1943
Corrado Di Pompeo (ADN)	1910 5-25-1957	M	Elementary school	Central Italy	10-1943
Emma Di Raimo (ADN)	1910 1979	F	Junior high school degree	Central Italy	1943
Danilo Durando (ADN)	9-1-1923 8-1-2001	M	Student	Northern Italy	2-19-1944
Fortunato Favai (ASP)	1899 1961	M	High school degree	Northern Italy	1939
Maria Fenoglio (ADN)	6-27-1905 1998	F	High school degree	Northern Italy	6-1922
Paolino Ferrari (ADN)	1899 1980	M	University degree	Northern Italy	1938
Leone Fioravanti (ADN)	1900 1970	M		Northern Italy	9-1943
Caterina Gaggero Viale (ADN)	1891 1959	F		Northern Italy	12-10-1943
Olga Garbagnati (ASP)	4-5-1928	F	Student	Northern Italy	7-26-1942
Barbara Garrone (ADN)	5-27-1891 1980	F		Central Italy	1943
A. G. (ADN)	6-13-1925	F	High school degree	Central Italy	6-25-1944
Vitruvio Giorni (ADN)	1915 1993	M	Elementary school	Central Italy	1940
Giacinto Mario Guala (ADN)	1912 1985	M	Elementary school	Northern Italy	9-12-1943
Aldo Lanzoni (ADN)	7-19-1908 2-26-1986	M	Elementary school	Northern Italy	4-16-1943
Lucio Macchiarella (ADN)	11-13-1915 11-11-1948	M	High school degree	Southern Italy	8-10-1941

Antonio Maestri (ASP)	5–26–1912	M		Northern Italy	1927
A. M. (ADN)	10–12–1921	F	High school degree	Northern Italy	7–25–1943
Zelinda Marcucci (ADN)	10–27–1923 2013	F	Elementary school	Central Italy	
Gualtiero Marello (Angela Delfino) (ADN)	8–14–1906 1971	M	University degree	Northern Italy	Epistolary
Ester Marozzi (ADN)	1885	F	High school degree	Northern Italy	4–1–1939
Pietro Massolo (ADN)	11–6–1921	M	Student	Southern Italy	1941
Anna Menestrina (ASP)	8–25–1883 3–16–1964	F	Elementary school	Northern Italy	7–26–1943
Michelina Michelini (ADN)	9–10–1914	F	High school degree	Central Italy	9–8–1943
Irene Paolisso (ADN)	1923	F	Student	Central Italy	9–1–1943
Angelo Peroni (ADN)	11–26–1925 2008	M	Student	Northern Italy	12–6–1941
Giulio Repetto (ALSP)		M	Student	Northern Italy	
Rinaldo Rinaldi Aida Rinaldi Gatti (ADN)	8–27–1910 10–31–1989	M F	University degree	Northern Italy	Epistolary
Antonio Rossi (ADN)	8–2–1912 2005	M	University degree	Southern Italy	8–24–1943
E. R. (ADN)	6–7–1887 2–6–1954	F	High school degree	Northern Italy	3–29–1943
V. R. (ADN)	12–26–1924	F	High school degree	Central Italy	
Albertina Roveda (ADN)	1927	F	Student	Northern Italy	1934
Liana Ruberl (ADN)	1–2–1925	F	Student	Northern Italy	3–5–1935
Luigi Serravalle (ADN)	3–3–1899 8–28–1979	M	Seminary	Northern Italy	1913
Gian Carlo Stracciari (ADN)	12–11–1925 2018	M	Student	Northern Italy	1943
Bruna Talluri (ADN)	6–12–1923 11–21–2006	F	Student	Central Italy	12–22–1939
Manilio Tartarini (ADN)	9–29–1905 5–31–1976	M	High school degree	Central Italy	10–15–1943
Gina Traverso (ADN)	1935	F	Student	Northern Italy	10–2–1942

Continued

Diarists	Birth dates	Gender	Education	Location	Start date
Mario Tutino (ADN)	1885 1968	M	University degree	Northern Italy	7-27-1943
Dino Villani (ADN)	8-16-1898 3-13-1989	M	High school	Northern Italy	7-26-1943
Luigia Visintainer (ASP)	1875 1965	F		Northern Italy	11-17-1937
Ada Vita (ADN)	10-28-1924	F	Student	Northern Italy	11-9-1942

Bibliography

Diary and Other Sources

Archivio Contemporaneo "Alessandro Bonsanti," Gabinetto G.P. Vieusseux
Archivio della scrittura popolare (ASP)
Archivio dell'Istituto di Storia Politica e Sociale V. Gabriotti
Archivio Diaristico Nazionale (ADN)
Archivio ligure della scrittura popolare (ALSP)
Museo Wolfsoniana, Fondazione Palazzo Ducale

Newspapers

Daily Express
Daily Mirror
Il Corriere della Sera
Il Mattino
Il Messaggero
Il Popolo di Roma
La Stampa
The New York Times

Books and Articles

Adamoli, Umberto. *Nel turbinio di una tempesta. Dalle pagine del mio diario: 1943–1944*. Teramo: Cioschi, 1947.
Adorno, Theodor. *Minima Moralia: Reflections from Damaged Life*. London: Verso, 1974.
Adorno, Theodor. "What Does Coming to Terms with the Past Mean?" In *Bitburg in Moral and Political Perspective*, edited by Geoffrey Hartman. Pp. 114–29. Bloomington: Indiana University Press, 1986.
Aga Rossi, Elena. *Una nazione allo sbando. L'armistizio italiano del settembre 1943*. Bologna: il Mulino, 1993.
Aga Rossi, Elena. *A Nation Collapses: The Italian Surrender of 1943*. Cambridge: Cambridge University Press, 2000.
Aga Rossi, Elena. *Una nazione allo sbando. L'armistizio italiano del settembre 1943 e le sue conseguenze*. Augmented edition. Bologna: il Mulino, 2003.
Aga Rossi, Elena, and Maria Teresa Giusti. *Una guerra a parte. I militari italiani nei Balcani (1940–1943)*. Bologna: il Mulino, 2011.
Agamben, Giorgio. *State of Exception*. Chicago: University of Chicago Press, 2005.
Aleramo, Sibilla. *Diario di una donna. Inediti 1945–1960*. Milan: Feltrinelli, 1978.
Aleramo, Sibilla. *Un amore insolito. Diario, 1940–1944*. Edited by Alba Morino. Milan: Feltrinelli, 1979.

Allam, Malik. *Journaux intimes. Une sociologie de l'écriture personnelle.* Paris: L'Harmattan, 2000.
Alvaro, Corrado. "Quaderno. Alcune pagine di un diario fra il luglio 1943 e il giugno 1944." *Mercurio* vol. 1, no. 4 (December 1944): pp. 9–19.
Alvaro, Corrado. *Quasi una vita. Giornale di uno scrittore.* Milan: Bompiani, 1950.
Amici del Museo del Risorgimento. *Il mito del Risorgimento nell'Italia unita. Atti del convegno: Milano 9–12 novembre 1993.* Milan: Edizioni del comune di Milano, 1995.
Ankersmit, F. R. *Sublime Historical Experience: Cultural Memory in the Present.* Stanford: Stanford University Press, 2005.
Antelme, Robert. *L'espèce humaine.* Paris: Gallimard, 1978.
Antonelli, Quinto. "'Bombe e Madonne': Vita quotidiana nel periodo dell'Alpenvorland (1943–45)" (conference paper).
Antonelli, Quinto. *Storia intima della grande guerra. Lettere, diari e memorie dei soldati dal fronte.* Rome: Donzelli, 2015.
Antonelli, Quinto, ed. *"La propaganda è l'unica nostra cultura." Scritture autobiografiche dal fronte sovietico (1941–1943).* Trento: Fondazione Museo Storico del Trentino, 2015.
Antonelli, Quinto, and Anna Iuso. *Vite di carta.* Naples: L'ancora del Mediterraneo, 2000.
Aquarone, Alberto. "Lo spirito pubblico in Italia alla vigilia della seconda guerra mondiale." *Nord e Sud* vol. 11 (January 1964): pp. 117–25.
Arendt, Hannah. *The Human Condition.* Chicago: University of Chicago Press, 1958.
Ariès, Philippe, and Georges Duby, eds. *A History of Private Life.* 5 vols. Cambridge, Mass.: Belknap Press of Harvard University Press, 1987–1991.
Aronowitz, Stanley. "Between Criticism and Ethnography: Raymond Williams and the Intervention of Cultural Studies." In *Cultural Materialism: On Raymond Williams*, edited by Christopher Prendergast, pp. 320–39. Minneapolis: University of Minnesota Press, 1995.
Arthurs, Joshua, Michael R. Ebner, and Kate Ferris, eds. *The Politics of Everyday Life in Fascist Italy: Outside the State?* New York: Palgrave Macmillan, 2017.
Artom, Emanuele. *Diario di un partigiano ebreo. Gennaio 1940–Febbraio 1944.* Edited by Guri Schwarz. Turin: Bollati-Boringhieri, 2008.
Asor Rosa, Alberto. *Letteratura italiana. La storia, i classici, l'identità nazionale.* Rome: Carocci editore, 2014.
Avagliano, Mario, ed. *Generazione ribelle. Diari e lettere dal 1943 al 1945.* Turin: Einaudi, 2006.
Avagliano, Mario, and Marco Palmieri. *Gli internati militari italiani. Diari e lettere dai lager nazisti (1943–1945).* Turin: Einaudi, 2009.
Avagliano, Mario, and Marco Palmieri. *I militari italiani nei lager nazisti. Una resistenza senz'armi (1943–1945).* Bologna: il Mulino, 2020.
Baggio, Serenella. *"Niente retorica." Liberalismo linguistico nei diari di una signora del Novecento.* Trento: Università degli Studi di Trento, 2012.
Baioni, Massimo. "Un mito per gli italiani: Il Risorgimento tra ricerca storica e discorso pubblico." *Italian Culture* vol. 30, no. 1 (2012): pp. 7–20.
Baldoli, Claudia, Andrew Knapp, and R. J. Overy, eds. *Bombing, States and Peoples in Western Europe, 1940–1945.* London: Continuum, 2011.
Baraitser, Lisa. *Enduring Time.* London: Bloomsbury, 2017.
Barthes, Roland. *Essais critiques.* Paris: Éditions du Seuil, 1964.
Barthes, Roland. *Writing Degree Zero.* London: Cape, 1967.
Barthes, Roland. *Critical Essays.* Evanston, IL: Northwestern University Press, 1972.
Barthes, Roland. *How to Live Together: Novelistic Simulations of Some Everyday Spaces.* New York: Columbia University Press, 2013.

Barthes, Roland, and Eric Marty. "Orale/Scritto." In *Enciclopedia Einaudi*. Vol. 10, *Opinione-Probabilità*, edited by Ruggiero Romano, pp. 60–86. Turin: Einaudi, 1980.
Bartoli Langeli, Attilio and Armando Petrucci, eds. *Alfabetismo e cultura scritta nella storia della società Italiana: Atti del seminario tenutosi a Perugia il 29–30 marzo 1977*. Perugia: Università degli Studi, 1978.
Battaglia, Roberto. *Storia della Resistenza italiana (8 settembre 1943–25 aprile 1945)*. Turin: Einaudi, 1953.
Battini, Michele, and Paolo Pezzino. *Guerra ai civili. Occupazione tedesca e politica del massacro. Toscana 1944*. Venice: Marsilio, 1997.
Bedeschi, Giulio, ed. *Fronte russo: c'ero anch'io*. Vol. 1. Milan: Mursia, 1987.
Belco, Victoria C. *War, Massacre, and Recovery in Central Italy, 1943–1948*. Toronto: University of Toronto Press, 2010.
Bellomo, Probo Bino. *Lettere censurate*. Milan: Longanesi, 1975.
Ben-Ghiat, Ruth. *Fascist Modernities: Italy, 1922–1945*. Berkeley: University of California Press, 2001.
Benveniste, Émile. *Problèmes de linguistíque générale*. 2 vols. Paris: Gallimard, 1966–74.
Bermeo, Nancy. *Ordinary People in Extraordinary Times: The Citizenry and the Breakdown of Democracy*. Princeton: Princeton University Press, 2003.
Bersellini, Guido. *Il riscatto: 8 settembre–25 aprile. Le tesi di Renzo de Felice, Salò, la Resistenza, l'identità della nazione*. Milan: Franco Angeli, 1998.
Betri, Maria Luisa, and Daniela Maldini Chiarito, eds. *Dolce dono graditissimo. La lettera privata dal Settecento al Novecento*. Milan: Franco Angeli, 2000.
Bianchi, Gianfranco. *25 luglio. Crollo di un regime*. Milan: Mursia, 1963.
Bianco, Dante Livio. *Guerra partigiana*. Preface by Norberto Bobbio, Introduction by Nuto Revelli. Turin: Einaudi, 2006.
Bidussa, David. *Il mito del bravo italiano*. Milan: Il Saggiatore, 1994.
Blanchot, Maurice. "Le journal intime et le récit." In *Le Livre à venir*, pp. 252–9. Paris: Gallimard, 1959.
Blanchot, Maurice. "Everyday Speech." *Yale French Studies* no. 73 (1987): pp. 12–20 (issue on Everyday Life).
Bloch, Marc. "Réflexions d'un historien sur les fausses nouvelles de la guerre." *Revue de synthèse historique* vol. 33 (1921): pp. 17–39.
Bloch, Marc. *The Historian's Craft*. Translated by Peter Putnam. New York: Vintage Books, 1953.
Bocca, Giorgio. *Partigiani della montagna. Vita delle Divisioni "Giustizia e Libertà" del Cuneese*. Borgo S. Dalmazzo: Bertello, 1945.
Bocca, Giorgio. *Storia dell'Italia partigiana, settembre 1943-maggio 1945*. Bari: Laterza, 1966.
Boerner, Peter. *Tagebuch*. Stuttgart: Metzler, 1969.
Boerner, Peter. "Place du journal dans la littérature moderne." In *Le Journal intime et ses formes littéraires. Actes du Colloque de septembre 1975*, edited by Victor Del Litto, pp. 217–24. Genève: Librairie Droz, 1978.
Bonacina, Giorgio. *Obiettivo: Italia. I bombardamenti aerei delle città Italiane dal 1940 al 1945*. Milan: Mursia, 1970.
Bonomi, Ivanoe. *Diario di un anno (2 giugno 1943–10 giugno 1944)*. Milan: Garzanti, 1947.
Bosworth, R. J. B. *Mussolini's Italy: Life under the Dictatorship, 1915–1945*. New York: Penguin Books, 2006.
Boyd-Bennett, Harriet. *Opera in Postwar Venice: Cultural Politics and the Avant-Garde*. Cambridge: Cambridge University Press, 2018.

Bravo, Anna, and Anna Maria Bruzzone. *In guerra senza armi. Storie di donne 1940–1945.* Rome-Bari: Laterza, 1995.
Brenta Brcic, Fedora. *Il diario dell'attesa. Storia di una famiglia 1943–1945.* Edited by Maria Trionfi. Rome: Bibliotheka Edizioni, 2013.
Breton, André. *Manifestoes of Surrealism.* Translated by Richard Seaver and Helen R. Lane. Ann Arbor: University of Michigan Press, 1969.
Bunkers, Suzanne L., and Cynthia Anne Huff, eds. *Inscribing the Daily: Critical Essays on Women's Diaries.* Amherst, Mass.: University of Massachusetts Press, 1996.
Burke, Peter, ed. *New Perspectives on Historical Writing.* 2nd edition. University Park: Pennsylvania State University Press, 2001.
Butler, Judith. "Giving an Account of Oneself." *Diacritics* vol. 31, no. 4 (Winter 2001): pp. 22–40.
Butler, Judith. *Giving an Account of Oneself.* New York: Fordham University Press, 2005.
Butor, Michel. *Répertoire.* 5 vols. Paris Editions de Minuit 1982.
Büyükokutan, Barış. *Bound Together: The Secularization of Turkey's Literary Fields and the Western Promise of Freedom.* Ann Arbor: University of Michigan Press, 2021.
Cacciaguerra, Perla. *Vinceremo…Mah!!! Diario di guerra, 4 ottobre 1943–4 maggio 1945.* Empoli: Ibiskos, 2000.
Calamandrei, Franco. "Piero Calamandrei mio padre." In Piero Calamandrei, *Diario, 1939–1945.* 2 vols, Vol. I, pp. vii–xxi. Edited by Giorgio Agosti. Florence: La Nuova Italia, 1982.
Calamandrei, Piero. *Diario, 1939–1945.* 2 vols. Edited by Giorgio Agosti. Florence: La Nuova Italia, 1982.
Cannistraro, Philip ed. *Historical Dictionary of Fascist Italy.* Westport, CT: Greenwood Press, 1982.
Canosa, Romano. *Storia dell'epurazione in Italia. Le sanzioni contro il fascismo (1943–1948).* Milan: Baldini and Castoldi, 1999.
Capogreco, Carlo. *I campi del duce. L'internamento civile nell'Italia fascista.* Turin: Einaudi, 2004.
Caporale, Riccardo. *La "Banda Carità." Storia del Reparto Servizi Speciali (1943–1945).* Lucca: Edizioni S. Marco Litotipo, 2004.
Cappelletti, Ugo. *Firenze in guerra. Cronache degli anni 1940–1945.* Prato: Edizioni del Palazzo, 1984.
Caracciolo di Castagneto, Filippo. *'43–'44. Diario di Napoli.* Florence: Vallecchi, 1964.
Carandini, Andrea. "Presentazione." In Elena Carandini Albertini, *Dal terrazzo. Diario 1943–1944.* Bologna: il Mulino, 1997.
Carandini Albertini, Elena. *Passata la stagione…Diari 1944–1947.* Florence: Passigli, 1989.
Carandini Albertini, Elena. *Dal terrazzo. Diario 1943–1944.* Bologna: il Mulino, 1997.
Carandini Albertini, Elena. *Le case, le cose, le carte. Diari 1948–1950.* Padova: Il Poligrafo, 2007.
Carazzolo, Maria. *Più forte della paura. Diario di guerra e dopoguerra (1938–1947).* Edited by Francesco Selmin with a preface by Ferdinando Camon. Caselle di Sommacampagna: Cierre edizioni, 2007.
Cardona, Giorgio Raimondo. *Antropologia della scrittura.* Turin: Loescher editore, 1981.
Carr, David. *Time, Narrative, and History.* Bloomington: Indiana University Press, 1986.
Cartosio, Bruno. "Memoria e storia: una famiglia tortonese nella guerra (1940–1945)." *Quaderno di storia contemporanea* no. 8 (1990): pp. 57–81.
Casoni, Gaetano. *Diario fiorentino (giugno-agosto 1944).* Florence: G. Civelli, 1946.

Castagnola, Raffaella, Fabrizio Panzera, and Massimiliano Spiga, eds. *Spiriti liberi in Svizzera. La presenza di fuoriusciti italiani nella Confederazione negli anni del fascismo e del nazismo, 1922–1945*. Florence: Franco Cesati editore, 2006.

Castiglioni, Ettore. *Il giorno delle Mésules. Diari di un alpinista antifascista*. Edited by Marco Albino Ferrari. Turin: CDA & Vivalda, 1993. [Milan: Hoepli, 2017.]

Casula, Carlo Felice. *Cattolici comunisti e sinistra cristiana (1938–1945)*. Bologna: il Mulino, 1976.

Cavallo, Pietro. *Italiani in guerra. Sentimenti e immagini dal 1940 al 1943*. Bologna: il Mulino, 1997.

Cavarero, Adriana. *Relating Narratives: Storytelling and Selfhood*. London: Routledge, 2000.

Cavarocchi, Francesca, and Valeria Galimi, eds. *Firenze in guerra 1940–1944. Catalogo della mostra storico-documentaria (Palazzo Medici-Riccardi, ottobre 2014–gennaio 2015)*. Florence: Firenze University Press, 2014.

Caviglia, Enrico. *Diario, aprile 1925–marzo 1945*. Roma: G. Casini, 1952.

Ceccarelli De Grada, Magda. *Giornale del tempo di guerra, 12 giugno 1940–7 maggio 1945*. Bologna: il Mulino, 2011.

Cecchi Pieraccini, Leonetta. *Vecchie agendine (1911–1929)*. Florence: Sansoni, 1960.

Cecchi Pieraccini, Leonetta. *Agendina di guerra (1939–1944)*. Milan: Longanesi, 1964.

Cecchi Pieraccini, Leonetta. *Agendine 1911–1929*. Edited by Isabella D'Amico. Palermo: Sellerio, 2015.

Cerutti, Toni. *Le vite dei Vittoriani. Breve storia dell'autobiografia vittoriana*. Bari: Adriatica, 1981.

Chevallard, Carlo. "Diario di Carlo Chevallard 1942–1945," edited by Riccardo Marchis. In *Torino in guerra tra cronaca e memoria*, edited by Rosanna Roccia and Giorgio Vaccarino, with a Preface by Alessandro Galante Garrone. Turin: Archivio Storico della Città di Torino, 1975.

Chevallard, Carlo. *Diario 1942–1945. Cronache del tempo di guerra*. Turin: Blu Edizioni, 2005.

Chiantaretto, Jean-François. *Écritures de soi et trauma*. Paris: Anthropos, 1998.

Chiodi, Pietro. *Banditi*. Alba: Ed. A.N.P.I., 1946.

Chocheyras, Jacques. "La place du journal intime dans une typologie linguistique des formes littéraires." In *Le Journal intime et ses formes littéraires. Actes du Colloque de septembre 1975*, edited by Victor Del Litto, pp. 225–33. Genève: Librairie Droz, 1978.

Cicchetti, Angelo, and Raul Mordenti. "La scrittura dei libri di famiglia." In *Letteratura italiana*, vol. III, 2. *Le forme del testo. La prosa*, edited by Alberto Asor Rosa, pp. 1117–59. Turin: Einaudi, 1984.

Cicchetti, Angelo, and Raul Mordenti. *I libri di famiglia in Italia*. 2 vols. Rome: Edizioni di storia e letteratura, 1985.

Cipolla, Carlo M. *Literacy and Development in the West*. Baltimore, MD: Penguin Books, 1969.

Cocco, Maurizio. *Qualunquismo, una storia politica e culturale dell'uomo qualunque*. Florence: Edizioni Le Monnier, 2018.

Colarizi, Simona. *L'opinione degli italiani sotto il regime, 1929–1943*. Rome-Bari: Laterza, 2009.

Collina Graziani, Giovanni. *Faenza nel baratro (8 settembre 1943–29 giugno 1945)*. Faenza: Tipografia Faentina, 1989.

Collotti, Enzo. *L'amministrazione tedesca dell'Italia occupata 1943–1945. Studio e documenti*. Milan: Lerici, 1963.

Collotti, Enzo. *Gli italiani sul fronte russo*. Bari: De Donato, 1982.
Collotti, Enzo. "L'occupazione tedesca in Italia." In *Dizionario della Resistenza*, edited by Enzo Collotti, Renato Sandri, and Frediano Sessi. 2 vols. Vol. 1, pp. 43–65. Turin: Einaudi, 2000–1.
Contini, Giovanni. *La memoria divisa*. Milan: Rizzoli, 1997.
Cooke, Philip. *The Legacy of the Italian Resistance*. New York: Palgrave Macmillan, 2011.
Corbin, Alain. "Backstage." In *A History of Private Life. Vol. IV. From the Fire of the Revolution to the Great War*, edited by Michelle Perrot. Translated by Arthur Goldhammer, pp. 421–667. Cambridge, Mass.: Belknap Press, 1990.
Corbolini, Mario. *Dall'Egeo al Baltico. Diario di guerra 8 settembre 1943–17 ottobre 1945*. Trento: Tecnolito, 1992.
Corner, Paul. *The Fascist Party and Popular Opinion in Mussolini's Italy*. Oxford: Oxford University Press, 2012.
Cortesi, Elena. *Reti dentro la guerra. Corrispondenza postale e strategie di sopravvivenza, 1940–1945*. Rome: Carocci editore, 2008.
Cortesi, Elena. *Sfollati, profughi, evacuati. L'Italia nella Seconda Guerra Mondiale*. Pisa: Pacini Editore, 2022.
Cossentino, Raffaele. *La canzone napoletana dalle origini ai nostri giorni. Storia e protagonisti*. Naples: Rogiosi, 2015.
Crainz, Giorgio. *Il diario di Giorgio Crainz*. Online: La Lampadina, 2019. https://www.lalampadina.net/magazine/2019/12/la-lampadina-archivi-di-famiglia-racconti-il-diario-di-giorgio-crainz/
Craveri, Piero. "Postfazione." In Benedetto Croce, *Taccuini di guerra, 1943–1945*, edited by Cinzia Cassani. Milan: Adelphi, 2004.
Croce, Benedetto. *Storia d'Europa nel secolo decimonono*. Bari: Laterza, 1932.
Croce, Benedetto. *Croce, the King and the Allies: Extracts from a Diary by Benedetto Croce, July 1943–June 1944*. Translated by Sylvia Sprigge. New York: Norton, 1950.
Croce, Benedetto. *Scritti e discorsi politici (1943–1947)*. 2 vols. Bari: Laterza, 1963.
Croce, Benedetto. *Taccuini di guerra, 1943–1945*. Edited by Cinzia Cassani. Milan: Adelphi, 2004.
Damiano, Andrea. *Rosso e grigio*. Bologna: il Mulino, 2000.
Darnton, Robert. *The Great Cat Massacre: And Other Episodes in French Cultural History*. New York: Basic Books, 2009 [1984].
David, Michel. "Il problema del diario intimo in Italia." In *"Journal intime" e letteratura moderna. Atti di seminario. Trento, marzo-maggio 1988*, edited by Anna Dolfi, pp. 79–108. Rome: Bulzoni: 1989.
Deakin, Frederick W. *Storia della Repubblica di Salò*. Turin: Einaudi, 1963.
De Certeau, Michel. *The Practice of Everyday Life*. Berkeley: University of California Press, 1984.
De Certeau, Michel. *La Fable mystique, XVIe–XVIIe siècle*. Paris: Gallimard, 1987.
De Felice, Renzo. *Mussolini l'alleato 1940–1945*. 2 vols. Vol. I. *L'Italia in guerra (1940–1943)*. Turin: Einaudi, 1990.
De Felice, Renzo. *Rosso e nero*. Edited by Pasquale Chessa. Milan: Baldini & Castoldi, 1995.
De Felice, Renzo. *Mussolini l'alleato 1940–1945*. 2 vols. Vol. II. *La guerra civile (1943–1945)*. Turin: Einaudi, 1997.
Degli Espinosa, Agostino. *Il Regno del Sud. 8 Settembre 1943–4 Giugno 1944*. Rome: Migliaresi Editore, 1946.
De Grazia, Victoria, and Sergio Luzzatto, eds. *Dizionario del fascismo*. 2 vols. Turin: Einaudi, 2002–3.

De Jaco, Aldo. *La città insorge (le quattro giornate di Napoli)*. Rome: Editori Riuniti, 1956.
Dekker, Rudolf, ed. *Egodocuments and History: Autobiographical Writing in Its Social Context since the Middle Ages*. Hilversum: Verloren, 2002.
Del Boca, Angelo. *Italiani, brava gente? Un mito duro a morire*. Vicenza: Neri Pozza Editore, 2005.
Del Litto, Victor. *Le Journal intime et ses formes littéraires. Actes du colloque de septembre 1975 (Grenoble)*. Genève: Droz, 1978.
Delfini, Antonio. *Diari, 1927-1961*. Edited by Giovanna Delfini and Natalia Ginzburg. Turin: Einaudi, 1982.
Della Santa, Nicola, ed. *I militari italiani internati dai tedeschi dopo l'8 settembre 1943. Atti del convegno di studi*. Florence: ANEI, 1986.
De Luna, Giovanni. *Storia del Partito d'Azione. 1942-1947*. Milan: Feltrinelli, 1982.
Delzell, Charles F. "The Italian Anti-Fascist Emigration 1922-1943." *Journal of Central European Affairs* vol. XII, no. 1 (1952): pp. 20-55.
de Martino, Ernesto. *Il mondo magico. Prolegomeni a una storia del magismo*. Turin: Boringhieri, 1973.
De Mauro, Tullio. *Storia linguistica dell'Italia unita*. Bari: Laterza, 1963.
De Nardi, Sarah. *The Poetics of Conflict Experience: Materiality and Embodiment in Second World War Italy*. London: Routledge, 2018.
De Simone, Cesare. *Venti angeli sopra Roma. I bombardamenti aerei sulla città eterna (19 luglio e 13 agosto 1943)*. Milan: Mursia, 1993.
Di Benigno, Jo'. *Occasioni mancate. Roma in un diario segreto, 1943-1944*. Rome: Edizioni S.E.I., 1945.
Didier, Béatrice. *Le Journal intime*. Paris: Presses universitaires de France, 1976.
Di Nolfo, Ennio. *Le paure e le speranze degli italiani (1943-1953)*. Milan: Mondadori, 1986.
Di Pompeo, Corrado. *Più della fame e più dei bombardamenti. Diario dell'occupazione di Roma*. Preface by Alessandro Portelli. Bologna: il Mulino, 2009.
Di Rienzo, Eugenio. *Benedetto Croce. Gli anni dello scontento (1943-1948)*. Soveria Mannelli: Rubbettino, 2019.
Dix, Hywel Rowland. *After Raymond Williams: Cultural Materialism and the Break-up of Britain*. Cardiff: University of Wales Press, 2008.
Dolfi, Anna, ed. *"Journal intime" e letteratura moderna. Atti di seminario. Trento, marzo-maggio 1988*. Rome: Bulzoni: 1989.
Domenico, Roy Palmer. *Italian Fascists on Trial, 1943-1948*. Chapel Hill: University of North Carolina Press, 1991.
Douglas, Mary. *Purity and Danger: An Analysis of Concepts of Pollution and Taboo*. London: Routledge and Kegan Paul, 1966.
Duggan, Christopher. *Fascist Voices: An Intimate History of Mussolini's Italy*. Oxford: Oxford University Press, 2013.
Eakin, Paul John. *How Our Lives Become Stories: Making Selves*. Ithaca, NY: Cornell University Press, 1999.
Ebner, Michael R. *Ordinary Violence in Mussolini's Italy*. New York: Cambridge University Press, 2011.
Eco, Umberto. "Ur-Fascism." *The New York Review of Books* (June 22, 1995): pp. 12-15.
Eley, Geoff. "Labor History, Social History, 'Alltagsgeschichte': Experience, Culture, and the Politics of the Everyday—a New Direction for German Social History?" *The Journal of Modern History* vol. 61, no. 2 (June 1989): pp. 297-343.
Eley, Geoff. *Nazism as Fascism: Violence, Ideology, and the Ground of Consent in Germany 1930-1945*. London: Routledge, 2013.

"Everyday Life in Nazi Germany." Forum. *German History* vol. 27, no. 4 (2009): pp. 560–79.

Fabre, Daniel, ed. *Par écrit. Ethnologie des écritures quotidiennes*. Paris: Éditions de la Maison des sciences de l'homme, 1997.

Fabre, Daniel. "Vivere, scrivere, archiviare." In *Vite di carta*, edited by Quinto Antonelli and Anna Iuso, pp. 261–84. Naples: L'ancora, 2000.

Fabre, Daniel, et al. *Écritures ordinaires*. Paris: Centre Georges Pompidou, 1993.

Falasca-Zamponi, Simonetta. *Fascist Spectacle: The Aesthetics of Power in Mussolini's Italy*. Berkeley: University of California Press, 1997.

Falasca-Zamponi, Simonetta. "Ordinary Antifascism? Italy and the Fall of Fascism, 1943–1945." *Journal of Modern Italian Studies* vol. 24, no. 1 (2019): pp. 171–89.

Falasca-Zamponi, Simonetta. "Is Democracy in Italy Secure? Fascism's Appeal to Italian Youth is a Worrisome Trend." *Public Seminar* (January 13, 2020), online. https://publicseminar.org/essays/is-democracy-in-italy-secure/

Falasca-Zamponi, Simonetta. "History, Ordinary Culture, and 'Structure of Feeling': Revisiting Raymond Williams." *Il Pensiero Storico* no. 7 (June 2020): pp. 99–118.

Falaschi, Giovanni, ed. *La letteratura partigiana in Italia 1943–1945*. Preface by Natalia Ginzburg. Rome: Editori Riuniti, 1984.

Faustini, Gianni, ed. *Per una storia d'Italia del 1943. Le cronache di Roberto Suster e altri scritti*. Trento: Museo storico in Trento, 2005.

Favai, Fortunato. *Opzioni, guerra e resistenza nelle valli ladine. Il diario di Fortunato Favai: Livinallongo, 1939–1945*. Edited by Luciana Palla. Trento: Museo storico in Trento, 2000.

Felski, Rita. "The Invention of Everyday Life." In *Doing Time: Feminist Theory and Postmodern Culture*, pp. 77–98. New York: New York University Press, 2000.

Ferioli, Alessandro. "Dai lager nazisti all'esercito di Mussolini. Gli internati militari italiani che aderirono alla Repubblica Sociale Italiana." *Nuova Storia Contemporanea* no. 5 (September–October 2005): pp. 63–88.

ffytche, Matt. "Psychoanalytic Sociology and the Traumas of History: Alexander Mitscherlich Between the Disciplines." *History of the Human Sciences* vol. 30, no. 5 (2017): pp. 3–29.

Fiori, Giovannino. *La memoria della gente comune. Nel cinquantesimo anniversario della Liberazione di Caprese Michelangelo*. Anghiari: I.T.E.A., 1994.

Focardi, Filippo. *La guerra della memoria. La Resistenza nel dibattito politico italiano dal 1945 a oggi*. Rome-Bari: Laterza, 2005.

Focardi, Filippo. *Il cattivo tedesco e il bravo italiano. La rimozione delle colpe della seconda guerra mondiale*. Rome-Bari: Laterza, 2013.

Focardi, Filippo, and Lutz Klinkhammer, "The Question of Fascist Italy's War Crimes: The Construction of a Self-Acquitting Myth (1943–1948)." *Journal of Modern Italian Studies* vol. 9, no. 3 (2004): pp. 330–48.

Folena, Gianfranco. "Premessa." *Quaderni di retorica e poetica*, issue on Le forme del diario, vol. 2 (1985): pp. 5–10.

Folkenflik, Robert, ed. *The Culture of Autobiography: Constructions of Self-representation*. Stanford, CA: Stanford University Press, 1993.

Forlenza, Rosario. *On the Edge of Democracy: Italy, 1943–1948*. Oxford: Oxford University Press, 2019.

Fothergill, Robert. *Private Chronicles: A Study of English Diaries*. London: Oxford University Press, 1974.

Foucault, Michel. *Language, Counter-memory, Practice: Selected Essays and Interviews*. Ithaca, NY: Cornell University Press, 1977.

Foucault, Michel. *The Care of the Self*. New York: Vintage, 1988.

Foucault, Michel. *Ethics: Subjectivity and Truth*. Edited by Paul Rabinow, translated by Robert Hurley et al. In *Essential Works of Foucault 1954-1984*. Vol. 1. New York: New Press, 1997.
Fucci, Franco. *Le polizie di Mussolini. La repressione dell'antifascismo nel "ventennio."* Milan: Mursia, 1985.
Gabriotti, Venanzio. *Diario 25 luglio 1943-4 maggio 1944*. Edited by Alvaro Tacchini, preface by Mario Tosti. Città di Castello: Petruzzi editore, 1998.
Gaggero Viale, Caterina. *Diario di guerra della zona intemelia 1943-1945*. Pinerolo: Alzani, 1999.
Gallerano, Nicola. "Il fronte interno attraverso i rapporti delle autorità (1942-1943)." *Il Movimento di Liberazione in Italia* no. 109 (1972): pp. 4-32.
Gallerano, Nicola, ed. *L'altro dopoguerra. Roma e il Sud 1943-1945*. Preface by Guido Quazza, with an Introduction by Enzo Forcella. Milan: Franco Angeli, 1985.
Gallerano, Nicola, ed. *La Resistenza tra storia e memoria*. Milan: Mursia, 1999.
Gallerano, Nicola, Luigi Ganapini, and Massimo Legnani. *L'Italia dei quarantacinque giorni. Studio e documenti. 1943. 25 luglio-8 settembre*. Milan: Istituto nazionale per la storia del movimento di liberazione, 1969.
Galli della Loggia, Ernesto. *La morte della patria. La crisi dell'idea di nazione tra Resistenza, antifascismo e Repubblica*. Rome-Bari: Laterza, 1996.
Ganapini, Luigi. *Una città, la guerra. Lotte di classe, ideologie e forze politiche a Milano, 1939-1951*. Milan: Franco Angeli, 1988.
Ganapini, Luigi. *Voci dalla guerra civile. Italiani nel 1943-1945*. Bologna: il Mulino, 2012.
Gargano, Pietro. "Simmo 'e Napule, paisà." *Il Mattino*. February 11, 2007.
Garofalo, Piero, Elizabeth Leake, and Dana Renga. *Internal Exile in Fascist Italy: History and Representations of Confino*. Manchester: Manchester University Press, 2019.
Garosci, Aldo. *Storia dei fuoriusciti*. Bari: Laterza, 1953.
Gentile, Carlo. *I crimini di guerra tedeschi in Italia, 1943-1945*. Turin: Einaudi, 2015.
Gentile, Emilio. *25 Luglio 1943*. Bari-Rome: Laterza, 2018.
Gentiloni Silveri, Umberto, and Maddalena Carli, eds. *Bombardare Roma. Gli Alleati e la "città aperta" (1940-1944)*. Bologna: il Mulino, 2007.
Gibelli, Antonio. "Pratica della scrittura e mutamento sociale. Orientamento e ipotesi." In *Per un archivio della scrittura popolare. Atti del seminario nazionale di studi di Rovereto 2-3 ottobre 1987*, pp. 7-20. Mori (TN): Editrice La grafica, 1987.
Gibelli, Antonio et al. *Per un archivio della scrittura popolare: Atti del seminario nazionale di studio: Rovereto 2-3 Ottobre 1987*. Mori (TN): La grafica, 1987.
Gibelli, Antonio. *La Grande Guerra degli italiani 1915-1918*. Milan: Sansoni, 1998.
Ginsborg, Paul. *A History of Contemporary Italy: Society and Politics, 1943-1988*. London: Penguin, 1990.
Gioannini, Marco, and Giulio Massobrio. *Bombardate l'Italia. Storia della guerra di distruzione aerea, 1940-1945*. Milan: Rizzoli, 2007.
Giovannini, Paolo, and Marco Palla, eds. *Il fascismo dalle mani sporche. Dittatura, corruzione, affarismo*. Bari-Rome: Laterza, 2019.
Girard, Alain. *Le Journal intime et la notion de personne*. Paris: Presses universitaires de France, 1963.
Gnoli, Antonio. "Fucilavamo i fascisti e non me ne pento." Interview with Nuto Revelli. *La Repubblica* (October 16, 1991).
Gobetti Marchesini Prospero, Ada. *Diario partigiano*. Turin: Einaudi, 1956.
Gobetti, Eric. *Alleati del nemico. L'occupazione italiana in Jugoslavia (1941-1943)*. Rome-Bari: Laterza, 2013.

Goebbels, Joseph. *The Goebbels Diaries, 1942–1943*. Edited by Louis Paul Lochner. Garden City, NY: Doubleday, 1948.
Goldmann, Lucien. *Recherches dialectiques*. Paris: Gallimard, 1959.
Goody, Jack, ed. *Literacy in Traditional Societies*. Cambridge: Cambridge University Press, 1968.
Goody, Jack. *The Domestication of the Savage Mind*. Cambridge: Cambridge University Press, 1977.
Goody, Jack. *The Interface Between the Written and the Oral*. Cambridge: Cambridge University Press, 1987.
Goody, Jack. *The Logic of Writing and the Organization of Society*. Cambridge: Cambridge University Press, 2001.
Gouldner, Alvin. "Sociology and the Everyday Life." In *The Idea of Social Structure: Papers in Honor of Robert K. Merton*, edited by Lewis A. Coser, pp. 417–32. New York: Harcourt Brace Jovanovich Inc., 1975.
Graff, Harvey J. *The Legacies of Literacy: Continuities and Contradictions in Western Culture and Society*. Bloomington: Indiana University Press, 1987.
Greppi, Carlo. *Uomini in grigio. Storie di gente comune nell'Italia della guerra civile*. Milan: Feltrinelli, 2016.
Gribaudi, Gabriella. *Guerra totale. Tra bombe alleate e violenze naziste. Napoli e il fronte meridionale, 1940–44*. Turin: Bollati Boringhieri, 2005.
Gribaudi, Gabriella. "The True Cause of the 'Moral Collapse': People, Fascists and Authorities under the Bombs. Naples and the Countryside, 1940–1944." In *Bombing, States and Peoples in Western Europe 1940–1945*, edited by Claudia Baldoli, Andrew Knapp, and Richard Overy, pp. 219–37. London: Continuum, 2011.
Gribaudi, Gabriella. *Combattenti, sbandati, prigionieri. Esperienze e memorie di reduci della seconda guerra mondiale*. Rome: Donzelli editore, 2016.
Guareschi, Giovanni. *Diario clandestino, 1943–1945*. Milan: Rizzoli, 1949.
Guglielminetti, Marziano. *Memoria e scrittura. L'autobiografia da Dante a Cellini*. Turin: Einaudi, 1977.
Gundle, Stephen, Christopher Duggan, and Giuliana Pieri, eds. *The Cult of the Duce: Mussolini and the Italians*. Manchester: Manchester University Press, 2013.
Gusdorf, Georges. *La découverte de soi*. Paris: Presses universitaires de France, 1948.
Gusdorf, Georges. *Speaking (La Parole)*. Evanston, IL: Northwestern University Press, 1965.
Gusdorf, Georges. *Auto-bio-graphie*. Paris: Éditions O. Jacob, 1991.
Gusdorf, Georges. *Les écritures du moi*. Paris: Éditions O. Jacob, 1991.
Halfin, Igal. *Terror in My Mind: Communist Autobiographies on Trial*. Cambridge, Mass.: Harvard University Press, 2003.
Hammermann, Gabriele. *Gli internati militari italiani in Germania. 1943–1945*. Bologna: il Mulino, 2004.
Hartog, François. *Regimes of Historicity: Presentism and the Experiences of Time*. New York: Columbia University Press, 2015.
Harvey, Elizabeth, Johannes Hürter, Maiken Umbach, and Andreas Wirsching, eds. *Private Life and Privacy in Nazi Germany*. Cambridge: Cambridge University Press, 2019.
Heilbrun, Carolyn G. *Writing a Woman's Life*. New York: W.W. Norton & Company, 2008.
Hellbeck, Jochen. "Russian Autobiographical Practice." In *Autobiographical Practices in Russia. Autobiographische Praktiken in Russland*, edited by Jochen Hellbeck and Klaus Heller, pp. 278–98. Göttingen: V & R Unipress, 2004.
Hellbeck, Jochen. *Revolution on My Mind: Writing a Diary under Stalin*. Cambridge, Mass.: Harvard University Press, 2006.

Heller, Agnes. *Everyday Life*. London: Routledge and Kegan Paul, 1984.
Higgins, John. *Raymond Williams: Literature, Marxism and Cultural Materialism*. London: Routledge, 1999.
Hitchcock, Tim. "A New History from Below." *History Workshop Journal* vol. 5, no. 7 (2004): pp. 294-8.
Hollier, Denis, ed. *The College of Sociology 1937-39*. Minneapolis: University of Minnesota Press, 1988.
Hunt, Lynn. "The Self and Its History." *The American Historical Review* vol. 119, no. 5 (2014): pp. 1576-86.
Imbriani, Angelo Michele. *Gli italiani e il Duce. Il mito e l'immagine di Mussolini negli ultimi anni del fascismo (1938-1943)*. Naples: Liguori, 1992.
Imbriani, Angelo Michele. *Vento del Sud. Moderati, reazionari, qualunquisti (1943-1948)*. Bologna: il Mulino, 1996.
Isnenghi, Mario. "Intervento di discussione." In *Per un archivio della scrittura popolare: Atti del seminario nazionale di studio: Rovereto 2-3 Ottobre 1987*, pp. 195-206. Mori (TN): La grafica, 1987.
Istituto Veneto per la storia della Resistenza. *Tedeschi, partigiani e popolazioni nell'Alpenvorland (1943-1945)*. Atti del convegno di Belluno 1983. Venice: Marsilio, 1984.
Janoff-Bulman, Ronnie. *Shattered Assumptions (Towards a New Psychology of Trauma)*. New York: Free Press, 1992.
Jay, Martin. *Cultural Semantics: Keywords of Our Time*. Amherst: University of Massachusetts Press, 1998.
Jay, Martin. *Songs of Experience: Modern American and European Variations on a Universal Theme*. Berkeley: University of California Press, 2005.
Katz, Robert. *Death in Rome*. New York: Macmillan, 1967.
Katz, Robert. *Morte a Roma. La storia ancora sconosciuta del massacro delle Fosse Ardeatine*. Rome: Editori Riuniti, 1967.
Kellner, Robert Scott, ed. *My Opposition: The Diary of Friedrich Kellner. A German against the Third Reich*. Cambridge: Cambridge University Press, 2018.
Klinkhammer, Lutz. *L'occupazione tedesca in Italia, 1943-1945*. Turin: Bollati Boringhieri, 1993.
Koselleck, Reinhart. *Futures Past: On the Semantics of Historical Time*. New York: Columbia University Press, 2004.
Koselleck, Reinhart. *Sediments of Time: On Possible Histories*. Palo Alto: Stanford University Press, 2018.
Kracauer, Siegfried, and Paul Oskar Kristeller. *History: The Last Things before the Last*. New York: Oxford University Press, 1969.
Kuby, Erich. *Il tradimento tedesco*. Milan: Rizzoli, 1987.
La ricerca folklorica. La Scrittura: Funzioni e Ideologie. Vol. 5 (1982).
Labanca, Nicola ed. *Fra sterminio e sfruttamento. Militari internati e prigionieri di guerra nella Germania nazista, 1939-1945*. Florence: Le Lettere, 1992.
Landes, David S. *Revolution in Time: Clocks and the Making of the Modern World*. Cambridge, Mass.: Harvard University Press, 2000.
Landi, Sandra. *La guerra narrata. Materiale biografico orale e scritto sulla seconda guerra mondiale raccolto a Certaldo*. Venice: Marsilio, 1989.
La Rovere, Luca. *L'eredità del fascismo. Gli intellettuali, i giovani e la transizione al postfascismo 1943-1948*. Turin: Bollati Boringhieri, 2008.
Lefebvre, Henri. *Critique de la vie quotidienne*. Tome I: *Introduction*. Paris: Grasset, 1947.
Lefebvre, Henri. *Rhythmanalysis: Space, Time and Everyday Life*. London: Continuum, 2004.

Lefebvre, Henri. *Critique of Everyday Life*. The One-Volume Edition. London: Verso, 2014.
Lejeune, Philippe. *L'Autobiographie en France*. Paris: Colin, 1971.
Lejeune, Philippe. *Le Pacte autobiographique*. Paris: Éditions du Seuil, 1975.
Lejeune, Philippe. *Le Moi des demoiselles. Enquête sur le journal de jeune fille*. Paris: Éditions du Seuil, 1993.
Lejeune, Philippe, and Catherine Bogaert. *Le journal intime. Histoire et anthologie*. Paris: Textuel, 2006.
Lepre, Aurelio. *L'occhio del Duce. Gli italiani e la censura di guerra, 1940–1943*. Milan: Mondadori, 1992.
Lepri, Sergio, Francesco Arbitrio, and Giuseppe Cultrera. *Informazione e potere in un secolo di storia italiana. L'agenzia Stefani da Cavour a Mussolini*. Florence: Le Monnier, 1999.
Leto, Guido. *OVRA. Fascismo-antifascismo*. Rocca San Casciano: Cappelli editore, 1952.
Levi, Primo. *I sommersi e i salvati*. Turin: Einaudi, 1986.
Levi, Primo. *The Drowned and the Saved*. New York: Vintage, 1989.
Levis Sullam, Simon. *The Italian Executioners: The Genocide of the Jews of Italy*. Translated by Oona Smyth, and Claudia Patane. Princeton: Princeton University Press, 2018.
Lignani, Antonella, and Alvaro Tacchini, eds., *Giulio Pierangeli. Scritti politici e memorie di guerra*. Città di Castello: Petruzzi editore, 2003.
Lo Biundo, Ester. *London Calling Italy. La propaganda di Radio Londra nel 1943*. Milan: Unicopli, 2014.
Lo Biundo, Ester. "'The War of Nerves.' Le trasmissioni di Radio Londra da El Alamein all'operazione Husky." *Meridiana. Rivista di storia e scienze sociali* no. 82 (2015): pp. 13–35.
Lo Biundo, Ester. "Voices of Occupiers/Liberators: The BBC's Radio Propaganda in Italy between 1942 and 1945." *Journal of War and Cultural Studies* vol. 9, no. 1 (2016): pp. 60–73.
Longo, Luigi. *Un popolo alla macchia*. Milan: Mondadori 1947.
Lorenzon, Erika. *Lo sguardo lontano. L'Italia della seconda guerra mondiale nella memoria dei prigionieri di guerra*. Venice: Edizioni Ca' Foscari, 2018.
Lowenthal, David. *The Past Is a Foreign Country*. Cambridge: Cambridge University Press, 1990.
Lüdtke, Alf, ed. *The History of Everyday Life: Reconstructing Historical Experiences and Ways of Life*. Princeton: Princeton University Press, 1995.
Lüdtke, Alf, ed. *Everyday Life in Mass Dictatorship: Collusion and Evasion*. New York: Palgrave Macmillan, 2016.
Lukács, Georg. *Soul and Form*. Edited by John T. Sanders and Katie Terezakis. London: Merlin Press, 1994.
Lyons, Martyn. *Ordinary Writings, Personal Narratives: Writing Practices in 19th and Early 20th-Century Europe*. Bern: P. Lang, 2007.
Lyons, Martyn. *The Writing Culture of Ordinary People in Europe, c. 1860–1920*. Cambridge: Cambridge University Press, 2013.
Maestro, Leone. *Meditazioni. Carte scelte di un medico ebreo (1939–1944)*. Livorno: Belforte-Salomone, 2015.
Mafai, Miriam. *Pane nero. Donne e vita quotidiana nella seconda guerra mondiale*. Milan: Mondadori, 1987.
Malgeri, Francesco. *La sinistra cristiana (1937–1945)*. Brescia: Morcelliana, 1982.
Mangoni, Luisa. "Civiltà della crisi. Gli intellettuali tra fascismo e antifascismo." In *Storia dell'Italia repubblicana*. Vol. 1, *La costruzione della democrazia*, edited by Francesco Barbagallo. Turin: Einaudi, 1994.

Marabini, Claudio. *Quell'autunno del 1943...Diario 1943-46 di Wanda Affricano-Marabini*. Self-published (2019).
Marchesini, Daniele. *Il bisogno di scrivere. Usi della scrittura nell'Italia moderna*. Rome-Bari: Laterza, 1992.
Marello, Gualtiero. *Prigioniero 589. Appunti di prigionia di un tenente medico*. Asti: Espansione Grafica, 2002.
Martinelli, Franco. *L'Ovra. Fatti e retroscena della polizia politica fascista*. Milan: G. De Veccchi, 1967.
Martinelli, Renzo. *Il fronte interno a Firenze, 1940-1943. Lo spirito pubblico nelle "informazioni fiduciarie" della polizia politica*. Florence: Dipartimento di storia, 1989.
Martini, Andrea. *Dopo Mussolini. I processi ai fascisti e ai collaborazionisti (1944-1953)*. Rome: Viella, 2019.
Mascuch, Michael. *Origins of the Individualist Self: Autobiography and Self-Identity in England, 1591-1791*. Cambridge: Polity Press, 1997.
Mason, Timothy W. *Nazism, Fascism and the Working Class*. Edited by Jane Caplan. Cambridge: Cambridge University Press, 1995.
Maynes, Mary Jo, Jennifer L. Pierce, and Barbara Laslett. *Telling Stories: The Use of Personal Narratives in the Social Sciences and History*. Ithaca, NY: Cornell University Press, 2008.
Melograni, Piero. *Rapporti segreti della polizia fascista, 1938-1940*. Rome-Bari: Laterza, 1979.
Menestrina, *Sotto le bombe, diario 1943-1945*. Trento: Museo storico in Trento, 2004-2005.
Merleau-Ponty, Maurice. *Phenomenology of Perception*. New York: Humanities Press, 1962.
Merleau-Ponty, Maurice. *Adventures of the Dialectic*. Translated by Joseph Bien. Evanston: Northwestern University Press, 1973.
Middleton, Peter. "Why Structure of Feeling?" *News from Nowhere* no. 6 (1989): pp. 50-7.
Misch, Georg. *Geschichte der Autobiographie*. Leipzig/Berlin: Druck und Verlag von B. G. Teubner, 1907.
Mitchell, W. J. T., ed. *On Narrative*. Chicago: University of Chicago Press, 1981.
Mitscherlich, Alexander, and Margarete Mitscherlich. *The Inability to Mourn: Principles of Collective Behavior*. New York: Grove Press, 1975.
Monchieri, Lino. *Diario di prigionia 1943-1945*. Brescia: Voce del Popolo, 1969.
Monelli, Paolo. *Roma 1943*. Rome: Migliaresi, 1945.
Moore, Barrington Jr. *Injustice: The Social Bases of Obedience and Revolt*. White Plains, NY: M.E. Sharpe, 1978.
Mordenti, Raul. *I libri di famiglia in Italia*, II, Geografia e storia. Rome: Edizioni di storia e letteratura, 2001.
Morgan, Philip. *The Fall of Mussolini: Italy, the Italians, and the Second World War*. Oxford: Oxford University Press, 2007.
Morris, Pam, ed. *The Bakhtin Reader: Selected Writings of Bakhtin, Medvedev and Voloshinov*. London: Arnold, 1994.
Nolan, Mary. "How Germans Saw Hitler." *The New York Times*. August 9, 1987.
Nubola, Cecilia, Paolo Pezzino, and Toni Rovatti eds. *Giustizia straordinaria tra fascismo e democrazia. I processi presso le Corti d'assise e nei tribunali militari*. Bologna: il Mulino, 2019.
Oakeshott, Michael. *Experience and Its Modes*. New York: Cambridge University Press, 2015.
Oliva, Gianni. *I vinti e i liberati. 8 settembre 1943-25 aprile 1945. Storia di due anni*. Milan: Mondadori, 1994.
Oliva, Gianni. *"Si ammazza troppo poco." I crimini di guerra italiani 1940-43*. Milan: Mndadori, 2006.

Olney, James, ed. *Autobiography: Essays Theoretical and Critical.* Princeton: Princeton University Press, 1980.
Ong, Walter J. *Orality and Literacy: The Technologizing of the Word.* London: Routledge, 2002.
Origo, Iris. *War in Val D'Orcia: An Italian War Diary, 1943–1944.* London: Jonathan Cape, 1947.
Origo, Iris. *A Chill in the Air: An Italian War Diary, 1939–1940.* London: Pushkin Press, 2017.
Osborne, Peter. *The Politics of Time: Modernity and Avant-Garde.* London: Verso, 1995.
Paggi, Leonardo. *Storia e memoria di un massacro ordinario.* Rome: Manifestolibri, 1996.
Paggi, Leonardo. *Il "popolo dei morti." La repubblica italiana nata dalla guerra (1940–1946).* Bologna: il Mulino, 2009.
Paliotti, Vittorio. *Storia della canzone napoletana.* Rome: Newton Compton, 1992.
Paolisso, Irene. *Un diario.* In Domenico Sciamanda, *L'autunno nero del '43. Fascisti e antifascisti a Regina Coeli.* Florence: Giunti Gruppo Editoriale, 1993.
Papa, Emilio R. *Storia di due manifesti. Il fascismo e la cultura italiana.* Milan: Feltrinelli, 1958.
Paperno, Irina. "What Can Be Done with Diaries?" *The Russian Review* no. 63 (October 2004): pp. 561–73.
Paperno, Irina. *Stories of the Soviet Experience: Memoirs, Diaries, Dreams.* Ithaca, NY: Cornell University Press, 2009.
Papini, Giovanni. *Diario.* Florence: Vallecchi, 1962.
Papini, Giovanni, and Ardengo Soffici. *Carteggio.* Vol. IV, *1919–1956. Dal primo al secondo dopoguerra.* Edited by Mario Richter. Rome: Edizioni di storia e letteratura, 2002.
Parkinson, Anna M. *An Emotional State: The Politics of Emotion in Postwar West German Culture.* Ann Arbor: University of Michigan Press, 2015.
Parisella, Antonio. *Sopravvivere liberi. Riflessioni sulla storia della Resistenza a cinquant'anni dalla Liberazione.* Roma: Gangemi Editore, 1997.
Passerini, Luisa. *Fascism in Popular Memory: The Cultural Experience of the Turin Working Class.* New York: Cambridge University Press, 1987.
Passerini, Luisa, and Alexander C. T. Geppert, eds. *Historein.* "Sprcial issue on "European Ego-histories: Historiography and the Self, 1970–2000" Vol. 3 (2001) (on "European Ego-histories: Historiography and the Self, 1970–2000").
Patricelli, Marco. *L'Italia sotto le bombe. Guerra aerea e vita civile, 1940–1945.* Rome-Bari: Laterza, 2007.
Pavone, Claudio. "La continuità dello Stato. Istituzioni e uomini." In *Italia 1945–48. Le origini della Repubblica,* edited by Enzo Piscitelli et al. Turin: G. Giappichelli Editore, 1974.
Pavone, Claudio. *Una guerra civile. Saggio storico sulla moralità nella Resistenza.* Turin: Bollati Boringhieri, 1991.
Pavone, Claudio. "Sulla moralità nella Resistenza. Conversazione con Claudio Pavone condotta da Daniele Borioli e Roberto Botta." *Quaderno di storia contemporanea* no. 10 (1991): pp. 19–42.
Pavone, Claudio. "Caratteri ed eredità della 'zona grigia.'" *Passato e presente* vol. XVI, no. 43 (1998): pp. 5–12.
Pavone, Claudio. *A Civil War. A History of the Italian Resistance.* Translated by Peter Levy with the assistance of David Broder. Edited with an Introduction by Stanislao G. Pugliese. London: Verso, 2013.
Pecchioli, Ugo. "Perché si è riaperto il dibattito su fascismo e antifascismo." *Rinascita,* no. 8 (March 9, 1985): pp. 6–9.

Perec, Georges. *Species of Spaces and Other Pieces*. Translated by John Sturrock. London: Penguin, 2008.
Perec, Georges. *An Attempt at Exhausting a Place in Paris*. Translated by Marc Lowenthal. Cambridge, Mass.: Wakefield Press, 2010.
Perfetti, Francesco. "Prefazione." In Ardengo Soffici, *Sull'orlo dell'abisso. Diario 1939-1943*. Milan: Luni, 2000.
Perfetti, Francesco. *Assassinio di un filosofo*. Florence: Le Lettere, 2004.
Peroni, Angelo, with Guido Petter. *Adolescenti particolari. Analisi psicologica del diario di un adolescente impegnato*. Gardolo (TN): Edizioni Erickson, 2005.
Petrella, Luigi. *Staging the Fascist War: The Ministry of Propaganda and the Italian Home Front, 1938-1943*. Bern: Peter Lang, 2016.
Petrillo, Paolo Emilio. *Lacerazione/Der Riss. 1915-1943: I nodi irrisolti tra Italia e Germania*. Rome: La lepre edizioni, 2014.
Petrucci, Armando. *La scrittura di Francesco Petrarca*. Città del Vaticano: Biblioteca Apostolica Vaticana, 1967.
Petrucci, Armando. "Per la storia dell'alfabetismo e della cultura scritta: metodi—materiali—quesiti." *Quaderni storici* vol. 13, no. 38 (2) (May–August 1978): pp. 451-65.
Petrucci, Armando. *La scrittura. Ideologia e rappresentazione*. Turin: Einaudi, 1986.
Peukert, Detlev. *Inside Nazi Germany: Conformity, Opposition, and Racism in Everyday Life*. Translated by Richard Deveson. New Haven: Yale University Press, 1987.
Pezzino, Paolo. *Memory and Massacre: Revisiting Sant'Anna di Stazzema*. New York: Palgrave Macmillan, 2012.
Piccialuti Caprioli, Maura, ed. *Radio Londra 1940-1945. Inventario delle trasmissioni per l'Italia*. Rome: Ministero per i Beni Culturali e Ambientali, 1975.
Piccialuti Caprioli, Maura. *Radio Londra 1939-1945*. Rome-Bari: Laterza, 1979.
Piscitelli, Enzo, et al. *Italia 1945-48. Le origini della Repubblica*. Turin: G. Giappichelli Editore, 1974.
Port, Andrew. "History from Below, the History of Everyday Life, and Microhistory." In *International Encyclopedia of the Social and Behavioral Sciences*. Vol. 11, edited by James D. Wright. Amsterdam: Elsevier, 2015. 2nd edition.
Portelli, Alessandro. *The Order Has Been Carried Out: History, Memory, and Meaning of a Nazi Massacre in Rome*. New York: Palgrave, 2007.
Porter, Roy, ed. *Rewriting the Self: Histories from the Renaissance to the Present*. London: Routledge, 1997.
Prendergast, Christopher, ed. *Cultural Materialism: On Raymond Williams*. Minneapolis: University of Minnesota Press, 1995.
Preti fiorentini. *Giorni di guerra 1943-1945. Lettere al Vescovo*. Edited by Giulio Villani, Preface by Pier Luigi Ballini. Florence: Libreria editrice fiorentina, 1992.
Prezzolini, Giuseppe. *Diario. 1942-1968*. Milan: Rusconi, 1980.
Quatermaine, Luisa. *Mussolini's Last Republic: Propaganda and Politics in the Italian Social Republic (R.S.I.) 1943-45*. Bristol: Intellect Ltd., 2000.
Quazza, Guido. *Resistenza e storia d'Italia. Problemi e ipotesi di ricerca*. Milan: Feltrinelli, 1976.
Quazza, Guido, ed. *Gli italiani sul fronte russo*. Bari: De Donato, 1982.
Radway, Janice. *Reading the Romance: Women, Patriarchy, and Popular Literature*. Chapel Hill: The University of North Carolina Press, 1984.
Rahimi, Sadeq. *Meaning, Madness and Political Subjectivity: A Study of Schizophrenia and Culture in Turkey*. London: Routledge, 2015.
Rahimi, Sadeq. "Haunted Metaphor, Transmitted Affect: The Pantemporality of Subjective Experience." *Subjectivity* vol. 9, no. 1 (2016): pp. 83-105.

Rastelli, Achille. *Bombe sulla città. Gli attacchi alleati. Le vittime civili a Milano*. Milan: Mursia, 2000.
Revelli, Marco. "A Fragile Political Sphere." *Journal of Modern Italian Studies* vol. 18, no. 3 (June 2013): pp. 296–308.
Revelli, Nuto. *Mai tardi. Diario di un alpino in Russia*. Cuneo: Panfilo editore, 1946.
Revelli, Nuto. *La strada del Davai*. Turin: Einaudi, 1966.
Revelli, Nuto. *L'ultimo fronte. Lettere di soldati caduti o dispersi nella seconda guerra mondiale.* Turin: Einaudi, 1971.
Revelli, Nuto. *Il mondo dei vinti*. Turin: Einaudi, 1977.
Ricœur, Paul. *Time and Narrative*. Chicago: University of Chicago Press, 1984–88.
Ricoeur, Paul. *Oneself as Another*. Chicago: University of Chicago Press, 1996.
Ripa di Meana, Fulvia. *Roma clandestina*. Rome: Edizioni Polilibraria 1945.
Rizi, Fabio Fernando. *Benedetto Croce and Italian Fascism*. Toronto: University of Toronto Press, 2003.
Rizzi, Loris. *Lo sguardo del potere. La censura militare in Italia nella seconda guerra mondiale 1943–45*. Milan: Rizzoli, 1984.
Robinett, Jane. "The Narrative Shape of Traumatic Experience." *Literature and Medicine* vol. 26, no. 2 (Fall 2007): pp. 290–311.
Rochat, Giorgio. "L'armistizio dell'8 settembre 1943." In *Dizionario della Resistenza*, edited by Enzo Collotti, Renato Sandri, and Frediano Sessi, Vol. I, *Storia e geografia della Liberazione*, pp. 32–42. Turin: Einaudi, 2000.
Rochat, Giorgio. *Le guerre italiane 1935–1943. Dall'impero di Etiopia alla disfatta*. Turin: Einaudi, 2005.
Rodogno, Davide. *Il nuovo ordine mediterraneo. Le politiche di occupazione dell'Italia fascista in Europa (1940–1943)*. Turin: Bollati-Boringhieri, 2003.
Rogari, Sandro. "L'opinione pubblica in Toscana di fronte alla guerra (1939–1943)." *Nuova Antologia* vol. 557, no. 2162 (April–June 1987): pp. 344–77.
Rossaro, Antonio. *Diario 1943–45. Il tempo delle bombe*. Rovereto: Museo storico italiano della guerra, 1993.
Rossi, Antonio. *Deportato n. 5500. 8 settembre 1943–6 settembre 1945*. Fasano (BA): Schena editore, 2005.
Rousset, Jean. "Le Journal intime. Texte sans destinataire?" *Poétique* vol. 14, no. 56 (1983): pp. 435–43.
Rusconi, Gian Enrico. *Se cessiamo di essere una nazione. Tra etnodemocrazie regionali e cittadinanza europea*. Bologna: il Mulino, 1993.
Rusconi, Gian Enrico. *Resistenza e postfascismo*. Bologna: il Mulino, 1995.
Salvati, Mariuccia. *Il regime e gli impiegati. La nazionalizzazione piccolo-borghese nel ventennio fascista*. Rome-Bari: Laterza, 1992.
Salvati, Mariuccia. *Passaggi. Italiani dal fascismo alla Repubblica*. Rome: Carocci editore, 2016.
Sammarco, Paolo. *Fronte interno*. Milan: Sonzogno, 1942.
Santomassimo, Gianpasquale. "Antifascismo Popolare." *Italia Contemporanea* vol. 32, no. 140 (July–September 1980): pp. 39–68.
Sartori, Giacomo. *Sono Dio*. Milan: Enne Enne, 2016.
Sassoon, Donald. "Italy after Fascism: The Predicament of Dominant Narratives." In *Life after Death: Approaches to a Cultural and Social History of Europe during the 1940s and 1950s*, edited by Richard Bessel and Dirk Schumann, pp. 259–90. Cambridge: Cambridge University Press, 2003.
Sassu, Aligi. *Un grido di colore. Autobiografia*. Lugano: Todaro, 1998.

Satta, Salvatore. *De profundis*. Edited by Remo Bodei. Nuoro: Ilisso Edizioni, 2003 [1948].
Savarese, Nino. *Cronachetta siciliana dell'estate 1943*. Caltanissetta: Salvatore Sciascia editore, 1963 [1945].
Scarry, Elaine. *The Body in Pain: The Making and Unmaking of the World*. Oxford: Oxford University Press, 1985.
Schmitt, Carl. *The Concept of the Political*. Translated by George Schwab. Chicago: University of Chicago Press, 1996.
Schreiber, Gerhardt. *I militari italiani internati nei campi di concentramento del Terzo Reich, 1943-1945: traditi, disprezzati, dimenticati*. Rome: Stato Maggiore dell'Esercito-Ufficio Storico, 1992.
Schreiber, Gerhardt. "Gli internati militari italiani ed i tedeschi (1943-1945)." In *Fra sterminio e sfruttamento. Militari internati e prigionieri di guerra nella Germania nazista (1939-1945)*, edited by Nicola Labanca, pp. 31-62. Florence: Le Lettere, 1992.
Scirocco, Giovanni. "Christian Schiefer: un fotografo a Piazzale Loreto." In *Le immagini delle guerre contemporanee*, edited by Maurizio Guerri, pp. 35-54. Milan: Meltemi, 2017.
Scott, Joan W. "Experience." In *Feminists Theorize the Political*, edited by Judith Butler and Joan W. Scott, pp. 22-40. New York: Routledge, 1992.
Scuola di Barbiana. *Lettera a una professoressa*. Florence: Libreria editrice fiorentina, 1967.
Seigel, Jerrold E. *The Idea of the Self: Thought and Experience in Western Europe since the Seventeenth Century*. Cambridge: Cambridge University Press, 2005.
Seldes, George. *Sawdust Caesar: The Untold History of Mussolini and Fascism*. New York: Harper and Brothers, 1935.
Serravalle, Don Luigi. *Il figlio dell'ubbidienza. Storia di un parroco: Don Luigi Serravalle*. Edited by Renzo Testori. Pavia: Casa del Giovane, 2008.
Setta, Sandro. *L'uomo qualunque, 1944-1948*. Rome-Bari: Laterza, 1975.
Sewell, William H. Jr. "Three Temporalities: Toward an Eventful Sociology." In *The Historic Turn in the Human Sciences*, edited by Terrence J. McDonald, pp. 245-80. Ann Arbor: University of Michigan Press, 1996.
Shashidhar, R. "Culture and Society: An Introduction to Raymond Williams." *Social Scientist* vol. 25, no. 5/6 (May-June 1997): pp. 33-53.
Sheringham, Michael. *Everyday Life: Theories and Practices from Surrealism to the Present*. Oxford: Oxford University Press, 2006.
Sherman, Stuart. *Telling Time: Clocks, Diaries, and English Diurnal Forms, 1660-1785*. Chicago: University of Chicago Press, 1996.
Simone, Raffaele. "Scrivere, leggere, capire." In *Alfabetismo e cultura scritta nella storia della società italiana. Atti del seminario tenutosi a Perugia il 29-30 marzo 1977*, pp. 91-107. Bologna: il Mulino, 1978.
Simonet-Tenant, Françoise. *Le Journal intime. Genre littéraire et écriture ordinaire*. Paris: Nathan, 2001.
Sinor, Jennifer. *The Extraordinary Work of Ordinary Writing: Annie Ray's Diary*. Iowa City: University of Iowa Press, 2002.
Soffici, Ardengo. *I diari della Grande Guerra. Kobilek. La ritirata del Friuli*. Edited by Maria Bartoletti Poggi and Marino Biondi. Florence: Vallecchi, 1986.
Soffici, Ardengo. *Sull'orlo dell'abisso. Diario 1939-1943*. Milan: Luni, 2000.
Soffici, Ardengo, and Giuseppe Prezzolini. *Diari 1939-1945*. Milan: Il Borghese, 1962.
Soldani, Simonetta. "La grande guerra lontano dal fronte." In *La Toscana*, edited by Giorgio Mori, pp. 344-452. Turin: Einaudi, 1986.
Soldani, Simonetta, and Gabriele Turi. *Fare gli italiani: Scuola e cultura nell'Italia contemporanea*. 2 vols. Bologna: il Mulino, 1993.

Sommaruga, Claudio. "Dati quantitative sull'internamento in Germania." In *Internati, prigionieri, reduci. La deportazione militare italiana durante la seconda guerra mondiale*, edited by Angelo Bendotti and Eugenia Valtulina. Bergamo: Istituto Bergamasco per la storia della Resistenza e dell'età contemporanea, 1999.
Spencer, Henry R. Review of *Sawdust Caesar* by George Seldes. *American Political Science Review* vol. 30, no. 2 (April 1936): pp. 384–5.
Starobinski, Jean. *La Relation critique*. Paris: Gallimard, 1970.
Sturani, Luisa. *Antologia della Resistenza*. Turin: Centro del libro popolare, 1951.
Suster, Roberto. *Per una storia d'Italia del 1943. Le cronache di Roberto Suster e altri scritti*. Edited by Gianni Faustini. Trento: Museo storico in Trento, 2006.
Tacchini, Alvaro. *Il fascismo a Città di Castello*. Città di Castello: Petruzzi Editore, 2004.
Tacchini, Alvaro. *Guerra e Resistenza nell'Alta Valle del Tevere (1943–1944)*. Città di Castello: Petruzzi Editore, 2015.
Talbot, George. *Censorship in Fascist Italy, 1922–43*. New York: Palgrave Macmillan, 2007.
Tartarini, Manilio. *Mio diario*. Pontedera (PI): DGS Servizi, 2013.
Taylor, Charles. *Sources of the Self: The Making of the Modern Identity*. Cambridge, Mass.: Harvard University Press, 1989.
Tecchi, Bonaventura. *Un'estate in campagna (Diario 1943)*. Florence: Sansoni, 1945.
Tecchi, Bonaventura. *Vigilia di guerra 1940*. Milan: Bompiani, 1946.
Tellier, Arnaud. *Expériences traumatiques et écriture*. Paris: Antrhopos, 1998.
Tombaccini, Simonetta. *Storia dei fuoriusciti italiani in Francia*. Milan: Mursia, 1988.
Tournier, Michel. *Journal extime*. Paris: La Musardine, 2002.
Trabucco, Carlo. *La prigionia di Roma. Diario dei 268 giorni dell'occupazione tedesca*. Turin: Borla, 1954.
Traverso, Enzo. *A ferro e fuoco. La guerra civile europea 1914–1945*. Bologna: il Mulino, 2008.
Trouillot, Michel-Rolph. *Silencing the Past: Power and the Production of History*. Boston: Beacon Press, 1995.
Turi, Gabriele. *Giovanni Gentile. Una biografia*. Florence: Giunti, 1995.
Valiani, Leo. *Tutte le strade conducono a Roma*. Bologna: il Mulino, 1983.
Ventresca, Robert. *From Fascism to Democracy: Culture and Politics in the Italian Election of 1948*. Toronto: University of Toronto Press, 2004.
Ventura, Angelo. *Intellettuali. Cultura e politica tra fascismo e antifascismo*. Introduction by Emilio Gentile. Rome: Donzelli, 2017.
Villani, Giulio, and Elia Dalla Costa, eds. *Giorni di guerra, 1943–1945. Lettere al vescovo*. Florence: Libreria editrice fiorentina, 1992.
Vincent, David. *Literacy and Popular Culture: England, 1750–1914*. Cambridge: Cambridge University Press, 1989.
Vincent, David. *The Rise of Mass Literacy: Reading and Writing in Modern Europe*. Cambridge: Polity Press, 2000.
Wagner-Pacifici, Robin. "Reconceptualizing Memory as Event: From 'Difficult Pasts' to 'Restless Events'." In *Routledge International Handbook of Memory Studies*, edited by Anna Lisa Tota and Trever Hagen, pp. 22–7. New York: Routledge, 2016.
Wagner-Pacifici, Robin. *What Is an Event?* Chicago: University of Chicago Press, 2017.
Ward, David. *Antifascisms: Cultural Politics in Italy, 1943–46. Benedetto Croce and the Liberals, Carlo Levi and the "Actionists."* Madison: Fairleigh Dickinson University Press, 1996.
Weintraub, Karl Joachim. *The Value of the Individual: Self and Circumstance in Autobiography*. Chicago: University of Chicago Press, 1978.

White, Hayden. "The Abiding Relevance of Croce's Idea of History." *Journal of Modern History* vol. 35, no. 2 (June 1963): pp. 109–24.
White, Hayden. *Metahistory: The Historical Imagination in Nineteenth-Century Europe.* Baltimore: Johns Hopkins University Press, 1973.
White, Hayden. *Tropics of Discourse: Essays in Cultural Criticism.* Baltimore: Johns Hopkins University Press, 1978.
Wildt, Michael. "Self-Reassurance in Troubled Times: German Diaries During the Upheavals of 1933." In *Everyday Life in Mass Dictatorship: Collusion and Evasion*, edited by Alf Lüdtke, pp. 55–74. Palgrave Macmillan, 2016.
Williams, Raymond. *Reading and Criticism.* London: Frederick Muller, 1950.
Williams, Raymond. *The Long Revolution.* New York: Columbia University Press, 1961.
Williams, Raymond. *Marxism and Literature.* Oxford: Oxford University Press, 1977.
Williams, Raymond. *Politics and Letters: Interviews with New Left Review.* London: NLB, 1979.
Williams, Raymond. *Keywords: A Vocabulary of Culture and Society.* Oxford: Oxford University Press, 1983.
Williams, Raymond. *Resources of Hope: Culture, Democracy, Socialism.* London: Verso, 1989.
Williams, Raymond, and Michael Orrom. *Preface to Film.* London: Film Drama Limited, 1954.
Woller, Hans. *I conti con il fascismo. L'epurazione in Italia, 1943–1948.* Bologna: il Mulino, 1997.
Zangrandi, Ruggero. *1943: 25 luglio-8 settembre.* Milan: Feltrinelli, 1964.
Zangrandi, Ruggero. *L'Italia tradita. 8 Settembre 1943.* Milan: Mursia, 1971.
Zunino, Pier Giorgio. *Interpretazione e memoria del fascismo. Gli anni del regime.* Rome-Bari: Laterza, 1991.
Zunino, Pier Giorgio. *La Repubblica e il suo passato. Il fascismo dopo il fascismo, il comunismo, la democrazia: le origini dell'Italia contemporanea.* Bologna: il Mulino, 2003.

Index

For the benefit of digital users, indexed terms that span two pages (e.g., 52–53) may, on occasion, appear on only one of those pages.

Adorno, Theodor 291–2, 295 n. 12, 303
Adriatic Littoral 95–6, 96 n. 10
Affricano Marabini, Wanda 94–6, 141–4, 147, 160–1, 163, 174, 179–81
A.G. 148–50, 289
Aga Rossi, Elena
   September 8 on 71–2, 72–3 nn. 57, 58
Agnello, Francesco 52–4, 78–9, 82
Agnese, Giacomo 134
Albertini, Luigi 196 n. 17
Alemanno, Maria 77–8, 99–100, 139–41, 147, 162, 169–70, 179–80
Aleramo, Sibilla 203 n. 51, 205 n. 56
Allied propaganda 94 n. 5
Allies the (*see* the English)
Alpenvorland 92 n. 2, 95–6
Alvaro, Corrado 201–9
   diary 201
   fascism 201–2, 205–9
   food 275
   Italians the 203–9
   July 25, 1943 203–6
   objectivity 204–9
   September 8, 1943 206–7
A.M. 52, 57, 73–4, 111, 120–1, 162, 180–1
anarchic chiaroscuro (*see* chiaroscuro)
Anglo-Americans the (*see* the English)
April 25, 1945
   and fascists' dead bodies 290–2
Ardeatine massacre 124, 200 n. 41, 259
Arendt, Hannah 29–30
Aronowitz, Stanley
   Williams's ethnographic approach 7–8
Aste, Pompilio 104–8, 128–9, 133–4

Bacci, Aldo 118–19
Badoglio, Pietro 2–3
   announcement of the armistice 72–3
   and corruption 133 n. 59
   and epuration 255–6
   loss of popularity 69 n. 49
   proclamation of October 13 86–7, 92–3
Baldi, Leo 76–7, 87, 288–9
"Banda Carità" 246 n. 22
"Bandits" 126 n. 47
Barile, Michele 132 n. 56
Barthes, Roland
   écrivains and écrivants 23 n. 70
   how to live 34 n. 108
Benveniste, Émile 17–18
betrayal 74–86, 93–6, 99–100, 234–5
   (*see also* September 8, 1943)
Blanchot, Maurice
   and chiaroscuro 34 n. 106
   on the everyday 34, 35 n. 109
bombings 69–70, 151, 154, 157–64, 171–2, 171 n. 18
   and waiting 163–4
Bonomi, Ivanoe 40 n. 124, 256 n. 55
Brenta Brcic, Fedora 87–8, 116, 174, 182–4
Brigham, Daniel T. 51–2 and n. 32, 52 n. 33
brother-enemy 117–25, 186
Brugnara, Cesarina 177–8
Bucciano, Concetta 52, 63–4, 75–6, 163, 171 n. 17, 172, 184–7

Cacciaguerra, Perla 98–100, 122–3, 127–8, 164, 289
Calamandrei, Franco 194 n. 11
Calamandrei, Piero 192–4, 210–17, 241 n. 7, 248–62
   on Croce and Gentile 250 n. 34
   diary 193–4, 210
   and the everyday 269–71
   fascism 192–4, 210–17, 303
   fascist Italians 216, 248–50, 260–1
   Germans the 212, 260–1
   Grandi, Dino 248–9

Calamandrei, Piero (*cont.*)
  Gentile, Giovanni 248–50
  Italians the 214–15, 271–2
  July 25, 1943 210–11
  liberation 284–5, 303
  Mussolini 192–3
  on the Puccioni brothers 249 n. 28
  Risorgimento 211–12
  September 8, 1943 214–15
  as "sfollato" 270–2
  trial of January 1944 216
Campregher, Massimo 106–7
Carandini Nicolò 196 n. 17, 280 n. 134
Carandini Albertini, Elena 195–6,
    220 n. 105
  diary 195–6, 280–4
  and the everyday 278–85
  fascism 280–1
  food 278–80
  Germans the 259
  Italians the 220 n. 105
  July 25, 1943 220 n. 105
  and political ambivalence 250–1
  September 8, 1943 280–1
Carazzolo, Maria 62 n. 44, 86 n. 75,
    101 n. 15, 113 n. 29, 130 n. 55,
    132 n. 56, 171 nn. 17, 18, 298–9, 306 n. 5
Carr, David 24–5
Casoni, Gaetano 200, 241 n. 7, 242–8,
  diary 200
  fascist Italians 242–8, 260–1
  Germans the 260–1
  and Giovanni Gentile 245–7
Castiglioni, Ettore 62–3, 66–7, 81–2, 110–11
Ceccarelli De Grada, Magda 56 n. 37,
    58–9, 63, 75–6, 103 n. 18, 124 n. 45,
    130 n. 55, 158–9, 290–1
Cecchi, Dario 242 n. 9
Cecchi, Emilio 194–5, 195 n. 14
  Carandini Albertini on 252 n. 40
Cecchi Pieraccini, Leonetta 194–5, 250–1
  and the everyday 275–8
  fascism 240–2
  food 275–8
  Italians the 205 n. 56, 271
  July 25, 1943 240–2
  and the lower classes 277 n. 118
  political hybridity 240–2
  and reporting 242

censorship 47 and n. 14, 48–9, 207
Chevallard, Carlo 37 n. 113, 50 nn. 26, 27,
    85 n. 73, 100 n. 14, 103 n. 18, 113 n. 29,
    114 n. 30, 117 n. 36, 130 n. 55, 161–2,
    306 n. 5
chiaroscuro (anarchic) 34 and n. 105, 39,
    236–7, 294
  Lukács, Georg 34 and n. 105
Ciseri, Carlo 81, 132–3, 170–1
Città di Castello (*see* Gabriotti, Pierangeli)
civil war
  De Felice, Renzo on 119–20
  and ordinary diarists 117–25
  Pavone, Claudio on 119–20
Cohen, Roberto 67–8, 179–80
Collina Graziani, Giovanni 180–1, 292 n. 5
Comitato di Liberazione Nazionale
    (CLN) 75 n. 61, 178–9, 243, 247–8,
    280 n. 134
Corbolini, Mario 107, 127–8
Corriere della Sera
  "Italy can finally smile" 56
Corsellini, Marisa 100–1, 169, 179–80
Crainz, Giorgio 88, 107–9, 131–2
Croce, Benedetto 196–7, 217–22,
    280 n. 134, 292–3
  on the announcement of peace 285 n. 154
  diary 196–7
  epuration 257–8
  and the everyday 282 n. 143
  fascism 3–4, 217–22, 258
  on Gentile 250 n. 34
  Italians the 220–1
  July 25, 1943 217–18
  Mussolini 219–22
  Parenthesis thesis 222
  "The Fascist Germ Still Lives" 4 n. 3, 219

Damiano, Andrea 198–9, 223–6
  diary 198–9
  fascism 223–6, 234–5
  Italians the 223–6, 234–5
  July 25, 1943 224–5
D'Amico, Fedele 242 n. 8
Darnton, Robert 7–8
Defascistization (*see* epuration)
De Felice, Renzo
  on betrayal 79 n. 66
  on civil war 119–20

on the gray zone 37 n. 115
September 8, 1943 74 n. 60
de Martino, Ernesto 274 n. 108
De Pedri, Agostino 106-7
Diaries 9-13, 16, 25-6
  and accounting (*see* history of the genre)
  addressee 17 n. 50, 27, 173-5
  auteurs and rédacteurs 22-4
  authenticity 16
  and autobiographies 28-9
  and capitalism 21
  Duggan, Christopher on 36 n. 111
  and the everyday 1-2, 28-30, 294-6, 299-300, 305-6
  family books (*see* memory books)
  history of the genre 13-17, 20-4
  interpretive challenges 16, 18, 297
  journal extime 15-16
  journal intime 15-17, 27
  memory and 305
  memory books 13-15, 17-18
  objectivity 16, 173-9, 202-9, 297
  and the ordinary 12-13
  and ordinary people 27-8
  pronouns 17-18
  punctuation 179-81
  recording (or reporting) 13-14, 20-4
  and the Resistance 36-8
  starting a diary 298
  and structures of feeling 9-11, 186-7, 297-8
  style 17-24, 173-81, 297-8, 306
  and subjectivity 17-18, 21-4
  as testimonial 16, 190-203
  and time 16, 294-6
  typographical devices 179-81
  writing 13-16, 22-6, 34-5, 147, 166, 181, 186-7, 227-8, 297-9
Di Pompeo, Corrado 144-7, 158 n. 9, 164-6, 171-2, 174
Di Raimo, Emma 288-90
Douglas, Mary 274 n. 108
drifters 110-12
Duggan, Christopher 36 n. 111, 126 n. 49
Durando, Danilo 130, 170-1

enemy the 94-125, 292
  and the Risorgimento 94 n. 6
  (*also see* the Germans)

enemy-brother the (*see* brother-enemy)
English the 50 n. 27, 93-6, 140-1, 145-7, 151, 171-2
  waiting for 164-6, 171-2, 274-5
  (*see also* liberators)
epuration 255-8
E.R. 77, 121-2, 163, 172, 179-81
eternal enemy the (*see* the Germans)
everyday the (*see also* normalcy)
  ambiguity of 1-2, 30-4, 39
  Arendt, Hannah on 29-30
  Blanchot, Maurice on 34, 35 n. 109
  Barthes, Roland 34 n. 108
  and diaries 1-2, 28-30, 294-6, 299-300, 305-6
  and fascism 1-2, 299-300
  Lefebvre, Henri on 33-4, 35 n. 110
  and Nazi Germany 30-2
  and normalcy 31-2
  and ordinary diarists 159-61, 181-9
  and routines 29-32
  and states of emergency 34-5, 39
  (*see also* Calamandrei, Carandini Albertini, Cecchi Pieraccini, Croce, hunger, Papini, Pierangeli)
everydayness
  and the political 27-35, 293-4
experience (*also see* Williams, Raymond) 1, 4-13
  Jay, Martin on 6
  Oakeshott, Michael on 7-8

family books (*see* diaries)
fascism
  Alvaro on 201-2, 31, 207-9
  Calamandrei on 192-4, 210-17
  Cecchi Pieraccini on 240-2
  and consent 3-4
  Croce on 3-4, 217-22, 258
  Damiano on 223-6, 234-5
  end of Second World War 292-3
  and the everyday 1-2, 299-300
  fatherland 126-30
  intellectual diarists 261-2
  malfeasance 132-3, 221-2, 227-8, 292
  ordinary diarists 64-9, 71, 86-8, 131-7, 140-1, 300
  Papini on 228-9, 234-5
  Pierangeli on 254-5

fascism (*cont.*)
  postwar normalization 293, 296, 300–2 and n.27
  and the RSI 300–1
  Soffici on 226–8, 234–5
  Tecchi on 230–5
  Trabucco on 251–3
fascist Italians 186, 257, 259, 262–3
  Calamandrei on 216, 248–50, 260–1
  Casoni on 242–8, 260–1
  Gabriotti on 266–8
  Pierangeli on 253–5
  Trabucco on 251–3, 259
fatherland
  and patriotism 126–30, 132 n. 56, 210–14
Favai, Fortunato 57–8, 80, 111–12, 132–3, 159–60
Fenoglio, Maria 179–80
Ferrari, Paolino 135 n. 60
Fioravanti, Leone 87–8, 124 n. 45, 132–3, 166–7
food (*see* hunger)
four days of Naples the 115 n. 31

Gabriotti, Venanzio 200–1, 262–8
  diary 200–1
  fascist Italians 266–8
  Germans the 263–5, 266 and n. 82, 275 and n. 109
  Risorgimento 262–5
  September 8, 1943 263–5
  and waiting 274–5
Gaggero Viale, Caterina 116–17, 117–19 nn. 35–37, 160–1, 164, 166, 168, 174–6
Galante Garrone, Alessandro
  the Resistance 37 n. 113
Garbagnati, Olga 59–60, 62, 94
Garrone, Barbara 73, 87
Gentile, Erminia 249–50
Gentile, Fortunato 245
Gentile, Giovanni 245–50
Germans the 75–6, 81–2, 84–5, 93–125, 146–7, 186, 192–3, 259–62
  Calamandrei on 212, 260–1
  Carandini Albertini on 259
  Casoni on 260–1
  Focardi on, as evil 100 n. 13
  Gabriotti on 263–6, 274–5

Papini on 272–3 and n. 103
Pavone on, as villains 98 n. 12
Pierangeli on 259–60
and the Risorgimento 94, 97, 126
Trabucco on 251–2, 259
Giannini, Guglielmo 296–7 and n. 19
Giorni, Vitruvio 73, 82, 179–80
'Giovinezza' 51 n. 32
Goebbels, Joseph
  July 25, 1943 56 n. 36
  September 8, 1943 79
Gouldner, Alvin
  on the everyday 33 n. 100
  on home and ordinariness 295 n. 12
  on Lefebvre, Henri 34 n. 104
Grand Council of Fascism 44 n. 3, 216
Grandi, Dino 248–9 and n. 29 and n. 30
gray zone 37 and n. 115, 38–9
  De Felice, Renzo on 37 n. 115
  Levi, Primo on 37 n. 115
  Pavone, Claudio on 38–40 nn. 122–123
Guala, Giacinto Mario 109–10

home
  Adorno, Theodor on 295 n. 12
  diarists on 294–6
  Gouldner, Alvin on 295 n. 12
  Lefebvre, Henri on 296 n. 14
  ordinary diarists 150–61, 184–5
hunger 166–9, 275–80
  (*see also* Alvaro, Carandini Albertini, Cecchi Pieraccini, Papini)

indifference/insanity 157–61
intellectual diarists 39–40 and n. 124
  diary editing 191
  diary keeping 192–203, 207, 285–6
  diary publishing 191
  diary as testimonial 192–203
  and the everyday 268–72, 275–8, 285–6
  fascism 191, 207–8, 235–6, 238, 285, 300
  and fellow Italians 271–2
  objectivity/reporting 202–3, 206–7, 242, 285–6
  and ordinary diarists 39–40, 188–9, 235–6, 285–6, 300
  political hybridity 194–5, 240–2, 250–1
  reflexivity 191, 198–9, 202–3, 235–6

war 192–4, 269–86
  (*see also* Alvaro, Calamandrei, Carandini Albertini, Cecchi Pieraccini, Croce, Damiano, Gabriotti, Papini, Pierangeli, Soffici, Tecchi, Trabucco)
Internati Militari Italiani (IMIs) 104–12
  and betrayal 110
Italians the
  Aleramo, Sibilla on 205 n. 56
  and fascism 37–9, 61, 71, 257, 292–3, 296–7, 300–3
  opinions, fluidity of 296
  ordinary diarists on 58, 63–5, 81–2, 86, 88
  Origo, Iris on 238–9 and n. 2
  (*see also* Alvaro, Calamandrei, Carandini Albertini, Cecchi Pieraccini, Croce, Damiano, Papini, Pierangeli, Soffici, Tecchi, Trabucco)

journal intime 15–16 n. 45, 17, 27
July 25, 1943 (*see also* Mussolini's fall) 2–3, 44–5, 51–69, 292
  announcement of 51 nn. 31, 32
  Chevallard, Claudio on 256 n. 52
  Eco, Umberto memories of 62 n. 45, 66 n. 46
  Goebbels, Joseph on 56 n. 36
  government response 56
  ordinary diarists on 51–69, 178–9
  strikes 54 n. 35
  (*see also* Alvaro, Calamandrei, Carandini Albertini, Cecchi Pieraccini, Croce, Damiano, Tecchi)

king Vittorio Emanuele III 55, 69 n. 49, 115 n. 32
kingdom of the South 87 n. 76

Lanzoni, Aldo 63–4, 179–80
Lefebvre, Henri
  everyday life 33–4, 35 n. 110, 137, 294;
    and ambiguity of everyday life 33–4,
    and material possessions 273–4,
    and rhythm in everyday life 35 n. 110
  home 296 n. 14
Levi, Primo
  the gray zone 37 n. 115

liberators (*see also* the English) 112–17, 146–7, 165
Lowenthal, David
  on time 24
Lukács, Georg
  anarchic chiaroscuro 34 and n. 105
L'Uomo qualunque (*see* qualunquismo)

Macchiarella, Lucio 114–15, 180–1
Maestri, Antonio 56 n. 37, 81
Manifesto of the Anti-Fascist Intellectuals 195 nn. 12, 14, 203 n. 51, 241 n. 6
Marcucci, Zelinda 51, 61, 73
Marello, Gualtiero 134
Marozzi, Ester 55, 69 n. 49, 75–6, 84, 111–12, 160, 163–4
Massolo, Pietro 70
M.D. 127–8
memory
  and diaries 305
Menestrina, Anna 59, 63–4, 73, 87, 91, 122, 124 n. 45, 150–3, 160–1, 163
Michelini, Michelina 100–1, 119–20, 168
Mussolini 58
  dead body 290–2
  fall 51 n. 31, 59–60, 61
  image 91
  irrelevance 93–4

narrative (*see also* time) 24–7
  Carr, David 24–5
  Fabre, Daniel 13 n. 36
  Lowenthal, David 24
  Ricoeur, Paul 24–5
  and writing a diary 25–7
normalcy (*see also* the everyday) 100 n. 14, 148–69, 185, 268–9, 273–5, 278–85
  and death 160–1
  and indifference 146, 157–61

Oakschott, Michael 7–8
October 13, 1943 86–90
ordinary the 9 n. 26
  historical studies 11–12
  ordinary people and the everyday 28–30
  Williams, Raymond on culture as "ordinary" 11–13
  and the extraordinary 11–13, 28, 32

336 INDEX

Ordinary diarists 24, 39
  addressee 173–5
  and betrayal 74–86
  and civil war 117–25 (*see also* brother–enemy)
  ending a diary 287
  and the everyday 159–61, 181–9
  and fascism 64–9, 71, 86–9, 131–7, 140–1, 300
  and freedom 61–9
  and history 146–7, 169–73, 177–8, 181–9
  and intellectual diarists 39–40, 188–9, 235–6, 285–6, 300
  and July 25, 1943 51–69, 178–9, 300–1
  and normalcy 148–66, 185
  objectivity 173–81
  and Piazzale Loreto (fascists' dead bodies) 290–2
  and power 139–40
  and the private (*see* the private) 139–47
  and reporting 139–40, 150–1
  and September 8, 1943 71–86, 99–100, 177–8
  starting a diary 139, 141, 144, 298
  style 173–81, 306
  and the subjective point of view 173–9
  typographical devices 179–81
  and the war 56–61, 70–1, 86–90, 139–40, 146, 150–2, 154
  writing 24 n. 72, 147, 166, 181, 186–8
  (*see also* bombings, brother–enemy, the English, the Germans, home, hunger, the Italians, liberators, Mussolini's fall, "sfollati")
Origo, Iris 203 n. 51, 238

Paolisso, Irene 71, 78, 102–3, 111–14, 134–5, 153–7, 160–1, 165–7, 171 n. 18, 171–2, 299–300
Papini, Giovanni 197, 228–9, 214 n. 84
  diary 197
  fascism 228–9, 234–5
  and food 278
  Germans the 272–3 and n. 103
  Italians the 214 n. 84, 228–30 n. and 142, 234–5
  and normalcy 275 n. 111
  as "sfollato" 272–3

Universal Judgment (*Giudizio Universale*) 228–9
Pavone, Claudio
  and the morality of the Resistance 38, 213 n. 83, 302–3
  and the Resistance as civil war 38, 119–20
Peace
  rumors 60–1
Pepys, Samuel 20
  Pepys, Mrs. 20
Perec, Georges 21 n. 64, 306 n. 4
Peroni, Angelo 58–9, 63, 65–7, 80–1, 157–8
Peukert, Detlev J. K. 30–2
Piazzale Loreto
  and photographs of dead bodies 292 n. 5
Pieraccini, Gaetano 240–2, 241–2 n. 7 and n. 8
Pierangeli, Giulio
  diary 190–1 and n. 2 and n. 3
  English the 274–5
  fascism 254–5
  fascist Italians 253–5
  Germans the 259–60
  Italians the 254–5
  and normalcy 273–4
  as "sfollato" 273
  and waiting 274–5
Prezzolini, Giuseppe 51 n. 32
prince Umberto 115 n. 32
private the 138–47, 294–6 and n. 14
Puccioni, Bruno 244–5, 249 n. 28
Puccioni, Uberto 243–5, 247–8

qualunquismo 296–7 and n. 19

Radio London 112–13
Rahimi, Sadeq 10 n. 28, 296 n. 15, 305 n. 3
"rebels" 119 n. 37
Repetto, Giulio 58
Resistance the 36–8, 75 n. 61
  Galante Garrone, Alessandro on 37 n. 113
  Pavone, Claudio on 38, 119–20, 213 n. 83, 302–3
  and September 8, 1943 74–5
Revelli, Nuto
  on fascists as foreigners 121 n. 41
Ricoeur, Paul 9 n. 26, 24–5
Rinaldi Gatti, Aida 124–5

Rinascita 263–4 and fig. 5
Rossaro, Don Antonio 51 n. 32
Rossi, Antonio 110 n. 26
Roveda, Albertina 73
Royal March 51 n. 32
RSI (Repubblica Sociale Italiana) 2–3, 91, 130 n. 55, 140, 216, 259, 300–1
Ruberl, Liana 62, 76

Sant'Anna di Stazzema 148–50, 289
sbandati (*see* drifters)
Second World War
   Italians' attitudes 45–50
   middle classes' attitudes 49
Seldes, George
   Sawdust Caesar 222 n. 109
September 8, 1943
   Aga Rossi on 71–2
   Alvaro on 206–7
   Badoglio's announcement 72–3
   Calamandrei on 214–15
   Carandini Albertini on 280–1
   Gabriotti on 263–5
   Goebbels on 79
   ordinary diarists 71–4, 99–100, 177–8
   popular response 73, 292
   and the Resistance 75 n. 61
   Tecchi on 234–5 and n. 165
Serravalle, Don Luigi 83–4, 87, 96–7, 119 n. 37, 129, 166–7, 179–80
"sfollati" 156–8
   Calamandrei as 270–2
   Papini as 272–3
   Pierangeli as 273
"Simmo 'e Napule, paisà" 253 n. 44
Soffici, Ardengo 197–8, 226–8
   diary 197–8, 227–8
   fascism 226–8, 234–5
   Italians the 226–8, 234–5
   on Mussolini 226–8
state of emergency 298
Stracciari, Gian Carlo 129–31
structures of feeling (*see also* Williams, Raymond) 3–6, 9–13, 19–20, 37–8, 235–6, 294–8, 306 n. 7
subjectivity, political 1–2, 294–6, 298–9
   Rahimi, Sadeq 10 n. 28, 296 n. 15
Surrealists the 293–4

Talluri, Bruna 52, 57–8, 63–5, 68, 84, 179–80, 296–7, 302–3
Tartarini, Manilio 121, 160, 164, 172–3, 179–80
Tecchi, Bonaventura 199, 230–7, 278 n. 125
   diary 199
   fascism 230–5
   Italians the 232–5
   July 25, 1943 231–3
   September 8, 1943 234–5
   war 232–4
time (*see* narrative) 24–5
Trabucco, Carlo 200, 251–2
   diary 200
   fascism 251–3
   fascist Italians 251–3, 259
   Germans the 251–2, 259
   Italians the 251–2
   July 25, 1943 252–3
   on Mussolini 251–2
   trial of January 1944 253
Traverso, Gina 287–8
trauma 148–50, 168, 270–1, 284–5, 289
trial of January 1944 122–3, 124 n. 45
   Calamandrei on 216
   Trabucco on 253
Turin strikes 50 n. 26
Tutino, Mario 61, 84–6, 88, 102–3, 122–3, 126–7, 162–3, 290–1, 301–2

Villani, Dino 52–4, 56 n. 37, 61, 80–1, 127–8, 132, 289–90
Visintainer, Luigia 56–7, 64, 178–9
Vita, Ada 62, 70, 76, 116–17, 120–1, 176, 180–1
V.R. 58, 115–16, 123–4

war
   the announcement 86–7
   and dehumanization 155, 169
   end 288–91
   and the everyday 280–6
   and insanity 157–61
   intellectual diarists 192–4, 268–86
   and material possessions 273–4
   and normalcy 273–4
   opposition to in Florence 45–8
   ordinary diarists 56–61, 70–1, 86–90, 139–40, 146, 154

war (*cont.*)
  rumors 61 n. 42
  and silence 163–4
  and waiting 164–6, 273–5
Williams, Raymond
  conventions (form and content) 10, 19–20
  culture as ordinary 11–13
  emergent 6 and n. 11
  ethnographic approach 7–8
  experience 4–11
  history and the past 8–10
  language 19–20
  literacy and literature 19–20
  the lived 5
  the personal 5
  practical consciousness 8–9, 12–13, 19–20
  the social 4–5
  structures of feeling 1–2, 4–7, 9–13, 19–20, 37–8, 297–300
  writing 13–14 and n. 39, 20
  and the popular classes 22–4, 27

Zuccarini, Oliviero 190–1